DENTON WELCH

Writer and Artist

JAMES METHUEN-CAMPBELL

James Methuen-Campbell has written extensively on classical music over a period of twenty-five years. Aside from several hundred reviews appearing in such publications as *The Times*, *Gramophone* and *Records and Recording*, his first book *Chopin Playing* came out in the US and in Japanese translation. This new biography derives from a long-standing interest in Modern British Painting.

Published in 2004 by Tauris Parke Paperbacks
an imprint of I.B.Tauris & Co Ltd
6 Salem Road, London W2 4BU
175 Fifth Avenue, New York NY 10010
www.ibtauris.com

In the United States of America and in Canada distributed by
Palgrave Macmillan, a division of St Martin's Press
175 Fifth Avenue, New York NY 10010

ISBN 1 86064 924 6

A full CIP record for this book is available from the British Library
A full CIP record for this book is available from the Library of Congress

Library of Congress catalog card: available

Printed and bound in Malaysia by SRM Production Services Sdn. Bnd.

Contents

Foreword
Alan Bennett

A good subtitle for a biography of Denton Welch might be *A Bike in the Hedge*, so much is his leisure and his *Journals* taken up with picnicking in fields, looking round country churches or exploring the overgrown parks of once grand houses. The bike would not be locked, as this was Kent in the 1940s, a county (though it had seen the Battle of Britain) still sunk in rustic tranquillity and seclusion.

June 7 1943 Monday
    I am sitting in the cool in Capel Church under the medieval fresco. Against a dim salmon pink ground two figures seem to be hanging long coats and gowns out of the windows of a castle turret. Other figures seem to be banqueting.

He had been banqueting too.

    I have been eating my lunch in the fields nearby (Ryvita, cheese, apricot jam, chocolate, bar of squashed dried fruits, coffee), sitting on my coral air-cushion, given me by May, reading for the fourth or fifth time an outline of the Brontë sisters' lives.

    Having just had his first book published he identified with Charlotte and the prospect of fame. Earlier, not untypically, he had been watching a loutish boy picking cherries and another mowing a field.

    . . . this is what goes on in nineteen-forty-three, the year of the greatest war to stop all wars, if I have the quotation right.
    Now I shall leave this cool church and this medieval fresco and get on my bicycle again.
    This may be read about in years to come and then people will know what I did on this June day.

    There was no forgetting what he had been doing on the same June day eight years before. Then his bike hadn't been in the hedge, but crushed on a Surrey road, when, as a young art student, he'd been knocked down by a car motorist, the injuries condemning him to the life of an invalid and leading ultimately to his death in 1948 at the age of thirty-three.

Tough, single-minded to the point of selfishness and often difficult to live with, he raged against the turn of fate that had wrecked his life and though it's tempting to say that without it he would not have been a writer, I'm not sure this is true. From early childhood, as James Methuen-Campbell's book makes plain, he seems to have had a particular slant on the world, and though his accident may have concentrated his energies it did not create his sensibility. A child who at the age of seven could remark 'in a slow, earnest, thoughtful voice that "a flea would despise the amount of lemonade I've got, Mother" ' was never going to be ordinary, and his experiences with his family in China made their contribution. After holidays spent rooting through the junk shops of Shanghai and on a solitary walk coming across a severed human head in the undergrowth it's hardly surprising if he failed to fit in at Repton.

When Denton Welch began to write, such occurrences were not slow to find their way into his stories and novels, which were nothing if not auto-biographical. What the accident did was add urgency to the process and though he regularly complained of how little his circumstances allowed him to accomplish, by the time of his death he had accumulated a substantial body of work and acquired a distinctive voice.

To begin with I knew nothing of his fiction, first reading about him when his *Journals* were published four years after his death. In those days I could afford few books, certainly in hardback, and so wrote my name in them as I seldom do nowadays. My copy of the *Journals* is also dated, with 'December 1952' written in my still childish hand. This was a few months after I had been conscripted. Utterly unlike any person I had come across, he seemed a sympathetic voice and—a characteristic of books read when young—seemed to be speaking particularly to me. So I took the book with me into the army as, I suppose, a token of a different sort of life, 'a civilised life' I probably thought of it then, though it was nothing like the life I'd known.

The military life meant regular kit inspections, your army belongings, boots, best BD, mess tins, etc. all laid out on the squared off bed. Nor was it just the army side of things that was on display, as your locker had to be open too, your whole life available for scrutiny should the inspecting officer so choose. I imagined the disdainful swagger-stick flicking the *Journals* open at some offending page and read out with sarcastic comments for the benefit of the other conscripts.

Still, his work wasn't entirely unsuited to the barrack-room, particularly during the war years, a time when reading (and writing) became almost an act of faith. Servicemen reading on barrack-room beds were testifying to their conviction that there was a world elsewhere. The early paperbacks slipped handily into the outside BD trouser pocket, as did *Horizon* or *Penguin New Writing*, and reading James Methuen-Campbell's account of Welch's life it almost seems as if even *Vogue* was a light in the darkness. So though Denton Welch took and almost prided himself on taking no notice of the war, wartime and the austerity that followed was the time of his life.

In this regard, though, it's a blessing that his accident banished him from the metropolis. How much less idiosyncratic would his life have been, certainly to read, had he landed up in Soho or Fitzrovia, the doings of which, particularly in that period are amply documented and over-described.

Kent, where he spent most of his invalid life might seem dull by comparison, but had much to recommend it. The setting of Samuel Palmer's valley of vision, now with its evidences of war, was one of those evocative landscapes that Piper and Ravilious were recording elsewhere. But the war didn't interest Denton Welch, not in its scenic aspects anyway, and it never obtrudes onto his own canvasses; no nissen huts here or surrealist barrage balloons, no bomb damage even, his paintings resolutely personal and obscure (and not always very good).

But his *Journals* are a different matter. Minor writers often convey a more intense flavour of their times than those whose range is broader and concerns more profound. Here the war is met with at every turn, but transmuted into an idyllic pastoral of soldiers bathing, prisoners harvesting and planes crossing the moonlit sky to the sound of distant singing from the pub. As drunken servicemen ride their girlfriends home on the handlebars his diaries sometimes read like the script for a documentary by Humphrey Jennings or notes for a film by Michael Powell.

In a letter to Barbara Cooper, secretary to John Lehmann, in October 1943 he gives his hobbies as 'old glass, china, furniture, little pictures and picnicking alone' and though Ryvita has never had many charms for me, lovingly detailed as one of the ingredients of his wartime picnics, even that gritty dimpled cardboard acquires glamour. Dashing off on his bike to antique shops (the prices absurdly cheap), exploring churches and dilapidated follies—to me in 1952 it seemed an ideal life. And a smart one too. To a boy brought up in the provinces this ailing ex-art student seemed to have moved effortlessly into a charmed circle, with letters from E.M. Forster, lunch with Edith Sitwell and tea at Sissinghurst with Harold and Vita. It was probably only her suicide that stopped Virginia Woolf from figuring here.

What I didn't appreciate then was the guts Welch must have had and needed to have. At eighteen I thought that to be 'sensitive' was a writer's first requirement—with discipline and persistence nowhere—whereas he never allowed himself to languish. His spinal injuries no more kept him off his bike than sickness and high temperatures did from the typewriter, and it was this no nonsense approach both to his disability and to his work that made him impatient of those occasional fans who sought him out expecting a wilting aesthete.

For the same reason he would probably have been uneasy to find himself on so many sensitive bookshelves in the late forties and fifties, when books perhaps said more about their readers than they do now. His writings would be found alongside such textbooks of proscribed affections as Housman's poems, the novels of Forrest Reid and Mary Renault and (as a chronicle of unhappy love) *The Unquiet Grave*; coded texts that spoke more plainly than their owners sometimes wanted or even knew.

Certainly, much of what Denton Welch wrote trembled on the brink of sex, which gave it much of its energy; though in the *Journals* it was never plain whether anything 'went on'. In 1952 I assumed he was of necessity exercising his discretion, but as James Methuen-Campbell makes clear, often catheterised and racked by his physical inabilities Denton Welch was very much an onlooker and non-participant. But at eighteen I was an onlooker and non-participant myself, so that probably rang bells too.

Though in describing the closeness between himself and his companion Eric Oliver (very little seems to have gone on, as it turns out) what was reassuring was his frankness about the intensity of their association, at least on Welch's side . . . and one-sided associations were the ones with which I was myself familiar. And he plainly wasn't shy. Sitting chatting to naked boys in hayfields seemed fairly unshy to me, though the mixture of his knowingness and their seeming naivety was typical of the times and would not last. By the sixties it's not only the nissen huts that have gone, but an innocence too.

Or perhaps not quite. In the early sixties I was in America for two years during which time my parents took to reading the books I had left at home. This made me slightly apprehensive, though all it meant was that my father became an early and unlikely fan of Nancy Mitford and it was my mother who first took to reading Denton Welch's *Journals*. What she picked up on were his visits to junk and bric-a-brac shop, since this was an inclination she shared. When he was younger my father had been a bit of a carpenter and made toys, so when she gave it to him to read what caught his fancy was the cleaning and restoration of the dolls' house. What I had been apprehensive about, the sexual undertones, seemed wholly to pass them by, leaving it, ironically, to Philip Roth's *Portnoy's Complaint* as the first book of mine to which my father took real exception.

Scarcely reaching middle age, it's hard to think that had he lived Denton Welch would now be in his eighties. To me he will always be that frail, curly-haired high-foreheaded young man who sits at the checkerboard table with the lustres and the candles in the frontispiece to the *Journals* that I bought in 1952.

His subject matter had a richness and a colour that links him with very unlike writers, such as Dylan Thomas, Edith Sitwell and Christopher Fry all of whom were standing out against the drabness of their times. The nearest he had come to active service was in the battle against beige, so it was fitting that in June 1945 he should have had a picture in the Victory number of *Vogue*, 'a rendering of a room in his cottage in Kent, where colour plays an important part.' He says '"Do not think that brilliant colour is difficult to live with. It is always stimulating and refreshing; and change to a neutral-toned, colourless room would be exhausting, lowering and depressing"'.

There was never much danger of that in his life or in his art; he went out still full of colour, and more than fifty years later it is unfaded.

Preface

Taking into account the brevity of his career and the relatively unambitious scope of his writing, it may come as a surprise to the reader that this is in fact the fourth book to be published on Denton Welch (although the first to consider his work as an author alongside his activities as an artist). Thankfully, each study has been rather different in its scope. In 1956 the Hogarth Press brought out Noël Adeney's curious book *No Coward Soul*, which in the guise of a novel (the names and in some cases the sexes of the characters were altered), tells of the authoress' often stormy relationship with 'Merton' (Denton) during the last five or so years of his life. It makes a fascinating read, even though one is left with the very definite impression that the purpose of the book was largely to justify various questionable actions that had in fact only added to the insecurity of Denton's last days.

A full-length work devoted to a critical survey of Denton Welch's writing appeared in 1974 with the American academic Robert S. Phillips' volume in the Twayne's English Authors series. It treats almost the entire published writings to a detailed and methodical analysis, leaning heavily on a Jungian interpretation of the narrative. It should be pointed out, however, that the conclusions arrived at might well be evident to anyone who had read the body of Denton Welch's work, and especially the uncut version of the Journals, which, admittedly, did not appear in print until 1984. Having said this, there can be little doubt that Phillips' study is valuable in considering Denton Welch's reputation within the context of international literature, and the exercise is sustained by a generous appreciation of the quality of the writing.

The most substantial book, indeed the first biography proper, is Michael De-la-Noy's *Denton Welch: the Making of a Writer* (Viking, 1984), which was timed to coincide with the publication and republication of many of the prose works. It is constructed principally through piecing together Denton's own writings, which are nearly all autobiographical and cover the great proportion of his life, with narrative to a great extent replaced by direct quotation. De-la-Noy also makes use of a series of letters that Denton wrote to friends, such as Eric Oliver, Noël Adeney and Maurice Cranston, and apart from the fairly minor contributions of around ten people who had known the subject at different stages of his short life, essentially the book allows Denton Welch to tell his own story. In keeping with the subtitle of his biography, De-la-Noy avoids much mention of Denton's artistic career, which, in fact, he was able to sustain at albeit a modest level, until the end of his life.

The present volume, aside from attempting to examine the factual background of these sometimes loosely autobiographical writings (and in doing so offering an insight into the subject's creative process), aims to explore the different influences and traits of personality that contributed to shaping Denton Welch into a writer of enduring charm and depth. In considering together his work as writer and artist (many of the pictures are reproduced here for the first time) one is better able to appreciate his output as a whole, since in many respects the two activities were related.

Introduction

There can be little doubt that initially Denton Welch turned to writing as a distraction from his wretched physical and mental condition. Garth Stacey, who was in the same house as him at Repton, and had been an exact contemporary, recalled that even as a schoolboy Denton had given the impression of being introspective 'almost to the extent of damaging himself', and this state of mind, coupled with the trauma of the horrific road accident that happened when he was an art student, left him extremely vulnerable to fluctuations of temperament and emotions.

The first months of 1940 found him living in a small modern house in Kent, with none of his troubles resolved. As a consequence of the War his friends were taken up with other concerns. He had failed to build on the success of having a poster design accepted by Shell and, more importantly, the one relationship that he coveted above all others had irretrievably come to an end, leaving him drained and neurotic. One or two people he knew living locally did suggest that he should try to write a book (he had always been an avid jotter-down of notes and lines of verse), and although he made an abortive effort at an autobiography starting with his earliest memories of childhood, it was in describing his running-away from Repton and the subsequent year spent out in China that he found his first effective vehicle for self-expression, at least in a literary form. The refusal to return to the school (he took a train from London in the opposite direction) had been a highly symbolic turning-point in his life. It was his bid to establish a definite identity and to register a protest that he did not accept the inevitability of following a prescribed course in the future. In writing *Maiden Voyage* Denton was able to affirm and take confidence in the significance of his action.

Critics have levelled the accusation of unpardonable self-indulgence at his writing and, of course, in the sense that he virtually always relied on auto-biographical material and wrote unashamedly about his own frequently rather ignoble impulses and obsessions, this is quite justified. It was not, however, that he negated the power of universal themes, but more that his style consisted almost exclusively of relaying his own feelings and observations with absolute candour and accuracy. In answering the letter of a fellow-author toward the end of his life, Denton stated that he believed the small, everyday happenings of one's existence were indicative of greater truths, and on the whole that he mistrusted writers who took it on themselves to peddle significant utterances.

Although in *A Voice Through a Cloud* one might be tempted to see the author as the archetypal 'doomed artist' (or even as an aesthete brought down to earth through experiencing the ravages of extreme physical pain), in reality Denton Welch the man, as many of his friends have testified, defied categorization. He was a mass of contradictions, the most obvious being the combination of extreme sophistication and palpable naivety. The latter surfaces especially in his writing, so that one can never quite guess what is going to be around the next corner.

It is true that Denton felt there had been an element of inevitability about the accident. One wonders whether the news of T.E. Lawrence's death following a motorbike crash made a deep impression (it happened three weeks to the day before Denton was knocked off his bicycle). And yet many of his Goldsmiths' friends have said that the trauma did not seem to have altered his personality at all. It was far more the publication of *Maiden Voyage* and the critical acclaim the book received that had the effect of maturing his outlook. He was made to think about what he was doing, and his life began to achieve a purpose that succeeded in sustaining him.

Denton Welch was, I believe, a writer and artist of considerably greater range than he is usually given credit for. In *Maiden Voyage* one warms immediately to the irrepressible teenage energy and wish to 'explore'; the second novel, *In Youth is Pleasure*, is an unashamed recreation of the author's troubled childhood (the hero gives the impression of being rather younger than fifteen), overshadowed as it was by the ghost of his mother, who had died when he was eleven. Here 'Orvil Pym' is wholly immersed in a Gothic reverie of nocturnal visits to an immense grotto on the one hand, and coping with his suppressed sexual impulse on the other. The *Journals*, again, are eminently readable, and filled with descriptions of food, churches and numerous, if tentative, encounters with young rustics. But then, if there is a single work that confirms Denton Welch's serious intent as an author, it is *A Voice Through a Cloud*. Nowhere else in his writings, save for the *Journals*, does he reveal so much of himself, and in so intense a vein. Stephen Spender was not alone in proclaiming it 'a masterpiece' and 'one of the most wonderful and terrifying books' that he had ever read.

Acknowledgements

In the seven years or so that I worked at researching and writing this biography of Denton Welch I met with extreme kindness, generosity and, in many instances, hospitality from a great many individuals. I hope that these few words will do justice to their immeasurable contribution to whatever interest this book may hold, but if I have omitted to mention any, I trust that they will understand that it is an oversight by me, and no reflection of any lack of appreciation for their input.

Denton Welch's companion, Eric Oliver, and the artist Gerald Mackenzie, who was closest to Denton during his time at Goldsmiths', have both sadly died before the publication of this book. They provided me with personal reminiscences of inestimable value, and I have made a particular effort to transmit these accurately. Eric, aside from this, had a wonderful memory for what happened to the various individuals associated with his friend, and in many cases this led me to pursue other contacts that proved valuable. Whatever questions I asked him about Denton Welch he answered without any reservation. His loyalty to the memory of his friend and soul mate was undiminished by the course of time. Gerald Mackenzie, thankfully, over the years kept a great deal of documentation, aside from his own diaries of the 1930s and 40s, that yielded a considerable amount of interesting material. His own memories of Denton were startlingly clear. I am grateful that he was able to read the manuscript of this book and allowed me to use various photographs that he had taken of his friend.

The late Helen Roeder and the late Joan Gresham (née Waymark), two fellow-students and intimate friends from Denton's years at Goldsmiths', passed on their warm memories, with Mrs Gresham allowing me to copy several photographs. The late Jack Easton, who sadly died in April 1994, was patient in answering over a dozen letters about his medical and personal association with Denton. I am very grateful for the opportunity of having met him, and regret that he will not be reading this book. He gave me real encouragement and was constantly asking after the date of publication.

Others who contributed significant personal material that I have used in the book—all former friends of Denton—were Nancy Quinlan (née Brooke), the late John and Griselda Lewis, the late D.B. Tubbs, Cedric Rogers, the late Professor Carel Weight, the late Betty Swanwick, the late John Bloom, Noel Cousins, the late Professor Maurice Cranston, Ronald Benge, Rosemary Kendall (née

Mundy-Castle), the late Jane Gardener, Elizabeth Hasell-Walker (née Plummer) and David Atkins.

Those who also knew or met Denton and have passed on their reminiscences, as well as in many cases kindly lending photographs, include John Hesketh, the late Dr Robert Sauvan-Smith, the late Bernard Hailstone, the late Edward Bawden, John Turner, Richard Adeney and his sister Charlotte Forman, the late Katharine Moore, Molly Townsend (née Ure), the late Derrick Sayer, Elizabeth Guyatt (formerly Nicholls), John Critchley, Joyce Brooks, his first cousins the late Thomas Kane, Lois Marson and the late Phyllis Timberlake. Mrs Judy Welch, who was married to Denton's elder brother, Bill, kindly gave me some photographs, as well as answering several letters.

The following either knew or met Denton or his family at different stages of his short life and provided further information: Marjorie Penton (née Parsons), the late Enid Saunders Candlin, who kindly gave me permission to quote a long letter from her sister, Pocetta, the late Lord Kadoorie, the late Julian Vinogradoff (formerly Mrs Goodman), the late Rowland Hilder, Lord Belhaven and Stenton, Michael Ford, Rosamund Owen, Dr Dawn Daniel (née Bosanquet), Sir Richard Beaumont, the Rev. Robert Crane, the late Rev. John Lisney, Michael Hely-Hutchinson, Monica Roberts-Jones (née Booth), Betty Walters (née Snow), Garth Stacey and the late Anthony Gilbert.

Without the co-operation and diligent attention of the staff at the Harry Ransom Humanities Research Center, the University of Texas at Austin, the project also would not really have been possible. Cathy Henderson and Kathleen Gee helped to make my three week stay in Austin worthwhile and pleasurable, and I was allowed easy access to their Denton Welch archive, which unquestionably contains the largest collection of his MSS and letters. The late Ronald Smoldon, whose Denton MSS and related photographs were especially useful, receives my belated appreciation. I am grateful to have had his permission to reproduce some material as illustrations.

I should also like to offer sincere thanks to Gordon Hooper, Benjamin Whitrow and Otto Stanton. All are Denton Welch devotees and have taken a great interest in the project, as well as contributing material. I must also mention the assistance of the staffs of the Berg Collection at the New York Public Library, the Reading and Bristol University Libraries, the Tonbridge and Sevenoaks Public Libraries, the First Church of Christ Scientist, Boston, the Redfern Gallery, Philip Athill of Abbott & Holder, Tom Sargant, the Rev. David Lockwood, Jean-Louis Chevalier, Michael De-la-Noy, A. Richard Carter, Elwyn Edwards, Stephen Gardiner, John Walker (the Old Reptonian Society), John and Alexander Plowright (the Archivist of Repton School and his son), Dr Dorothy Miller and the late W.H. Boomgaard. Janet Green and the Modern British Pictures department at Sotherby's have been unfailingly generous and helpful, allowing me to scour their catalogues and collection of reproductions of pictures. Assistance and in many cases hospitality have been proffered by the late Phil Swales, Peter Knapton, C.V. Bones and his son, Jonathan Cannon, Charles Williams, Guy Roddon, Guy Dearlove, Barbara Christie-Millar, Professor Peter Dickinson, Julian Nangle, Dennis Hawkins, Mrs John Thornton, the late R.J.L.

Smith, the Rev. Frank Seymour Skelton, Elizabeth Rayner and Adrian Goodman.

The late Richard Newton did quite a bit of pioneering research into Denton Welch's life back in the 1970s, some of which I found useful. I thank his nephew, Dr John Newton, for allowing me access to his papers, which are housed in the Heslop Room, the University of Birmingham Library. Of invaluable help in constructing the Bibliography was Dr Charlotte Laughlin's 'Catalogue of the Denton Welch Collection at the University of Texas' (doctoral dissertation, 1975).

I am greatly indebted to Alan Bennett for contributing the foreword, which is written in his inimitably perceptive and personal style that I so much admire. I thank warmly my mother and especially my elder sister Joanna Martin for offering suggestions about the style of the book and for discussing grammatical points. Joanna has been through the MS with a fine-tooth comb, and yet in no way do I wish her to share responsibility for any errors that may have crept in. It was another sister, Lucinda, who first introduced me to Denton Welch's work, and I thank her for doing so. Also, I thank my friend Louisa Poole, for her forbearance and encouragement, and particularly for driving me around the country to seek out locations and interview several of the above-named individuals. The project has been a source of great interest for me and, I like to think, has broadened my mind.

List of Illustrations

Archive Photographs
1. Denton Welch and his parents, Shanghai, c.1923.
2. Denton, Brendon and Betty Parsons, Shanghai, 1925.
3. School photograph, Brook House, Repton, 1931, with Denton behind his housemaster, Mr Snape.
4. Denton and his brother Paul (front row) on holiday at Zoute, Belgium, 1931.
5. With Joan Waymark at Brixham in Devon, 1934.
6. Oatlands Park Hotel, Weybridge, Surrey (the setting for the novel *In Youth is Pleasure*), where Denton, his father and brothers stayed in 1930.
7. The house was formerly the Southcourt Nursing Home in Broadstairs, where Denton convalesced from October 1935 to January 1936.
8. At the piano, 1937/8.
9. Dr Jack Easton.
10. Evelyn Sinclair
11. Self-portrait, c.1938. *Courtesy of the National Portrait Gallery, London.*
12. In his flat at Hadlow Road, Tonbridge, 1937.
13. Gerald Mackenzie resting on one of Denton's carved wooden angels, 1937.
14. Alex Comfort. Photograph by Howard Coster. *Courtesy of the National Portrait Gallery, London.*
15. Edith Sitwell, 1934. Photograph by Howard Coster. *Courtesy of the National Portrait Gallery, London.*
16. May Walbrand-Evans.
17. John Henry 'Monty' Bones.
18. Noël Adeney. *Courtesy of Mr Richard Adeney.*
19. Eric Oliver, 1946.
20. Denton at the Hop Garden, St Mary's Platt, 1940.
21. Middle Orchard, Crouch. *Photograph by Mr Richard Adeney.*
22. At Middle Orchard, 1946.
23. With the doll's house, 1946.
24. With Eric Oliver, 1946.

Colour Illustrations
25. Portrait of Denton Welch by Gerald Mackenzie Leet, 1935.
26. Flowers on a Table, c.1940/1 (cat. no. 45). *Courtesy of the Harry Ransom Humanities Research Center, the University of Texas (HRHRC)*
27. 'A Cat Waiting for its Master', a watercolour, 1946 (cat. no. 81). *Courtesy of*

Chapter One

Childhood

A bespectacled and rather thin art student called Denton Welch was cycling south to visit an aunt and uncle for the Whitsun holiday. Having successfully negotiated the heavy traffic of London's suburbs, he was now on the main Brighton road. A railway line ran parallel on the left-hand side. Not used to cycling in a built-up area, one can imagine Denton heaving a sigh of relief as only the countryside and one or two small market towns of Surrey now lay ahead of him on his long journey.

He was approaching Hooley—today, as then, an insignificant village with tired brick houses straddling the highway. Suddenly, and for no apparent reason, a car driven by a Mrs Annie Hutley crashed into him from behind throwing Denton violently onto the verge.[1] He sustained a fractured spine, amongst other less serious injuries. Thus began thirteen years of physical and mental agony that eventually came to an end with his death at the age of thirty-three.

As if unable and certainly unwilling to come to terms with his post-accident predicament, Denton Welch made extensive use of his memories of childhood and adolescence during his brief career as a writer. He had lost his mother at eleven, and in many ways his emotional development became retarded, so that for him the world seen through the eyes of a child was not so remote as is usual with a twenty-year-old. And when in 1940 for the first time Denton attempted to write a book, it was only natural for him that it should be an autobiography starting with his very earliest recollections of infancy.[2]

Denton Welch was born on 29th March 1915 at the Victoria Nursing Home in Shanghai. His adoring mother Rosalind already had two fine healthy sons, Bill and Paul, and she might well have wished that this time the baby had been a girl.[3] The Welches were well-off and travelled about a great deal, making regular trips to England. They could afford to be cosmopolitan in their outlook.

A partner in the general trading firm of Wattie & Co., Denton's father Arthur Welch had risen to become one of the pillars of Shanghai's business community. The late Lord Kadoorie remembered that it was thanks to Mr Welch and to his own father, Sir Elly Kadoorie,[4] that more than forty rubber companies had been saved from liquidation during the severe slump in rubber of 1911.

There was plenty of money around in the city and the successful Europeans, eight thousand or so of whom were British, lived in considerable luxury—to the envy of the frequently impoverished White Russian refugees and the mass of the still poorer Chinese. The social life of the foreign community, in particular, was comfortably well organized. The British, when in need of relaxation, tended to congregate at the Country Club, situated in Bubbling Brook Road. It boasted a swimming-pool, tennis courts and an expanse of mowed lawns, flowerbeds and ornamental brooks. Arthur Welch was on the committee.

Nor were those with a sophisticated taste for Western culture neglected: the expatriates were able to offer high fees to tempt world-class artists to visit the city, and during the First World War Kreisler, Elman, Godowsky and Pavlova all came to Shanghai. It had its own Municipal Orchestra, as well as various ballrooms and eight excellent cinemas. There were also racecourses that catered for those with less elevated interests. A number of the Russian immigrants added to the rich mix of cultures and they could often be found playing in night-club bands or, in the daytime, offering music lessons to the young girls of the house.

Denton's parents were an incongruous couple: he very much the businessman, reluctant to bestow affection on his children, she a lively American—a devout Christian Scientist with an impish sense of humour. Her maiden name was Rosalind Bassett and she was six years younger than Arthur Welch, whom she had known for quite some time before their marriage. As a young lady in her early twenties Denton's mother had stayed at a convent in Florence; she went there for a month or two each year between 1901 and 1903, most probably to round off her education.[5] The Bassett forebears were New Englanders, but Mrs Welch did not have an American accent, nor was she ever an habitué of the American set in Shanghai; for friendship she would turn rather to fellow members of the Christian Science Church, a sect that had been founded in Boston by Mary Baker Eddy in the 1870s.

A childhood friend of Denton's, Nancy Quinlan, recalls the contrast between his mother and father:

> She was a sweet and friendly person, who struck one also as being very intelligent. We didn't seem to see terribly much of our parents at that age, because they were always out and we were left with the Chinese servants, who really had quite an important role in bringing up the children. I remember Denton's mother playing the part of the little girl Margaret in Barrie's play *Dear Brutus* for the dramatic society. Denton's father, on the other hand, was rather grave; he didn't sparkle. I think he understood the two older boys, Bill and Paul, but not Denton.[6]

One of the reasons why Mr Welch had a lack of sympathy for his youngest son was Denton's unusual behaviour. From his very earliest years the little boy displayed a passion for collecting trinkets. Whether it was Victorian knick-knacks lying unloved in an old dressing-case at the Welch's house in Shanghai or his own collection of 'treasures', which consisted of a painted snuff-bottle, a filigree box inlaid with kingfishers' feathers and a small ivory netsuke (all unceremoniously labelled by his father as 'junk'), Denton would lavish hour upon hour of loving attention on them and a choice selection would travel with him wherever he went.

By the age of ten Denton had visited Korea, Canada and Switzerland on holiday and three times had made the long journey to England. The normal passenger route to London took five weeks, with three sailings out of Shanghai every month. Stopping-off ports included Hong Kong, Singapore, Penang, Colombo and Port Said; thereafter the liner passed through the Suez Canal and then crossed the Mediterranean. The price of a first-class ticket was well under £100. Alternatively, there was another route via Canada and the Atlantic.

For a young child the time spent on board must have seemed endless, especially when the grown-ups were engaged in their own social activities. Denton, already solitary by nature and disinclined to join in with the rough-and-tumble games of other boys, would while away the long hours by fixing his eyes on a particular passenger who appealed to his romantic imagination. A sufficiently dramatic expression or an exotically 'historical' surname was quite enough reason for an innocent lady or gentleman to become the object of his curiosity.

Denton made his first visit to England as a four-year-old child in 1919. It was not as he had expected it to be. 'I had known there was a war between England and Germany and could not understand why my parents wanted to go back to a country that must surely be nothing but a mass of gaunt and smoking ruins'.[7] The Welches were lent a house at the seaside resort of Frinton in Essex, famous for its pleasant beach and golf courses. Denton retained remarkably vivid memories of the holiday, as he demonstrated when answering a fan letter from a Major Dougald McGregor in 1946:

. . . I did not remember that the house [in Frinton] was called 'The Willows', but I know that it had queerish, crackled tiles in the porch, because the crackle was a source of wonder to me. I could never quite decide whether it were intentional or a mistake. Then too I remembered the wind howling around a corner of the drawing-room, while I was huddling in the cushions on the sofa all alone. And there was a grown-up called Phyl who upset me a great deal by saying that I should be kept upstairs in the nursery with the nurses.

There was a tiny butcher's shop in the house. It fascinated me and I loved to hook and unhook the miniature cuts of meat. They were carved out of wood and gruesomely real-seeming. One night I woke up and found myself at the bottom of my bed, under the clothes. I imagined that I was going to suffocate and began screaming for my mother or my nurse. It was a terrible moment for me. I thought that nobody would be able to hear and I would be left to die slowly.

There was a girl who painted the *most* beautiful violets and put real silver paint on the vase. She also covered a box with silk and made cherries out of silk and cotton-wool to decorate it. I admired it enormously. It was for her mother's birthday and I well remember the great to-do and hiding that took place when the mother was heard to be approaching the nursery door while she was working on it.

One night there was a fancy-dress party and before it began I was able to see my eldest brother Bill dressed as a cave man in a leopard-skin. He pretended to pull my mother along by her hair and to hit her with his club. It was all a little too realistic for me and I tried to get her away from him as quickly as possible. There was another boy at the party dressed in one of the girl's frocks and with the most grotesque kiss-curls drawn on his forehead and cheeks with an eyebrow pencil. He was also a little terrifying to me, but amusing too. I had to watch his preposterous dancing and hand movements. It was a sort of Douglas Byng act. Could this have been you? Or have I got my people hopelessly mixed? I wish I could remember each person more perfectly. Only the impression remains of several other children all older than myself, and so friends of my brothers and not of me. I know that my mother had a large mustard-yellow velvet bow on her hat and that I thought it the dirtiest colour in the world. I know too that she lost one of her lapis earrings and that the nurse went with me to the police station to enquire about it. On the way she terrified me by telling me that she was taking me there to be locked up, wicked woman.

You may remember a mine on the beach. I have been told that it was harmless, but I still expected it to explode, and whenever Paul went too near I was in a fever of anxiety. We caught tiny flat fish, which I looked on as plaice, designed by God for dolls. . . [8]

As Denton relates in the autobiographical fragment, 'I Can Remember', they spent Christmas of that year with his grandfather Joseph Welch at Waphams in Henfield, within sight of the Sussex Downs. The old man, now seventy-five, had himself gone out to Shanghai in 1866 as an apprentice in the tea trade and after some years had been successful enough to establish his own business in the rapidly expanding city. When the Boxer Rising came in the summer months of 1900 old Welch had decided that it was a propitious moment to retire and so he returned to England. His firm, Welch & Co., had been made over to Denton's father, but shortly after taking on a new partner the concern collapsed, the two having over-reached themselves. It was then that Arthur Welch had joined Wattie & Co., firstly as an accountant.[9]

Grandfather Welch lived with his spinster daughter Dorothy (or 'Aunt Dolly' as Denton refers to her) and was very much the Victorian in outlook and manner. Denton liked the quaintness of Waphams, years later writing, 'I was pleased that my grandfather's house was so old-fashioned; it gave me a feeling of experience, of having lived longer than I had'.[10] However, the place was quite frequently called upon to play host to young people, since Dolly's sister, Daisy Kane had married a naval chaplain from Ireland and there were nine children. In contrast to the Welches, the Kanes never had much money, but were a close-knit and happy family, often on the move from one home to another. For them going to Waphams was a great treat; aside from being fond of their grandfather, the house had a very pleasant and spacious garden, lovingly tended by Fred Coles.

The three Welch boys on the other hand, being used to the fast and colourful life of Shanghai with its far more relaxed attitude to social convention, as they got older most probably came to find the place rather tame, although Denton, with his great curiosity about history and his love of the old-world English village, appreciated Henfield just because it was a small, typically quiet Sussex town.

Paul, the middle Welch brother, was Aunt Dolly's favourite. Perhaps it was this that in time encouraged Denton to play the 'difficult nephew'; when writing about his aunt in his first novel, *Maiden Voyage*, he portrays her as having been no more than dutifully affectionate towards him. Thomas Kane, one of the first cousins, understood how the over-sensitive nephew came to feel this: 'Aunt Dolly wouldn't stand any nonsense and could be severe at times. We all had to button down. But she was basically a kind person'.[11] Normally, however, Mr and Mrs Welch would only inflict their three sons on the rather staid household for short visits—their custom was to rent a house in the country. Trips to England were only worthwhile if they lasted for a few months.

After the Christmas season Mrs Welch and the boys stayed on at Waphams until the late spring of 1920. Bill was now old enough to go to prep school and once he had been installed at Darley Dale in Derbyshire, Rosalind, Paul and Denton set off for Canada, where they spent the summer months as guests of friends who owned a ranch.[12] When at last they did return to Shanghai—they had been away for well over a year—everything must have seemed quite different to Denton, his mind now sensitive to the feel of two radically contrasting cultures.

He described the year that followed as having been 'the last stage of infancy, a quiet time of playing with my brother in the garden, building houses in the bushes and hiding in the branches of the camphor tree'[13] In the afternoons it was the boys' delight to take a ride in an ancient carriage drawn by a twenty-three year-old horse 'Girlie'; it had belonged to their Welch grandmother. An old mafoo in a green-braided coat with capes and a conical hat would look after the horse, whilst Denton and Paul stood on the steps each side of the vehicle, pretending to be firemen. A somewhat alarmed nurse sat in the middle of the back seat trying to keep an eye on them.

The four rooms that made up the attics of their home in Shanghai were a constant source of interest, especially the three that were kept locked. Sometimes Denton's mother would go up there in search of this or that and he relished the chance to see still more belongings of his grandmother, a lady who had died on board a ship as it was passing through the Red Sea. He remembered 'strange, thick, gold bracelets, a great mourning ring with a fleur-de-lys on it in fire-opal, a brooch of jet and pearls, a long necklace of white sapphires fitted into a chain, scent bottles, chatelaines, vinaigrettes and belts of cast silver. The whole case seemed filled with treasure to me, and I never tired of undoing the little leather boxes and unwrapping the faint-mauve cotton wool'.[14]

Plenty of children, of course, are intrigued by old things, but with Denton a pretty ivory or a decorated snuff-box would give him more pleasure than almost anything else in life. Such objects represented a fantastic world of mystery and colour and around each piece he would weave an exotic story. But it would be wrong to think he led an entirely solitary and cossetted existence. Like any other child he was high-spirited enough to enjoy playing with his brothers and their friends and he found that the kindergarten, where he was sent at the age of six, far from being 'the Jaws of Hell' that he had expected it to be, offered a number of quite congenial pastimes alongside the laborious copying out of numbers from one to ten. Each summer the Welches would take an extended holiday and in 1921 Rosalind and her two younger sons set off for Wei-hai Wei, an island near the Shantung Peninsula, some 480 nautical miles north of Shanghai. It was leased to the British from 1898 to 1930. O.M. Green in *The Foreigner in China* paints a most attractive picture of the settlement: 'with its exquisite climate, russet mountains, blue sea and lovely bays, Wei-hai Wei as a summer resort could not be surpassed and every year numerous foreigners journeyed thither from the fierce heat of Shanghai and Tientsin'.[15]

Denton's memories of the island were somewhat less idyllic. In the short story 'Narcissus Bay', which he wrote in 1944, he tells of his first encounter with human brutality. He had wandered off by himself and had witnessed a scene wholly alien to the world of innocent pleasure that was all he had hitherto known:

> . . . I remember seeing four men and one woman coming down through the woods from the mountain. Two of the men had their hands tied behind their backs; their chests were naked, and they had thick ropes round their necks. The other two held these ropes, which they made to curl and ripple as they drove their prisoners on. The woman walked behind. Her dusty black hair was torn down over her face and shoulders. Blood oozed from the cuts on her scalp; a patch of oiled paper had been stuck over one gash, and her lips were swollen and bruised. White cotton puffed out of the sharp tears all over her quilted clothes. She was crying and shaking her head exaggeratedly.[16]

Although it is possible that this horrific experience was taken from a later period in his life and has been transposed here for literary effect, the extract does indicate that alongside the delicate beauty of the landscape and the refinement of its porcelain, Denton also grew up with some appreciation of the underlying violence and inhumanity that was as much a part of the reality of China.

England must have seemed very predictable and safe by comparison. However, with his Shanghai background, he inevitably saw this country and its society through eyes very different from those of a boy born and bred here. He took nothing at its face value. The fact that Arthur Welch had a very large family that was dotted about England added to a feeling of belonging, but as Denton grew older this notion proved to be illusory—the aunts and uncles and cousins were never quite able to live up to his ideal of what a family should be.

There was always some relation that the Welches could call upon to look after them when they came over. In 1922 it was the turn of Denton's great-aunt Blanche, who lived at Birchington on the north coast of Kent.[17] She found them a house to rent and a local governess was hired to deal with Denton. 'Miss T.', as he refers to her, fancied herself as being 'artistic' and decided rather ambitiously that she would try to teach the seven-year-old to draw:

She set up some drapery and gave me a piece of charcoal. I laboured and smudged and rebelled, I ran with my charcoal into the garden. I can see the impatient whisk of her skirt as she turned her back on me and went into the house, clutching the board and the paper. Soon after this she left and I was allowed to go on with my childish drawing.[18]

From this time onwards Denton no longer had his brother as a regular playmate. They were very close in age—less than two years separated them—and had done everything together. Paul, generous-spirited and easy-going, was boyish and keen at games. Denton writes that he was 'desolate' when at the age of eight Paul was sent away to join Bill at prep school.

But the sense of dejection did not last long. Suddenly, a new character, Wooly, burst in on his life. She was the new governess and it was her job to take him in hand, leaving Rosalind free to catch up with her own circle of friends. Wooly was quite unlike anyone he had known:

She wore pince-nez and had two wings of hair that left her ears exposed. She took Kruschen salts, and I always remember the queer feeling I had on the first night when she bathed me. . . . She was energetic and full of anecdotes, always about herself and her past. She managed me very much more than I had ever been managed before. . . . My life became defined. There were special ways of drying oneself, eating, sleeping, brushing one's hair, folding one's clothes, and these rules must not be broken. [19]

Despite this change in his life, Denton liked Wooly. She gave him a great deal of attention and had been employed specially to look after *him*, yet she was nothing like his mother. There were all the stories Wooly would tell about her own family. On walks Denton was shown wild flowers, which he pooh-poohed until one day she took him for a picnic in a bluebell wood. Wooly told him all she knew about history, a subject for which he had already developed an insatiable appetite.

The family travelled around Kent taking in the sights: the ruined flint church at Reculver, forlornly looking out to sea, and the overpowering majesty of Canterbury Cathedral both made a lasting impression on Denton. They also went to Broadstairs, the town that was to play such an important part in Denton's recuperation after the accident. Little could he have guessed that in twelve years time he would be lying in a state of desperate misery at a nursing-home in a back-street of the resort. It is chilling to think of the two visits—the first as a happy, carefree child, bombarding his mother with questions; the second as a twenty-year-old in terrible pain and with a future so uncertain as to appear virtually hopeless.

Wooly accompanied Denton and his mother when they returned to China. Back at the house in Shanghai her lessons were now to be taken seriously. It seems that Denton, who throughout his life had a deep loathing of authority, was neither a willing nor a particularly talented pupil:

Wooly has told me since that it was almost impossible to teach me sometimes; I would just sit, weeping sullenly until my face was red and swollen. Only, when my sums were right, everything was changed and I felt a quiet delight.[20]

Although he had begged his mother to let him have piano lessons, these too did not run very smoothly. Even so, a genuine love of music remained with him for the rest of his life, and despite not being especially talented, Denton continued taking music lessons for many years. Eventually, when he had his own home, he bought a little harpsichord.

Writing about his days as an art student at Goldsmiths', Denton mentions that when he was alone in his room he would often dance around, as if celebrating his freedom. Certainly it was not the dancing classes on his agenda in Shanghai that were responsible for this. His teacher, Miss Sharp—that was her real name—was a stern harridan with a biting tongue. However, Denton recalled that her instruction had been infinitely preferable to that at the riding-school run by Cossacks. 'There I would solemnly ride round the covered ring, first trotting and gradually going faster and faster, trying all the time to do everything correctly. . . . Wooly would sit, watching critically and telling me not to be a jelly'.[21] His horse was called Whiskers, and one day, to his extreme satisfaction, it escaped from the stable at their home and demolished a number of flowerbeds in the garden.

Had Denton's experience of China been restricted solely to the grossly Europeanized and decadent city of Shanghai, one feels that his aesthetic sense could never have been so richly developed. It was the journeys out of the city into the stunning countryside that were never to be forgotten. One such experience that is described at length was a trip he and Wooly made to the mountain resort of Mokanshan ('Isolated Peak') near Hangchow to stay with two American missionary sisters, the Misses Allen; this summer Mr and Mrs Welch had decided to go on holiday to Java.

After a long rail journey Denton and his governess rested for a night at the home of a Dutch consul, who, pressing a killing bottle into the boy's hand, asked Denton to find various beetles that he might add to his collection. The next day was spent in taking a motor launch along a series of canals, although for the final leg Denton and Wooly were carried in sedan chairs:

We left the watery rice fields, the pools between the rocks, and passed by the neglected tea terraces. The path was steep and narrow, the efforts of the coolies were agonizing; the sedans swung from side to side and I was terrified. I thought I was much too heavy for them and that they would lose their balance and throw me down a gully.[22]

However, they safely reached the Allens' house up in the mountains and were greeted with a meal of tomato soup and pumpkin pie, something that Denton had never before tasted.

In the days that followed Denton tried out his lethal bottle on the insects and was allowed to bathe in the pool of a mountain spring. He had learnt to swim in Wei-hai Wei. His style was breast-stroke. When the weather was fine he and Wooly went on walks with the maiden sisters; when it was not, the four of them would sit in the house playing mah-jong. Wooly taught Denton to knit, which, unlike most boys, he took to without thinking it in the least bit odd.

Captivated by this world of deserted Buddhist and Taoist monasteries, romantic hills and the occasional abandoned European house, Denton was loving the holiday. And when the news came that his mother was back from Java and that she would come up to Mokanshan to stay with them, his joy was complete. Rosalind appeared bearing presents for Denton, which he undid in a frenzy of excitement. The next evening the Allen sisters organized a moonlight picnic around a pool, at which, to Denton's amazement, his mother, in a moment of caprice, pushed a young girl into the water.

Denton was eight. He had reached the age at which a boy of his upbringing would normally be sent away to a prep school in England, as his brothers Bill and Paul had been. However, what with all the travelling to and fro between England and China, his education to date had been extremely sporadic, consisting mainly of Wooly's idiomatic lessons. Matters might have been more clear cut if Denton had shown more aptitude, but it seems that he was so wrapped up in his own little world that lessons really had scant meaning for him. However, the time had now come to prepare for what lay ahead, and so once back in Shanghai he went to a school for British children run by a Mrs Paul. From Denton's account of the place, however, it seems the pupils learnt little more than rudimentary spelling.

So far books were only of interest if they had pictures. The first mention Denton makes of having looked at one was when he went to a pre-Christmas eighteenth-century costume party that year. He writes of how he had gone dressed in 'a blue suit with knee-breeches and powdered hair'. After feasting on rather too many cream cakes, he and the other children go into the drawing-room of the house where there is a huge tree weighed down with presents. Denton finds that the one handed to him is a nicely bound book of Greek myths:

> I turned the pages idly, for I could not yet read, until my eyes fell on a picture of Prometheus chained to the rock, a vulture hovering over him. He was nearly naked, his athlete's chest and arms pinned to the rock, his powerful legs straddled apart, his perfect features contorted with pain. It gave me the same feeling that crucifixes did. I felt shame and admiration. I shut the book quickly. I did not want anyone to see me looking at the picture.[23]

This small incident evidently achieved some significance in Denton's mind for him to have remembered it so vividly. Possibly he saw it in retrospect as a fledgling confirmation of his homosexuality, although to an observer it could just as well reveal an inhibited and slightly morbid attitude towards sexuality in general. Whatever the case, it was very characteristic of Denton's nature as a child that things he did not understand would be stored away, unresolved and bothersome.

In writing of his early years it becomes clear to the reader that Denton is intending to portray himself as having been a secretive child, separated from other boys by a sensitivity that led him to rely on his own reserves of knowledge and inner strength. His account of an incident that happened on Christmas Day itself confirms this.[24] Mr and Mrs Welch together with their youngest son were spending the holiday on a house-boat. The plan was to go up river from Shanghai. Denton had his own cabin with two bunks in it.

Before getting down to the main event of the story, he describes how he dropped his strange gollywog-like doll out of one of the portholes into the river. Nancy Quinlan remembers the toy as having been 'chocolate-coffee brown'; it was usually to be found in his sitting-room. Although upset at losing his doll-companion, one visualizes his half-purposeful abandonment of it as being a symbolic shedding of childish things.

Just as he had come quite unexpectedly upon the scene of the brutalized woman being humiliated at Wei-hai Wei, his confrontation with a decayed corpse this Christmas afternoon must have been equally traumatic. After their lunch on board the boat, the Welches went for a walk in the countryside:

The hills were honeycombs, the cells of which were tombs. There were mounds of earth and small shrines with top-heavy roofs. Many were excavated in the shape of a horseshoe, with an altar in the middle. Here the families would come to worship their ancestors. The ground was littered with gold and silver paper money which had been offered as a sacrifice.[25]

Denton tells how he leaves his parents and strolls off by himself. He notices one of the ruined tombs has split open and that inside there is a coffin in a state of disintegration. With that curiosity for the macabre so typical in children, he cannot resist investigating: 'I went nearer and saw a skull, the reddish hair and livid flesh still clinging to it in strips. I was covered with fear which held me tight inside'.[26] Denton runs away from the chilling sight, scratching his legs in distraction, until he finds his mother and father—but he does not tell them of the incident. The degree to which this experience made an indelible impression on him can be measured by the fact that aside from writing it up in 'I Can Remember', it forms the basis for the short story, 'The Coffin on the Hill' and he also painted a picture using the same title.[27]

If the boy had been asked at this stage of his life whether he regarded England or China as being 'home', he would undoubtedly have chosen the latter. Denton knew, however, that before very long he would be sent away to school in England—there was no other socially acceptable alternative—and since he never envisaged being remotely interested in pursuing a business career, it seems likely that from an early age he realized that in all probability he would end up living in London or some other part of the country. It was a world with which he needed to feel more familiar.

Now nine, Denton was able to take in much more when in 1924 his parents brought him over to England once again. Someone had found them a house to rent in the village of Benson a few miles south-east of Oxford. The plan was that before moving into Brookside they would tour around in a new car that Arthur Welch had hired. He was the driver. Rosalind sat with him in the front; Denton, feeling a little sick, in the back.

Pressing on through Northamptonshire, they made for Repton, where Bill was now at school. On the way Denton was given a great treat. Derbyshire's three great houses are all close together and the family visited each one. The romantically situated Haddon Hall, then empty, was the first stately home that Denton had been to. 'The gardens were wonderful, in terraces, falling into the woods, lost in the early summer haze;' he remembered, 'I was enchanted'.[28] Next came the late seventeenth-century Chatsworth with its palatial grounds, and lastly Hardwick Hall, that extravagant monument to a formidable Elizabethan lady. The opulence and sheer wealth of historical association must have been overpowering for the child. However, as if reacting against the *embarras de richesses*, after staying at a Georgian hotel in Burton-on-Trent, which was near Repton, Denton quite rapidly began to form a definite aesthetic allegiance that was to remain with him throughout his life:

This was a new period to me. So far we had only stayed in Tudor places. My mother told me what she knew about the eighteenth century and I became absorbed. Something inside me told me that this sort of architecture was greater than all the beamed cottages put together, which I had had such a mania for.[29]

Fortunately, the prospect of going to Repton was distant enough in the future for Denton to enjoy the richly historical setting of the public school unhindered. He liked the idea of having an Art School housed in what had once been the ox-stables of the twelfth-century priory and inside the building he was delighted to come across plaster casts of Greek and Roman sculpture, objects that he already admired from a collection of photographs Rosalind had kept from her time in Florence.

It was still term-time, so very soon Denton and his parents drove south to settle into their rented house; Bill and Paul would join them later. Benson is a small and quite dull village, marked only by a trickling stream that runs alongside its main road. Nor did Brookside where they were going to stay seem exactly attractive from the exterior, Denton recalling that 'it had a very repressed unmarried look'. The family to whom the house belonged had fallen on hard times and had decamped to what was virtually an army hut in the village, letting out the property.

As soon as the Welches moved into the house there began a great spring-cleaning. Denton, determined not to be left out, set about applying a nailbrush and his father's shaving soap to some of the darker oil paintings; he used Adam's furniture polish to restore a shiny surface, since the varnish had been made dull by his scrubbing. That job done, he went around the rather squalid place energetically waxing any piece of furniture that seemed in need of his dedicated attention.

When his brothers arrived for the school holidays life became more boyish. Paul taught Denton to ride a bicycle and was determined that his pupil should be able to produce a creditable skid-mark on the lawn. Denton's first day out on the road was fine until a car appeared, at which he immediately lost his newly acquired confidence and went into the ditch. The weather was not especially good during their stay at Benson and there were evidently days when Mr and Mrs Welch did not feel up to taking their three boys sight-seeing. One rainy afternoon, having nothing better to do, Denton decided to go and explore the disused barn that lay across the cobbled stable-yard outside the house:

I entered by the huge, crazy door and shut it behind me. I was in darkness with the smell of dust and mice and hay in my nostrils. The light came in through the cracks in the doors and the walls. I climbed up onto some boxes and hung onto a beam, pretending I was a monkey. I took my raincoat off and jersey, to be freer. I gnashed my teeth and made contorted faces, I gibbered and tried to hang on with one hand as I scratched myself with the other.[30]

Quite soon Denton thought it would be fun to imagine himself as a slave from Ancient Greece, and so he shed his remaining clothes. Paul came in, undressed himself too, and joined in the game. Denton writes that the two of them were 'dancing and swinging like mad mice'.

This old farm building, symbolic of a timeless, hidden aspect of rustic life that appealed greatly to Denton's imagination, was the setting of his short story, 'The Barn', which he completed in 1943.[31] It is centred around a tramp coming to the house on a wet night and asking if he might bed down in the barn until morning. Denton wrote a brief paragraph describing the events as they actually occurred in 'I Can Remember' and he tells how he rose early the next day to see the man go, recalling that 'he was grey and unwashed and quite young'.

In 'The Barn' a contrast is made between the comfortable life of the young boy (Denton), deeply engrossed in polishing his own possessions inside the house, and the tramp, who owns nothing and just has need of the most basic requirement—a good night's sleep out of the rain. The boy decides that he must go and sample the other life. Quite late at night, when his parents are about to retire, he steals out of the house, taking some blankets and sweets and goes to the barn across the wet yard. The tramp is asleep in the hay, only to be woken by Denton shining a torch in his eyes. Initially suspicious, the young man relaxes and is quite friendly, jeering a bit at the child's idealistic notions of what a life on the road must be like. Denton cannot resist sleeping there with him. He tells the story as if they are two innocents at one with nature—the man as the father-protector figure and Denton as his child-pet:

Deep, deep into the hay I sank, until we were in one nest. He did not wake again, but stirred a little in his sleep, turning towards me. I drew as close as I dared to him and lay, my head close to his chest, so that I could feel the rhythm of its rising and falling.[32]

In the morning he wakes up to find the tramp's arm over him. The young man looks at him and smiles—'he had accepted me'. Denton feels that they now have a bond. He yearns to sustain it a little longer, but the tramp is soon on his way. He is followed for a while by his new admirer, but finally has to throw him off, the story concluding with a return to hard reality: 'At last he stood up, and looking at me harshly, compellingly, he said, "Now go back, you silly little sod".'[33]

Although the story has its factual basis, it is impossible to determine whether the fiction of a relationship with the tramp was thought up when the event actually occurred, or whether, as with the case of the picture of Prometheus that he looked at in a book, the incident achieved a significance only retrospectively in the light of Denton's acceptance of his sexuality. Whichever is the case, one can be certain that Denton's feelings about the barn and the tramp are evidence that his romantic sympathy for working-class men, especially of the land, existed from a very early age and that it was something embedded in his need to find emotional acceptance. He sought in such figures the strong but gentle fatherly care that Arthur Welch could not provide.

At the end of the summer Mr Welch returned to Shanghai and Bill and Paul to their respective schools, so that Denton and his mother were left alone. It had been arranged that he should attend a Christian Science day-school in London and one was found at Queen's Gate in South Kensington. Denton was to lodge with a family, giving Rosalind the freedom to visit friends and relations in other parts of England. This was the first time Denton would be completely separated from his family and he balked at the prospect.

Fortunately, Mrs Spencer, with whom he stayed, did her utmost to make him feel at home and he managed to get on well with her daughter Gwen, who was also a pupil at the school. But as soon as Denton was left alone in his new room that evening he was overcome by sickness and depression and went to bed crying bitterly. He felt abandoned.

In the morning the children set out for Queen's Gate:

Inside the door of the school was a subdued buzzing of girls' voices and the insistent smell of turpentine and beeswax. This was a girls' school where a few small boys were also taken. In the clean-smelling darkness of the hall I saw all these girls with their soft brown hair, and one in particular caught my eye. She must have been about sixteen. She was quite olive coloured, as smooth as rubber, with big animal's eyes and tight curled hair as dark and shining as black treacle. She was quite beautiful and very arresting.[34]

Denton wrote that this school was the only one he ever liked, especially since 'everything seemed to be done for the interest of doing it'. Elsewhere, he confesses that he 'adroitly avoided the one or two other little boys'. The pupils were taught drawing, they could listen to poetry being read, they could sing songs in rounds and even try their hands at elementary sewing. Just before lunch came the half-hour of the day Denton most eagerly awaited—his form mistress would read to them:

> She had pale gold hair done in a plait round her head, and I think she wore thin rimmed glasses, but I am not sure. She had a delightful mildness and serenity. . .
>
> After morning school was over, we would all cluster round her and implore her to go on with the fascinating story of some children who discovered by chance an ancient crypt under some medieval ruins, and how later they also discovered that it was being used as a storehouse by criminals. The rivières of diamonds! The emerald rings! The rubies that had belonged to Indian princes; birds with jewelled eyes that flapped their wings when wound up; the kegs of brandy and almost legendary liqueurs; laces, satins, cloth of gold.[35]

This exotic Aladdin's-cave world so atmospherically described in the book must have made Denton all the more frustrated that he was still unable to read. It was irksome for him to be with children of the same age who already had a three years' start on him.

Twice a week organized physical exercise raised its ugly head and the pupils would travel by train to some playing fields. Denton hated having to join in the games of hockey. This was, nevertheless, a useful introduction to the communal sporting activity from which there would be no escape once he went to boarding-school. Although always happy to take up a tennis racket, team games really did not appeal to him in the least.

Whilst his mother was away, Denton was taken out on Sundays by two of her friends. One of these was Cissie Carpmael, a bright-eyed, middle-aged Christian Scientist. Denton had known her since he was four. Mrs Carpmael was a painter rather in the English Impressionist mould, and she had a studio at Cheyne Row in Chelsea. It was here that Denton was first able to sample something of the life of an artist. 'We would often have tea in her studio, where the smell of paint intoxicated me. The size of her paint tubes thrilled me too. They were as large as my toothpaste tube'.[36] The enthusiastic boy was taken to Rowney's art shop, near Harrods, where she bought him a little easel. The seed of his ambition to become an artist was sown. Over the next twenty years Denton saw Cissie Carpmael regularly and shortly before her death in 1947 he managed to persuade a London gallery to show some of her paintings.

Rosalind Welch's return to London meant that Denton no longer had to board with the Spencers and soon mother and son had installed themselves at the smart Hotel Vandyck, a long-since-disappeared establishment that occupied three houses in Cromwell Road overlooking the gardens of the Natural History Museum. This should have been a happy time with Rosalind taking Denton sight-seeing around the capital and going into the country at weekends[37]—he would have her entirely to himself, uninterrupted either by his father or brothers. Yet, despite the distraction of being taken to Harrods to buy a fairy-cycle, which he rode with delirious abandon around the pavements in Knightsbridge, Denton began to notice a change in her.

There were moments now when she was no more the carefree, energetic person that he knew and loved. She had to take rests, and, naturally, he could not understand why. After school it was decided that he should be read to by Molly, a middle-aged friend, but he resented not being able to spend this time with Rosalind. 'This arrangement is chiefly made, I think, because my mother wants to help her friend,' he wrote, 'but I have the sneaking fear that it may also be because my mother is bored of me'.[38]

The situation would have been difficult for any child to accept. She looked much the same to him. 'with her wonderful gold-brown curls and the brick-dust colour of her cheeks', but now she tended to become tired by quite modest physical exertion. In his Journal entry of the 7th December 1942, he recalled an evening when he went to see her after a reading session was over:

> I go into our room and find my mother lying on the bed in the half-light. I go up to her and see that she is clearly not well, for her face is buried in the pillows and I think that she has been crying.
>
> 'Love me, darling,' she says, turning towards me. 'Love me, love me, and I shall be all right.'
>
> I am terribly disturbed. Tears start to run down my cheeks and my mother sees them shining on my face.
>
> 'Don't cry, darling; I didn't say cry.' My mother laughs and teases me so that it is unbearably sad.
>
> 'Sing to me,' she says. 'Sing "O Gentle Presence, Peace and Joy and Power" or "Saw ye my Saviour? Heard ye the glad sound?"'
>
> I try to sing the Christian Science hymns, but break down completely and hug my mother fiercely. Gradually she seems to get better. At last she sits up and says laughingly, "How silly to behave like that! It's only Error trying to get hold of me!'[39]

Although a lively boy, Denton was small for his age and not very strong. This was probably the reason why his mother did not yet consider him ready to face the rigours of boarding-school life, even though he was already over nine-and-a-half. It is possible too that Rosalind, having been told of the potential seriousness of her illness, thought that Denton, almost clingingly devoted, should at least be allowed to remain with her whilst she still had tolerably good health.

. With the spell at school in Queen's Gate over, Mrs Welch and her three sons went off to Switzerland for the Christmas holidays and some time after that she and Denton left Europe altogether and made the long journey back to Shanghai.[40] It was about this period that the Welches moved, Arthur using mainly his wife's money to buy 585 Avenue Foch, a comfortable house in the French Concession. Nancy Quinlan's thumb-nail sketch of Denton at this age reveals a little boy still doggedly individualistic:

When we met up at the more modern house they had, after we had been to England, there was no longer a magnolia tree, so we used the flat roof of the garage to play on—that was our pirate boat. We were brigands and we took beautiful maidens hostage and these games went on for days. Then in the winter we used to play in a spare bedroom. We used to put on all his mother's evening dresses and shoes. We left a terrible mess everywhere and the Chinese boy had to clear up afterwards. Denton was bubbling over with fun and ideas all the time.

We couldn't play in Denton's own room, because there were fans, feathers and shells in it, all displayed on little tables, and you daren't move about in case you knocked something over. That was why we had to play in the spare room. I think all the things were arranged out after he had been to Peking. In those days in Peking there were lots of special streets—you'd have a silk street, a street of semi-precious stones, and so on. Everybody bought beautiful things there.[41]

She also recalls a Wendy House that Denton had in the garden. He writes about it in the short story, 'The Packing-case House and the Thief', one of his least-known published works. Here, once again, he recaptures the childish pleasures of these years, when life was still protected, unsullied by boarding-schools and the tragedy of his mother's early death (see Appendix One for the full text of the story, and Bibliography no.39).

Eventually, though, the evil hour could be postponed no longer and Denton, aged eleven, was sent to prep school. The place chosen was St Michael's, in Uckfield, Sussex. A fellow-pupil of Denton's, Michael Astor, described the initial impact of going there as 'like being thrown into an ice-cold bath straight out of a warm bed'. Aside from taking a large proportion of Christian Science children,[42] St Michael's had the double advantage of being only about twenty-five miles from his grandfather's house at Henfield, from which it was easy for Aunt Dolly to drive over and take him out or collect him at the end of term. But whatever arrangements had been made in his favour, Denton was desperately unhappy to go, especially since his mother was at the other end of the globe and in failing health. From Rosalind's point of view, Denton would need all the support that Christian Science had to offer if he was to cope with what lay ahead.

English prep schools have always been infamous for being staffed by eccentrics and St Michael's was no exception. The large red-brick house overlooking the gently undulating fields of the Vale of Sussex, bordered to the north by Ashdown Forest and to the south by the Downs, was run by a very strange Anglican clergyman called Harold Hibbert Herbert Hockey, whose chief distinction in life had been that he gained a half blue in association football when at Cambridge. The place had originally been built as an agricultural college in the late nineteenth century, but now the school brochure could boast a gymnasium and a small indoor swimming-pool; another photograph displayed lots of small boys busily running about in scouts' uniform. School dress was grey trousers and a grey jersey with a pink V at the neck.

There were about ninety pupils in all and they came from very different backgrounds. The well-meaning headmaster, Mr Hockey, whose wife was a Christian Scientist, was wholly inept at managing the financial side of running the school—it fell to the butler, apparently a crook, to look after the bills and wages. Generally the parents of the Christian Science children were the wealthiest (St Michael's had a good reputation for getting boys into Eton) and so to encourage them Hockey engaged three Scientists as teachers. These men were also relied upon to take charge of the boys' spiritual welfare. A former pupil of the school, the author Jocelyn Brooke, who was seven years Denton's senior and had left by the time he came, wrote very scathingly about 'St Ethelbert's' in his autobiographical book, *The Military Orchid*:

> Every morning before breakfast we 'Scientists' congregated in a sort of catacomb in the basement, where the day's 'lesson' was read to us by one of the assistant-masters, Mr Learoyd, a 'keen Scientist' himself. His 'keenness' showed itself at times in other ways: he had a singularly well-developed knack of twisting arms and ears during his arithmetic classes. However, as he believed that pain was an Error of Mortal Mind, he could afford to laugh pleasantly at the tears of anguish and humiliation which his 'keenness' too often provoked.[43]

Denton, on the other hand, having no real wish to recall what had been one of the most miserable phases of his life, wrote nothing about the experiences he had endured as a pupil; the three glimpses he left of St Michael's are concerned rather with character-studies of some of the people he encountered there. None of these fragments extends to more than three pages in print. 'A Child Meets Church and State in Strange Places' describes Lady Astor descending on the school to see her son Michael acting in *The Mikado*, whereas another piece records a conversation between a boy called 'Marshall' (this is Denton) and an older pupil as they stroll around the Big Field arm in arm.[44] Lastly, there is the account of his mother visiting the school to take him out. It is in this latter fragment that Denton paints a very funny portrait of the headmaster's wife:

> Mrs Hockey met us at the foot of the stairs. She had just come down in a new dress. It was brilliantly patterned and coloured, and she carried an eighteenth-century quizzing glass with an enormously thick lens through which she peered. The legend in the school was that she was so blind that she had given the prize for the best boy's garden to a quite neglected one almost completely overgrown with huge dandelions. I wondered how much her eyes hurt her, and whether she would ever go quite blind. [45]

It is more than likely that Denton had to face the usual prep school indignity of being told what to put in his letters home to his parents. To the author's knowledge, none of these has been preserved. What have survived, though, are eight of Rosalind's replies, dating from the winter months of 1926, and these give a valuable insight into her relationship with Denton. Needless to say, generally she did her best to write about things that he wanted to hear, such as details of the improvements she had made to the decoration of the new house, but when she went on to describe how Taffy was missing him and how well the pup was getting on with a new kitten they had been given, Denton very probably felt even more homesick and isolated.

The first of the letters was written on board the Canadian Pacific liner, the *Empress of India*. Mrs Welch had just been in Vancouver.

> We have had tea-parties nearly every afternoon in Mr Matthews' cabin. I wonder if you remember him? He lived next door to us last winter and came in for a cocktail once or twice. We got hold of a gramophone and some good records and it has been such fun trying to dance in the cabin with the ship rolling and about ten people in the cabin as well. Needless to say, we could not all dance at once.
>
> I had a tea-party in my room, which is the drawing-room of a suite in a deck. My bed is the sofa, and they put in rather a smelly little washstand. I never use it, but go to the bathroom. It [i.e. the room] has tapestry panels and looks very nice, but there are no hooks, no place to put books, except on a table, and as it has been rough, they have been on the floor part of the time. One night my wardrobe trunk fell over against the table and that slid over towards my sofa and the books fell on me.[46]

It seems that Denton felt very sore when he read of Mr Matthews' attentions to his mother and the reaction was remembered into his adult life: in 1944 he wrote a short story, 'At Sea', which is constructed around the above incident.[47] Here Denton has placed himself on board the liner with his mother, and he takes an instant dislike to 'Mr Barron' (alias Matthews), who is unflatteringly characterized as 'so delicate and spectacled and poor and gentlemanly looking'. Barron has a smile that reminds him of a skeleton. Predictably, the invitation for his mother to come to a tea-party in Barron's cabin throws the little boy into a fit of jealousy and he scolds her that if she accepts she will almost certainly be forced to compromise her Christian Science principles. 'Robert' (Denton) takes himself off in a sulk, but after a while starts chatting to a certain Princess de Bourbon, who accompanies him to Mr Barron's quarters, where the party is in full swing. Several of the guests offer Denton a sample of their drinks, and after eating a cherry soaked in brandy and some of the Princess's pistachio chocolates, not surprisingly he feels rather ill and starts to cry.

> Robert's mother immediately left Mr Barron's arms and went up to the bed.
>
> 'What is wrong?' she asked rather coldly, bending down.
>
> 'Go away, pig,' he screamed, then turned over on his face and buried it in the eiderdown.
>
> He felt his mother's hands on his shoulders and her warm breath on his neck. He wriggled his shoulders violently and kicked back his legs. He

knew that he was about to make the most terrible scene. He had the sudden fear that his nervous excitement would make him lose control of his bladder. The shame, if this happened, would be terrible, but he also thought with detachment that it would be funny to wee-wee on Mr Barron's soft bed.

'Don't be troublesome, Robert,' his mother said briskly. 'It is so bad to make scenes in public. People never do it. They think it very ugly and in very bad taste.'

This mention of good taste, correct behaviour and public opinion struck Robert as extraordinarily frivolous and wicked.

'I don't care what anyone thinks,' he shouted into the thickness of the eiderdown; then he sprang up and ran into the centre of the cabin. The two or three dancing couples stared at him. He felt with horror the sudden warmth on the inside of his leg. His mouth fell open. He screamed some abuse at his mother, then with tears pouring down his face he ran from the cabin, slamming the door behind him.[48]

'At Sea' comes to an end with a moving reconciliation between Robert and his mother; here Denton appears to have drawn on the account of what had happened in the room at the Hotel Vandyck for his material. She comes back to their cabin after dinner and prepares to go to bed. Robert is pretending to be asleep, but glances at her and notices that she is miserable and clearly feeling unwell. Even the act of undressing is exhausting, so she lies down on the bed and tries to draw strength from Christian Science maxims, intoning, 'There is no life truth, intelligence or substance in matter. All is Infinite Mind and its infinite manifestation'. Robert is desperately upset and tries to console her with some hymns:

He wanted to sing something so consummate and wonderful that his mother would turn over and smile and be happy for ever; but he knew that she was dying and that she could not save herself. He only knew this sometimes in a flash.[49]

But in reality Denton was not with Rosalind to offer her comfort and his aching worries about her must have made the daily routine of lessons and games at St Michael's seem cruelly banal and irrelevant. In her letters his mother tried to sustain his morale as best she could, mixing in religious exhortation with her news about life in Shanghai: 'Darling, I hope you use what you understand of Science. It will help you so much with your work and your play at school. I'm sure you use some by your letters, but go on using more and more'. On one occasion Denton must have written to say he was having problems with one subject in particular, Mrs Welch advising, 'After all, why should French be any more difficult than any other lesson you have—just Error trying to make you think that'. And shortly before the start of the Christmas holidays, when he and his brothers were about to go again to Switzerland, Rosalind wrote, 'I can't tell you how happy I am that you use your Science. Do read with Molly at Wengen and use it to know that you are always God's child and that you are never separated from Him. As you said in your letter, there is no separation.' [50]

In November Rosalind wrote to Denton saying that she had just been to book the passage to England for 14th May the following year and that she expected to see him some time in the middle of June. One can imagine Denton's feeling of warmth and comfort when he read this letter around Christmas-time. The anticipation would be something to keep him going during the Easter term at St Michael's.

It was a reunion that never took place. Rosalind Welch died on 3rd March 1927 at 585 Avenue Foch, in Shanghai.[51] About three weeks afterwards Denton celebrated what must have been the most miserable birthday in his life—his twelfth.

Twenty years later, writing in his Journal, he remembered his reaction to hearing the tragic news:

C. came then in the car with Irene[52] to the school to fetch me away to the Oast House for a few days. I went into the headmaster's drawingroom. I didn't cry. I was very stiff and still and smiling. I held my gloves, straightened my coat and waited to be taken out to the car.

The chauffeur, Garrard, was there holding open the door. We got into the rather old fashioned Humber and lay back on the large, loose, puffy cushions. We swept away from St Michael's down the steep drive, and I was watching, watching all the time the streets, the houses of Uckfield, the people walking, shopping. . .

That night I sat with the earphones on my head—the new loud-speakers were no use to Cecil in her deafness. There was some music on the wireless, romantic music, and I remembered the ancient gramophone in China which had played a record of just such music. Why can I not remember what it was now? It seemed alive to me forever then. The music floated to me and melted me, and I wanted to listen to it, but Irene saw me there so near to tears, sitting by the stove in the long, low room that had once been the bottom storey of the barn, and she smiled and gently put her hand up to take the earphones off my head. I did not want her to, I wanted to listen; but I let her. And then I began to cry and gulp, and she began to tell me Christian Science truisms and words of comfort. She did it very well, with great conviction.

Later, when I went to bed in the little larkspur blue room with its oblong flowery-painted lampshade, I cried and cried again and thought that I was lost.[53]

Chapter Two

Repton and China

Denton went to Repton School in the Autumn term of 1929. He was fourteen and a half. Initially he may have enjoyed being fitted with the picturesque school uniform of black pin-striped trousers, waistcoat, tailed jacket, butterfly collar and stiff, wide-brimmed straw hat, but the move from the relatively sheltered life at St Michael's to the boisterous public school in Derbyshire, with the older boys almost grown men, must have seemed extremely daunting. There were 425 pupils at the school and they were divided up into eight houses.

Denton, who, as has already been described, had been shown around some years earlier, was the third Welch brother to enter Brook House. Bill had been there from 1922-27, rising to the status of a school prefect, and Paul came the term after his elder brother left; he was in Brook House with Denton during his entire stay at the school. Paul's presence greatly lessened Denton's feelings of insecurity—he could keep an eye on him for the first term or so and see that he escaped being bullied.

As was typical of public schools in the old days, little concession was made to a boy's comfort and Derbyshire can be a bitterly cold county in the winter. Nor was Repton an institution that laid any great emphasis on academic achievement. After all, it is less demanding and certainly cheaper in terms of the outlay of staff to drum up a sense of comradeship through organizing sports activities than it is to cultivate a high level of scholarship. Each house had three football teams, and these would vie for supremacy when playing against their equivalent team in another house and so bring credit to the unit. As a result of this rivalry there was little mixing between boys of different houses. Beatings, especially from the senior boys, were part of the daily routine and even Denton, distinctly quiet and well-behaved, was not always able to escape the cane.

Paul and Denton's housemaster was Harold John Snape ('Mr Bird' in *Maiden Voyage*), who was nicknamed 'Bulldog' Snape because he kept a mastiff. Indeed, he bore some resemblance to the animal, with his short, thick-set neck and slightly fierce appearance. John Critchley, who was one of the seven new boys to enter Brook House the term Denton came, considered the man to have been excellent at his job. He would always stand up for the boys under his charge. Critchley remembers especially that in the matter of inculcating discipline and good behaviour he would 'put you on your honour' and appeal to a boy's instinct for decency and fair-play.

Another contemporary of Denton's, though in Priory House, was the writer Roald Dahl. Despite having been in the same form for some of their time at Repton, Dahl was not able to recall having had one significant conversation with him. Also in that class, however, was David Atkins, who had known Denton as a fellow-pupil at St Michael's, and he remembered Dahl's association with him quite well:

> Welch was a natural target for cruelty, and Dahl was sometimes protective, but also enjoyed hurting him. Welch, surely a masochist, would pretend to run away; Dahl would catch him and twist his arm behind his back until tears came. He also applied Chinese burns to the skin of Welch's wrist. The rest of us stood and watched; we were all a little frightened of Dahl.[1]

Another incident that stuck in Atkins' mind was the time when the form was reading through a Shakespeare play and the master, John Crommelin Brown, gave Dahl the lead male role and Denton the female. The choice, David Atkins thinks, was mildly ironic, since on his first day at the school he had seen Dahl making a determined grab at Denton's private parts!

Roald Dahl has left some interesting, if acerbic, vignettes of their school in his book, *Boy*. The teaching staff, in particular, do not come off well. 'There were about forty or more masters at Repton,' he wrote, 'and most of them were amazingly dull and totally colourless and completely uninterested in boys'.[2] However, Dahl's most damning criticism perhaps is reserved for the then Headmaster, the Reverend Geoffrey Fisher, later Bishop of Chester and in 1945 elevated to the see of Canterbury (as had been, by some quirk of fate, his predecessor as Headmaster, William Temple). Dahl's recollections were of 'a rather shoddy bandy-legged fellow. . . this was the man who used to deliver the most vicious beatings to the boys under his care'.[3] Fisher would often fill his pipe between strokes of the cane and, after the ritual was over, a basin and sponge would thoughtfully be provided to wipe away the blood! Fisher's signature can be found on the presentation bookplate in a leather-bound copy of Kipling's *Stalky & Co.* awarded to Denton as the form prize at the end of his first term.

But he was never considered to be an outstanding pupil. Any bias that existed in the academic field at Repton was definitely towards the classics and although one can imagine Denton recreating in his mind the different hero-figures from antiquity, the study of a dead language *per se* did not interest him. The memories of Sir Richard Beaumont, also in Brook House, succinctly confirm the impression of a boy out of step with the ethos of the system: 'he would probably be called a "wimp"—small, thin, unco-ordinated in his movements. He was the reverse of the sporting type. He did not appear to be particularly intellectually bright either, and doubtless, as things proved later, he was sustained by an interior life'.[4]

Fortunately for him there were other boys in the house who were also not entirely devoted to games. A number of these found Denton to be pleasant company. Nevertheless, in such an environment he was vulnerable. The late Kenneth Blackburn, in adult life a doctor, recalled this aspect and seems to have succeeded in making his life a little easier:

Academically he was not very good. I used to help him with his prep nearly every night. . . Although very young, I realized he was entirely unsuited to public-school life, and indeed I did not agree with a great deal of it myself. I can say with truth, I think, that I took it on myself to protect him. I realized he was quite different from the rest of us. I only wish I could have known at the time that he had greatness in him. . .[5]

To Michael Hely-Hutchinson, who entered Brook House the same term, Denton was 'a very gentle and quiet little boy', not at all attuned to the hurly-burly of Repton. 'Although he may look "precious" in the house photographs,' Hely-Hutchinson continued, 'he was not really like that'.[6] Garth Stacey, another boy who had come the same term, recalled him as having been 'reserved and extremely quiet—a loner'. Also in that year, the late Rev. John Lisney remembered how Denton was reluctant to muck in with the others. For instance, when they were in a hurry to get ready in time for the roll-call in the school yard, Denton would often empty the previous bath and run a new one for himself, thus making the muddy footballers, who were really dirty and in need of a proper wash, late—and they would sometimes be punished as a result of his fastidiousness.

Denton's greatest friend at Repton, though, was Geoffrey Lumsden, who later in life became a successful actor. He was a few months Denton's senior and even at this young age had a developed theatricality. In *Maiden Voyage* he appears as 'Geoffrey Forbes'. Lumsden added a welcome dash of colour to Denton's life and the two of them were rather exuberant and iconoclastic in their opinions, although sometimes Denton took it on himself to act as a tempering force in curbing his friend's behaviour. They used to go for walks together in the countryside around the school:

> As we had both been at school for two years we were allowed to carry umbrellas. I never had one, but Geoffrey always flourished his. He would wave it and recite to me as we walked along. Suddenly he would stop in the middle of the road and ask me if I had enjoyed Hamlet's speech. If I showed no pleasure he would begin to shout, 'You little sissy, you can't think about anything but yourself.' He would poke me with the umbrella, and once he tried to tie me to a tree with my scarf.[7]

On other occasions Lumsden would sing Schubert songs to him. It was a relationship in which both of them managed to escape from the grind of school routine.

Although he sometimes found the gym to be a quiet haven away from Brook House, Denton's favourite retreat was the Art School, the building he had admired so much during his visit in 1924. On Saturdays he would get permission from the duty prefect to go over there. He liked to immerse himself in the atmosphere.

> Now, in the evening it was sombre and mysterious with casts of the Elgin Marbles floating on the gloom and partitions of heavy drapery thrown over the beams. There was a huge sink where the taps dripped and next to it a cupboard stuffed with paint-boxes, dead singing-birds, owls, brushes, milk-jugs, drawing-boards, plaster noses, ears and eyes, flower-bowls, pencils, saucers and shells.[8]

Periodically models too would be drafted in from the village; usually an old man or woman, but only the more senior pupils were allowed to draw them.

We do not know to what extent Denton was able to develop his artistic talent at the school. Before he had gone to St Michael's he had been given an easel and some oil paints and in his Journals he states that his first proper picture was a still-life, which consisted of holly and beech leaves. This was done when he was nine years old. In his writings he makes no reference to any work that he did at St Michael's, but in *The Reptonian*, the school magazine, it is noted that he participated in the school art shows and John Lisney had the memory that most of his pictures were of the old buildings around the school, and landscapes.

Whatever work was accomplished, a number of Old Reptonians in Brook House at the time associated Denton very much with the Art School. The master in charge was Arthur Norris, who taught there for thirty years from 1922. He had trained under Henry Tonks at the Slade between 1907-10 and, according to Roald Dahl, was, like his teacher, an admirer of the French Impressionists. Dennis Hawkins, who succeeded Norris as art master, remembered him as a gracious man, tall, slim and elegant—'he was for me an elusive character from the past; an old-fashioned laissez-faire Liberal'. From *Maiden Voyage* it is evident that Denton got on well with him, although he creates a very different impression of the man's personality to the one in Dahl's book.

The evidence is that Denton's work in the Art School was his only real accomplishment. An interest in music was much less developed; on Sunday mornings he would join an informal group of boys who met to sing under the direction of the headmaster's sister-in-law. These two activities were infinitely preferable to playing games, or to cross-country running, one of which had to be borne every afternoon to fulfil the school rules. Denton was hardly the first choice a football captain would make for his team and so usually he found himself struggling across the fields instead—and sometimes taking a short cut.

When in the 1940s Denton came to write about this stage of his life, he drew on what occurred in the school holidays as an equally rich source of material. With Bill now up at Oxford, it was only during these periods that the three of them would be reunited. Denton's relations with his eldest brother, however, were never easy and he felt that Bill's presence to a large extent blighted these valued weeks, a spell that should have been free from discipline and the threat of punishment. Writing to Peggy Kirkaldy in 1945, he told her his brother had been 'a sort of bogey-man to me in those school holidays. . . I felt very much under his domination '.[9]

In the summer months of 1930 Arthur Welch paid one of his periodic visits to England and with him Denton toured about the country, taking in Stratford-upon-Avon, Winchester, Oxford, Salisbury, Chichester, Teignmouth and also Brooklands race-track (the latter most probably for Bill's benefit, since he had a liking for fast cars). It seems almost certain it was on this holiday that the family stayed at Oatlands Park Hotel near Weybridge on the Thames, a visit which Denton used as the setting for his second novel, *In Youth is Pleasure*. He kept a postcard album as a souvenir of the tour with his father, and in the early pages of the novel, which begins with the statement that he was then fifteen, it is mentioned that the two of them had been to Salisbury to see Paul at his school army camp and also that just before this they had stopped off at Oxford to try and track down Bill, who tended not to tell anybody of his plans.

During the Christmas break that year Denton spent some days with his mother's old friend Mrs Carpmael, whose country home was a converted oast-house at Trottiscliffe, an attractive Kentish village on the edge of the North Downs with views out over the Medway Valley. On the 20th December he began his grandiosely titled 'Catalogue of Miniatures in the Collection of D. Welch',[10] and the first item on the list is a watercolour of the actress Mrs Siddons by Mrs William Avorne ('she was very intimate with the Countess of Huntingdon', Denton noted), which undoubtedly was given to him by Mrs Carpmael as an early Christmas present. At the end of the carefully penned entry he has added a value of £25 30s, which indicates that he must have shown it to an expert at a later date. The miniature remained in his possession up to the time of his death. The following Christmas an ever-generous Cissie Carpmael, who had taken on the role of a surrogate aunt, gave him another picture, this time an oil painting on copper of the Colossus of Rhodes, supposedly painted by the well-known late sixteenth-century German artist, Hans Rottenhammer.

Up to this time Denton, who celebrated his sixteenth birthday in March of 1931, had really made very little impression on his contemporaries. He had never done anything notable and by many was just regarded as being Paul's slightly wet younger brother. Things were about to change.

It was soon after returning from a seaside holiday in Belgium that Denton decided for the first time in his life to make a stand. The Christmas term began in September and on the appointed day he and Paul, each wanting to do something different in London, arranged that they would meet at St Pancras Station to be in time for the dreaded school train. Instead, in a moment of caprice combined with desperation, Denton took a bus to Waterloo and boarded a train going to the other end of the country—to Salisbury. Successfully passing himself off as younger than fifteen, he bought a half-fare ticket and once inside a carriage locked himself in the lavatory, so as to evade the imagined adversary.

> I suddenly felt terribly glad. I looked at my face in the glass. I was so anxious and happy that I thought I looked mad. I pulled my hat this way and that, wondering how to disguise myself. I thought I might dress up as a woman if I could get any clothes. I knocked the dent out of my hat, making it look like a girl's riding-hat. I was so excited that my face was red, with sweat on it.[11]

Denton's first published book, *Maiden Voyage*, begins with this adventure. It was written ten years after these events occurred and the title was decided on after the weaker options of 'Youth's Journey' and 'I Had No Razor' were rejected.[12] In the book he tells how he had originally been to Salisbury with his mother years before. They had stayed at The George, a half-timbered Tudor hotel that lies within a stone's throw of the Cathedral grounds. Denton now made his way there and timidly booked a room for the night: 12s 6d for bed and breakfast, 5s for dinner. He was asked to pay the sum in advance, since he had no luggage. It was only the next day, having spent a night disturbed by unwelcome dreams, that he registered the full import of what he had done.

Ambling around the immense interior of Salisbury Cathedral, he paused in the Lady Chapel to consider his dilemma:

> I sat down on one of the oak chairs and started to pray. I grew more and more unhappy; there was nothing that I could do. I could not go back and I could not stay away for long, my money would run out. I felt hopeless and very lonely; I longed for someone to talk to me but nobody did, they were all too busy looking at the sights or praying.'[13]

Suddenly, in a state of agitation, Denton knew he had to move on. The next cathedral on his whistle-stop tour would be Exeter, but once he had mounted a train for the city he found to his dismay that it was filled with boys going back to another public school, Sherborne. 'As I passed a group of three, one called out to the others in a mocking voice, "There's a pretty boy for you!"' [14] and before long, and for the second time in twenty-four hours, Denton had resorted to locking himself in the W.C.

After taking a room at The Royal Clarence Hotel in Exeter—it does not seem to have occurred to him that if he had lowered his sights and stayed at less expensive hostelries his money would have lasted longer—he sent off a postcard to Aunt Dolly in Henfield, attempting to put her mind at rest:

> I hope you have not been worrying about me. I am quite all right but I will never go back to school. I have a very nice room here with hot and cold water. The cathedral is lovely, I have been wandering all over it.[15]

In a way there appears to have been some symbolic purpose behind his flight; it was rapidly taking the form of a pilgrimage to places he had visited with his mother. He was trying in vain to recapture something of the happiness he experienced when they had been together on holiday. And so off he went in search of Exeter's antique shops, which he remembered having seen with her. Back at the hotel, however, it was necessary to face the prospect of sleeping a second night in his clothes, which were now becoming increasingly dirty.

The following day Denton made the short journey to the coastal town of Budleigh Salterton—with less than £1 in his pocket. The situation was getting rougher by the hour. A couple he had met in Switzerland happened to live in the resort and, concealing the truth from them, he managed to cadge a lift back to Exeter, where, in a state of dejection, he was forced to pawn his watch. By now the only thing Denton wanted to do was to buy a ticket to London, but he had at most sufficient money for a half-fare to Salisbury. When he returned there just 10d was left—certainly no use whatever in paying for a bed. Disconsolately, Denton sat down in a dark corner of the Butter Cross[16] to wait for daybreak.

As things transpired, he did not have to sleep out in the open. He was approached by two policemen, who, taking pity on him, allowed the puzzling teenager to spend a night in one of the cells at the police station. When morning came he managed to remember the name of a family who lived in the city and, after a kind bobby had looked up their address, he succeeded in borrowing £1 from the husband to pay for his fare to London.

In the capital Denton first of all tried the bell of a friend's flat (almost certainly Irene Dallas), but there was no answer and so he went to look up a distant cousin, May Beeman, whose house was off the Fulham Road. May was the daughter of his grandfather's sister, Christine Welch, who had emigrated to Australia where she had married an Isaac Beeman. May lived with a brother, Stanley, and had been awarded a C.B.E. for her good works. She treated the unexpected young visitor with real kindness and, to Denton's relief, made light of the situation. A telegram was sent off to Aunt Dolly and another to Bill, assuring them that Denton was safe and sound. After that she let him go off to do some shopping.

Later that day Cousin May and Denton turned to discuss weightier matters:

> My cousin was asking me what I wanted to do in life. I said that I was interested in history and architecture, and that I liked drawing and painting. The words made me feel embarrassed.
>
> She listened quietly, then said: 'Tomorrow we'll get Miss Billings to drive us to some of the art schools.'
>
> I felt very grateful; my cousin seemed to be taking it for granted that I should not back to school.[17]

The trip around the various institutions took up most of the morning —their last port of call was the Royal College of Art—and then Denton had to wait for his aunt and brother to appear after lunch. Now he would know his fate. He sensed that if he wavered in his resolve to leave school they would seize upon his weakness and the impact made by running away would be completely wasted. The situation was all the more troublesome because he had little idea of how they might react to his defiance.

It turned out that Aunt Dolly was quite bewildered and had no real appreciation of the reasons why he had run away; Bill, who arrived on the scene a few minutes later, however, was impressed. 'He shook my hand extravagantly, saying, "I never thought you had it in you."'[18] Denton managed to maintain his bold front when the family meeting began, but became irritated when the three grown-ups proceeded to talk about him in the third person, completely ignoring his presence.

What on earth could be done with him if he did leave school? It was only Cousin May who was able to consider his future intelligently and she came up with a cunning proposition that he could hardly turn down:

'Would you go back just for this term, Denton?'
I suddenly felt cornered. I knew that my cousin expected me to be reasonable.
'There isn't any point in going back just for this term,' I said, still fighting. 'Why can't I leave now?'
'Because they'd think you were afraid,' she answered softly; and as she spoke, the words 'Harmless as doves and wise as serpents' sprang up in my mind. I saw them spelt out as if they were written round the walls of a chapel. I felt that I had been betrayed, that I had to do right against my will. Slowly and miserably I said that I would go back till the end of the term. I did not know how I would do it, but I said it. I could not argue any more.[19]

Little did Denton know that in his absence Brook House was buzzing with gossip about what had happened. On returning to Repton he was surprised to discover that he had achieved a notoriety and even respect such as he had never previously experienced. Naturally, there would be a great deal of explaining to be done, but in the meantime he was fascinated to hear of the various rumours that had been going about. One of the first boys he met, 'Peach', blurted out, ' "Good God, Welch, have you come back? I heard that you'd got hold of forty pounds and had gone off to France, and someone else told me that Iliffe had taken you to Italy," ' 'Iliffe' being a recent leaver who 'had shown a frank interest in people younger than himself'.[20]

Luckily, his housemaster Mr Snape thought the best thing to do was to forget the whole affair (he had told the pupils under his care not to mention it after Denton's return) and Denton was rescued from having to confront the others in the house when Mrs Snape packed him off to the school 'san' for a few days' rest, saying he struck her as looking a bit feverish.

But school life could not be avoided for long. After lunch on the first day back in Brook House Denton found his brother Paul waiting for him in the passage.

'You are a bloody fool, Denton. I couldn't think what had happened to you. When I turned up here without you Bird was furious. He sent me back the next morning to look for you, and I had three days in London with Bill, so I didn't mind. We rang up all the hospitals and told the police; we thought you might have been run over. You were a sod to disappear like that!'[21]

The Art Master, Mr Norris ('Mr Williams' in *Maiden Voyage*) on the other hand, poked fun at him, asking sarcastically whether he had preferred Exeter to Salisbury. Denton writes that 'Everywhere I met with more tolerance than I had ever known before,'[22] and this, together with the almost certain knowledge that he would be leaving the school with Paul at the end of the term succeeded in making the two and a half months that lay ahead more bearable than he had dared imagine.

Other events mentioned in *Maiden Voyage* as having occurred that term include the news that his friend Geoffrey's mother had died (although he had been through the same dreadful trauma himself, Denton was too young to offer any help) and also a trip he made to Chatsworth with a party of other boys in the charge of Mr Norris. This outing is the setting for his short story, 'John Trevor'[23] When he returned to the school from the stately home, according to the version in *Maiden Voyage*, he was ignominiously beaten by the Captain of House Games for not obtaining permission to skip playing in the Third Eleven.[24]

Arthur Welch seldom wrote to his youngest son. Any letter from him was something of an occasion, since it usually dealt with plans for what they might be doing in the holidays. One afternoon Denton came into Brook House after playing games and saw there was an envelope from Shanghai waiting for him. Rather than opening it at once, he went for a walk and, choosing a congenial spot, sat down on his raincoat to read it. With mounting excitement he realized that the letter contained the best possible news. When the term finished he would accompany Paul back to China. It meant that the five years' misery in boarding-schools was coming to a definite end. Freedom was in sight at last.

> I was so full of joy that I ran down the lane and over the fields until I was exhausted. I felt like a person full of power and skill. I was no longer a part of the dead old system. I could bear anything now till the end of term.[25]

The sense of being liberated brightened his whole attitude to life. Whatever he said now could never be held against him in the future and out on a walk with a boy he calls 'Brophy', who wore a truss (in real life Garth Stacey—he had entered Brook House the same term), Denton let down his guard far more than he would normally have dared to:

> 'I can't believe, Brophy, that I shall never come back here again. After two years of being a fag and being beaten and hustled about, it seems too good to be true. I know I shall never send any of my children to a public school. Not that I shall marry or have any children,' I added as an after-thought.
>
> 'Don't you ever want to marry, Welch?' he asked.
>
> 'Not unless I found a very old woman with plenty of money.'
>
> 'What a swine you are, Welch. Besides, you'd have to go to bed with her.'
>
> 'No I shouldn't. There'd be an arrangement that we only met at meals or when other people were there.'
>
> 'Then what do you think she'd marry you for?' he jeered.

'She might like to have young life about the place,' I answered
weakly.[26]

For some reason Aunt Dolly thought that her nephew had got into bad
company at Repton and she wrote to Paul telling him as much. Denton
intercepted the letter and penned a furious reply, which only prompted his aunt
to write again to Paul telling him that she would have 'nothing more to do' with
Denton unless she received an apology. It was not forthcoming. However, it
seems that there had been a reconciliation between them by the end of term.

Denton, of course, had not taken any matriculation exams and during his
final days at school he was very happy to receive what amounted to some
definite career guidance from the one person whom he felt was qualified to give
it:

> . . . I stopped at the Art School to collect my drawings and say good-bye
> to Mr Williams. He was in a corner, bending over someone's drawing,
> giving it a big, grey wash. The boy was hating it. His work was being
> spoilt for him. Masters never understand this.
>
> When Williams saw me he pushed his round shoulders back and said,
> 'Well, good-bye, Welch. Go on with your drawing. Don't let them make
> you do anything else.'
>
> I felt flattered. I decided that I wanted to be a painter. I collected my
> drawings and went out feeling warm and comfortable.[27]

The inevitable meeting with the Headmaster out of the way, the last item
on the agenda was the House Supper, a pre-Christmas event that boys relied
upon to produce the most palatable food of the term. As a leaver it was
Denton's duty to make a speech, but being the youngest and least accomplished,
his turn was left to the end. An old boy 'with a strange cast in his eye' briefed
him to say some lines that he thought might go down well, and so Denton stood
up and, deeply ashamed, came out with an arrangement of phrases including:
'Since brevity is the soul of wit—I will not repeat myself—like the humble
onion—Everything has been said—.'[28] The other boys fed him with dates and
gave him a congratulatory thump on the back.

Denton parted from his friend Geoffrey in memorable fashion at Derby
Station. Lumsden still had another five terms ahead of him.

> He said good-bye with mock sentimentality, putting his arms round me
> while we were in the great lavatory, and trying to thrust his tongue right
> down my throat. He screamed with laughter when I ran away, rubbing
> my face with my handkerchief.[29]

Paul and Denton, once they had arrived at St Pancras, immediately made for
Scotts, where they had a sumptuous meal; afterwards they went on to see Bill.

They spent a quiet Christmas that year with their grandfather and aunt at
Henfield, Denton having also stayed with Mrs Carpmael for a few days
beforehand.

In January there was snow and Denton's memories of tobogganing with Paul demonstrate how his senses were heightened by the general feeling of elation—he recreates the winter scene with startling clarity:

> I sat on the toboggan and Paul pulled me across the Common. The sun was shining and I began to sing and feel very happy.
>
> We heard shouts and saw the flick of a coloured scarf before we reached the top of the slope. The scene on the other side was exciting. Sitting people or people flat on their stomachs tore down the hill, narrowly missing the frozen pond and the tangle of black hedges at the bottom.
>
> They were mostly young men and boys. The snow brought colour to them and made them look more lusty and strong. Hot breathing and pipe smoke made little clouds in the air, and mouths opened wide and teeth flashed when jokes were told. Some of these were not to be understood by strangers.[30]

Denton decked himself out with suitable clothes for his stay in China and some time in February or early March he and Paul set sail for Shanghai, travelling on this occasion via the Suez Canal. Denton was not yet seventeen—too old to be sent to another boarding-school, but still much too young and academically unqualified to progress to the next stage of education—university. No doubt on the long journey out to the Orient the two brothers had many discussions about what they intended to do in the future; Paul, who was perhaps rather conventionally-minded and unimaginative, knew he was destined for a career in his father's business, an idea which, needless to say, his younger brother still could not countenance. So how was Denton going to occupy his time? No advance plans had been made. It would be up to him to create his own niche.

In *Maiden Voyage* Denton describes the long sea journey with all the freshness of someone who at last has found relaxation after a great burden had been lifted from their shoulders. He could now observe people at leisure; he could savour the quirky side of life on board the liner without having to worry that everything he did was being overseen by the beady eye of authority. Aside from mentioning several of his co-passengers in the book, he also gives a picturesque flavour of the various ports at which they stopped on the way, and in doing so it seems as if he is describing places that he has never before visited.

It is likely that Denton had not been to Shanghai since his mother's death over five years earlier. In the meantime, his father, finding the family home at Avenue Foch far too big just for himself, had moved to an apartment at Rivers Court, which Denton tells us was 'set almost in the country, with the remains of a tiny Chinese village not far away'.[31] Once he enters the spacious flat he has the urge to reacquaint himself with all his mother's belongings, things that would bring back her memory with poignant immediacy. Waited on by the Chinese servants, his father's home now became a secure base from which Denton could venture into the city. Mr Welch and Paul were working at the office during much of the day, leaving him free to roam around as he liked.

With its myriad of shops, many of which sold antiques and more utilitarian second-hand goods, Denton was able to rely on Shanghai to provide him with as much material as he could wish for to satisfy his enthusiasm as a collector. On the other hand, when in need of company he always had the English-speaking community to turn to. Apart from having to fulfil certain social obligations, such as being at home to meet his father's guests at dinner (and trying not to appear bored, or worse, giggly), Denton spent quite a bit of time catching up with various families he had known either in his childhood, or who had been especially close to his mother.

For instance, there was Mrs Parsons and her four daughters. Marjorie, the eldest, although about eight years older than he, had been popular with Rosalind and so became a trusted companion. She remembered Denton at this time as 'a friendly, lively young man'. Then there were the Saunders girls—Christian Scientists from America—whose mother had also known Denton's. Pocetta and Enid were again both older, but he came to know them well and spent many days in their home.

It was Pocetta ('Vesta Fielding' in *Maiden Voyage*)[32] who rapidly became his closest friend. She had a strong sense of humour and did not hesitate to poke fun at him. Underneath, however, she was a sympathetic person and, having recently married, didn't care a jot about his lack of masculinity. Throughout his life Denton found relief in female company and Pocetta appeared to be perfectly happy to accept him just as he was. Their first meeting, though, had not gone too well:

> I saw a figure coming across the lawn. It was small and graceful, but top-heavy from the load it was carrying. I went to take some of the things from her, and saw the pale, compact face and dark curls behind the pile of rugs.
>
> 'You're just as I imagined you'd be,' she said disconcertingly. 'And Muddy tells me you're crazy about old things. Have you bought anything yet?'
>
> 'Yes,' I answered. 'I bought an old ivory gourd-shaped scent bottle at Hong Kong, and I went down the town the other day and found a small wine-cup of very good Fukien ware or blanc-de-Chine as it is called.'
>
> My nervousness must have made me sound pompous, for her eyes opened wide as she said maliciously, 'Oh, you do know a lot; you're quite a connoisseur.'
>
> I felt slapped, and was resentful. Surely she could see that I had not been trying to impress her. She smiled very charmingly. . .[33]

Denton soon became a regular visitor and on one occasion he acted as a chaperon for Pocetta when she went to have a cello lesson from a slightly suspicious-looking Hungarian emigré. And so his rather aimless life went on: seeing someone here, visiting a shop there, but never really doing anything in particular. One day, however, he arrived at the Fieldings' house in a state of great excitement to announce that his father had just arranged for him to make a long journey into the interior with a 'Mr Butler', who was a dealer in porcelain and other antiquities. It was just the sort of thing that would suit him. He set about preparing for the trip with gusto, buying all manner of clothes to accommodate changes in the weather.[34]

Initially, Denton was a little frightened that Mr Butler, 'a mild, well-covered person, with crinkly hair and rather piggy eyes',[35] might have some homosexual interest in him, but once his fears had been laid to rest, he found the man to be an interesting companion, especially since there was no doubting that he was a genuine expert in his field. Denton became greatly impressed by Butler's skill at recognizing fakes, of which there were many around.

Before they set out up river to the city of Nanking—a journey of some 210 miles—Arthur Welch gave his son $100 to buy whatever curios he fancied. Denton was delighted. Now he too could take an active interest in the trip, instead of having to stand back and watch Butler handing over bundles of bank-notes for rare artefacts. Once they had reached Nanking Denton in his enthusiasm very nearly spent most of the money on a stained ivory carving, until the older man advised him against it.

After a few days the two of them pressed on by train for Kaifeng Fu, where they were met at the station by a young Chinese student, who was Mr Butler's secretary—from now on he joined the party. In watching his behaviour Denton came to appreciate something of the complicated class structure of Chinese society. The Chinaman could not bear to lose face in his dealings with a foreigner and Denton learnt that a degree of tact was always called for when enlisting Li's co-operation. Xenophobia had been quite strong in Nanking (Denton only just escaped being detained by a ferocious soldier when he had gone to explore a part of the city's famous thirty-two-mile-long wall), but in Kaifeng the situation was still more dangerous. Although Li showed him the sights of the town, Denton, restless as usual, was determined to ignore any instructions to stay in his quarters for the remainder of the time. The urge to roam about was just too strong. However, this attitude shifted drastically when the proximity of violence and danger was brought home to him in a most alarming way. One afternoon whilst wandering along a road that led to the nearby hills, he stumbled across a severed human head lying in the track, surrounded by a haze of flies. At first disorientated, Denton fled in horror to the safety of the house where he was staying.

Meanwhile, Mr Butler was spending thousands of dollars purchasing porcelain. One day he and Denton were invited by a dealer to lunch at a local restaurant, a meal that is described in *Maiden Voyage* with all the writer's extraordinary gift for evoking atmosphere:

> In the courtyard of the restaurant was a tank of fishes. They were the colour of black pearls and their flesh seemed soft and plushy, like moleskin. We went into a little private room where servants dipped towels into boiling scented water and then, after wringing them out, held them to our faces. The scent was lavender, reminding me of bread-and-butter and

unbecoming English shoes. When our faces dried they looked shiny and
tight.

We were led into the adjoining dining-room. A round table, covered
with little dishes, almost filled it. There was much shuffling and politeness,
and I found myself sitting next to the dealer.

The meal began with sweet rice soup. Then came a little procession of
servants bearing dishes. Nothing was left long enough to be finished. We
were only supposed to pick delicately and then pass on to something else.
The dealer treated me charmingly. He found titbits for me and tossed them
gracefully into my bowl, making noises at the same time to stimulate my
appetite. He reminded me of a woman saying 'Swoop, swoop, sup, sup,
nicey, nicey!' to her lap-dog.[36]

From Kaifeng Denton and Mr Butler moved on and made an expedition by
train to visit the manager of some coal mines. The Murrays were a British
couple, and the wife, starved of convivial company, immediately took Denton
into her confidence, telling him how greedy her husband was. But the next day,
after he had spent a very restless night and was probably not in the best of
moods, she blotted her copybook by remarking how much he reminded her of
her own brother whose voice had not broken until he was twenty. Denton hated
people who, just on the basis of his looks or behaviour, took it for granted that
he belonged to a particular 'type', for he knew that the 'arty' or 'sensitive' male
was frequently talked of in derogatory terms. His lack of ease with the situation
in the Murrays' house was heightened still further when the lady suggested that
he should come and work with them at the mine—she assured him that he
would have plenty of time for his painting and collecting. Denton excused
himself by saying that he expected to be returning to England before very long.

A welcome diversion came in the person of a young Canadian missionary
doctor, 'Jim MacEwen', who had been invited over for lunch. At last there was
somebody that he found physically attractive and easy-going. MacEwen thought
Denton might like a change of scene, and so when it was time for him to return
to Yiching[37], where he lived, he asked Denton if he would like to accompany
him. This was quite a different sort of rail journey. Once more he saw the other
side of life in China. The lacquered view of a country full of exoticism, colour
and peculiarly quaint behaviour now gave way to feelings of utter revulsion as he
was confronted with the squalor of many ordinary people's lives, some suffering
from syphilis, others broken by an addiction to opium. This was far removed
from the comfortable life he knew in Shanghai. It was only MacEwen's company
that made the experience bearable and, reading between the lines, the
opportunity of watching the sturdy young doctor stripped to the waist as he
concentrated on shaving himself was the high-point of Denton's entire trip into
the interior.

Once Denton had come back to the Murrays at the coal-mine it was time
for the party to return by rail to Kaifeng, but the only means of transport
available proved to be a cattle-truck. Nor was this the only hardship they had to
endure on the journey. In the middle of nowhere some hostile Chinese soldiers

forced them to leave the primitive truck and they ended up having to spend the night in an exceedingly seedy 'hotel'. Denton tells how he used his jacket to cover the harsh light in his room, only to wake up finding himself in a cloud of smoke: 'I wanted to laugh. To be burnt while serving as a lampshade in a Chinese opium den and brothel was such an extraordinary end for a school blazer. It seemed to make the evening amusing, instead of vile and frightening.'[38] Understandably, he got little sleep. His description of the episode ends with a masterly picture of the eventual sunrise: 'It came in a little thread, like an inflamed eyelid against a grey face. The morning seemed dead and old and tired before it had begun.'[39]

Before long Mr Butler and Denton were on their way back to Shanghai. There was the prospect of life returning to the rather predictable routine he had known before. If one is to believe the escapades that comprise the rest of Denton's account of his stay in China, however, his adventures to the interior appear to have given him a new determination to branch out and explore the city more thoroughly; he was hungry for experience. If at times there was an element of risk involved, so much the better.

When tired of drifting about the fields, the little villages and the old graveyards in the vicinity of Rivers Court, he used to walk into the heart of Shanghai, purposefully not taking a bus or tram so as to see as much of life as possible. Although there were quite smart curio and antique shops in Yates, Bubbling Well and Nanking Roads, it was one street in particular, Peking Road, that offered the most exciting array of stores, chiefly selling second-hand European goods, and here Denton could put his observations of Butler's skill at bargaining to good use. *The Shanghai Yearbook* of 1934-35 gives the following advice to foreigners about to visit the thoroughfare: 'Don't pay the first price asked; perhaps the third or fourth will be about right. Even then you may be "taken"'.[40] Denton, naturally, was on fairly safe ground when it came to picking out the odd piece of Georgian silver and once, to his extreme delight, he found 'a most beautiful lustre jug', which was added to his ever-burgeoning collection of treasures.

During the summer months the temperature often rose to around 90-100°. This was the season when the young 'Shanghailanders' flocked to the various swimming-pools. One afternoon Denton decided he would go and see what was on offer at the Country Club, where his father had enrolled him as a junior member. Young men went there for tennis and squash, neither of which he was inclined to pursue in earnest; nevertheless, he thought, the swimming-pool might be a pleasant relief from the heat.

People sipping drinks sat at tables around the edge of the bath; it was necessary to pass by them to reach the changing-rooms. Denton remembered this experience as having been especially embarrassing. 'As I did so, I heard one woman whisper piercingly to another, "My dear, sandals!"',[41] a remark which at first he did not appreciate had been aimed at him. Initiated into the pool by 'a very strong and lusty' friend of Paul's, after his swim he was introduced to the young man's sister. It turned out that she was just as offensive as the woman who had insulted him about his footwear: when he tried to stroke her comparably unfriendly dog, she smiled and said ' "he hates children." ' 'I wondered why she disliked me so much,' Denton mused, 'perhaps she realized that I thought her buttocks were like full wine-skins.'[42] And so, after his short encounter with the patrons of the Country Club, Denton left the place and vowed never to set foot inside there again.

Throughout his short life he was attracted in particular to people whose behaviour and conversation were not inhibited by the observance of the social niceties that belonged to his own class. One cannot say, though, that Denton felt any more at ease with a working-class man than with friends whose background was similar to his own, but he had an almost romantic curiosity about 'how the other half lived'. He wanted to be accepted by such people, just as he had with the tramp; he wanted them to be friendly and undemanding. Needless to say, Denton would be the one who was in control of the relationship, and it was kept casual enough to avoid any lasting disappointment when the other party lost interest.

In *Maiden Voyage* Denton tells how one day, whilst taking a walk in a public park, he starts talking to an English soldier and asks him if he would like to come along to his father's flat for tea; they fix up a rendezvous for later. Back home Denton orders the Boy to get things ready and he himself fusses around in preparation for the visitor, then returns to the park at half-past-three to show the man the way. He is in a state of great excitement. 'I had never had a guest of my own before.' The soldier has considerably smartened himself up and is now in his summer uniform. 'His belt sparkled and twinkled with pipeclay and polished brass.' He gave Denton 'the most extravagant salute.'[43]

Once in the flat Denton asks tentatively if he would mind drinking china tea, but the soldier says he hates it and so the Boy is told to fetch the whisky decanter. A number of refills are pressed on the man and soon he is attempting to teach Denton how to smoke. The time passes by innocently enough until, to Denton's horror, there is the sound of a key turning in the front door. Expecting it to be his father, he tries to hurry the now half-drunk man into the kitchen—but fortunately it is only Paul. Denton tells how he begged his brother to open a new bottle and replace what had been drunk, but Paul refuses. He manages to bustle the soldier down the back stairs of the flat, and returns to find that, much to his relief, Paul is helping to cover his tracks. 'He tilted the spirit into the decanter savagely, so that it plopped and gurgled'; Denton concludes the chapter, 'he was furious'.[44]

It is impossible to determine whether this incident really happened, or whether in writing *Maiden Voyage* Denton was portraying himself as a more daring seventeen-year-old than actually he had been. One assumes that his first book is a genuinely autobiographical account, though coloured with partially fictionalized incidents, some of which could have occurred in a different context. Denton was to use this device throughout his writings. Another striking story that he tells in *Maiden Voyage*—about a day-trip that he made on a house-boat with the 'Barbours'—however, is certainly based closely on fact and the person who could corroborate the account was Marjorie Parsons herself ('Margot Barbour' in the book). Some fifty years later her recollection of the day was still quite clear:

I had watercolour lessons from a White Russian artist in his fifties, a Mr Leibney. A friend had lent Mr Leibney his house-boat for the day and my mother, myself, two sisters and Denton were invited to spend the day on the Whangpoo River to sketch and paint junks and sampans.

Mr Leibney (having lived in India) was a student of yoga—long before it was recognized in the West. He used to say to me, 'Miss Marjorie, you will never be able to paint unless you can control your thoughts.' 'But,' I replied, 'I can't control any of my thoughts for a moment!' He then proceeded to teach me about concentrating the mind 'between the two eyes', or else to breathe in the Goodness of the Universe, down to the solar plexus, at the same time breathing up the goodness in oneself to meet 'at the centre of one's being'. He also practised controlled breathing. We saw the effect of this on him during that day on the Whangpoo.

We were all on deck, tied up to the wharf, lazing in the sun, when suddenly there was raucous shouting through a megaphone, and to our horror we saw the high black steel bow of a steamer, out of control, bearing down towards us. The loadah (the man in charge of the house-boat), the crew and all of us were frozen with fright, but Mr Leibney, despite being rather stout, leapt onto the wharf, shouting to the loadah to do the same, and as quick as lightning unfastened the rope at the bow, while the loadah did the same at the stern, and pushed us into the river, where the current took us away.

As we watched, a heavy-laden barge of coal was cut in half by the oncoming ship before it crashed into the wharf where we had been. The Whangpoo was a fast-flowing river with dangerous whirlpools and the poor men flung into the yellow waters were undoubtedly drowned.

We all felt unnerved, except Mr Leibney, who had taken charge, and whose calmness and clarity of mind had saved our lives. It was a fine demonstration of what a man with 'collected thoughts' can do.[45]

Denton's account, written approximately ten years after the event, differs slightly in detail, especially in that he emphasizes the danger of their predicament —he places the trapped coal barge directly between them and the steamer, so that their boat is slightly damaged too. He also heightens the impact by describing how one of the crew standing on the bow of the steamer had treated what happened to the barge with callous nonchalance. When 'Mr Mantovic' (Leibney) berates the man for most probably causing the death of the coolies, the only answer he gets is, '"What's the matter? You ain't hurt."'[46]

After dinner, if there were no guests, Denton was in the habit of letting himself out of his father's flat and going to explore other parts of the city. One such night when he is in the French Concession he watches a fair-haired young man loading furniture onto a barrow, and, after seeing him shut up shop, in a spirit of adventure, decides to follow him. The man walks to a stadium used for boxing and other sports. If one can believe the story, Denton climbed onto a wall and spied on him through the window. But he was spotted. The man darted out of the building and cut off his exit, forcing a confrontation. 'I knew at once that if he had not been there,' Denton writes, 'I would have run home and regretted it always.'[47] He is asked into the stadium to have a go at boxing, and although coming off with a bloody nose and a sore lip from 'Ernst', he enjoys the experience and so returns for more punishment at a later date, only to find the place deserted. On another occasion Denton meets an American marine who insists on taking him to 'St George's Cabaret',[48] near Bubbling Well Road, where he is made to have 'a good time' and even has a dance with a Chinese girl.

In September 'Vesta' and her husband went away to Peking, and 'Mrs Fielding', thinking that Denton might welcome a break from the sombre and constricting atmosphere of his father's flat, invited him to spend a few days at her house on the perimeter of the French Concession; he would have Vesta's room. In his book Denton describes how, apparently with no feelings of guilt whatever, he carried out a leisurely inspection of his friend's belongings. Her Chinese jewellery, in particular, caught his imagination. Very soon a fantastic plan grew in his mind.

> It was while I looked at these things that the temptation to dress up came to me. . .
> I had everything I could want now for the experiment. With rising excitement I opened the wardrobe to look at Vesta's clothes. How many there were! I did not know what to choose. At last I decided on a thin woollen dress with a wide scarlet leather belt. I slipped it over my head and it tickled my skin, as I had nothing on underneath. It fitted very well, except of course for the fact that I had no breasts. I buckled the belt and then stuffed two bunched-up handkerchiefs into my bosom, but they looked so outrageous that, laughing quite hysterically, I pulled them out again.[49]

He found it still more difficult to apply Vesta's make-up with discretion and, casting a final glance into the mirror before letting himself out of the window onto the porch, he registered that he looked like a whore rather than any respectable woman. Out in the street the high-heel shoes proved to be unexpectedly tricky and after a brief saunter around the neighbourhood, Denton had to beat a hasty retreat to the Fieldings' house when a Scotsman jumped from a rickshaw and asked him if he was on the right road for the Avenue Roi Albert!

Time was marching on. The year 1932 was nearly at an end and as yet no one had broached the subject of how Denton might occupy himself in the new year. In his usual carefree attitude of mind he made the journey to Peking that Christmas to stay with his Uncle Harry and Aunt Dos, who lived in some style inside the diplomatic legation. Unfortunately, the holiday came to an abrupt end when his uncle, Sir Harry Fox,[50] suffered a stroke. Denton returned at once to Shanghai; It was during his first evening back that Arthur Welch asked him if he had given any thought to his future:

'Well, what are you going to do now? You must decide what you want to do.'

'I want to go to an Art School.' I had to say it very quickly, because, for some reason, the words made me feel ashamed.

My father made a face.

'I don't think that's at all a good idea,' was all he said. And after that we talked of other things.

The next day I went to ask Vesta what I should do.

'You should go to a University or an Art School,' she said. 'You can't just play around.'[51]

The realization that a new chapter of his life was about to begin struck Denton forcibly when his father booked the passage back to England a few days later. Events were already moving very rapidly.

My thoughts buzzed and jumped about as if hot water had been poured on them.

I would have to live in rooms in London or with relations who disapproved of me. Sometimes the English food would be horrible. There would be so little sun. I would belong again to my surroundings and would understand what people said. I would be able to go anywhere without fear, and I would see again the places I loved.

The pros and cons darted one after the other; but, deep down under all my thinking, I knew that I was glad.[52]

Inevitably, packing all the things that he wanted to take was a major operation. New clothes could always be bought (he had almost certainly left some at his grandfather's house in Sussex). It was not these that concerned him—but more his treasures, which were now an inseparable part of his identity. He wanted to take as many of them as possible. If they were left behind in Shanghai the probability was that he would not set eyes on them again for a very long time indeed. And so Denton busied himself wrapping up the different bits and pieces he had collected since his childhood, as well as the more valuable curios bought on the trip with Mr Butler.

He showed no qualms either in grabbing many of the smaller things in the flat. There were his grandmother's delicate and exquisitely coloured flower-paintings,[53] an old table-cloth they used only once a year at Christmas, family silver, and so on. Denton thought he might find more in the basement, where each tenant had his own cubicle for storage; he went down to have a look. When he returned to the flat he learnt to his embarrassment that his father, extremely angry at having had several of his belongings taken without his permission, had unpacked his trunk. All the pieces of cotton-wool and the tins he had found for the more breakable items were undone and emptied. Later Denton had to face up to Mr Welch:

'Punky, what the devil do you mean by packing up those things without telling me?'

I thought it was a strange moment to use my pet name.

'Oh, I didn't think you'd mind,' I said in a futile, casual voice. 'You've got so much stuff here, and you know that I treasure those things more than you do.'

'That's nothing to do with it. You should have asked me first.'

This was so true that it acted like a blow, making me want to retaliate.

'They were my mother's, so they are really just as much mine as yours now,' I said. 'If she were alive she'd give them all to me!' I wanted to hurt him.[54]

Denton made one of his furious exits and went off into the city to find some distraction from the unpleasantness. He returned to the cabaret club, had a fair amount to drink, and later set out for home in the company of three soldiers. To avoid the sentry, two of the men had to climb over a fence to get into their barracks and Denton was nearly caught in the escapade when an Indian watchman clung onto his coat, which, in a state of panic, he managed to jettison. He ran back to Rivers Court terrified that he was being pursued.

The following morning Denton was still worried. Would there be a visit from a detective making enquiries about the night before? He might have to appear in court. Would he be leaving China under a cloud, unreconciled with his father over the business with the silver? He was getting things very much out of proportion. Paul told him that if he asked his father nicely that evening, he might be pleasantly surprised at the response. And so, swallowing his pride, Denton took the bull by the horns. He found now that Mr Welch was quite happy for him to have nearly everything he had originally wanted. He added more china and his mother's books to the list; from the collection of silver that had belonged to her family the only piece he seems to have rejected was a huge soup-ladle.

The day of his departure finally arrived. Denton was to bid farewell to Pocetta (Vesta) on the quay. Arthur Welch and Paul drove him to the dock, where he duly met his friend and her husband, and all of them, excepting his father, went on a motor-launch to board the liner. Denton and Pocetta soon found his cabin and after a short while Paul appeared. He had bought Denton a miniature bottle of Cointreau, which was opened then and there, with each of them taking a sip of the rich, sickly liqueur from a toothbrush glass.

Then the hooter sounded, and everyone jumped up convulsively.

Vesta left with the others but ran back into the cabin afterwards. Her face, even her lips were pale, as I had seen them sometimes on cold days. I knew suddenly that she was my greatest friend; and I had the grotesque idea that her husband might imagine us to be in love. It was so funny, I wanted to laugh.

'Good-bye, darling,' she said, kissing me desperately, half afraid, I think, that I might pull away. When she stepped back, her hat was a little crooked and some more tight curls had pushed out onto her forehead.

We looked at each other for a moment, then she turned and ran away.[55]

Denton waved to her in the motor-launch. They both cried. Perhaps he would never see her again. He was leaving behind one of the few people he could relate to. He was also leaving China, never to return.

Some months after the publication of *Maiden Voyage* in 1943, Pocetta ('Vesta') wrote to Denton from her home in Seattle giving her impressions of the book. This letter gives a compelling insight into Denton's personality at what had been a transitional stage of his life:

> . . . All through I was so moved by what I had never known in you. I was thinking of you so much more than the book. I never dreamt that you felt the world's horror so keenly. I always thought of you as an Ariel—dew and sunlight—free as air and gay as morning.
>
> I kept wondering how much of it had really happened, which was entirely beside the point, as the spirit of everything was very clear and accurate, it seemed to me. I think I remember about the soldier, but I didn't realize the times you weren't with us were as weighty as those you were. Did that boxing really happen? It was so vivid. And did you crawl out of the window and go mincing down the street as a gay lady? Why are the poor things called Gay? Must be a pretty loathsome sort of life. . . It seemed to me that in order to paint your picture of our family you were transposing events and putting in things that never happened. . .
>
> You knew, and every day it was being impressed deeper on your quiveringly receptive consciousness how cruel the world is. You were, and I expect still are, in the mood I was in when you knew me. I felt that humour, and so on, were escapist and that tragic, terrible music and literature—portrayals of misery—were the truth and must be expressed. You were the highlight of joy in my life at that time, when you were really suffering so, and I didn't know you were. I felt you were lonely in spirit elsewhere, at least for deep anchorage, and yet you were such a joy to have around.
>
> But, Dearest Denton, you did not bring that head wrapped in a piece of paper from Kaifeng Fu, or paint me a picture of it and put it in a gold frame over my dressing-table. When you came we were happy and had brightness instead of darkness. For us you put behind you your sufferings and cruel knowledge and gave us gaiety.[56]

Chapter Three

Goldsmiths'

If one accepts the sequence of events recorded in *Maiden Voyage* as being accurate, Denton returned to England some time around the beginning of February 1933. One can imagine that a whole variety of thoughts were running through his mind as once again he stepped onto the reassuring solidity of British soil. Uppermost, perhaps, was a determination to free himself from the supervision of his family.

Although letters or telegrams must have been exchanged between Arthur Welch in China and his sister, Dorothy ('Aunt Dolly'), it is unlikely that any definite plans had yet been made for his future. Mr Welch was adamant that Denton should not fritter away his time, and even if he had let it be known that he viewed a training in art as being highly unsuitable for any member of his business-orientated family, it was better that his son should be doing 'something', rather than nothing.

It appears the choice of Goldsmiths' came about purely on the strength of a chance encounter. Whilst at a party in Steyning, a village near to Henfield, Aunt Dolly had been chatting to Gerald Mackenzie, who was a senior student at the college. The young man listened to her anxieties about what she should do with her 'problematic nephew'; the teenager's one ambition in life, she explained, was a wish to study painting. Could he suggest something? At once Gerald advised Miss Welch that she might like to consider sending him to Goldsmiths'. Not only were students accepted at well below university entrance age, but more importantly, the staff took an enthusiastic and enlightened approach to teaching and the general atmosphere was quite relaxed. Aunt Dolly was reassured to learn that the institution listed Stanley Anderson as a member of staff: she had one of his wood-engravings.[1]

It seems that Denton enrolled as a student at the Goldsmiths' School of Art for the summer term, which began on 9th April and extended to the end of June. The plan was that he should lodge with Bill, who had rooms in a house just a few hundred yards from the Wallace Collection in Manchester Square. As far as Denton was concerned, this was not at all a promising start:

> When I knew that I was going to live with my eldest brother in Adam Street I was horrified. I had wanted to be on my own, and this arrangement would not be the same thing at all. It was the last thing I could have wished for.[2]

Nevertheless, the landlady provided 'excellent breakfasts', which fortified him for the day ahead.

Denton would then set off for Goldsmiths' on a No.36 bus, which took him all the way. It was a long journey, the college being situated at New Cross in the suburbs of South London. To pass the time, he would note the various historical landmarks along the route and in between these he glanced at the faces of people going about their daily business. Denton tried to fathom their thoughts as they walked self-containedly along the pavements. And in his mind's eye he created vignettes of the life that was going on behind the façades of shop windows and in the privacy of the terraced house. Eventually he reached his destination, and his attention shifted to other matters:

> The Marquis of Granby was my stop. I would get off the bus, cross the road and enter a large building which had dusty evergreen bushes round the door. The main part was devoted to the training of schoolteachers, so I would run down a long, dark passage till I reached the stairs which led to the art school. I would climb up as quietly as possible, for I was usually late, get my drawing-board and pencil, and glide silently into the Antique Room. Students already astride their 'donkeys' would glance up at me, then down again. They seemed both curious and uninterested. I was too new to have any friends.[3]

Goldsmiths' College had been affiliated to London University since 1904, the Goldsmiths' Company having purchased the property in New Cross a few years previously for use as a Technical and Recreative Institute. The scheme was to provide classes in art and music on the one hand, and to prepare students for external university degrees in engineering and science on the other. At this time, however, the Art School and the teacher-training sections were entirely separate.

By the early 1930s the curriculum contained few indications that the Art School had ever taught any of the skills specifically associated with the goldsmiths. The making of jewellery, for instance, did not feature. Only the etching process remained of the tradition, but this was not a compulsory course and at the time when Denton came, perhaps as a reflection of changing public demand, there was less emphasis on it than there had been in previous years, when Graham Sutherland, for one, had benefited so much from instruction in the craft.

Clive Gardiner's appointment as Headmaster of the Art School in 1929 marked the evolution of Goldsmiths' from a rather stuffy academic institution into a thoroughly vibrant environment within which the latest trends were discussed by students and staff alike. Modern Art was not treated as a threat to the established order, but more as an exciting and challenging movement that could expand the scope for self-expression.

Gardiner, at forty-two, had already been teaching there for twelve years when Denton arrived. Initially, he had made a name in designing posters for the London Underground, the first of which appeared in 1926. After visiting Paris as a schoolboy of sixteen, he developed a special sympathy for French art and, as was very evident to his students, he admired Cézanne above all others. Gardiner possessed the keenest eye for harmonious composition in his own pictures, and the preference can be seen as reflecting a strongly mathematical bent.

Of the then more avant-garde artists, Gardiner admired Picasso and was also interested in the works of de Chirico, Magritte and the other Surrealists—in short, he was a man with a thoroughly catholic taste in art. However, over and above this, as his son recalls, he 'believed utterly in the ability to draw', and the students were encouraged to develop their powers of observation to the utmost. In a letter to his nephew, Richard Robbins, he gives a clear outline of his priorities as a painter, priorities that fortunately were entirely compatible with a person of Denton's temperament:

> I would say that it doesn't matter a scrap whether one's pictures are done in the same style, or colours, or tone, provided that in each individual case one knows what one is trying to do. . . I hope you will just go on painting what interests you and if you do, you will find you get better and every now and then you will change your style, and your colours, simply because that's the only means you have of getting something into your pictures that you didn't get before.[4]

The painter Carel Weight, a friend of Denton's at Goldsmiths' and also afterwards, recalled Gardiner as having been a man of considerable intellect who 'managed to run the school making as little fuss as possible'. Students were allowed to attend whichever classes interested them and the freedom offered was perfectly suited to Denton with his very low threshold for boredom.

Quite naturally, though, the success of the enterprise did not rely solely on the personality of one man, and Denton came into daily contact with a number of different teachers, each of whom can be seen as having contributed something to his development as an artist. Edward Bawden, then thirty years old and thought of very much as a designer and illustrator, was in some ways the star teacher (he would appear only on Tuesdays and tended to be surrounded by a coterie of admirers), but it was more figures such as James Bateman, E.M. Dinkel, John Mansbridge[5] and Gardiner himself who were the ones responsible for developing the basic skills.

One could generalize and say that the Art School was made up of two different categories of student: there were those who were training to become either fully-fledged artists or teachers equipped with a certificate from London University—a number of these came from working-class backgrounds—and there were others, often admitted on the personal whim of Clive Gardiner, who were more nebulously 'continuing their education', perhaps with the idea of becoming semi-professional painters or maybe of teaching at a lower school level. The fairly large proportion of these more casual students, of whom Denton was one, can be explained by the fact that there was a shortfall of applicants at that time.

Some members of the first group were scholarship students undertaking a four-year course; these would have their fees paid, as well as the cost of the artists' materials they used. Denton could not have joined this course, since he

1. Denton Welch and his parents, Shanghai, c.1923.

2. Denton, Brendon and Betty Parsons, Shanghai, 1925.

3. School photograph, Brook House, Repton, 1931,
with Denton behind his housemaster, Mr Snape.

4. Denton and his brother Paul (front row) on holiday at Zoute, Belgium, 1931.

5. With Joan Waymark at Brixham in Devon, 1934.

6. Oatlands Park Hotel, Weybridge, Surrey (the setting for the novel *In Youth is Pleasure*), where Denton, his father and brothers stayed in 1930.

7. The house was formerly the Southcourt Nursing Home in Broadstairs, where Denton convalesced from October 1935 to January 1936. His room can be seen lower left.

8. At the piano, 1937/8.

9. Dr Jack Easton.

10. Evelyn Sinclair.

11. Self-portrait, c.1938.

12. In his flat at Hadlow Road, Tonbridge, 1937.

13. Gerald Mackenzie resting on one of Denton's carved wooden angels, 1937.

14. Alex Comfort. Photograph by Howard Coster.

15. Edith Sitwell, 1934. Photograph by Howard Coster.

16. May Walbrand-Evans.

17. John Henry 'Monty' Bones.

18. Noël Adeney.

19. Eric Oliver, 1946.

20. Denton at the Hop Garden, St Mary's Platt, 1940.

21. Middle Orchard, Crouch.

22. At Middle Orchard, 1946.

23. With the doll's house, 1946.

24. With Eric Oliver, 1946.

had not passed, or even taken, the School Certificate examination. He was a fee-paying student, a person who would eventually leave Goldsmiths' without any qualification, other than having been taught at a well-known college by a highly professional staff. Understandably, at times there was some tension between the two camps. Whereas the poorer students often had to struggle to get by, Denton, with a substantial allowance from his father, could afford to live in comfort and purchase whatever artists' materials he thought were needed.

At first he found himself slightly intimidated by the often boisterous atmosphere at Goldsmiths'. After all, it was only eighteen months since he had run away from school. During the break for lunch, rather than joining the other students and the trainee teachers in the communal refectory, he would go out into the streets of New Cross and buy himself a modest picnic, which he ate on the steps of a nearby church, St James's. When the working day was at an end he went back to the centre of London on his bus.

It soon dawned on Denton that by living so far away and in such a different style to the majority of the other students he was missing out on much of the social life surrounding the school, and so he reached the decision to move to somewhere in the vicinity of New Cross. Because he had not yet succeeded in making any real friends at Goldsmiths'—he was still shy—Denton made use of his Christian Science contacts when looking about for a new place to live and it was almost certainly on Irene Dallas's suggestion that one afternoon he went round to a couple of houses in Greenwich, which was the most agreeable residential area close to the college. The first lady Denton tried didn't seem quite suitable, but she gave him another address, and presently he found himself at the door of 34 Croom's Hill, an imposing old house that overlooked the park. He was immediately attracted by the situation of the building. He rang the bell and waited.

> . . . a woman of perhaps thirty-eight or thirty-nine opened the door. Her hair was bobbed in the fashion of the 1920s. She wore a white knitted jersey, so long that it was almost a tunic dress, and one of the dark brown eyes had a slight cast in it, so that she seemed to be looking away shyly and engagingly as she confronted him.[6]

Evelyn Sinclair, the curious spinster who played such a significant behind-the-scenes role in the rest of Denton's life, was, like her architect brother Braxton, a Christian Scientist, although she had been born into a family of Plymouth Brethren. She was quite well-educated and for a time had worked at the Admiralty. Rather reserved by nature (and fundamentally an eccentric), the tiny woman always struck Denton as being unfathomable—someone locked away in a private world that she had no wish to share with anybody else.

Once she liked a person, though, her toleration of their behaviour would be boundless. In general preferring young men to women, the new landlady took Denton's colourful taste in clothes and his fussiness over food in her stride; he did not bother her in the least. She felt quite at home with unconventional people.

Even so, it was some time before he was able to settle down. In his final novel, *A Voice Through a Cloud*, he wrote of the loneliness of those early days at Goldsmiths':

> When I had first gone there I had known nobody; and my evenings in my room on Croom's Hill were spent all alone. I used to come back and climb the stairs and throw myself down on the bed, sprawling out my legs and burying my face in the pillow. I would be thinking of the pleasures and the pain in the day that had just passed. Then, turning over, I would stare at the uneven ceiling and wonder how much longer my life would lack direction, how much longer I would be cut off yet searching for my true place in the world. I thought of the hours wasted at the art school, with the drawing-board in front of me and the pencil in my hand, the feeling of uselessness that came upon me as I sat there, staring into space.[7]

However, Greenwich is a district that has its own definite character, derived from historic buildings such as the Naval College and the Royal Observatory (not to mention the seemingly arid expanse of Blackheath, which lies at the top of Croom's Hill), and within a relatively short space of time Denton was discovering it to be a congenial and relaxing area to live in.

A long walking tour in the West Country during the summer holidays of that first year helped increase his confidence in mixing with people of the same age group—Denton stayed in youth hostels and to a certain extent was forced to muck in with the other holiday-makers[8] —and when the Michaelmas term came he found himself much better equipped to form friendships with fellow students, most of whom either lived or lodged in the locality of New Cross, Lewisham or Greenwich.

It was chiefly in the company of a group of the girl students that Denton felt at his most secure. There were Joan Waymark and Corinne Snow, both rather frivolous and good for light-hearted, undemanding conversation, Valerie White, a gifted graphic artist and later to become a well-known actress, the tall and large-boned Betty Swanwick, more serious-minded and certainly regarded as one of the most talented students at the school, and lastly Helen Roeder, a dark-haired girl Denton came to know particularly well when they worked together in Mr Wooller's fabric-printing class each Friday.[9]

Betty Swanwick, who shared a work-room with Denton during his first year, remembered that he did not seem to be taking the course at all seriously and that at times his behaviour could be downright stupid. This opinion was also confirmed by Edward Bawden, who, when approached to share his memories of his erstwhile pupil, failed to come up with anything at all complimentary.

> I am sorry to have been so slow in sending you a reply to your letter asking me about Denton Welch when he was a student at Goldsmiths' Art School and I had the honour of having him in my class. The truth is that I never saw him for more than two consecutive minutes, because he spent his time rushing about from room to room. I regarded him as a disruptive

influence and best left alone. No doubt he had talent as an artist, but chose not to reveal it.[10]

Denton gives his side of the story in a letter to Peggy Kirkaldy, written in 1945: 'Edward Bawden used to teach me drawing once, but I found it terribly difficult to do anything or to get on with him, because of his amazing shyness. It was quite paralysing.'[11] In Betty Swanwick's words, the two 'just did not hit it off' and she did not think that the man who was her own mentor had had any real influence on Denton's development as an artist. Nevertheless, on occasion he did try his hand at something that bore a very close resemblance to Bawden's lighter style, as one can see in a cartoon-like pen and ink drawing of a few years later.[12]

The charge that Denton had done little work at Goldsmiths', however, was unfair. It was just that he tended to accomplish things in a different way to other people. Joan Waymark, perhaps closer to him than any of the others during this period, was aware that he did have real application, but everything went on behind the scenes; he was not at all ostentatious when it came to parading his work. Indeed, throughout his career Denton was at pains to avoid giving the impression that he treated his painting as much more than a diversion—except to those who he felt were sympathetic to what he was trying to achieve. His constant façade of being cheerful and 'larking about' at Goldsmiths' was merely a ruse to protect himself from being taken seriously and then being expected to produce work of quality, which, at this stage, he almost certainly sensed was beyond his capabilities. He hated to think he could be tied down. Joan, looking back on those years, considered that to a great extent Denton had been 'feeling his way'—and perhaps more tentatively than most.

A glance at the Goldsmiths' prospectus for 1933-34 reveals that the basis of the teaching derived from the traditional skills any budding artist needed to develop; in attending the various classes listed below Denton could be quite sure that he was 'doing the real thing'. These extracts from the syllabus encapsulate the core of this training:

The course of instruction, which is progressive in character, includes drawing and painting from the Antique, from Still Life, and from Plant Form; Perspective, Anatomy; drawing and painting from the Nude Life Model; Portraiture and Figure Composition.
Constructive draughtsmanship and an understanding of the principles of light and shade, of perspective, and of the formal relationships of tone and colour provide the general basis of a teaching which aims at the fullest development of personal expression.[13]

In the Antique Room the students would draw the plaster casts of statuesque marble busts, with their idealized forms and perfect physiques. Amongst those on offer were the Eye of David, the Clapping Faun and the Venus de Milo. However, about a month after his arrival Denton decided to venture into the Life Room, so that he could make a drawing from a nude model. Generally, it was the more advanced students who would work in there: those undertaking the formal course had to spend two years in the Antique Room before they were admitted to the class. Denton, on the other hand, as a fee-paying student, was free to wander about where he liked, though on this occasion, when faced with a naked lady of an uncertain age, he had slight misgivings at having taken the plunge.

> The shock was as great as he supposed it would be. The sight of all that mauvish flesh with the hank of dark hair sent a tingle of horror right through his body. Madame David, with her elaborate arrangement of pulleys, had slung herself from the ceiling in one of her poses from the old masters. One arm and one leg were supported in nooses while she reclined on the dais, cupping her chin in her other hand—it was contortionist—and through his panic, Robert [Denton] wondered if she was supposed to be Venus floating on a cloud. Madame David looked up and smiled broadly at him. She seemed to be cracking nuts between her teeth. He felt the furious wave of red spreading over his face. In desperation he bent over his board and began to try to draw the amazing figure.[14]

The master in charge of the class that day was James Bateman, who appears as 'Mr Bridgeman' in 'A Novel Fragment'. A highly accomplished artist, and later elected a Royal Academician (he was noted for painting idyllic English landscapes), one senses from the following extract that he had a strongly disciplined approach to draughtsmanship; something that Denton needed to cultivate.

> He stopped by each 'donkey', or easel, for a moment, sometimes drawing a little diagram, sometimes only muttering a few words and passing on. Robert waited for him in sweating anxiety. He was horribly ashamed of his drawing and he tried blindly to hide it from the master by leaning forward and almost crouching over it.
>
> 'Let me see what you've been doing,' Mr Bridgeman said, mildly enough. Robert sat back and smiled shamefacedly. He could say nothing and waited for the master to speak.
>
> 'This is just fun,' Mr Bridgeman said at last. 'I don't mind your having fun, but it isn't the way to learn drawing.'
>
> He took the pencil from Robert's hand and sat down on the donkey. Robert stood over him, watching uneasily.
>
> 'In drawing you must learn to construct, not just to depict surfaces.' Mr Bridgeman started to draw in a corner of Robert's paper. Madame David was soon turned into a series of tubes which exaggerated and brought out her volume and stance. Mr Bridgeman suddenly got up in the middle of his drawing and passed on, saying no more.[15]

Given a modicum of talent and application, it was almost impossible not to benefit from the instruction at Goldsmiths'. As it turned out, the emphasis on the attainment of practical skills worked well for Denton; later in life, aside from selling a dozen or more paintings, he also managed to earn some money from undertaking small commissions to supply illustrations for periodicals and magazines.

Other than the fabric-printing already mentioned, he experimented a little with sculpting,[16] though it would seem to have been the presence of the odd sturdy male sitter that attracted him to the class, rather than any loftier ambition. There was one man, an all-in wrestler, who drew him like a magnet. Stepping down from his dais during one of the rest-periods, the burly fellow laid a hand on Denton's shoulder to steady himself and a conversation followed. Denton had plenty of questions he wanted to ask about the man's profession—especially all the gory bits—and then suddenly he found himself being used for demonstration!

> He caught hold of Robert purposefully and twisted him round so that he fell on the floor; then, before he had time to collect himself, the model had got him into some impossible position between his legs. Next, Robert found himself hanging over the model's back, being held by one leg.
> The rest of the students began to laugh. 'Look at Sonny Boy being treated rough!' shrieked Madge and Jane gleefully. The model began to march up and down the room with Robert, like some trophy, still hanging down his back.[17]

Although Denton does not attempt to mask his sexuality when writing about the time he spent at art school, his 'leanings' were not generally perceived by the other students, at least, not on a conscious level. Perhaps, too, he himself did not give the matter very much thought, but accepted the feelings as being integrated into his personality. Cedric Rogers, who features as 'Billings' in 'A Novel Fragment', always thought of him, rather, as an inconsequential figure:

> Reading his books and comparing my recollections (fortified by my diaries, which are not confused by hindsight), it is quite remarkable to me that his homosexual inclination, so overt in his books, was not at all clear in those days. . . . In spite of thinking him as soppy and affected and 'not having an original idea in his head', I was aware of an unshakeable integrity. Also he did not fit into the ready-made image of a 'pansy boy' that was prevalent at the time. Certainly one associates him with an entourage of female students most of the time he was there.[18]

Whilst Rogers, who according to Denton appears to have spent much of his time crooning to the other students, was not a particular friend—more an affable person he saw each day—there was one of the male students who became close to him during these years: this was Gerald Mackenzie, the young man who had in the first place recommended Goldsmiths' to Aunt Dolly.

Gerald recalled that Miss Welch wrote to Clive Gardiner expressing a concern that her nephew should not be allowed just to drift, and consequently the Headmaster asked him, as a responsible and serious-minded senior student, to keep an eye on Denton and lend him as much encouragement as possible.

The Antique Room was the place where they first came into contact with one another. Gerald had come in late one afternoon to set up a still-life for the evening-class that he taught as part of his course; Denton was the only student left in the room. He was struggling with a drawing of the Clapping Faun.

> He looked across at Robert and saw *De Profundis* lying on the donkey in front of him.
>
> 'What d'you think of that?' he asked smiling.
>
> 'Not very much; I bought it off a stall at lunch-time; I've read somewhere that it was all cut about before it was published. That's what's wrong with it, I expect—most of it's left out!'
>
> They both laughed and went on talking about Oscar Wilde. Neither of them knew very much and there were pauses.
>
> 'What do you do in the evenings?' Hope [Mackenzie] asked at last.
>
> A little taken aback by the direct question, Robert answered hurriedly, 'Oh, I don't know; I read and go for walks over the heath.'
>
> 'That sounds rather gloomy. Don't you ever get depressed?'
>
> 'Sometimes—but I don't think it's what I do that makes me depressed.'
>
> 'What is it, then?' asked Hope rather sharply. Robert could not answer, and again there was a slight pause.
>
> 'I have to spend most of my evenings going round to my various friends and cheering them up,' said Hope, showing a little too much gaiety and brightness.[19]

Within a few days they were seeing a great deal of one another. Gerald, who was two years Denton's senior, would arrive at Croom's Hill after supper and they would get down to animated conversation. There was much to talk about. They could discuss their likes and dislikes in the fields of modern art and literature or, in a lighter vein, swap stories about the enormities of various professors and students.

It seems that to begin with Gerald did not disclose his connection with Aunt Dolly. Had he done so, one suspects that Denton would have regarded him as a spy. Moreover, to a certain extent Gerald did take an interest in him that was over and above the usual. In a notebook he jotted down a brief memo of his new friend's character:

> Shows tendency towards fantastic things. Drawing though very rough and messy shows something. Aunt has opinion that he has the mind of a child—sure she is quite wrong.
>
> Shows promise at Mr Wooller's class. Bold in design—not fiddly. Cannot resist buying antiques—hates reproductions. Has unfortunately frequent attacks of 'ennui'. Aunt believes that Miss Dallas has a bad effect on Denton.[20]

At a later date Denton may have turned against Gerald to some extent—in *A Voice Through a Cloud* and the essay 'Sickert at St Peter's' he becomes the butt of the author's malice—but when they were together at Goldsmiths' his friend did not sense there was any underlying animosity between them; in point of fact, they shared many of the same interests and found each other to be witty and entertaining company.

The relationship was helping to divert Denton from his normal mood of introspection. By the spring of 1934 they were making weekend trips into the country. Strolling about and maybe stopping off at a tea-shop for refreshment, Denton and his friend would have frequent light-hearted arguments about the foibles that each perceived in the other's personality. An invitation from Aunt Dolly for Gerald to come down to Waphams for the Easter break helped to cement the bond between them. It appears that during all his years at St Michael's and Repton Denton had never had a friend to stay in the holidays.

Yet there was no emotional attachment on his part. This impression is confirmed in an extract from his Journals written in 1945. Here Denton is reliving the time spent at Croom's Hill in 1934:

> Over the wide floorboards my light rubber shoes would move, leaving faintly dulled marks. I would sit on alone with the perfect book, feeling the warmth of my smooth stomach separate itself from my shirt and my navy sweater as I drew in deep breaths.
>
> And in the winter the fire would snap and I would long for the perfect friend who I knew could never exist. (For in those days even the possibility of a day-to-day friendship seemed utterly remote.) I lived young, alone, secret in my room or at the Art School, walking over the dark heath at night, staring down at London and the puce glow it made in the sky.[21]

Though he did get to know a young man called John Russell during this period (he had introduced himself to Denton in the lavatory of a pub—apparently with quite innocent intentions), it was the social life connected with the art school that was slowly becoming his real sphere. For a while he even had a go at fencing lessons, following the example of Anthony Gilbert, a student whom he rather admired (they stayed in touch for many years), and occasionally he would join in a game of hockey.

Gerald caught a few seconds from one of these none-too-serious games on a cine-film, and after the short clip one momentarily gets a glimpse of Denton and a few of the other students engaging in a sort of mock wedding. Denton is holding Joan Waymark's bridal train. Gerald then turns the lens directly on his friend, and Denton, camera-shy, looks away in embarrassment. One is struck not only by the lightness of his build, but also by an irrepressible vivacity, something that is poignant when considered in the context of the rest of his life. His clothes are casual and comfortable: it was only when he dressed up for some special occasion that he would, for instance, sport a silver-topped cane, as if emulating an eighteenth-century fop.

He had already begun to collect antiques in earnest. From the year in China Denton knew that interesting odds and ends could be found in the most unlikely of places and, armed with a highly developed nose for sniffing out bargains, he was soon adding to his possessions at an almost alarming rate. These were the inter-war years when many people were badly off and had faced a decline in their living standards. Few people had any real knowledge about the rarity or potential value of antiques. The type of shops that Denton frequented were often crammed full with the contents of house clearances.

In the article 'Strange Discoveries', Denton writes that his method of unearthing things was to scour the junk shops of the neighbourhood every afternoon when school was over. 'I used to jump on a bus and then get off at any street that looked promising.'[22] His ambition was to furnish the room at Croom's Hill entirely with his own belongings. A Victorian work-table he had carried home on his shoulders from the other side of Blackheath could be a dressing-table; the bottom of a Chippendale tallboy served as a chest. More decorative pieces included a small Flemish cabinet and a spoon-backed Regency chair he had come across one weekend in the country.

Of course, these were items of furniture that could be found in many a home. They were nothing special. Their role was chiefly functional. Rather more exotic was the pale skin of a lioness that Miss Sinclair had allowed him to borrow and Denton eulogized the trophy in what is the only piece of verse that is known to survive from his Goldsmiths' days:

> The Lion,
> A shaggy beast,
> Lies on the floor
> Flattened out
> The colour of straw;
> While on either side
> Of his curved hide
> Stretch blue rugs.
> O there the royal lion lies!
> Model head and glassy eyes.[23]

With his extraordinarily acute eye Denton now and again turned up something really significant. The pride and joy of his collection was a fifteenth-century Southern Italian panel of The Nativity, very small and painted in tempera. He discovered it in a Greenwich shop during November 1933. At first the man asked a price of £10, but Denton managed to wheedle it down to just £4.[24] There was also a Rajput Hunting Scene, depicting two women bringing offerings to a priest. This dated from the early eighteenth century and came from a shop in New Cross. In a list of his most treasured possessions Denton states that it was bought in June 1934 for the modest sum of 10s.[25] Both paintings were taken to experts, who verified their authenticity. The Nativity remained in Denton's possession until the end of his life.

A rather more bizarre acquisition was the crimson alderman's robe that had been spotted 'hanging on a rusty hook with some beaded loincloths and a soldier's felt-covered water-bottle'[26] in the same New Cross shop. Denton intended to use it as the basis for an elaborate fancy-dress costume for the party that ended the Easter term of 1934. In spite of high expectations (Gerald went dressed as 'a sinister harlequin') the event itself proved to be a severe anti-climax. Denton's only moment of glory came when a rather drunk cockney taught him some new dance-steps. In 'A Novel Fragment' he tells how the man, taking him under his wing, 'clapped their bellies together and started to prance and sway in the most extravagant but masterly way'. Denton received the superfluous advice that 'if you want your partner to know what you're going to do next, you must hold her as tight against you as you can; then she can feel every little twitch of your body all the way down'.[27] After continuing the tutoring for a while, the cockney's eye was caught by one of the art school models, and so Denton, with his purple whiskers and sparkling dagger (which Gerald had cleverly fashioned from a ruler), was hastily abandoned.

A similar festivity took place at the home of Betty Swanwick on 25th May 1935. Denton describes it in his short story 'A Party', which he worked up from a much earlier piece in the last year of his life.[28] The first version differs very considerably in style. This is not the work of Denton Welch the fluent writer of the mid-1940s, but rather of a young man in his early twenties having a go at describing what had been a memorably entertaining evening:

> It was the crack-pated sort of party that very young art students give. Everyone was to appear in a bathing suit or less. Ian [Denton] bathed and put on slowly the faded mauve jansen [?] bought two years ago. He had liked it because it was the only mauve bathing suit he had ever seen. It had a skirt, which was so reassuring, and had been much reduced in the sale. Last of all, it was good, and known to be good and Ian had a passion for what was good and recognized to be good in others.
>
> As he drew it up over his thin, tight hips, he had the desire to tuck it in round his waist and so convert it into what the shop man would have called 'trunks', then he would mark all over it instead of unprocurable vine leaves, and make of it and himself something truly pagan. Prudence, quickly knocking on the door, put an end to these little half-formed plans—only the bold can afford to be pagans, and at the age of nineteen[29] one is acutely conscious of small hairs on the chest. One feels that one must be looked on as a sort of gorilla and one knows that it is impossible to live up to these signs of virility.
>
> So Ian pulled up the mauve wool, so that it covered his nipples and the offending hairs, slipped each slender strap over each slender shoulder and looked at himself in the glass. His get-up was dull, but would have to do. Perhaps he would just sew a leaf or two on round the skirt to make things a little more romantic, then he would brush his hair. This, at least, he felt was truly pagan, since it was short and curly and would always be an asset until it fell out. Ian shuddered!
>
> When he had done his hair, he soon put on his grey flannel trousers

very carefully over the leaves and then a white shirt and navy blue sweater, buckled on his childish brown sandals, and was ready to get on the bus for Catford. Arriving at Bertha Swan's,[30] he found that the cats already had other collars on and were tied up in the garden. This was because they did not like visitors and Ian could tell by the noise that most of the guests had arrived. Bertha always treated her cats as if they were dogs.

Bertha opened the charming door, heavy and swart, dressed in union jacks, her bunchy brazier divided from her little frilly skirt by the round, blond pillar of stomach. He was introduced to Bertha's mother, then he was free to look at the other guests. They were nearly all from the art school and well-known to him, but he had never seen them in their present state of undress and was surprised how well it suited some of them. There was that stocky little Bobby Davis,[31] looking quite amazingly masculine and primitive in that strip of leopard skin; Ian supposed it must be due to being Welsh. With him was Veronica Tooth,[32] solid, pretty and uncoloured, reminding one somehow of a piece of oatmeal soap.

Ian's eyes quickly took in several others, including Bertha's younger sister, Baby,[33] who, against all the rules, was very well-covered in a man's jacket and trousers, with a rather dirty scarf round her neck. She was seventeen years old, had a passion for collecting books, which she hardly read and affected a briar pipe when she felt the occasion demanded it.

It was after noticing all these that Ian suddenly saw the nun and was for a moment almost convinced of her genuineness. There seemed to be nothing missing from or incorrect about her appearance, but the face was not a nun's face; it was brown, a little freckled and masculine. She was talking to some others, who were inspecting her clothes and Ian heard *her* say, 'Yes, even the crucifix. I've got everything on. Do I look holy?' At this moment the others broke in with all sorts of remarks, The poor nun was asked if she bathed in a shift, and many other different questions.

Ian, still not knowing who it could be, left the drawing-room and went out into the hall. There was nothing here but a great coarse hanging of needlework done by Bertha. It was of lions sitting amongst arum lilies and went strangely with the corrupt and civilized paper frieze of autumn leaves, which hung round the walls. He went into the dining-room and looked at the food, which they were just about to eat. It was childish and appetizing. After he looked at it he looked at Baby's books, which lined the walls. Here they all were, book after book, from *Treasures of Peru* in one corner, until one came right round again to the *Proceedings of the Sexual Reform Congress*.

The room was filling up now. Soon everyone was eating and talking. Forks were all in use and trifle was disappearing. Some people were eating their silver balls and some were not. Ian wondered for the thousandth time if they might possibly be silvered with mercury. The hot sardine toast was appreciated and much lemonade and cider were drunk.

Bertha's mother, in her upholstery of black velvet with the worn imitation pearls around her neck, moved weightily about, suggesting to people that they should have a stuffed egg or perhaps a cucumber sandwich. Gradually the forks became less active and smoke curled in the air. People sat down now and there was peace for a little.

This was not like a party, and Bertha knew it so. Jumping up, she shouted, 'We must all play sardines.' The bustle began again and soon the lights were put out. Ian found himself wandering from the dark dining-room into the dark kitchen. There the tap dripped slowly and the ghosts of yellow soap and potatoes were in the air. Ian felt in the corners, but there was nothing soft, so he felt his way up the two steps again and tried to make towards the bathroom. At last he found it. The air was full of whispers.

There were moving bodies round him, but in the bathroom was only the cold white reflection from the bottom of the bath and the smell of mature sponges. 'I must not be the last. To be the last is always humiliating,' thought Ian. 'I will try the lavatory.' There was silence in the lavatory; it was not a natural silence. Ian felt slowly along the wall until he came to a bare leg. There was an excited start and giggle, and Ian knew that he had found what he was looking for. They were all round the seat, pressed against the wall, some standing on the seat. Ian put one foot on the seat and gradually got up. 'There must be four up here already,' he thought, 'I hope my foot won't slip.'

It was tense waiting in the stifling little room and there were giggles and smirks as people tried to move their bodies. Suddenly Ian felt a hand exploring him. He put out his own and touched a crucifix. He felt Bertha's deep breaths near him and he realized that the nun must think that he was Bertha. The nun was tightly holding his hand now and tickling him seductively at the same time. Ian could not think what he ought to do, but was saved from deciding when the last person arrived and he was able to break away quickly.

Sardines went on until people were tired of it and the murder, of course, took its place; more movements in the dark and that stealthy walking and breathing that was becoming so repressive. Ian was becoming what his aunt would have called 'morbid'. He longed for quiet. Suddenly he heard the clock in the dining-room strike twelve. With a jerk he realized that he had missed the last bus.

When the lights went on he went up and told Bertha. The nun was standing with her and replied, 'I can put you up if you like.'

It took a second for Ian to adapt himself to this idea and then he decided—'That is very good. Are you sure you don't mind?' Perhaps this was the friend he'd been waiting for. He must wait and see. He wanted so to talk to him alone. . . .[34]

This version continues with approximately the same text as 'A Party'. What makes the extract so interesting is that another of the guests, Cedric Rogers (who appears in the final version as 'Treff Rowse'), wrote his own account—and just a couple of days after the event had taken place. In comparing the two one gains a rare insight into how Denton would set about elaborating a story that was based on fact. Rogers, who was in no sense a professional writer, tells his tale:

> I got very little done today; roughs this morning—writing in the afternoon. Mum and Dad went out to tea, to the Alexanders. (In the morning I made a G-string out of a bit of tweed coat material.)
>
> At six I shut up Bunjie and left. Just outside the front door I saw Nick with a tiny mouse in his mouth.[35] He put it down rather guiltily and it was still just alive, so I trod on it and made a nasty mess.
>
> I met Smith[36] at the end of the road (where Betty's home was) and found our way to Betty's. Betty was not nearly so indecent as I had expected and I felt terribly nervous about wearing my G-string.
>
> Mrs Swanwick is a quaint, slightly pathetic woman—very big and fattish and not very strong, with a voice that becomes unhappy quite a lot, whatever she's talking about. But she's a very kind and sweet person, I should say.
>
> Betty was hysterical with laughing when she saw what I was going to wear; I think she must have been drinking a bit. When Smith and I were getting ready someone belched loudly outside the door. This surprised me greatly, but was nothing to what followed. I said I was nervous of wearing my costume and said I'd like to wait until someone else from Goldsmiths came. So when Appelbee[37] was ready, I emerged. Smith was dressed as a Black Mammy, a marvellous one he made, and some of my drawings had worn off (I had done some imitation tattoos in coloured inks, as I remember). I drew them in again with grease-paint. It made things very crude and the previous delicacy was lost, but it helped cover things up a bit. Smith drew things on my back too.
>
> Smith took a little of the attention off me when we met the company. But it was a very extraordinary position, to go to a strange house, meet a lot of strange people and be practically naked at the same time. All the same, no-one seemed to worry very much.
>
> Betty's sister had a coarse, superficial manner, which hides a very shy nature. She was dressed as a parson. We played the questions and answers game, and then Bobby and Monica came, dressed very well as fauns, leaves sewn on shorts, etc. and browned all over.
>
> I had two drinks, a cocktail and a Martini, thrust on me during the evening. Welch was there, and I must say in the right company he is quite reasonable and unobtrusive.
>
> We played a game called 'Artist's Model', which I saw through and arranged to my advantage. A game called 'I see a light', which Smith and I started one lot, I mucked up by giving the word away as soon as I opened my mouth. They played 'Animal, Vegetable, Mineral'. Bobby chose one that also had a symbolic meaning. The thing was Appelbee's Adam's Apple, but the answers were so confusing that I got nowhere near it and it was almost shown to me.
>
> We had supper then and it was very good and filling. Betty's sister

said, 'Don't be afraid to belch' and she and her boyfriend proceeded to set
the pace. Appelbee said 'Cummon Rogers, let's show 'em what Goldsmiths
can do!' When we'd finished, Betty's sister said, 'I don't think much of
Goldsmiths' effort', but all in a terribly self-conscious way. A few minutes
later I brought one out that made Appelbee shout for joy.

Just before we went home I saw a door open leading into a passage
where some people were running up and down, so I went out there and
found I was dancing up and down the garden with Welch and Appelbee
(Bobby and Monica were having their fortunes told). We got bolder and I
jumped over the garden gate and sprinted up and down the street, danced
in the lights of a parked car and came in.

A girl visitor was playing the piano just as I left. I was asked to croon;
they'd all heard about me, and I did so in a very subdued manner (negro
spirituals); of course 'Dinah' had to be resurrected (I was then dressed very
smartly in a thin grey flannel coat and trousers, and must have presented a
curiously different aspect). I got home about 11.30.[38]

By now Denton was fully accepted as a definite personality at Goldsmiths';
He had built up his own circle of friends and it would appear that he was
happier than at any time since his mother's death eight years earlier. He had left
Repton with the ambition of training as an artist and this was precisely the
course he was following. Although he may not have had any real plans for the
future, at least he was trying to develop his talent. Goldsmiths' offered a way of
life that suited his eager and lively temperament.

Chapter Four

The Accident

The accident that shattered Denton's life happened almost exactly a fortnight after the party at Betty Swanwick's. It was the Whitsun weekend and the students of course had the Bank Holiday Monday free as well. Denton planned to ride down to the country on his bicycle. He would spend a night with his aunt, Edith Kane, at Leigh Vicarage, near Betchworth on the way. Apparently they had no idea he was coming. There were so many brothers and sisters that one extra, he thought, would hardly make much difference. He knew he could rely on the Kanes to give him a bed.

Denton and Betty Swanwick had agreed to meet at the post office in Cuckfield, probably the next day; the intention was that they should cycle over to Waphams and have tea with his grandfather and Aunt Dolly. Maybe Denton meant to leave his bicycle there, so that it would be ready for the summer holidays—he could then return to London by train. The trip down to Aunt Edith's would certainly be a very long ride, but it was not as daunting as it might have been; the previous summer Valerie White and he had cycled a far greater distance—to Brixham in Devon.[1] The only doubt in Denton's mind now was the prospect of having to face heavy traffic.

Whatever the details of his plan were, he set out from 34 Croom's Hill on the morning of Sunday 9th June.[2] First of all Denton passed over Blackheath, windy and exposed, and then, before getting down to the journey proper, he paid a visit to Joan Waymark at her home in Lewisham. She remembered having waved him off on his way south along the road that is today the A2.

He had the complete freedom to stop whenever he wanted to. First it was Lewisham's peculiarly designed Catholic Church, with its hard red brick and tall thin tower, and then, further along the main road Denton spotted some intriguing park gates that promised, perhaps, a house of some significance. Light refreshments were advertised. He decided to make a small detour. He followed a drive through the park, which had been neatly groomed into a golf course, and then came upon Beckenham Lodge, an attractive neo-classical Georgian house. Having admired the well-proportioned façade, Denton went in and had some coffee and biscuits in an oval saloon, now rudely converted into a cafe, resplendent with tea-urns and advertisements for cigarettes.

Soon he was away again. He thought he might make the vicarage in time for tea. He pedalled on to Bromley[3] and then must have continued through Croydon until he reached the Brighton road. The area was already rather built up, with the towns of Purley and Coulsdon providing little centres for shopping along the route. Once he had passed by South Coulsdon Station on the left, the scene became more countryfied, although there was still a railway cutting bordering the road. At this point one can imagine Denton assuming that the worst of the journey was behind him.

It was just a short way further south that he was knocked off his bicycle. Some time afterwards his brother Bill told him what was known of the actual circumstances of the accident: 'A private car, driven by a woman, had run into me from behind. The road had been straight and wide, with little traffic on it. It had, of course, been broad daylight. There appeared to be no reason for the accident, except the gross carelessness of the driver. There were several witnesses. . . .' [4]

A policeman was soon on hand and fortunately Denton regained consciousness long enough to give the man his name and tell him where he was going.

> I heard a voice through a great cloud of agony and sickness. The voice was asking questions. It seemed to be opening and closing like a concertina. The words were loud, as the swelling notes of an organ, then they melted to the tiniest wiry tinkle of water in a glass.
>
> I knew that I was lying on my back on the grass; I could feel the shiny blades on my neck. I was staring at the sky and I could not move. Everything about me seemed to be reeling and breaking up. My whole body was screaming with pain, filling my head with its roaring, and my eyes were swimming in a sort of gum mucilage. Rich clouds of what seemed to be a combination of ink and velvet soot kept belching over me, soaking into me, then melting away. Bright little points glittered all down the front of the liquid man kneeling beside me. I knew at once that he was a policeman, and I thought that, in his official capacity, he was performing some ritual operation on me. There was a confusion in my mind between being brought to life—forceps, navel-cords, midwives—and being put to death—ropes, axes and black masks; but whatever it was that was happening, I felt that all men came to this at last. I was caught and could never escape the terrible natural law. [5]

A front-page story in *The Coulsdon and Purley Times* of 14th June tells what had happened next:

> In Brighton-road, Hooley on Sunday afternoon, Mr Denton Welch, 34 [sic] of Cromes-hill [sic], Greenwich, sustained multiple injuries when he was knocked from his cycle by a motor vehicle. He was taken in the Coulsdon and Purley ambulance to Purley Hospital, and subsequently to Greenwich Hospital. [6]

The first evening in St Alphege's, Greenwich, was not quite so much of a blur in his memory as it might have been. Denton remembered his Aunt Edith and her son Bernard coming to see him. [7] With a strange concern to appear composed, he had attempted to make sensible conversation, but she had told him not to talk. Within a few seconds he was left alone again; alone to come to terms with a severely damaged body and also with what he soon realized was a cruelly alien environment. Nobody told him what had happened—he had to ask a nurse if he was correct in thinking that he had been run over; nobody told him the extent of his injuries and nobody told him how long the blinding pain that was wracking his body would last, or whether there could be any relief from it. All Denton could do was to cry out in agony, and eventually he was given an injection of what was probably morphine.

When morning came there was the quick realization that any humanity one might reasonably expect from the nursing staff had long since been sacrificed before the god of daily routine. Denton regarded their ruthless professionalism as savage and inappropriate. He could put up with being washed—that was rather a novelty—but then came the special nurse with her trolley to change his dressings:

> After giving me one preoccupied witch-like glance, she undid the tapes at the back of my neck and the night-shirt was pulled down again. She stared at my cut body, then, without any warning, stretched out her hand and ripped off one of the dressings.
>
> My mouth jerked open and I heard my own shuddering intake of breath. The shock made me feel sick.
>
> 'Don't!' I implored, when I saw her stretching for the next dressing. 'You can't, Nurse!'
>
> 'Can't what?' she asked, affronted. 'This is the right way to do it. I've got too much to do to waste my time playing about. Just you show me what you're made of instead of creating.'[8]

Denton was forced to give in. When the nurse pulled back the bedclothes still further, he saw for the first time that his leg was in a splint. He had a broken ankle. But this was really the least of his worries. A small bone in the spine had been fractured. The results of this injury would remain with him for the rest of his life.

Part of Denton's very deep distrust and dislike of anyone associated with medicine can be attributed to his Christian Science upbringing. He had a desperate need of someone he could count on for comfort and moral support; at once he thought of Hilda Dallas. Aside from having been a close friend of his mother, she was a Christian Science practitioner. Denton concocted a story that he had been about to have tea with her on the day of his accident, and having told the untruth to the Ward Sister, he asked her to telephone Hilda and explain what had happened. He knew the ploy would have its desired effect, and within a short time 'Clare', as she appears in *A Voice through a Cloud*,[9] was at his bedside.

> I tried to lull myself to sleep, to forget everything and wait for Clare, but all the pleasant things that only yesterday I liked so much rose up to

haunt me. I thought of eating delicious food, wearing good clothes, feeling proud and gay, going for walks, singing and dancing alone, fencing and swimming and painting pictures with other people, reading books. And everything seemed horrible and thin and nasty as soiled paper. I wondered how I could ever have believed in these things, how I could even for a moment have thought they were real. Now I knew nothing was real but pain, heat, blood, tingling, loneliness and sweat.[10]

Finally Hilda came and she promised to visit him regularly. Taking heart, Denton undid one of the knots that had been tied to secure the splint to his leg. The relief from the pressure of the iron contraption was marvellous while it lasted, but the Ward Sister soon discovered what he had done and was exceedingly cross. It was put back in place as painfully tight as it had been before and Denton, after undoing it one more time, was finally thwarted by another nurse who fixed the knots beyond his reach at the lower end of his leg.

Night was a period of lonely despair and unremitting pain and he had to wait until the afternoon of the second day to experience a modicum of relief from the dreadful situation: he caught sight of two friends from Goldsmiths', Corinne Snow and Joan Waymark, looking anxiously around the ward to find his bed. Joan had a vivid memory of the event:

St Alphege's in Greenwich was a terrible hospital—it looked like a workhouse really. We went upstairs and found our way to him. We nearly fainted when we saw him. We didn't say anything about it, but his whole face and his eyes were blacked all over. He also had a bad leg and was very bruised indeed.[11]

Denton cheered up momentarily. He borrowed a mirror from Joan to have a look at his face. How grotesque and ironical it was that the two girls had greeted him with his nickname, 'Sonny Boy'! They stayed for a short time, left some small presents, and then went on their way. From now on, at least, Denton had a regular flow of visitors, including other students from the art school, his relations, Miss Sinclair and, of course, the indispensable Miss Dallas.

His description of the first few days in hospital expresses both a morbid curiosity about his own physical state and also a feeling of utter degradation. Denton was surrounded by the vulnerable sick and became very aware of the absolute power wielded over them by the female nurses. One day, to his extreme satisfaction, a chap who had been pushed beyond the limits of tolerance rebelled. Denton remembered how two young men were brought in after having been involved in a serious motor-bike accident—they had been riding pillion. One of them, Joe, died during the night. The following morning his friend was telling another patient about what had happened, when, as Joe's death began to sink in, he broke down, crying quietly.

A nurse rustled by busily. 'You mustn't carry on like that you know,' she said; 'we're all very sorry about your friend; but you can't upset the other patients. Just take a hold on yourself. Men mustn't cry.'

There was a silence; then the man burst out, 'Bloody well sod off! Bloody well sod off!'

His voice mounted to a plaintive, outraged howl, as if he had been baited beyond endurance. Tears rained down his face again.

The nurse stood at the foot of his bed, too dumbfounded to speak. All at once she turned on her heel and hurried away.

She returned with Sister. Both women bore down on the man with the set, grim faces of executioners.

Sister insisted on the man apologising; she stood over him until he said, 'I beg your pardon, Nurse.'

His crushed, humbled tone stung me. I longed for him to burst out against the women, to swear again.[12]

As a method of escaping from the permanent discomfort, Denton would often float off into a reverie, or he might amuse himself by doodling in a drawing-book that Hilda had brought, sometimes writing down lines too that had a special significance at the moment.[13]

Miss Dallas it was who successfully instilled in Denton the will to get better and her regular visits were the most important factor in his recovery from the immediate effects of the accident. After he had been at St Alphege's for about a month, the specialist who was looking after him pronounced Denton well enough to be moved. Bill informed his brother that the next destination would be the Hospital for Nervous Diseases in Bloomsbury—then he was to be packed off to a nursing-home in the country.

In early June he was transferred to the somewhat forbidding hospital in Queen's Square. When the ambulance arrived, Denton saw three girls, all friends of Bill's, waiting for him on the steps, but their cheery gaiety did not prevent him from forming a rather negative opinion of the place. To make matters worse, the first nurse he encountered greeted him with a combative, 'Well, and what's wrong with you?', thus confirming all his fears that the Hospital for Nervous Diseases was no more humane than the one he had just left.

Because of the specialized nature of the hospital, many of the men on the ward were mentally disturbed and the overall atmosphere was very dismal. Quite a few had suffered head injuries.

The ones with open eyes looked even deader than the ones who slept; these at least appeared to be living inside their own heads. But the ones with open eyes had nothing within or without; their very eyeballs were as unmysterious and hard as uncooked bullaces. [14]

And so, not for the first time, Denton found himself retreating into daydreams; all the while they were becoming more and more elaborate. One in particular that he mentions in *A Voice Through a Cloud* was centred round a beautifully furnished country house. He would be sitting in an old, panelled room, whilst a dainty kitten played on the floor nearby. There was a succulent meal laid out before him and outside the house he was free to roam in the stillness of the garden, with its evocative scents of damp grass and humid soil. The mansion had disused wings that he could explore. The whole experience of the daydream filled Denton with intense pleasure.[15] He knew that he could always linger in this enticing world when he needed to insulate himself from the sufferings of the people round about him.

Nevertheless, in the right mood Denton was quite happy to talk to the other patients on the ward and he even tried helping a man who had lost his memory to read again. 'Ray', as his new friend was called, was discharged before him. Denton wrote him a letter from the hospital, but received no reply. Some time afterwards one of the male nurses told Denton that he had died. His reaction to hearing of the death reveals the extent to which the introverted side of his nature was becoming more pronounced; it was beginning to engulf his personality. Everything was now seen in a distorted and morbid light, which, though being exquisitely creative in itself, was taking Denton further and further away from reality. From his immediate sadness at Ray's death Denton moved on to imagine the coffin.

I watched tiny creatures crawling in and out of the flowers, falling into the coffin, trying to climb out again with a terrible patience. The breath from the flowers was so sweet that it seemed to coat the inside of my nostrils.

I could not rid my mind of these white flowers, so melodramatic, so obvious, waving falsely over the corruption, trying to hide the sight and the smell of it.

Under the lilac plumes were the utterly still features. They looked like some rather timid wax sculpture. Somehow the skull was beginning to smile its way through the drawn flesh, which had grown almost as clear as a sheet of carpenter's glue.[16]

But as time wore on he became more immune to the sufferings of the other patients. There tended to be disturbances in the night and deaths were not uncommon. Denton realized that he had to dissociate himself from these upsets. It was his own survival that counted and becoming too involved in the lives of the other patients would only lead him up a blind alley.

Now and then his thoughts turned to Goldsmiths'. One thing kept puzzling him. Why hadn't he seen anything of his friend Gerald? He had been in hospital for weeks and weeks now, yet he was the one person who did not come. They had spent so much time together. Denton thought that quite possibly he had said something to offend him; he had been unnecessarily churlish on occasion.

The reasons why his friend had stayed away were, in fact, quite different.

I went to see Denton only once in hospital—at Queen's Square. I think he was rather unkind in writing about the incident as he did in *A Voice Through a Cloud*. My brother had been killed just a month before and at that stage I had a thing about hospitals. It wasn't that I didn't want to see Denton, it was just the thought of entering the door of one. I went in to see him anyway and I remember thinking how normal he looked, except for a graze on his forehead. But of course, down below the nerves in the spine had been injured and he was paralysed; the bladder had ceased to work.[17]

In *A Voice Through a Cloud* Denton writes how he spotted 'Mark Lynch' (alias Gerald) hastily scanning the ward for his bed. They were soon reunited and Gerald's absence was explained. Denton too felt a little guilty at being unable to come up with the right things to say in response to the sad news about his brother. It was obviously a difficult meeting for both of them and this may be part of the reason why it was not until Denton had moved to a nursing-home that they saw one another again.

By early autumn Denton had made sufficient progress to be taken into the day-room. Sitting up in a wheelchair was a very unpleasant experience at first—all the blood seemed to be rushing into his legs. By now his weight had dropped to under five stones and even his arms were emaciated through lack of movement. This state of complete physical helplessness was keenly brought home to him when one night the ward filled up with smoke after the first fire of the season had been lit.

> I heard feet running and the sound of urgent voices. I decided that it would be unwise to wait for somebody to carry me out, and since I could not walk or even crawl, there was nothing left for me to do but roll. I thought for one moment of trying to climb out of the window behind me, but realized that I would be trapped in the well and perhaps roasted if the fire began to rage.[18]

In the event nobody had to leave their beds. The windows were opened and to celebrate his supposed lucky escape Denton ate some chocolate. He writes that he 'felt glad that the night had been made shorter by the excitement'.

It is curious that in describing his life during this period, Denton makes virtually no mention of having read books, or even of attempting to obtain them. It is possible his physical condition made the angle of holding a book tiresome, but he does not tell us this was so. Considering that one day he would become a writer, one might have expected him to have taken advantage of the opportunity to expand his knowledge of literature, something that had certainly been a great solace to him during his years at school.

One day, however, there arrived a book on English china, three bottles of sherry and a letter, all from his brother Bill. Denton skimmed through the book and then devoted his attention to the letter. It brought news of the arrangements that had been made for the next stage of his recovery. Very soon he would be moved to a nursing-home at Broadstairs on the south-east coast, chosen on account of its proximity to his uncle and aunt, Sir Harry and Lady Fox (these were the relations who had entertained him for the Christmas in Peking shortly before his return to England.) The project was a great boost to Denton's spirits:

> Now that I knew I was going, I looked on the ward with different eyes. Everything, even the light and air, seemed changed. Figures suddenly lost their depth and darkness and became harmless marionettes seen only from one angle, watched only for their interest as spectacle.[19]

Around the beginning of October 1935, Denton was deemed to be well enough to leave hospital. Already four months had elapsed since the accident. In recent days he had been trying to walk again, but it was no easy matter getting his feet to respond. Initially, he could only move them an inch at a time.

Miss Dallas, helpful as ever, came along to oversee the arrangements and she travelled with him in the ambulance on the long journey down to the south coast. First of all, however, they called in at Greenwich so that Denton could collect some of his belongings. The ambulance men carried the feather-light invalid up to his room on the top floor and there he managed to steal a few moments of privacy with his collection. The things had remained unseen and unattended for so many months. Denton was in a bit of a quandary as to which he should take. He really had no idea what sort of place the nursing-home might be. In the end he settled on the Italian primitive and three favourite pieces of china.

Soon the ambulance was passing through many towns that reminded him of earlier periods in his life, a life over which, for the moment, he had lost control. Denton did not know whether he would ever recover his health. It seems that some medical students had inadvertently told him that his condition was virtually incurable.[20] At least, he had left the hospital and was beginning to contemplate the possibility of becoming mobile again; that was something.

Broadstairs lies very near the south-easternmost tip of England. Looking out over the Strait of Dover, it had originally been a small fishing town. The ancient jetty can be found below the picturesque Bleak House, with its Dickensian associations. But to someone of Denton's background the place, apart from being quite a popular holiday resort, was known almost exclusively for providing two different types of service: the education of the young sons of the wealthy and homes for the recuperation of the sick (especially those suffering from tuberculosis, and children who were recovering from rheumatic fever). The air was bracing.

The ambulance's destination was the Southcourt Nursing Home, only a stone's throw away from the well known prep school, Wellesley House. It was not considered to be one of the better convalescent homes, though the owner-matron, Miss Widdop, had built up a reputation as a capable nurse. The modest building still stands in an unprepossessing road that is quite some distance from the esplanades of the sea front. Denton's first impressions did not bode well.

She led the way through the dark hall, her heels clapping on the polished wood-block floor. I saw a brass jug gleaming and some late zinnias in a bowl; then I was carried down a narrow passage and found myself in a bedroom with a french-window as big as a garage door. Perhaps the room had once been a garage, for it was at the side of the house, cut off from all the other rooms.[21]

Miss Dallas duly returned to London and Denton was left alone to ponder his new surroundings. In an early draft of *A Voice Through a Cloud* he reveals that to begin with he 'lay there in the bed, gazing at the fire and crying'.[22] Despite these feelings of misery, he soon pulled himself together and was able to look on the bright side. No more would he have to put up with the noises from the hospital ward. He could concentrate on his enjoyment of the improved food. His life was starting to become his own again.

That evening the new doctor, Hugh Raven, dropped in. He was also the Foxs' physician, though the practice was not the best one in town. Raven was a man enthused by a disconcertingly eccentric type of religiosity, and Denton recalled that on this first visit the doctor had told him of a poem he had written about Ethiopia. When asked if he intended to have it published, Raven replied 'Not on your life!' and smiled secretively.

The next morning Denton climbed upstairs to have a bath. At this stage he was only able to drag himself around by holding on to furniture or banisters. Before he had time to get back to his room, 'Nurse Goff', who was charged with taking care of him, came and said that Lady Fox would soon be looking in. Denton was slightly anxious. As things turned out, he needn't have been. His aunt only stayed long enough to hand over a large box of chocolates and a bunch of flowers. Since her husband had suffered a severe paralytic stroke, she was probably not over-enthusiastic at the idea of spending much time visiting a distant relation. Denton knew immediately that she wasn't the person to help him in his recovery.

And so he became very aware of the dimension of time stretching out endlessly before him. He had no idea how to fill it. The situation was very different from being at Greenwich or Queen's Square. Broadstairs lies a long way from London and not many of his friends would be able to make the rail journey down to visit him. It was already the Michaelmas term at Goldsmiths'. The sense of isolation must have been acute.

Denton managed to cope by turning his attention purely to thinking about his life in the home. Fortunately, he was given a physiotherapist whom he liked. 'Miss Pierce' may have looked somewhat masculine, but she talked freely about her own life and this was interesting. Soon Nurse Goff opened up too and almost immediately she told him of the love affair with her 'dark and solid' fiancé, who, as it happened, had been the previous occupant of Denton's room.

Things might have progressed in a slow, unremarkable way, with Denton gradually improving within the confines of a controlled environment in which nothing out of the ordinary ever occurred; but this was not the way it was going to be.

On the third day at Southcourt Gerald put in an appearance. With great generosity he promised he would visit Denton weekly. When he was coming down next, he said, he would bring more paints, brushes and an easel, so that Denton could start painting again. The two friends spent a pleasant afternoon together, exchanging news.

It was eventually time for Gerald to make his way back to London. Denton got out of bed, put on his dressing-gown, and escorted him through the french windows into the garden at the front of the house.

Just at that moment a small car drew up and a man carrying a doctor's bag got out. As Denton was making his way back to the room, he heard the front door close and the young doctor, whom he had seen go inside, instead of returning to his car, came up to him:

> He was tall and dark and dressed in dark clothes. His body seemed elastic but not light. As he came nearer, I saw that he was looking into me with eyes that could not pierce, because they were too brown and soft, too like a stag's eyes. His chin was cleft, his lips square and good; but a harshness from nose to mouth reminded me of Charles the Second's portraits. His expression was too concentrated and searching. He did not conciliate me. I thought of him as an inquisitor; and, smiling with anxiety and annoyance, I lifted my head to confront him and keep him at bay.[23]

Denton learnt that the doctor, Jack Easton, who appears in *A Voice Through a Cloud* as 'Dr Farley', was the junior partner in Raven's practice. Easton would be treating him from now on. Soon Denton was telling him about the accident and his time in hospital. When he had finished his story the doctor said, '"Well, you *have* had a bad time."'

These simple words of sympathy had a profound effect. Up till now no member of the medical profession had shown any real recognition of the degree to which he had suffered. Denton felt instantly that this was the person he was searching for, a doctor who understood his plight and would try to help him get better.

But strangely his initial reaction to Easton had been quite mixed. Just after the doctor had waved his bag in a friendly gesture to say goodbye, all sorts of emotions had been churning around in Denton's mind. 'I kept saying to myself, "I wonder why I didn't like the look of him. What was wrong with him? Or is there something wrong with me? Am I suspicious of everybody?"'[24]

Jack Easton was in his early thirties. He had come to Broadstairs three years previously, having been a senior registrar at King's College Hospital in London. From this post he could easily have moved on to become a Harley Street consultant, but he preferred the thought of general practice. The reason why he landed up at Broadstairs was that Roger Raven, his housemaster at Rugby, a man unusually sympathetic and supportive of boys who were unhappy at school (as Easton had been), took an interest in his career and encouraged him to join his brother Hugh's practice.

With his obvious success at King's behind him, Dr Easton had hoped that he would have been able to branch out into accepting some consultancy work in Kent. However, he quickly discovered the new practice was not all that it might have been. Dr Raven was so unpopular amongst the local medical fraternity that it was impossible for him to get on the staff of either the Ramsgate or Margate Hospitals. To make matters worse, his senior partner's blind prejudice against female physicians meant that Mrs Easton, herself a doctor, effectively could not practise in the area.

Raven had already told Easton he didn't think Denton could live long. A case such as his was considered to be hopeless—it was to all intents and purposes untreatable.[25]

For Denton to urinate, a catheter had to be passed into his bladder through the urethra. This process, when performed regularly, nearly always led to the patient getting an inflammation of the kidneys and a symptom of this was the blinding headaches from which Denton suffered for the rest of his life. Also there would be high temperatures. Antibiotics had yet to be invented, so that to clear up the infection it was necessary to prescribe sulphur drugs, but these could only be taken for three days or so at a time.

Dr Easton eventually managed to teach Denton to empty his bladder by squeezing his stomach, but for much of the rest of his life he had to wear a catheter. It had to be sterilized each time it was replaced. The paralysis also affected his bowels, and at this stage these had to be cleaned out. One can understand Denton's feelings of degradation at being unable to exercise control over these functions. It was all so alien to his self-image. He was no longer a person of elegance and vitality; this had gone for ever.

When Easton reappeared the following day Denton could scrutinize him once again and explore more exactly what his feelings were. Having asked a great many questions, the doctor remarked on his patient's extreme thinness and then said it would be a good idea if he had cream with his porridge; he wrote out a list of foods that the matron was to give him.

> To be ordered such things was like being a child again, with someone above you who brooded over your welfare and took all the responsibility. Little attentions after the indifference of hospital struck me as almost too refined, too delicate. This was not true, hard-headed doctoring, but cossetting, coddling.[26]

But really Denton was grateful for the consideration and he desperately wanted Easton to stay a little longer and chat, but, as nearly always happened, duty called and the man went away. Denton felt frustrated.

Supported by Nurse Goff and two walking sticks, he begin to totter around the streets in the vicinity of the nursing-home. At least it was flat and they were divided up into convenient blocks.

One Saturday, just when he was about to make one of these afternoon jaunts, Aunt Dos (Lady Fox) arrived. She was accompanied by his brother Bill, whom she had invited down for the weekend to see how Denton was progressing. As his closest relative in England, Bill now shouldered some of the responsibility for seeing to his affairs. Unfortunately, because of the great difference in their temperaments, when left alone they could find little to say to one another. Bill kept on asking if Denton had everything he wanted and whether the place was satisfactory or not. Tea was brought in, but the atmosphere remained dead. Denton became more and more depressed. Finally, seeing that it was quite pointless detaining Bill any longer when he so obviously wanted to escape, Denton let him return to the comfort of Corlismore, Aunt Dos's large house on the sea-front.

The whole meeting had been disappointing and very unsatisfactory. Fired with an almost superhuman determination, Denton reached the decision then and there to go over to Lady Fox's home. He would show his family that he had to be taken seriously, that he was still capable of doing things for himself.

As he passed by her office, Denton told Matron that he was just venturing out to practise some walking. The extraordinary feat that he then accomplished involved him turning left out of the home, going several hundred yards to the end of the street and then taking a rough footpath that led down to a road behind the one where his aunt and uncle lived.

> I began to see my aunt's house as a goal—a goal like the Cross in that child's prayer book picture, where a woman with streaming hair is shown clinging to the base in utter exhaustion, while storm clouds part, the sun breaks through and one sees the terrible length of her pilgrimage.[27]

Denton reached his destination.

Though the outing was unquestionably foolhardy—his relations at Corlismore were horrified to see him—the incident did tell Denton that, given time, it would be possible to get about again. He had not collapsed. He had made a bid for independence that was crucial in the progress of his recovery.

Easton did all he could to ease his patient's feelings of tedium and loneliness. He became more than just a doctor; Denton was rapidly coming to regard him as his only true friend. One gets an idea of the light-hearted nature of their relationship at this time in an incident that is recalled in *A Voice Through a Cloud*. Denton apparently told Miss Widdop that he had a craving for a pineapple—and she must have gone out and bought one in the town—for one day, when Easton was about to leave, Denton heard a bustle outside his room and then the sound of him rushing back in again:

> The door flew open and I saw him holding the great cockaded fruit as if it had been a baby in arms. He was laughing silently and his thick eyebrows curled like furry caterpillars. All at once he slung the horny, scaly pine on to the foot of my bed, then made an extraordinary face at me and was gone.[28]

The doctor also lent Denton his gramophone and after the effects of his over-exertion had worn off, offered to take him out in the car for a change of scenery. Later, they retired to his house for tea. It was whilst they were relaxing and tucking into hot toast and dripping that Easton asked him what he intended to do with himself when he had regained his health. Denton thought the question too precipitate. Rather than launch into a complex explanation of how he felt, he considered it would be easier if he gave the impression that he had no ambition at all. Easton was disappointed. He thought Denton was gifted. As is made evident in *A Voice Through a Cloud*, the chief reason why the question threw him was that at this stage Denton found it almost impossible to make the necessary adjustment to his physical state:

> What could I say? How could I tell him of all the things that I wanted to—things I was ashamed of because I wanted them so weakly, so confusedly, yet so persistently? The cloudy beckoning things had been knocked to pieces by the sudden violence of the accident. They had lost all their worth and fascination at first, but now they were growing again. The ghosts were losing their greyness and were trying to draw me from the lulled muted life of bed; but I rebelled, still wanting to be left in my nothingness, not wanting anyone to talk to me of plans and futures.[29]

Looking back over the doctor-patient relationship at this time, Jack Easton recalled that there had been no one else on the spot prepared to give Denton the attention that he needed. Unfortunately, the doctor was not able to perceive the extent to which he was becoming dependent on him. Denton was focusing his emotions on the one person who showed an almost fatherly consideration for his welfare. Indeed, one might speculate that the choice of the surname 'Farley' for Easton reflects this.[30]

From the doctor's point of view, the relationship, of course, was entirely professional. He was the caring physician intent on doing what he could for his patient. Nevertheless, as the incident with the pineapple suggests, Easton did have a certain fondness for Denton, who was a good deal more interesting and challenging than the usual run of elderly convalescent cases and schoolboys.

Denton, however, was slowly clawing back what he could of his mobility and by early November he felt sufficiently confident to make another trip out on his own. This time he took a bus into the centre of Broadstairs and bought himself some truffles. There were very few shops near the nursing-home. Afterwards he hobbled along one of the esplanades till he found somewhere to sit. Denton writes that he had the impression of a town 'full of almost useless men moping at street corners'.[31] Resting in a small pavilion, he got into conversation with a fellow convalescent, but very quickly discovered the man didn't have a spark of life left in his personality; the two of them went their separate ways without Denton having the opportunity of telling *his* story. In an early draft of *A Voice Through a Cloud*, however, he includes a paragraph about their parting, and it demonstrates a depth of compassion that several commentators have refused to credit as being part of his personality:

He stood still for a moment, then I heard him following me. This was a moment of creeping alarm in that soft tender mist blowing so delicately, thickening, eddying, enveloping and dispersing. I looked back, trying to put sharpness and authority into my frightened face. Then I saw that he was crying. The tears were swelling out of his weak eyes and running down the pink cheeks. He wore a terrible child-like look of distress and hopelessness and without saying anything, but only looking into my eyes, he caught hold of my hand and held it tightly, as if he must hold something human or collapse. Standing there in the brown trilby, the sporty reefing-coat, with the tears streaming down and the mouth open in the tragic square Greek statue shape, he seemed to me infinitely more stricken, more floundering than I was myself or than all the other people in the London hospital.[32]

Before long Denton was venturing out of the Southcourt Nursing Home quite regularly. By now he knew the subdued neighbourhood rather well. The Romanesque-style Catholic church, Our Lady of the Sea, held a certain fascination. In the building, which had been erected in 1931, he would observe the toings and froings of an altar-server who had been struck on the head by the one bell falling from the tower while he was ringing the Angelus. It never ceased to amaze him that this horrifying accident, with its almost gothic overtones, had not deterred the lad, whose real name was Teddy King, from returning to his sacred duty. Another outing was when he went to pay a social call on Mrs Noote. She was the mother of his Aunt Dos, and her house, Upton Lodge, stood near the church on land that bordered onto the property of Wellesley House. The last time he had seen the eccentric old lady was when he was six. With his extraordinary powers of observation, Denton made a mental note of as many aspects of the house as he could remember from his childhood visit.

But he spent most of his time and energy in thinking about Jack Easton. One gets a glimpse of just how much he had become obsessed in reading his description of an evening when the matron took him along to see the doctor take part in an amateur dramatic production. For some reason the whole setting had a very peculiar effect on him and when he saw Easton smile (a smile that he felt almost belonged to *him*), something akin to jealousy was aroused:

> I distrusted it, not because I thought it false, but because I felt it pleased me too much and so falsified my judgement. I told myself that it was a trick of his and that he knew it pleased, just as a child sometimes knows that its childishness is endearing. I waited for him to overdo the smile and repel me. But he never did, or if he did I embraced the extravagance wholeheartedly.[33]

Only after the performance was over and Matron had returned Denton to his room did the curious mood break. All the frustrations that had built up inside him rose to a peak of unhappiness. He burst into tears.

The next morning Matron must have told Dr Easton of his patient's behaviour. He came in to see Denton and asked for some explanation.

'Well,' I said slowly, trying to spin out mild bantering expressions until he left, 'it was rather peculiar to see you on the stage.'

'Why peculiar?' he asked, refusing my banter.

'I don't know; I kept looking at you, wondering about you, watching your smile spreading and shrinking, wondering what it was all for. What did the other people think? Then, when it ended and we were going home, I began to imagine what it was like at your end. I saw it all, the dog, your wife, the lights on, hot drinks.'[34]

Denton rambled on for a few more minutes, trying blindly to express his feelings. Dr Easton listened with patience. He had the first inkling that the relationship was becoming awkward. It had almost reached the level of a transference. Denton too could sense that what he was saying would alter things. 'I know now,' he wrote in *A Voice Through a Cloud*, 'that this slight talk was unfortunate, for my most desolate time dates from it. Unhappiness seemed to be fixed on me as my part, and I took it up and accepted it. I thought that Dr Farley began to treat me with more anxious care and less easy friendship.'[35]

Appreciating something of Denton's generally muddled emotional state, Easton thought the best remedy would be for him to meet someone of his own age with whom he shared a common interest. It was nearing Christmas and various university students would be returning home for the holiday season. The doctor hit on the scheme of introducing Denton to the son of one of his patients. Martin Miles, who was up at Oxford, turned out to be a much more pleasant and easy-going companion than Denton had imagined, even though he may not have been the answer to the problem. The Miles's home, St Ninian's, just a few streets away, had a cosy atmosphere—there was a Christmas crib—and to begin with Denton allowed himself to be distracted from his obsessive worries. Martin's mother was German. When they had tea, in a rather un-English manner, a girl started to recite poetry, especially for his benefit. Afterwards he went up to Martin's bedroom, where his new friend showed him an assortment of books, one of which was an autographed copy of poems by Walter de la Mare. Denton registered that there existed a gulf between them, though, when he saw that Martin in no way shared his passion for possessions. There was a lack of intensity in the young man's personality that did not appeal to him. Nevertheless, he was someone he would be perfectly happy to see on occasion.

But something else rather more significant had bothered Denton. The neat and happy household reminded him of all the things that he himself lacked. He did not have a family home where he could go for Christmas. He had no mother. He could never be a student again. Christmas celebrations were not for him. The opening words of the chapter in *A Voice Through a Cloud* that follows the description of the Miles's home underlines the degree to which he felt cut off from conventional society. 'Therefore it was to the outcasts and wanderers that I was attracted',[36] he writes—and then goes on to recall how he had walked unsteadily about the area watching people, even staring at them. Sometimes he was asked for a cigarette, at other times for money; one or two people wanted to know why they were being examined so intently. It was as if he had the need to sample a little aspect of their lives, their sexuality and their state of mind. Denton's role may have been that of the voyeur, but the interest was genuine, even if fleeting.

Gerald came down for Christmas and he stayed at a house on the sea-front with a family called Macfarlane. Much to the mirth of the two friends it was called 'Lesbia'! Aunt Dos graciously invited them over for lunch on Christmas Day. It turned out to be a strange affair, not helped, perhaps, by Sir Harry crying during the King's Speech. Gerald was duly solicitous to Lady Fox, but he made rather a *faux pas* when requested to give an opinion of some pastel portraits of his hostess. Denton did not appreciate being given a walking stick as a present, even though it had a silver band round the top engraved with his initials. On leaving the house he noticed an identical one belonging to his uncle, but this with a gold band. Once they were out on the Western Esplanade he threw the rubber ferrule into the Channel and some time afterwards the present itself was left on a bus.

Exactly ten days after Christmas he made his celebrated visit to Walter Richard Sickert. The old man, then regarded as the doyen of British artists, had recently moved to St Peter's, a village on the perimeter of Broadstairs—and only a mile or so away from Denton. Initially, though, there were difficulties in obtaining an invitation. Dr Raven approached Sickert, asking if he would be prepared to go and see this young invalid who had been an art student, but the famous painter brushed him off with the remark that he didn't go in for 'district visiting'. Denton was naturally very disappointed. It appears that mention was made of the rebuff when Gerald and he went over to see Martin Miles on Christmas Eve—by a stroke of good luck it turned out that the young man's mother knew Sickert well, and she assured them it would be quite easy to arrange a visit.

And so, on Saturday, 4th January 1936[37] Denton and his friend set out for 'Hauteville', the dark red-brick house where the great man lived with his third wife, Thérèse Lessore. They arrived in an old taxi. Almost immediately things took a rather bizarre turn. 'One entered through what at one time had been the "cloakroom"!' Denton writes in his essay 'Sickert at St Peter's'; 'I remember with vividness the slight shock I received on being confronted with a glistening white "W.C." as soon as the door was opened.'[38] The artist's wife was there to greet them and the guests were led through to the rather more salubrious comfort of the drawing-room, where they were handed cups of tea. Denton had plenty of time to make a mental note of all the different things in the room. Just as he was looking in some puzzlement at a picture of a miner kissing his wife, Sickert came in.

My first sight of him was rather overwhelming. Huge and bearded, he was dressed in rough clothes and from his toes to his thighs reached what I can only describe as sewer-boots.

He had seen me staring at the picture and now said directly to me, 'That picture gives you the right feeling, doesn't it? You'd kiss your wife like that if you'd just come up from the pit, wouldn't you?'

I was appalled by the dreadful heartiness of the question. I found myself blushing, and hated him for making me do so.

Sickert came right up to me and looked me all over.

'Well, you don't look very ill,' he said. 'I thought you'd be in a terrible mess. Didn't you fracture your spine or something?'[39]

Denton's attention was momentarily distracted when he heard another guest, someone who had been talking to Mrs Sickert, utter the intriguing words '. . . couldn't pass water for six days' as he was being shown out. Always preferring to occupy centre stage, Sickert proceeded to launch into an extravagant dance in front of the fire. 'He lifted his cup and, waving it to and fro, burst into a German drinking song.'[40] Denton was flattered to know that the spectacle was being put on for his benefit. The charade only came to an end when the doorbell rang.

The fifth person to join the party was Roger Raven, Easton's former housemaster at Rugby. He was staying with his mother, who also lived in St Peter's. By coincidence, Raven then held a senior administrative post in the teacher-training section of Goldsmiths' and Denton states that they had already met.

The ex-schoolmaster attempted to interest Sickert in a tiny photograph of his mother. Evidently he hoped the artist might want to make a painting from it. Denton had a look at the print too and it seems he must have given the impression that he thought it too small to be of much use. Sickert, prone to outbursts of temper, took this as an insult to his professionalism and boasted that he could paint a picture of any size he liked from it.

The old man started to talk to Gerald. Up to this point Denton makes no mention of him having taken part in the conversation. Gerald recorded in his diary that 'he told us a lot about the Edens and how he'd spanked Anthony Eden's bottom.' There was the perhaps inevitable reference to the politician's famed good looks and then, speaking to Denton, Sickert came out with the malicious remark, 'Ugly ones like us haven't a chance when there's someone like Eden about, have we?'[41] Now it was Denton's turn to be affronted.

Soon they were leaving. Denton writes that as they walked down the road, Sickert, 'in great good humour', had cried out, 'Goodbye, goodbye! Come again when you can't stop quite so long!'[42] In his diary, written on the day of the event, however, Gerald noted down the actual words as having been, 'Run, run, run, run; this is how you get killed!'

As it transpired, Denton did not have long to savour the experience. Just a few days afterwards everything was thrown into confusion with the wholly unexpected news that Jack Easton would imminently be leaving Broadstairs for a more interesting and demanding practice at the other end of the county.

Although completely taken aback, to some degree Denton too had been growing increasingly dissatisfied with his existence. When Matron cautioned that 'things would become very serious indeed' if he did not look after himself properly and that he would have to be 'extremely careful' with his health for some time to come, he came to realize that by staying on at Southcourt he was providing her with a valuable source of regular income; it was in her interest to keep him there for as long as possible. The prospect of having to remain in the establishment without Dr Easton being there to attend him, filled Denton with misery.

By this stage he had become so reliant on his physician that at once he set about devising a plan for continuing the relationship. An obvious solution would be for him to find somewhere to live in the same area as Easton's new practice; then he would be able to carry on being his patient. After all, Denton reasoned, who else knew his case so well?

Easton's reaction to the scheme was not nearly so negative as Denton had feared it might be. The doctor even said that possibly he could put him up while Denton was looking around for a new home. This co-operative attitude seemed almost too good to be true. Now Denton felt he had something specific to latch onto; there was really nothing to keep him in Broadstairs any longer.

It is significant that his adoration of Easton coincided with Denton's final break from Christian Science. Perhaps subconsciously, he realized that the Church's denial of the conventionally accepted concept of illness was incompatible with his vision of Easton as being the ideal 'healer'. A Christian Scientist, after all, could hardly hero-worship a man dedicated to a profession that was in itself 'erroneous'. Towards the end of *A Voice Through a Cloud* Denton reveals that his disillusionment had reached the point of no return.

> Now that I looked at it coldly, from a distance, Christian Science suddenly assumed all the forms of a burlesque madness. There was the jargon of *mortal mind, error, passing on,* and a hundred other set phrases. Christian Scientists juggled them about until they became as jaded as the little pieces of gristle that people put out on the sides of their plates after desperate chewing. I never doubted that they were right in stressing love; but again the word was used so mercilessly that it became monstrous, unmeaning, a swelling sound in the ears, a senseless flapping of the tongue .[43]

Denton decided the best course of action would be to take the bull by the horns and write to Miss Dallas clarifying his change of attitude. It was no easy matter—she had done so much for him—but he felt he no longer wanted to live a lie.

> I saw all at once that sooner or later the grateful person must show ingratitude in order to regain his integrity. To bite the hand that feeds you is unnecessary, but at least you must stop kissing it. If you don't,

everything will become slimed over with your mawkish thanks and you will secretly begin to hate. This came to me as a blazing truth, because I had discovered it for myself in the middle of my confused, unhappy thinking. I felt freed already.[44]

The split with Christian Science, the ideology that had played such a strong moral and philosophical role in his upbringing, was also perceived as being a feature of Denton's new, post-accident life. When he had regained consciousness in the hospital, the bed had been surrounded by tall screens and the nurses brought a cradle-shaped device to protect his broken ankle. In his delirium he had associated these things with the act of giving birth (as he had when receiving the ministrations of the policeman). And so one has the impression that the accident had achieved the status of being something rather more than just a physical and mental trauma—it was as if a new existence had been born of his suffering.

Little is known about his last days at Broadstairs. On 12th January Gerald dutifully paid another visit, bringing with him the Hon. Richard Cary, someone who had been with Denton at Repton. Gerald was in the process of painting his portrait.

On Friday the 17th a paragraph appeared in the press that gives one a clue as to how Denton had been able to establish his independence:

CYCLIST KNOCKED OVER. £4,000 DAMAGES
The victim of a terrible accident, leaving a young man of considerable promise with several permanent injuries, was granted £4,000 agreed damages today. Maurice Denton Welch, aged 20, of Sloane Avenue Mansions, S.W., was knocked off his bicycle by a car driven by a woman on the London-Reigate road. Mr Justice Lawrence approved the agreement, but said it could not compensate adequately the young man for the injuries he had suffered.[45]

Chapter Five

Hadlow Road

A mere two days after the Eastons had moved to their new home, Denton, whose walking was still shaky, got himself onto a train at Broadstairs and, despite feeling extremely weak, made the journey to Tonbridge. This involved changing trains at Ashford. The episode is described in the last pages of *A Voice Through a Cloud*. He tells of meeting Miss Sinclair at Tonbridge Station and the two of them visiting an estate agent in the town. Apparently they went to look over a property in a village that was a short bus-ride away, but it proved to be unsuitable, since it was already furnished. The book ends with 'Dr Farley' himself taking Denton to see another place after they have dropped into his house for tea.

According to Dr Easton, what in reality happened was that Denton had got into such a parlous state by the evening that it was necessary to put him into the Tonbridge Nursing Home for a night or two. The doctor then telephoned his former colleague, Hugh Raven, and also Lady Fox, to say that he would make sure Denton was returned to Broadstairs the following day—he asked Lady Fox to meet the train.

Thinking he had seen the last of him for a while, imagine Easton's surprise when his night-bell was rung the next evening by a policeman supporting an exhausted Denton. He had been spotted in a state of near-collapse in the doctor's garden, having alighted from the train at Paddock Wood and taken a bus back to Tonbridge. After all, Jack Easton was the only person who he felt understood his agonized state of mind; and the only person on hand that he loved. As the doctor remembered, 'much to Dr Raven's and Lady Fox's annoyance, I felt he had to stay, and he went back to the Tonbridge Nursing Home.'[1]

On 8th February Gerald visited him there and Denton confided in his friend that just thinking of Easton's neck and hands would evoke a burning desire for his presence. This poem, written during these days, bears witness to his feelings of frustration and loneliness:

> When I die
> and fall sick
> to the ground;
> When I lie
> quietly sinking,
> I shall be longing

For your eyes,
which never touched my own.
I shall be breathing out my love,
Which gasps for you always.[2]

The obsession was to remain with him for another three years. During almost the entire period that he lived at Tonbridge Denton was liable to wander up to the Eastons' house in Pembury Road, where he would peer in through the windows—or even break in, as happened later. One gains a clear insight into his profound unhappiness from a reference in the Journals to 'Those endless days and nights of 1936 alone and desperate'.[3]

In truth, it was mainly a spiritual isolation. He was not entirely by himself: Miss Sinclair was an ever-faithful guardian, even though she may have been on quite a different wavelength to his own. After Denton had spent a while in the nursing-home, the two of them succeeded in finding a ground floor flat at 54 Hadlow Road, on the outskirts of Tonbridge. The tall Victorian house, which has recently been demolished, stood on the main road out to Maidstone. At the time Gerald thought it surprising that his friend hadn't taken somewhere more 'classy'—the choice was certainly one of convenience. Perhaps the long flat *was* a little dark inside, but its proximity to the banks of the River Medway made the position quite pleasant and, more importantly, it lay within walking distance of the town centre.

It seems that Miss Sinclair had only once been down to Broadstairs to see Denton. In her totally unpractical way she had made a mess of letting out rooms at Croom's Hill and now the idea of devoting herself entirely to one person seemed quite appealing. She was a Christian Scientist too, but unlike him she had remained faithful to the principles of the Church. Her view of illness as something that was morally unacceptable ensured he did not live in an environment where self-pity was encouraged. Maybe Evie's eccentricities— particularly a total vagueness concerning time—came to annoy Denton, but he appreciated in her a quality of loyalty and an absolute dedication to protecting him.

Other than the presence of Easton, Denton's connection with Tonbridge was tenuous. The only person he knew really well living in the area was Mrs Carpmael, but her home in Trottiscliffe lay several miles away, and so he did not get to see her very often. Tonbridge society, such as it was in the 1930s, centred round the boys' public school, which is in the middle of the town. A friend of his in those early days described it to the author as having been 'outwardly respectable, but with an air of raffishness underneath'.[4] Predictably, Denton was never to mix in the circle of the school masters; he was drawn more to the various literary and artistic personalities such as could be found in a small provincial town.

His new life, based on the slightly dreary flat, must have seemed daunting at first. It was vital for his sanity that he should make new friends. By a stroke of good luck, he discovered an ideal meeting-place almost on his doorstep. Just a few hundred yards away from the flat was a public house, The Mitre. A group of people, mainly living close by, had founded an amateur dramatic society that met regularly in a large, bare room above a garage next door to the pub. It became known as the Mitre Theatre Club.[5] It functioned by producing plays in local villages, and once a year some of the members would put on an exhibition of paintings. Denton soon joined—most probably at the instigation of Dr Cedric Tuckett, who after a very short time took him on as a patient when relations with Jack Easton had become too awkward—and it was here that he came to know various people in the neighbourhood. Tuckett, regarded as being something of 'a lad', but eminently likeable, was a member of the club and acted in some of their plays. It was in the same setting that Denton came to know Mrs Joyce Brooks, whose husband was a local estate agent, and also John Nicholls, the Art Master at Tonbridge School. Nicholls's wife, Elizabeth, rapidly became a close friend and she and Denton used to make expeditions into the countryside to sketch. Fortunately, she drove a car.

Denton exhibited for the first time at the club's annual art show, which was held at the school. It was by no means a wholly amateur affair. The distinguished watercolourist Martin Hardie, himself a native of the town, used to put in a few of his pictures (he had been Senior Keeper of Paintings at the Victoria and Albert Museum), as did Harold Hailstone, who also helped design some of the sets for the drama productions.

Always on the lookout for a romantic personality to add a little colour to his existence, Denton came to hear of a rather extraordinary Russian nobleman who lived within a short walking distance of his flat. The seventy-year-old Lt-General Prince Serge Belosselsky-Belozersky had left his native land after the 1917 Revolution and had settled, presumably through lack of funds, in the relative backwater of Tonbridge. The Belosselskys could hardly have been a more intriguing household, consisting of an American wife, who was sadly deranged, her personal maid Mrs Abramara, and a Mr Lomakin, reputedly one of the men who had helped drag the dead Rasputin from the river!

Belosselsky was someone he just *had* to cultivate. It is interesting that when he describes the old man in his Journals, Denton makes no mention of the fact that a few years earlier he had painted his portrait, a picture that is now stored in the Harry Ransom Humanities Research Center at Austin, Texas.[6] However, relations between them were never quite the same after Denton offended the venerable nobleman by offering to buy some of his mementoes from Czarist Russia.

A more frivolous acquaintance was the authoress Peggy Whitehouse (Mrs Mundy-Castle), a near-neighbour whom he met through the Nicholls.[7] Although in later years a frequent target of his malicious humour, there were really many reasons why Denton should have been grateful to her, not least because it was she who initially gave him the idea of writing a book. Peggy's motto in life, 'Everybody's got their own spiritual Monte Carlo', was certainly unique, and an air of dottiness seems to have prevailed in the relationship. Denton always felt quite at ease in her company—there was no inclination whatever to mother him. The Mundy-Castle children consisted of a son and two daughters, one of whom, Rosemary, features several times in the Journals.

Some of the Goldsmiths' brigade, especially Joan Waymark and Helen Roeder, came down from London when they could—Tonbridge was more accessible than Broadstairs had been—but Denton's most frequent visitor continued to be Gerald, who happened to know a number of people living in the town. At weekends they would devote much of their time to painting, and Denton, still in many respects an apprentice, greatly valued having on hand an accomplished artist to whom he could turn for advice. He was very keen to expand his knowledge of technique. The enigmatic Miss Sinclair would wait on them. She was always to be found hovering somewhere in the background, locked in her own world. Although totally formal, discreet and polite, Evie, as Denton called her, tended to give people the impression of being his 'unwelcome keeper'.[8]

This period, when he was setting up home for the first time, was without doubt the most insecure time of Denton's whole life. In the past it had never been necessary for him to fend for himself, coming as he did from a privileged middle-class background. Until the accident he had imagined that one day he would find a niche in the art world, if not actually as a painter. Now he was obliged to adapt to a different pace of life, with horizons dramatically curtailed. In *A Voice Through a Cloud* he wrote that 'the thought of what I should try to do in the world came as a black face looming nearer and nearer. I could never look into the eyes for more than a moment.'[9] The accident had undermined the self that he had so meticulously fabricated and nurtured and this imposed change of direction was a traumatic blow. It was, needless to say, one of the factors that led him to escape into the fantasy-world of his relationship with Jack Easton.

And so, despite the occasional visitor, time again began to weigh heavily on Denton's shoulders. Whereas in the nursing-home there had been the specific aim of improving his mobility and putting on weight, no such structured programme existed any more. Dr Easton, who dropped in to see him sometimes, still kept up the pressure for him to get on with his life, and one learns that in June of 1936 Denton attended a crammer in Tonbridge called Eton House. It was run by the less-than-inspiring Mr E.C. Macintosh, B.Sc. A couple of exercise books that Denton used there have survived, and these bear witness to typically dull lessons in Latin and History. There are numerous corrections in red ink by the tutor. After a very few pages the exercises cease and the remainder of the book is filled with poetry and prose jottings, written at a later date. One gets the impression that Denton only managed to persevere for a very short time indeed. After this abortive attempt at continuing his schooling, his mind quite naturally returned to his painting, and from now on this activity was pursued with considerable zeal.

The two years of training at Goldsmiths' had, as we have seen, been strongly orientated towards making life studies and the drawing of busts and suchlike in the Antique Room. At Hadlow Road, quite naturally, since he was so often housebound, Denton found it necessary to look around for other types of subject to use. Although there was always Evie—he drew and painted her several times—it occurred to Denton that no more willing and available model existed than himself: the search for his own identity henceforth came to manifest itself in a series of self-portraits.

The most finished of these now hangs in the National Portrait Gallery in London. It is a faithful image, if somewhat romanticized. The first time the public had an opportunity to see it was at the 1954 posthumous exhibition of Denton's paintings at the Leicester Galleries in London, which was organized by the artist Guy Roddon.[10] Mr Roddon remembered that prior to the show, he advertised the picture for sale in *The New Statesman*; it failed to find a buyer. One man who had seriously considered adding it to his collection, told the author that it would have been just too much to have had those eyes staring right into him every time he passed it!

The stylistic roots of the National Portrait Gallery picture (see illustration) can be traced back to Denton's frequent visits to the National Gallery, both during his holidays from school and from his time as an art student. Its fifteenth-century origins are apparent both in the studied aloofness and in the smooth and highly finished application of paint. Antonello da Messina's 'Portrait of a Man' in the National Gallery[11] demonstrates the same slightly quizzical relationship between artist and viewer; in the eyes of the nobleman one senses a reserve that borders on suspicion. The varied choice of colours for the extravagant layers of clothing is reminiscent of pictures by the Van Eycks of Flanders (although friends do remember Denton himself wearing embarrassingly garish scarves).

It seems that he never showed the self-portraits to anybody who visited him. Their essentially private nature is revealed in the fact that even at the end of his life, when he was at the peak of his fame as a writer and was short of pictures that he could send to exhibitions, he never considered putting one of them forward for a show. They were early works that did not demonstrate enough individuality of style for him to think them worthy extensions of the interesting personality that he wished to project. The beginning of Denton's career as an author in 1941 coincided with his abandonment of the self-portrait as a useful medium of expression. He had come to visualize writing as the most effective means of discovering and developing his personality.

Whereas there exist about seven self-portraits in all, three of which are oil paintings,[12] the number is easily outweighed by paintings that take their inspiration from Denton's ever-growing accumulation of antiques and bric-à-brac. The preponderance of still lifes is very striking, and these frequently contain rather bizarre domestic items, such as brushes, tape-measures and pipes, alongside the more conventional brightly coloured plates, chairs and pieces of cloth. One of the pictures that Denton did in the Broadstairs nursing-home had featured a specimen bottle with the yellow urine glowing radiantly in the sunlight. Many of the still lifes are painted with an intensity that underlines Denton's fascination with man-made objects; he loved most of all things that had been well-used by other people.

With a liberal monthly allowance from his father and the income generated from the £4,000 compensation, Denton was free to indulge his passion for collecting.[13] Once his walking became easier, he would avidly hunt around the shops of Tonbridge, and more particularly Tunbridge Wells, for anything that might beautify his home. Porcelain, as ever, was his speciality, and when it came to painting a vase or a teapot he took the greatest pains to capture just the right quality of reflection on the glaze, or the exact line of an elegant curve. Although he had yet to evolve an individual style (one notices the very definite influence of Mark Gertler in the still lifes), Denton still managed to create quite arresting pictures through the skilful juxtaposition of the artefacts he had chosen. Moreover, his impeccable and faultless eye for design ensured that there was a certain strength to whatever he tried to accomplish in paint.

But by no means all of Denton's pictures from this time belong to the limited indoor world. On 6th August 1936, he began an ambitious painting of three male nudes drying themselves after bathing (see illustration). Gerald recorded in his diary that the central figure was drawn from life; the anatomy is quite sound. It is, however, a sensitive feeling for skin texture that ranks as the most remarkable feature. Denton more than once wrote of the 'creamy' colour of normally unexposed skin and this description exactly matches what he has achieved here. If the genitals and nipples appear to be shaped with greater care than any other part of the body, then one must see this as a reflection of Denton's homosexuality and also of the fact that for the span of his convalescence he had been deprived of gazing at the beauty of the male form, which previously he was able to admire at leisure in the life class.

Taking into account that Denton's artistic talent had really made very little impression at Goldsmiths', the speed at which he developed into an unusual and distinctly idiosyncratic artist is very remarkable. The accident seems to have had the effect of concentrating his mind. Within a few months of coming to Tonbridge, Denton settled into a way of life in which drawing and painting were pursued with all the dedication of a professional. The largely sedentary existence, of course, suited his physical state.

In the Autumn the unexpected news came that Arthur Welch had remarried.[14] It was almost ten years since Rosalind's death. The newly-weds spent six weeks in England for their honeymoon and Denton took the train up to London a number of times to meet them. He told a friend some years later that he suspected his father had had an ulterior motive in wanting him there: the couple seemed to be relying on Denton to make amusing conversation whilst they were getting to know one another better. Probably this was over-cynical. Whatever went on behind the scenes, Denton, by nature exceedingly curious about people, welcomed the opportunity to meet his stepmother. It was nice, also, to be entertained in style, as he had been in the old days; there was the secure feeling of returning to the bosom of his father's affluence.

Arthur Welch already knew of Denton's friend Gerald Mackenzie, and once or twice he was invited along to make up a party. On 4th November he and Denton introduced Mr Welch to a rather pretentious young man called Marcus Oliver, whom Gerald had met at a country-house party. Marcus worked for the whisky distillers John Haig, and he was also a first-rate bridge-player. His brother, Peter, had achieved some fame as a mountaineer and thus constituted a useful topic for manly conversation. Mr Welch confided in Gerald, though, that he found the intelligent man-about-town to be 'very polite, but rather Jewish'. Denton and Marcus were to write regularly to one another over the next twelve years and the correspondence bears witness to a gossipy and 'camp' side to Denton's character, an aspect that became diluted once he had found glory and self-esteem as a published author.[15]

The first few months of 1937 saw Denton working on a large-scale panel of Hadlow Castle, a building some three miles east of Tonbridge. Although the main part of the house dated from the end of the eighteenth century and had been inspired by Strawberry Hill, the 170-foot tower, built between 1838-40, was modelled on William Beckford's Fonthill.[16] The whole ambience of the place appealed greatly to Denton's love of the Gothic. His naive painting, which shows the puny tower rising above the other parts like a coffee-iced wedding-cake, was designed specifically to be reproduced as a poster. Jack Miller, a fellow-student at Goldsmiths' and a native of Tonbridge, had been successful in selling a work to Shell Mex the previous year (his 'Summer Shells—Mermaids' depicts an assembly of crustacea dancing about a beach in gay abandon) and through his good offices Denton came to the notice of Jack Beddington, the man in charge of commissioning art work at Shell. Beddington accepted the Hadlow Castle picture for the series of lorry posters, 'Visit Britain's Landmarks'; it featured as No. 496[17]. This was almost certainly the first work that Denton ever sold (see illustration).

The success was a tremendous boost to his morale: he was now well above the first rung of the ladder towards becoming a professional artist. One only has to glance through the names of those who had designed Shell posters since 1930 to appreciate something of the prestige associated with the acceptance: Denton could mention himself in the exalted company of Graham Sutherland, Duncan Grant, Paul Nash and Lord Berners! It must have amused him also to discover that four of the staff members at Goldsmiths' had all gained considerable kudos from their Shell posters in the same series.

Spurred on by his good fortune, Denton began to take driving lessons, his father having promised to buy him a car. The Baby Austin turned out to be an invaluable asset in broadening his spheres of interest. For one thing, it enabled him to make a thorough exploration of the Kentish countryside, with its picturesque views of oast-houses and the beauty of the North Downs seen across the patterned rows of hop-fields and apple orchards. The Medway Valley is an area rich in history—there were endless churches that could be visited. And Denton now had the freedom to attend any odd private auction that took his fancy; he became even more selective in what he bought.

When taking a walk along the banks of the Medway, which stretched from just below his flat in Hadlow Road to Maidstone, Denton would customarily be on the look out for some young farm worker to chat with. His romantic image of the 'naturalness' of the working man was undiminished—indeed, one suspects this had been heightened as a result of having had his own body ruined by the accident—and it was a thrill for him to come across someone responsive and willing to make human contact. As ever, he had a great love of the unexpected encounter. In those days the young were frequently less suspicious and it was much easier to fall into conversation with a complete stranger.

One does not really know the extent to which Denton ever became involved with such people. There are references in letters to Marcus Oliver that suggest he did have the occasional sexual fling, and Eric Oliver (no relation to Marcus), who knew him more intimately than anyone, remembers Denton telling him that once he had been questioned by a policeman for loitering in or near a gentleman's public lavatory. The shame of such a confrontation, together with his general feelings of persecution, almost certainly deterred him from ever trying anything like that again.

In the winter of 1937 there was a novelty in store when Gerald came down to Tonbridge with a camera. He was a keen and highly skilled photographer. The flat in Hadlow Road was rapidly transformed into an elaborate studio with all manner of props taken from Denton's collection. A dozen or more photos were taken, one or two by Denton himself, with Gerald posing. One notices the bronze Estruscan head, the pair of hermaphroditic wooden angels, the marble topped table with its chessboard design, a vast French cartoon that they used as a backdrop and also the delicate harpsichord which Denton had bought from the Dolmetsch family at Haslemere (see illustrations).

The results of these sessions confirm the impression of an almost shameless preciosity; but this was a character trait Denton was quite ready to recognize in himself. In one of the shots he chooses to strike a decidedly 'literary' pose—it features him wearing a rough tweed jacket and an exuberant cravat—in another he has taken off his glasses (he was only very slightly short-sighted) and is seated at a table beside his Second Empire 'Head of Apollo', a rather gaudy monstrance-like ornament that glistens in the candlelight. This latter image must have appealed to Denton's vanity, since he made a pen and ink drawing from the print and used it as the frontispiece for his book, *Maiden Voyage*.

Whilst the closing months of 1937 found him working steadily at his painting, there was a slight shift in Denton's social life. One day, when coming away from the Public Library, he was engaged in conversation by a man called Francis Streeten, someone who indirectly happened to play an important role in his future.

Streeten, a few years older than Denton, could justifiably be described as having been the archetypal dilettante. Though his father was a pillar of the establishment and a governor of Tonbridge School, and though he had had a brother who was a brilliant sportsman, Francis and his mother were a little unstable. He was the black sheep of the family, spending his time dabbling in literature and anarchist politics.[18] The rather dubious Fortune Press some years earlier had published a book by him with the title *Frolic Welcome: A Picture of Life in Great Britain in 1930* (it is all about a distinctly affected young man called Denzil!),[19] but when Denton knew him, Francis was incapable of settling into any sort of work.

The strange man's interest had been aroused on hearing of this young artist with a reputation for strolling around and talking to any available young rustic.

In the short story, 'A Picture in the Snow', Denton outlines the exact circumstances of their first meeting:

> . . . I became aware of footsteps behind me. They seemed to be hurrying, then a shadow loomed over me and I looked up to see a very tall, very plump man of about thirty-five passing close to me on the pavement. . . Before I knew quite what was happening he had turned, bent down towards me with a tentative smile, and was saying in a surprising baby voice, 'Oh—you look interesting; do tell me about yourself.'[20]

The new acquaintance quickly achieved the status of Denton's most prized oddity: he would introduce Streeten to his friends partly, one suspects, to shock them with the contrast between himself as 'the beauty' and Streeten as 'the beast'. Gerald commented that in relationships Denton frequently liked to be both attracted and repelled at the same time. Streeten was a pathetically inadequate person, indecisive and physically broken and Denton's pen-and-ink drawing of him accentuates this description (see illustration).

This having been said, Denton was not the only one who took an interest in the rather grotesque man. Whatever his failings may have been, Streeten certainly possessed an agile mind and could be entertaining on a number of topics. One person he introduced to Denton was the young Maurice Cranston, who today is recognized as having been a leading authority on the philosophy and literature of eighteenth-century France. Since Denton wished that he had been born into that age of grace and gentility, he was very happy to talk to someone with an informed knowledge of the subject. In other respects, though, the two of them didn't have much in common, and Denton was really far happier gossiping naughtily about mutual acquaintances than he was in discussing any political idea or theoretical concept.

Maurice Cranston, in what is the most evocative memoir of Denton, devoted a paragraph to the reasons behind the ultimately rather unsatisfactory nature of their association:

> . . . Friendship was not easy for Denton. He was too fastidious, and worse, he was not trusting. He knew a fair number of people, but he admired not more than three or four, and he liked perhaps seven or eight. I never knew whether he liked me or not; it seemed too much to hope for. But he was always very sweet to me, and I was happy in his company. Because of his illness, and for less obvious psychological reasons, Denton was deeply suspicious. In a room with other people I have seen his eyes flash from one face to another, watching for malice. He could be malicious himself, but only to enliven conversation, not to hurt. If he was unkind in his books, he always wanted to be truthful.[21]

Cranston goes on to write that although Denton had a penchant for 'worldly conversation', his rather puritanical Christian Science background meant that he tended to disapprove of the people who were responsible for drawing him into it; 'thus the society he chose to mitigate his loneliness only drove him further inward'. Few of his other friends, perhaps, had an awareness of this dichotomy, which, if it is a correct analysis, must have had the effect of forming a barrier which prevented him from achieving contentment.

Another member of this unlikely circle, someone who also knew Cranston, was Ronald Benge, then a librarian in Tunbridge Wells. Although he came over to the flat in Hadlow Road on several occasions, Benge was rather less enamoured of Denton than either of the other two had been. In reading his comments, one senses that even though Denton had an irrepressibly compelling personality, ultimately everything was very much on *his* terms and he did not really possess the capacity or ambition to broaden his mind beyond fairly specific horizons:

> . . . One was impressed by his *intense* interest in everything and everybody. There was, of course, most noticeable this extraordinary *vivid* quality, compounded by his appearance and high-pitched excitable speech. He was like some exotic tropical bird and his dress too was flamboyant, so that some of his acquaintances were embarrassed to be with him in public—the small slight figure limping along and full of spontaneity and laughter. His sufferings were never alluded to. Yet one could not accurately label it as *typical* gay camp—it was beyond that stereotype—an almost Shelleyan quality—childlike, perhaps. He would listen from his couch to the chatter and the patter of the company with a *quizzical* look—yes, that is the word. His responses were not cluttered up by idealistic and ideological baggage. I think it is fair to say that abstractions meant nothing to him and that is his strength—not a common thing. He was not impeded by 'traditional' and cultural assumptions, and attitudes which characterize those (especially the English) who have grown up in one place and country.
>
> The main reason why I remained on the fringe of the group was that, as a typical thirties left-wing activist, I was impatient with what I regarded as their frivolity. Denton's indifference to social or political issues and the impending War appalled me and I had no sympathy with his passionate—everything was passionate—interest in antiques. He was, of course, not 'literary' in the usual sense—as I was—not 'intellectual', since ideas bored him. I can see now that his work survives precisely because he never dealt in abstractions or ever wanted to—it was an almost palpable *physical* perception.[22]

Despite a lack of receptiveness in considering many of the deeper questions concerning humanity, there can be little doubt that Denton *was* influenced through coming into contact with intellectuals such as Cranston and Benge. In the past the majority of his friends had been art students; now he was frequently keeping company with a group of people interested in literature.

It was in this changed environment that Denton felt the urge to discover whether he possessed any literary talent of his own. He had always been an avid reader, and to date it appears that he had written quite a number of poems. Maurice Cranston informs us that around the time of the Munich crisis (September 1938), Denton asked him if he knew someone who would be able to type out one or two:

> I was rather surprised. Denton was then a painter, and I had been brought up to believe that painters can't write. What sort of poetry, I wondered, would he produce? He was rather reluctant to show me. When I persuaded him I was rather surprised again. They were really rather good, but they gave no hint of what he was later to achieve in prose.[23]

It is not known whether Denton's intention was to get these verses published or if he just wanted to begin making a tidy collection of what he had written. The Harry Ransom Center at Austin has typed copies of eight poems that date from the Hadlow Road years, and each of these has appeared in print (though only one in Denton's lifetime).[24] However, since on his own admission he destroyed the majority of his early writings, one can presume that there originally existed a much greater quantity.

Despite this broadening in the range of his interests, it would seem that Denton's obsession with Jack Easton had lost very little of its intensity: on 19th December 1938, the doctor felt compelled to send him a letter aimed at terminating the unbalanced relationship once and for all. 'I do very definitely say,' Easton wrote, 'that I must see no more of you and that this business of seeing you occasionally is no good.'[25]

One finds an explanation for this uncharacteristically firm line in 'A Fragment of a Life Story'.[26] Denton recalls how one day he had surreptitiously broken into the doctor's house and had concealed himself behind a curtain—he then began to cry. The doctor, unnamed in the short story, hears the sobbing, comes into the room and makes him leave the house by the french windows. With a manic persistence, Denton goes round to the front door, where he is readmitted by an innocent maid; when the doctor appears Denton starts to swear. There follows an extraordinary scene in which Denton clings onto the bannisters in the hall, whilst Easton is trying to throw him out into the street.

This version of the incident continues with Denton returning home and taking an overdose in an attempted suicide. In 'A Fragment of a Life Story', however, it appears that he has worked together various different episodes from his life at that time: Denton gives an account of what actually had taken place in his Journals (2nd December 1942). Here it is revealed that he did not in fact enter the Eastons' house, but spied in through one of the windows.[27] Dr Tuckett was telephoned by Miss Sinclair when Denton took the Prontosil tablets, and afterwards the physician told Easton that he hadn't been very impressed by the seriousness of his patient's gesture.

It was most probably as a direct result of the melodrama that Denton was spirited away again to Broadstairs. This time he spent four months or so at the Cliff Coombe Nursing Home on the Eastern Esplanade, a far grander and more comfortable establishment than Southcourt had been. He describes his sojourn in another short story, 'Leaves from a Young Person's Notebook'.[28]

For much of the time he was desperately unhappy, although things did improve slightly when Dr Easton wrote a warmly supportive letter which, to some extent, revised his previously stern attitude. The words contained just the sort of common-sense advice Denton needed. 'It wouldn't be a bad plan,' Easton suggested, 'to concentrate on getting fit physically, and then seeing whether life is worth living or not.'[29] Denton's psychological difficulty seems to have manifested itself in severe swings of mood. He possessed an almost hyperactive mind that demanded there should always be something to occupy and entertain it. He had been like this since childhood, but the accident had made the condition more pronounced; no longer could he burn off energy by taking a brisk walk or making an impromptu trip to wherever he chose. A symptom of his restlessness was the compulsion to doodle.

In writing what exists as the only published article on Denton's work as an artist, the author Jocelyn Brooke attempted to find a term that would neatly encapsulate the essence of his style. He settled on 'prettified surrealism'.[30] Although I think this definition is both inaccurate and limiting, one has to concede that it can be applied with justification to the drawings and watercolours that were done during these months.

Of course, the Surrealist Movement had been a topic of heated conversation at Goldsmiths'. Rowland Hilder recalled that Denton had ribbed Cedric Rogers for his early attempts in the genre. However, since the landmark International Surrealist Exhibition of June 1936 had been held only four months or so after his move to Tonbridge, one can be almost certain that Denton was not able to attend it. None of his friends remember him having done so. It was chiefly through reading magazines and the like that he could keep abreast with the latest trends in modern art, and Gerald recalled that a number of times he used a magazine illustration as the starting-point for one of his pictures.

Denton toyed with the more grotesque images associated with surrealism, but he never involved himself in any of the philosophical ideas associated with the movement. For instance, he believed that objects had an intrinsic aesthetic value that was closely related to their manufacture and use by man, and very seldom did he invest them with any obviously deeper significance.

Whilst at Cliff Coombe on this second visit to Broadstairs, Denton drew an elaborate and quite large pen and ink work, 'Faces at the Stage Door'[31] (see illustration), which is described at length both in the short story 'Leaves from a Young Person's Notebook' and also in another prose fragment. The latter text in particular gives one a rare insight into the seemingly random flow of his creative inspiration whilst putting a picture together. Although it is possible that the fragment was written some time later, Denton's attempt to make some interpretation of what he had drawn is significant.

> I lay in bed in a nursing home overlooking the sea. Only three things happened to me there and these were all animal: Eating, Going to the Bathroom and Treatment. My mind was an uneasy bog through which

pushed shapes and forms that had been buried and sucked under. I could not ever read. It seemed a waste of eyesight.

Slowly, when Sister had gone and my room was too still to bear, I pulled my book of cartridge paper towards me.

My fountain pen had 'Jet Black Quink' in it, which is really the colour of Royal Mourning gone dirty.

I began a fantastic face with little Greek lips and a mask. I will have all different faces, I thought. I did next a boy whose face was much darker than the flesh on his chest, as if he had taken off his shirt after, not before, long exposure in the sun. I did him. I did all the faces. They were terribly sad. They were all waiting outside closed doors. The bluestocking woman with 'Russian' hair had grown a megaphone from each eye, she was so keen on piercing into the future. The boy with the sunburnt face had tattooed on his chest two hearts pierced by an arrow, and on the hearts was written 'Alfie and Maisie'. But that was last year and now he had nothing left but resentment against these silly marks on his white body.

They were all waiting outside the stage door. Their parts were learned, but they did not know what they meant.[32]

One can see this picture as being powerfully symbolic of Denton's situation, with each face representing a different facet of his troubled personality. The door leading to the 'stage'—the stage of life—is an opening through to the unknown. Although each figure has a certain role prepared, it is impossible to see what significance this might hold for the future. Taking the three main faces one by one, the figure on the left with the elaborately coiffured hair and mask could well symbolize Denton the Artist, attempting to please with visual beauty, but essentially superficial and unwilling to let the eye express the deeper state of the soul. Although Denton himself has given us a basic explanation of the face with megaphones coming from its eyes, in confusing the visual and aural senses he is perhaps underlining a dilemma about his vocation in life—the girl is labelled a 'bluestocking' and therefore a person of serious intent, bound up in a career. But it is the sunburnt boy with his tattoos that is the tell-tale figure. He represents the current state of Denton's emotional life: the finality of the break with Dr Easton had left him marked or scarred and now, looking back, he resents the degree to which he had allowed himself to become so obsessed with a fantasy. The darkness or redness of the face is surely indicative of embarrassment. In drawing this picture Denton sensed that although his new life had been born of the accident, it was not yet under way. How much easier it would be if, when the door did eventually open, one integrated person was ready to go through it.

He was in a much improved state of health when he returned to the flat in Tonbridge. 'I had been lying naked on the roof of a nursing home at Broadstairs for four months,' he wrote 'so I was very brown and felt extremely well and lively.' The sentence is taken from the opening pages of 'Touchett's Party', a story that tells how Francis Streeten had invited him and a couple of others out for a meal.[33] One of the guests was Maurice Cranston, who in his article on

Denton gives us a factual outline of the episode. Cranston remembered this evening as being the first time that Denton disclosed to him the potential gravity of his illness.

> In the summer of 1939 Oswell won £13 on the Derby. Very generously, for he was not well-off at the time, he proposed to give a dinner party with his winnings. Denton and a Blackshirt called Edward and I were to be his guests. The dinner was at Penshurst—the Leicester Arms—where we ate and drank exceedingly well. It was a gay evening, and a great success. It was the only time, I believe, that I ever saw Denton almost, if not quite, drunk. That same evening, just before we went home, with Edward at the wheel of Denton's Baby Austin, Denton told me that he had to wear a catheter, that he was crippled and that he could not live long.[34]

Denton soldiered on, keeping up his usual enthusiastic correspondence and continuing to expand his range as an artist. The previous year one of his flowerpieces had been shown at the Redfern Gallery and now for their Summer Exhibition he contributed a similar oil, also of flowers; both were priced at ten guineas. One suspects that neither sold. He would make the occasional jaunt up to town so as to maintain some contact with the art world, or to meet friends, and it is known that some time in 1938 he went to see a psychiatrist at 86 Brook Street,[35] where many of the King's College Hospital specialists had consulting rooms. Later on Gerald was given a report of the meeting and he remembered his friend's sense of outrage at the way he had been handled. Apparently, as soon as Denton was ushered into the psychiatrist's presence, he was greeted with, 'Hello old man—or should I say "old girl!" Do you take it up the back passage?'[36] Denton was quite speechless and it seems he fled in terror as fast as his semi-crippled legs would carry him. The idea of seeking further 'help' in this direction became anathema to him.

At the beginning of September 1939, Great Britain went to war. Denton was having a late breakfast at the back of the flat when Miss Sinclair, having just heard Chamberlain's speech on the wireless, rushed in to give him the news.

> The sirens started to drone, and the air was filled with such terror by their rising and falling that he [Denton] lurched out of the deck-chair and stood up gulping. The next moment he had dashed into the house and shut the French windows after him.
>
> . . . Through the window he saw a woman running, pushing a perambulator madly before her. Her heel turned over, her hat slipped drunkenly. It was horrible to watch. He darted to the front door and shouted, 'Come in here, come in here!' but she heard nothing, she lurched on desperately.[37]

Within a couple of months he was making plans to move. The Hadlow Road flat had never been anything more than a functional home and now it was time for a change. Through his friends the artists Robin and Fay Pearce Denton heard of a small house for rent in the village of St Mary's Platt near Borough Green, some seven miles away.[38]

It seems that he gave no serious consideration to finding a house in a less exposed part of the country. Personal safety really came very low on Denton's list of priorities. By this stage he had developed a philosophical attitude to death. It was only when he had achieved acclaim as a writer that the thought of it came to torment him—but by then his time was running out.

Chapter Six

The Hop Garden

There was a striking contrast between Denton's rather dingy flat in Tonbridge and his new home at St Mary's Platt. 54 Hadlow Road had been a heavy Victorian house on a busy main road out of the town; The Hop Garden was an ultra-modern cottage lying along a leafy lane on the edge of a quietly attractive village. Denton wanted to forget about the recent past, about what he later described as 'the frightful mess' of his relationship with Jack Easton. He would now devote all his energies to painting—and maybe expand into doing some more writing as well. With its large windows letting in plenty of light, The Hop Garden was an ideally optimistic setting.

The house, properly named The Hopfield, dated from 1933 and had been constructed entirely from reinforced concrete. For the date the design was nothing if not innovatory. The less usual features included an external staircase leading up to a balcony onto which opened a sleeping-porch. The latter was separated from the main bed-sitting-room of the first floor by a glass partition. The walls of the house were only five inches thick, insulated with Celotex wallboard. The ground floor consisted of a kitchen, a lounge and a dining-room.

The architect, Colin Lucas, designed The Hopfield as a holiday home for his own use, but he decided to rent it out because he had a young family and the area was considered to be dangerous because of the risk of bombs. From the outside, even making allowances for its modernity, the house must have looked a trifle odd, as the rendering on the exterior was coloured with a subdued green distemper, supposedly to blend in with the countryside.[1] The place was heated by electricity. The downstairs lounge flaunted an aluminium stove with large round holes to allow for the maximum circulation of heat. Denton branded the fitting as 'preposterous' and his overall verdict on The Hop Garden was that there existed 'an unfortunate air of affectation hanging about the place'[2]

One can imagine him enthusiastically unpacking all his antiques and deciding where each should go. The collection had multiplied considerably during the four years he had been in Tonbridge. And now there was a further addition to the household—a Siamese cat—which appears to have been bought shortly before the move. Noel Cousins recollects that Denton treated it 'as if it were one of his bizarre possessions'.[3] He would play around with the animal and sing to it. There is a photograph of them together, with the cat, a blurred shape, sitting on his knee and struggling to get free. Unfortunately, it did not live long, and Denton vowed that he would never have another pet.

The first months of their occupancy did not augur well. The winter brought the hazard of burst pipes, and Denton, as usual, took out his frustration on Miss Sinclair. They had an almighty row. He wrote a letter to Maurice Cranston reporting that she had taken herself off 'saying that her whole soul rebelled against my wickedness'.[4] Much to his relief, she reappeared after three nights. Marcus Oliver came down a number of times to lend moral support, and he was put up on a camp-bed that his friend kept in the garage.

It was presumably as a result of Denton sending out notices of his changed address to all and sundry that, very shortly after he had moved, his old governess Wooly came to stay for the weekend. They had not met for twelve years, and waiting on the platform at Borough Green station, he was even a little fearful that she might not recognize him. Denton needn't have worried. Wooly was very much her old self. She had the firm determination to impress on her ex-pupil just how successful she had been since leaving the Welches' employ.[5]

By now the war was well under way and inevitably Denton lost touch with many of his old friends. Some would come to visit him when they were on leave from the forces, but by and large he had fewer visitors than before. Even the Tonbridge crowd were several miles away; with the scarcity of petrol, people generally were less inclined to be sociable.

And so, once the excitement of moving house had worn off—and it did so very rapidly—Denton again sank into a mood of deep depression. His attempt to regain some degree of emotional stability proved to be an uphill struggle. Gerald saw him over several days in March 1940, and recorded in his diary that he had found his friend in a very low state.

> He has developed a very cynical attitude towards human nature. . . he is very difficult and aggravating. . . almost rather strange. . . Miss Sinclair is apprehensive. . . he becomes violent at the least provocation—baits one until a first-class row ensues. . . tells me to get out of the house because I lock the bedroom door. . . he wishes to publish some poems and I suggest that I show them to J.M. and F.F. to read. He says that I only pretend to know people and that I have no real intention of helping him. When I protest, he says, as usual, that people are blind to themselves—no-one, he contends, does anything for anyone else in an unselfish way. Everyone pretends to be unselfish, etc. . .[6]

Gerald had not been exaggerating when he wrote that Denton was liable to become 'violent at the least provocation'. On one occasion he threw a heavy cut-glass custard-bowl at Evie Sinclair. Luckily it missed the intended target, hit the door-surround and shattered on the floor. In calmer moods Denton realized the outrageousness of his behaviour and would try to make amends. After all, his housekeeper was the one person who was always there to look after him. Helen Roeder, very conscious of Miss Sinclair's unfathomable loyalty in standing by him, saw her as having been a person absolutely vital to his existence at this time.

I think Evie was a remarkable person. She had such fanaticism. Denton was a fanatic too and they both had hard edges. She also had terrific grit and they used to fight like anything. I remember Denton coming up to London one day—it was in the Blitz. There was a very charming shop called Footprints—they used to do hand-printed dresses—and Denton wanted to buy something for Evie there. Evie had left; she had swept out again. He said, 'I've been absolutely horrid to her, Helen. I must buy her a frock,' and he bought her a lovely dress there.[7]

Anyone but the supremely tolerant Miss Sinclair might have been very surprised when one day, around April 1940, Denton brought home a young woodman called Tom, with the intention of painting his portrait. A couple of days previously he had been walking in the woods that rose in a bank behind The Hop Garden and, noticing a column of smoke rising in the air, had worked his way through the maze of little paths to investigate.

Behind a huge smoking bonfire I saw a half-naked man with a wide brass-buckled belt round his riding breeches. His shoulders were thick and broad, and his skin had turned to a tawny brown. His hair was all in his eyes and dusty with wood ash. He looked extraordinarily glowering and wild. We grunted at each other and then we talked, and afterwards he came to the Hop Garden and I tried to paint him several times. He was gentle and strange and came from Yorkshire. I still see his hands black with turpentine from the wood and his hair full of minute twigs, needles, skeletons of leaves and buds.[8]

The meeting with Tom the Woodman, whose real name was almost certainly Tom Fletcher, is told in the short story, 'The Fire in the Wood', one of Denton's longest works in the form.[9] It was not completed until the end of 1947, and appears to have given him considerable trouble to write. Indeed, amongst his manuscripts and papers in Austin there exist fifteen or so slightly different opening paragraphs: this was highly uncharacteristic—within quite a short time of starting his writing career Denton was able to develop an enviable fluency.

In each of the versions of the short story, save one, Denton has portrayed himself as a woman. Had he not made this transformation the work would have read as a homosexual love story, and as such would not have been acceptable to his publisher. Although Denton might have liked the idea of telling the story in its true, unadulterated form, the image of himself as a submissive girl caught up in the strong embrace of a virile young forester was not unappealing.

Accordingly, in 'The Fire In the Wood' one has to accept Denton as 'Mary', a young girl who is living in a house on the edge of the wood. She is middle-class, artistic and vulnerable. Having met 'Jim' (alias Tom) by the fire that first time, she returns the next day to draw him and his father at work, sawing down one of the Scots pines[10] (see illustration). After a while, the two men take a break and Jim, looking over in Mary's direction, speaks to her. ' "When

I'm having my dinner," ' he says, ' "I'll keep still and you can do my photo lying down." ' [11] She starts another sketch of him. Before Jim and his father go back to their sawing, Mary, wanting to keep up some sort of momentum in developing the fragile relationship, asks the young labourer if he will come home with her later so that she can do a proper painting of him. He agrees. The Yorkshireman accompanies Mary to her house at five o'clock. They have a large tea that has been prepared by 'Mrs Legatt' the housekeeper, and then Jim sits for Mary in the large upstairs room that she uses as a studio. The immediacy of Denton's description of Jim's behaviour inside what is so obviously The Hop Garden leads one to think that this is a near-factual account of what really happened:

> On that first afternoon she got to work almost at once, arranging Jim on a stool near the window, with his axe across his knees. . . Jim sat with a rigidity which became so strained that he looked like a piece of frozen meat or a dead man. A vein in his heavy throat pulsed and the open flap of his shirt waved very slightly, as if there had been a breeze on that area of his body. . . Jim's tenseness had turned him into almost a caricature of himself. His head had gone right back and he gripped the axe on his knees as if it were a spar and he a drowning man. [12]

On the evening of the sixth day that Mary has been working at the portrait—by now the incongruous pair have become quite friendly—Jim is even more tired than usual. He rolls Mary a cigarette as they relax before the fire, and she takes time to study the man and mull over in her mind exactly what she finds so attractive in him. It is in writing the following description that Denton reveals the extent to which his sexuality was concerned with archetypes, rather than real individuals:

> Looking down at the length of Jim's body on the sofa, Mary thought he looked like Gulliver. His knees were higher than his head; he was pinned down by his tiredness, just as Gulliver had been trussed and strapped across with the Lilliputians' spider-thread ropes. She saw him with the eyes of a Lilliputian. He was some giant of enormous size and weight. And his skin was not skin; it was too tough, too permanent. . .
> Why was Jim always reminding her of the pictures in her nursery books? Sinbad, Gulliver, even Rip van Winkle, when his hair was full of the woods, his hands black as peat, and his Wellingtons caked with mud and grass and moss. Was it because of his clear outlines, his separation from her? Did these give him the legendary quality? He was a woodman, and woodmen were linked with charcoal burners, with bears, wild boar, Robin Hood and venison pasties. [13]

Mary gets on with her painting, but she becomes increasingly aware of the strain on Jim. He is exhausted, yet is maintaining the pose with almost stoic fortitude. She suggests that they take another few minutes' break. Jim says that he really must be going home; he has a bicycle ride of twenty miles ahead of him. Just as he is about to leave, Mrs Legatt comes into the studio to collect the tea things, and she suggests that it might be best if he stayed the night. He could sleep on the camp-bed. At once Jim warms to the idea; ' "but I wonder what the wife'll think," ' he adds.

Mary eases off his boots and they sit down together. Mrs Legatt is preparing a proper meal in the kitchen. Highly relieved at having been spared the journey—darkness has already fallen—Jim begins to reminisce about his childhood days in Yorkshire. After a while he turns to Mary, who is next to him.

> 'But you—I've never known anyone like you before; you treat me more like a brother than anything else—and me only a rough chap you saw in the wood last week.'
>
> Mary stirred uneasily in her corner. How glad she was that Jim could not see her face! His voice had changed—he was urgent and faltering, a little ashamed of putting his feelings into words.[14]

One would have thought that this was the moment Mary/Denton had been waiting for. But in the event nothing comes of it: after Jim has said ' "I think I shall have to stroke you" ' and then proceeds to run his fingers through her hair, she feels compelled to reject the advance. She has no idea how to respond. She jumps up from the sofa and changes the subject of the conversation.

Mary and Jim go out to the garage to fetch the camp-bed. Just as they are about to mount the external staircase, Jim flings the couch to the ground and embraces Mary almost violently, forcing her back onto the wall of the house. Nowhere else in Denton's writing does one find such a torrid scene. The following description is taken from an early draft of the story, which, thankfully, was rejected in favour of something slightly less unseemly.

> Mary felt the brass clasp press against her navel, his knee dug into her thigh. 'What does it feel like to be a woman,' he asked, 'to lie back and take it like a woman?' His voice rasped and was husky. And in the garden there he had her while the moon for a moment shone on the concrete wall, then was hidden by the dark clouds.[15]

After a supper eaten in near-silence Mary retires to the sleeping porch and Jim beds down in the studio room; they are separated by the glass doors of the partition.

The following day they go together into the wood. It is a chilly spring morning. Jim's mother is there, helping to clear up sticks. 'Mrs Archer' has heard about the progress of her son's portrait and she asks Mary if she can see it, even though it is unfinished.[16] Mary takes her back to the house.

As they are talking, Jim's mother drops the bombshell that all three of them will be leaving the district the next day, their work in the wood completed. Mary's illusions about Jim are then shattered as Mrs Archer continues to give her a detailed history of the many problems that have beset their family. She has an epileptic daughter. Jim only married his wife to make an honest woman of her. They had a mentally retarded child. Mary feels burdened with this information that tarnishes her image of Jim. He is not a fairy-tale character at all; the romance is false and soured. Again, it is in an early draft that Denton expresses his feelings with least restraint.

> She would never see Jim again or finish his picture from the life. He was over there working with his father, perhaps fifty yards away.
> The pink-brown pines were down, ninety years of life ended. There were the white bases, the amputated arms bleeding their true blood.
> Tom's [sic] baby was an idiot
> His wife a pretty whore. . .
> The lines seemed to wish to form themselves into a verse; Mary quite disinterestedly began searching in her mind for a clinching, biting final couplet:—
> No pleasure's coming after
> He's had it all before
> (He's bitten through his apple
> and reached the rotten core.)[17]

The sheer hopelessness of this fleeting relationship made a considerable impact on Denton. Although, of course, it is impossible to know just where fact ends and fiction begins, it would seem that for a few moments he had experienced a particular type of homosexual contact that previously had only existed in the realm of his fantasy. Although there is one other reference to Tom in the Journals,[18] it is highly improbable that they ever saw each other again; the encounter was one that Denton could do little more than hug to himself as a memory.

One of the more endearing traits in Denton's personality was his capacity for friendship. Aside from the people of his own age connected with the world of art and literature, there was another category that began to achieve an ever-increasing significance once the war was under way: these were his middle-aged 'ladies'. Peggy Mundy-Castle may have been the first to qualify, but now the circle had expanded. Properly installed at The Hop Garden, Denton was in a much better position to play host to visitors in the manner he felt appropriate—and he was not to be outdone in gentility.

He had known Ellen Easdale since leaving Tonbridge. Indeed, it was in the unlikely setting of his flat in Hadlow Road that Denton introduced her daughter, Frida, to Noel Cousins, the man whom eventually she came to marry. Ellen was something of a writer herself—the autobiography of her early life had been published several years previously[19]—and she would often invite Denton along to her home in the nearby village of Crouch to meet various literary people down from London.

They shared a particular feeling for the Kentish countryside. The author Katharine Moore, who first met Denton in September 1940, remembered how the two friends had been extremely keen on a special part of the Mereworth estate, where Peckham Old Church stands isolated on a hill, virtually engulfed by the trees of the park.[20] The church was supposed to have been built on a pagan site, and Ellen Easdale and Denton liked to think there still existed some element of magic hanging about in the air. The myth was reinforced in his mind when he came across one or two peculiarly grotesque headstones in the graveyard.

Understandably, a few of Denton's neighbours in Platt were rather hostile to this fey attitude towards life, nor did they approve of the frequent comings and goings of 'arty' visitors. Since Denton kept his disability a secret, no one had any particular sympathy for him on that score. Captain and Mrs Turner did not like him a bit. When asking the good lady for her memories of having lived near Denton Welch, the author was met with a stony silence, followed by the question, 'Well, he was a queer, wasn't he?'

The Turners had a young son, John, still in his 'teens, whom they probably regarded as being 'of an impressionable age'. He used to go over to the Hop Garden quite regularly at this time and recalls Denton as having been 'good at gaining one's confidence'. He always felt perfectly comfortable in his presence. John was flattered that a grown-up should treat him as an equal.[21] There was no sexual element in the relationship—it was just that the teenager found him to be unusual and stimulating company, and Denton in turn admired John's independence of mind and his strongly-held pacifist convictions. To a certain extent, each recognized in the other a fellow rebel. Amongst a clique of the less sympathetic villagers, though, Denton with his love of china and his 'artistic ways' earned the soubriquet 'Doulton Wench'!

Of all Denton's middle-aged lady friends there was none to compare with May Walbrand-Evans; she became the most stalwart of companions. He had first come to know her in 1938, before the move to Platt.[22] By temperament they may not have been especially compatible—she could be brassy and insensitive —but her iconoclastic sense of humour and her eccentricity in filling her home with mountains of furniture and china all contributed to make her a person whom he found irresistible. Throughout the entire war she and Denton would go around Kent digging out antiques from a junk shop here, a sale there.

Another factor in May's favour was that she had an impeccable artistic pedigree, having studied at the Slade School alongside such distinguished painters as Augustus John and William Orpen. On two or three occasions she had sat as a model for Lavery.[23] May was in the habit of describing herself as having been 'an Edwardian beauty'.

Following a break of many years, May returned to painting, and when Denton first knew her she was giving drawing lessons to one or two neighbours. Although he used to speak disparagingly of her efforts, in many ways she was by far the more accomplished draughtsman, particularly in portraiture. It was at May's home, The Brown Jug, a converted pub lying on the main road between Tonbridge and Hadlow, that he was introduced to two of her pupils, Elizabeth Plummer and Margery Gardener. Elizabeth became a good friend and she has left many valuable reminiscences of Denton's activity as an artist.

One notices a distinct shift in his style following the move to The Hop Garden. The very modern design of the house itself seems to have been conducive to experimentation and now Denton felt that he wanted to abandon the use of a rather 'muddy' palette in favour of purer and more brilliant colours in general. Things looked far more effective in the sunny upstairs studio than ever they had at the flat. The new approach can be seen not only in Denton's flowerpieces, but also in the more progressive paintings.

An abstract collage, now stored at the Harry Ransom Center in Austin,[24] exemplifies the extent to which he was prepared to experiment with a style that would at the time have been considered to be avant-garde. Although there is some allegiance to the still-lifes of Braque, the picture was almost certainly prompted by Denton's purchase of an oil by the British artist Blair Hughes-Stanton, a work that is written about in the prose fragment 'A Mews Flat in the Country'. Denton tells how some of his friends labelled Stanton's oil 'the stomach picture', since this seemed to be the only recognizable form in the predominantly abstract composition. 'I, by gazing long and living with it,' Denton recorded, 'have found many other and more interesting portions'.[25]

Even if his own abstract, so closely modelled on the type of work Hughes-Stanton was doing about 1936-38, does contain references to other definable forms, the overall impression is of a huge phallus (see colour illustration). Nevertheless, there does exist some ambiguity. The central shape could just as well represent a joint of meat lying on a kitchen table, and the door on the left of the picture, an oven. Pieces of linoleum and ply-wood have been inlaid into the panel. In using this collage technique with such sophistication one senses a level of creative energy that was previously missing in Denton's work; here is a mind seeking out new horizons for self-expression.

One would like to think that the periods of depression were becoming less acute, but if the following poem is representative of Denton's state of mind during the autumn of 1940, this does not appear to have been the case.

> Arch-whisper in the night time said to me
> From your deep melancholy you'll be free
> Only when all is dead and past
> For though you live, you cannot last.[26]

Possibly one of the problems was that, as before, he had too much time on his hands. However keen Denton may have been on his painting, there were other things that he wanted to do as well; and given the circumstances of the war and the various restrictions imposed by it, to have spent the rest of the day burrowing around for antiques was virtually an impossibility. What is more, collecting was his hobby, not his profession.

It was in this context, having been told by his friend the artist Fay Pearce that 'he was a parasite, living on unearned income, while the proletariat was sweating—or starving',[27] that Denton decided the time was ripe to make his first attempt at writing a book. One learns something about how the project got under way from an entry in his Journals, written many years later. Denton had just been re-exploring the Platt Woods: the extract follows on directly from the description of his meeting with Tom.

> There was the pine where I sat looking out to a village of chicken houses, which I tried to draw at the end of the exercise book that was really given up to the book I began before *Maiden Voyage*. It was to be an autobiography from my birth. Through the months of 1940 I plugged at it. Then it suddenly died on me. . . .[28]

The work he struggled with appeared in print only posthumously under the title 'I Can Remember'.[29] It is to be found in Penguin's anthology of his short stories and prose fragments. Running to just over fifty pages, 'I Can Remember' is an account of his early childhood, ending with a visit to the wheelchair-bound James Wattie at his home near Guildford. The author has reached the august age of nine when the narrative breaks off. Denton never worked up the chapters for publication and yet, although he presents little more than a string of vignettes bound together by chronological sequence, the colour and naive simplicity of his style is in several instances typical of his most characteristic writing.

Denton was always quick to learn from experience and one suspects that he fully realized the reason why 'I Can Remember' had fizzled out was because it lacked form; there was nothing to bind the narrative together. Although he may have felt some sense of failure, in getting down this quantity of writing on paper at least he had proved to himself that he had the staying power necessary to attempt a full-length book.

Coincidentally or not, it was only after Denton had experienced first-hand something of the violence of war that his real career as a writer began.[30] On Thursday, 15th August 1940, he happened to be in Tonbridge with May and Peggy Mundy-Castle. There was an air-raid. It was the first he had experienced. Someone said they could see a bomb landing in the direction of Platt, at which Denton said laughingly, 'I expect it's the Hop Garden'.[31] He thought little more of it and went off to The Angel, a hotel near Tonbridge station, where he spent the rest of the evening in the congenial company of three cadets. It was late when he returned to Platt. Just as he was about to put away his Austin in the garage there was the most almighty explosion. A time-bomb had landed in the garden only eight yards or so from the house. It left a very considerable crater. Miss Sinclair came out and at once began to calm him down. Aside from broken windows, the damage was slight. None of his treasures had suffered.

Within six weeks of this Denton started work on his first autobiographical novel, *Maiden Voyage*. In the Journals he tells how it had come into being.

> . . . several tiny things suddenly crystallized into the determination, by hook or by crook, to finish a book that began with my running away from Repton and ended in China.
>
> I remember the complete conviction that this was what I should do. It came to me after I had read *Hindoo Holiday*, which I liked, and after I

had seen somewhere that true books of travel are always interesting. I knew instinctively that my book would be nothing like Ackerley's, and nothing like a travel book either, but there were commonplace pegs that I badly needed; they somehow made all simple, only leaving hard work and perseverance to be cultivated.[32]

Although J.R. Ackerley's *Hindoo Holiday*,[33] first published in April 1932, had recently appeared in a Penguin edition, it seems that Gerald had lent Denton a copy some time before 1940. The book—it is a journal rather than a novel—tells of the author going out to India to fulfil the role of private 'secretary' to an eccentric old maharajah. The latter is intent on using the moderately well-educated young man as a sounding-board for his own ideas about Western culture. Ackerley makes no attempt to cloak his interest in certain youths belonging to the retinue of the undisguisedly homosexual potentate, but over and above this, *Hindoo Holiday* gives the reader a highly-coloured and irresistibly witty glimpse of a small Indian state presided over by a charming, if bizarre, ruler.

Unlike Denton, Ackerley had a broad personality that could respond with generosity to humour in others. In terms of underlying mood, *Maiden Voyage* and *Hindoo Holiday* are indeed poles apart, Denton's book being propelled by a combination of teenage angst and the determination to seek out fresh experience. His intensity is quite foreign to the much more relaxed style of Ackerley. Taking into consideration all of Denton's problems, his disaffection with society and the unresolved emotional needs, it seems very likely that for him writing soon became a useful means of therapy; the accuracy of this idea is more than supported by the fact that nearly everything he penned was autobiographical. Instinctually he set about exploring the origins of his own unhappiness. He needed to survey and put into some order his formative years, so that he might be able to reflect on them from the standpoint of an adult. Only then could his life be seen in perspective and some of his feelings of insecurity mitigated. In the event, the process took him along an unexpected path—following on from the success of *Maiden Voyage*, Denton allowed himself to become almost addicted to recalling and writing about the early part of his life; he found it to be the most effective way of escaping from having to confront the pain of the present and the hopelessness of the future.

He settled into working on the new book with a keen sense of purpose and discipline. We learn that every morning he would stay in bed and write until it was time for lunch.

It gave me a serenity which I had not had since childhood, although I dared not read what I had written, for fear of disgusting myself. All that mattered seemed to be that I should finish it, doing each piece as well as I could.[34]

Before long Denton was well into filling a succession of lined exercise books with his rather untidy, immature, left-handed scrawl.

Since the events described in *Maiden Voyage* had occurred less than a decade earlier, one presumes that they were still relatively fresh in the memory. We do not know if he had kept a journal of some sort during his stay in China; nothing of the kind has survived. It is interesting, however, that just before he sets off into the interior with Mr Butler, we read of Denton visiting the Fieldings' house, and the daughter Elaine telling him that he should keep a diary of what happens. It is entirely conceivable that the very detailed descriptions of this trip in particular are based on some such written source.[35]

Whilst he was busy with the book, Denton started a new painting which exists today as his largest known work. The panel, now in the Tate Gallery, depicts a quasi-mythological scene with a dark horse, a dancing female, an old man with a beard and a tree that obscures the head of a second female who is standing on a plinth (see illustration). An undulating cornfield fills much of the background. The stance of the animal strikes one as odd—its knees are too high up the leg—and the general impression is that the artist has made a conscious decision to paint something 'archaic'. There would appear to be some definite symbolic meaning, and yet Denton's reference to it as 'my harvester picture'[36] seems to preclude any definable allusion to mythology. One sees the work, therefore, as a pastiche, owing something to André Derain's paintings of the late 1930s[37]—though the horse is definitely more reminiscent of those bulky steeds favoured by Renaissance artists. The mélange of derivations could also be expanded to include Magritte, particularly in the figure of the headless lady. Denton attempted a number of less ambitious works along the same lines. They are scenes of Elysium brought down to earth by a certain uglification in his drawing of figures and by the shaping of trees and foliage into idiosyncratically stylized forms.

On the borders of his property, where the short drive to The Hop Garden meets the village lane, there is a wooden house which was then used as a studio. A man called Peter Bishop lived there.[38] He was by profession an industrial psychologist, but he devoted his spare time to painting. Whatever his own talents might have been (one neighbour would talk jokingly of 'the history of art from Leonardo to Peter Bishop!'), he did manage to bring to fruition the enterprising idea of getting together as many local artists as possible with the aim of them showing their pictures in pubs, village halls and the like. And Bishop succeeded in building up a rather impressive array of talent. Amongst those who participated were Graham Sutherland, William Scott, the sculptors Trevor Tennant and Karin Löwenadler,[39] and watercolourist Tom Hennell, together with lesser lights such as Robin and Fay Pearce, Wilfrid Sloane (he signed his works Matutinovich, a family name), Harold and Bernard Hailstone, Mrs Carpmael and, of course, Denton himself, who knew Bishop as a neighbour.

A person working behind the scenes to ensure that things ran smoothly was Bunnie Tubbs, a keen lover of art, who incidentally had known Denton as a fellow-pupil at St Michael's. Because of his disability he was permitted to have a larger allowance of petrol than most, and so he offered to ferry round the various works of art to whichever location had been selected for an exhibition. The first show they put on was at The New King's Head in Wateringbury, a village near Maidstone, and on this occasion Trevor Tennant displayed his striking sculpture of St Francis, hewn from a tree-trunk. Not surprisingly, the more avant-garde pieces caused a great deal of chatter and merriment amongst the men in the public bar!

Most of the works were for sale, with prices generally around the £10-15 mark. The most successful show of all was held at the Sir Thomas Wyatt on the A20, and Mr Tubbs recalled that Denton contributed a picture or two for this. He was quite sure that Denton was not being patronized when invited to contribute his work. The others treated him as an artist in his own right. It is in a letter to Elizabeth Nicholls of 24th May 1941, that he gives his own account of the project:

. . . Did you know that the Sutherlands lived near here? I met them first some months ago and have seen them once or twice since then. I think they are charming. I told them that I knew you and they asked me if I had heard from you lately.

We have been having some picture shows round here in pubs and public halls and someone else took me to their house to ask Sutherland for some pictures.

The shows have been really rather a success. We've made quite a lot of money for The Red Cross and, incidentally, nearly all of us have sold pictures. I sold two. One of two centaurs and the other a pen drawing of an evil and contented looking cat licking its behind.[40] Miss Sinclair said it looked like a Pekinese-pug, whatever that may be!

Jan Gordon mentioned our efforts in *The Observer* and we were going to have some photographs in *Picture Post*, but they wriggled out of it by saying that they were too bad to print! I didn't see the photographer at work, but I'm told he took one of a big buck nigger leaning on a bar and solemnly discussing my picture over his beer with Robin Pearce, another painter! I didn't really like the work of any of the other painters round here, except Sutherland and a person called Tom Hennell, who does really very interesting landscapes in pen and watercolour.[41]

Despite this evidence of artistic activity, he reveals in the same letter that in recent months he had been giving far more attention to completing the first draft of *Maiden Voyage*.

Since last summer I have been busily writing a book, more or less autobiographical as first efforts usually are! It is about the time when I ran away from school and was sent back for a term and then went to China with my brother and the things I saw and did in China.

I've written every morning in bed for two or three hours and now at last I've finished it; I think I've got about two more pages and I dread doing them. I meant to do them this morning, but I'm so glad I've got your letter to answer instead. They seem far more trouble than the rest of the book put together. Of course, my next task is making a fair copy and correcting and revising. I shall probably hate every word of it when I read it through again.

. . . *Sunday June 8th*. I've been keeping this letter to add to it. . . I've finished my book at last and am reading it through. Fred Beale, a friend of Peggy's, is going to type it for me. God only knows what it will read like to other people. . .[42]

Nor was the novel the only piece of writing occupying him; in the course of this long letter we also learn that one of his poems had been accepted for *The Abinger Chronicle*, a thin, modest magazine edited by a Sylvia Sprigge, who lived at Abinger Common near Dorking in Surrey. This was to be Denton's first time in print and he tells Elizabeth Nicholls that he was 'childishly excited' at the prospect of it coming out. The poem, 'Where I Wander' appeared in the June 1941 number.

> Where I wander
> By the sea. . .
> Where birds float. . .
> And where pools
> Are black and sleek,
> Where, in the upturned sand
> So many feet have been;
> Amongst those brittle rocks and slime
> I feel the passing of all time.

'Where I Wander' did not feature in either of the anthologies of Denton's poetry that appeared after his death, and one has to admit that it is much less striking than another, 'Jane Allen', which Miss Sprigge held over for the next edition of her magazine.[43]

> Our maid, Jane Allen,
> Fly-by-night,
> Left the dishes
> Shining white—
> Took her stockings
> From the horse,
> Darned the heels
> With stitches coarse—
> Drank a cup
> Of Indian tea;
> Then dropped a letter
> In a tree:
> And this is what
> The letter said
> 'When you get this, I'll be dead.'

Denton's initial contact with *The Abinger Chronicle* had been through his friendship with an acquaintance of Mrs Carpmael, Mildred Bosanquet, who lived in the village of Seal, near Sevenoaks. She was a regular contributor to the magazine and must have shown him a copy before he sent off his poems to Miss Sprigge. The April/May number included an article by Mrs Bosanquet, tracing the history of selected nursery rhymes. One that she quotes is 'The Ballade of the Bad Black Sheep'. Further on in the essay, attempting to give her subject some sort of topicality, she writes that 'remains of Anglo-Saxon is found in a rhyme that seems quaintly appropriate to black-out nights: when sent through a dark passage, the Devon children used to chant—

> Buckee Buckee, Biddy bere
> Is the way now fair and clean?
> Has the goose ygone to rest?
> Has the fox ygone to rest?
> Shall I come away?

Denton—one cannot determine whether it was on a subliminal or conscious level—made use of this rhyme in one of his own poems from 1941:

Condemnation in the Castle Gardens

> Bah, Bah, Blister Sheep,
> All the pigeons in the Keep,
> All their eggs between the cracks,
> All the office girls in slacks,
> All the daisies on the lawn,
> All the duckweed and the spawn
> Floating in the concrete pool,
> Tell me I'm a bloody fool.
> All the children on the swings
> Shout the message till it rings.
> 'Bahing, Bahing Bladder Sheep
> The animal-doctor should put you to sleep!'[44]

The setting of this poem is Tonbridge Castle: the imposing yellow-brown ironstone keep sits on a massive rocky mound in the middle of the town's high street. One can still see the concrete pool, one can hear the pigeons flapping noisily about their territory and there are still the office girls passing by, though perhaps no longer in slacks. The playground lies just beyond the river walk that skirts the base of the castle mound.

It is perfectly evident, however, that this poem is no picturesque recreation of a town scene. Denton himself is the sheep—and a sheep does not belong in such a place. He sees himself as the one who is shunned by society. The children's cry, 'Bahing, Bahing Bladder Sheep/the animal doctor should put you to sleep!' is a reference to his injured body, the 'bladder' being his catheter.

In 'Jane Allen', Denton places himself in the role of a domestic servant about to commit suicide; in 'Where I Wander' he is the restless artist. The one sentiment that all three poems have in common is the same old all-pervasive sense of detachment from the rest of humanity.

The increased camaraderie that the war engendered in everyday people almost certainly accentuated these feelings. Denton could not identify with the shared sense of purpose that bound together the majority of the country. To have done so, he would have had to compromise his beliefs. Although he did don an Air Raid Precautions warden's helmet for a time—people remember him rushing about on a bicycle—as the poem 'Panacea' demonstrates, he made virtually no effort to correct the misconception that somehow he had managed to wriggle his way out of things.

Panacea

In Total War I lead a life
Epitomized by Chinese Chippendale.
I still am Gothic on a painted bed,
Rococo in a grotto underground,
Baroque in cloisters pillaged from dead Spain,
Enjoying what will never live again.

In Total War I'm idle in the sun,
Eat mangoes underneath a feathered fan,
Catch sounds from Paganini's violin,
Suck pips from fancy, spitting out the fruit,
Toy with my monkey by the stagnant pool;
For I can read, so am no Army's tool.[45]

His friend of later years, Eric Oliver, when asked about what view Denton had taken of the hostilities, recalled:

The war didn't seem to affect him. He took little interest in it and never read the newspapers. In fact, he disliked them. He thought the war was just stupid. Neither Evie or he was afraid. Denton certainly worried that his brother Paul might have been killed; but apart from that I don't think he gave it very much thought; he did not feel the least bit guilty about being out of it.[46]

However, as one can judge from the last line of 'Panacea', and also from the title itself, this is by no means the whole story. Denton did hold strong, if unconventional, views about what was going on. Refusing to concern himself with the moral issue of his country going to war to uphold freedom, he felt much more strongly that the nation's jingoistic patriotism was in itself something revolting and sub-human. In his eyes, the attitude of the British

25. Portrait of Denton Welch by Gerald Mackenzie Leet, 1935.

26. Flowers on a Table, c.1940/1 (cat. no. 45).

27. 'A Cat Waiting for its Master', a watercolour, 1946 (cat. no. 81).

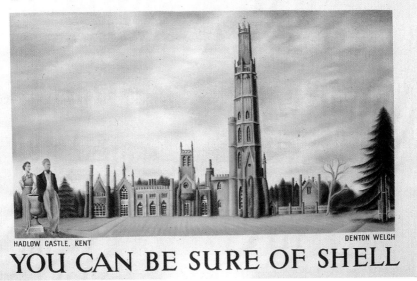

28. Hadlow Castle, a Shell poster, from a painting by Denton Welch, 1937 (cat. no. 23).

29. A road, farm buildings, with a chimney, possibly c.1933 (cat. no. 26).

30. A church (unidentified), c.1936-9 (cat. no. 25).

31. Landscape with a cottage and a road, c.1936-9.

32. 'The Gilded Serpent', c.1940/1 (cat. no. 42).

33. An abstract collage, c.1940 (cat no. 43), influenced by Blair Hughes-Stanton.

34. 'Dinner Serenade', c.1937 (cat. no. 36).

35. 'By the Sea', oil painting begun early 1940s and later adapted by the artist (cat. no. 53).

36. Portrait of a lady with crossed arms (cat. no. 35).

37. Still-life with a spotted cloth, c.1937 (cat. no. 15).

38. 'The Bust and the Toadstools', c.1942-6 (cat. no. 87).

39. A cottage surrounded by trees, c.1947 (cat. no. 93).

establishment precluded it from having any moral standing whatever. He appears to have been incapable of seeing that it was all merely a means to an end: the government's affirmation to the people that they were superior to the enemy.

For Denton the whole affair of the war was something so meaningless that it did not deserve the attention of a person who had dedicated his life to art. The idea that young men in their prime should be sacrificed in order to maintain the status quo was deeply offensive to the homosexual side of his nature and he could not understand how armed conflict might be viewed as anything but profoundly evil. His vehemence can be sensed in this extract, which was prompted by listening to a war-time broadcast:

Jan 6th Wednesday

I always remember the first war-joke I saw. It was in an old *Punch* and I was a little boy in my Grandfather's drawing-room. The *Punch*, unusual and therefore fascinating because it had no colour on its cover, I had picked out of the cupboard under the stairs. I took it with me and sat down in the bow-window.

Then I opened it and saw the war-joke. I think some wretched soldier in slovenly rolled puttees groped and slopped through the mud while Very lights or shells burst above him. Underneath was something incomparably British, middle-class, sordid, manly, and false—stinkingly false—something jolly and vomit-making.

I stood up in amazement. It seemed horribly dirty and wicked to me—another example of the horrible devil-worship of grown ups. I am not exaggerating, only the words are too flashy, but there are no others.

I was frightened and I always shall be at that sort of thing.

Why don't they laugh and joke when the torture of the boot is applied—when the trap-door opens and the 'last offering to Venus', so beloved of novelists, is made by the kicking victim? Why don't they laugh and joke in the hospitals when the patients scream and vomit? Why don't they laugh when the poor lunatics sit in trances of melancholy for days or when the homosexuals and other unchangeable neurotics weep and shout and build new façades even more brittle, more ginger-breadish than the older ones?

Now this stinking broadcast shoots its obscene pantomime. Slimed over with this filth everything is Gilbertianly villainous and oh so good-humoured.

This is what makes the war possible. We have such a wonderful sense of humour. So wonderful that it is quite grisly.[47]

As Denton had written in his letter to Elizabeth Nicholls, the initial draft of *Maiden Voyage* was completed at the beginning of June 1941. Little did he realize how much work lay ahead before the manuscript could be submitted to a publisher. 'I thought that to revise my first writing would only take a few weeks'; he wrote in the Journals, 'I never dreamt it was by far the longest and most arduous part of the proceeding. I even suggested, half-heartedly, dictating it to Freddie while he typed!'[48]

One afternoon, most probably in the early summer, there was a pleasant break from his labours when Helen Roeder came down from London to take him to tea with the famous designer and promoter of the Arts and Crafts Movement, C.R. Ashbee, who lived at Godden Green, a village only a short distance from The Hop Garden. Maybe he was not quite such a lofty figure as Sickert, but Denton still relished the idea of meeting the seventy-eight-year-old who, besides having known William Morris, had published books on such diverse topics as modern silverwork and rural architecture, as well as two or three about his years in Palestine as 'civic adviser' to the administration. Ashbee also knew a great deal about ecclesiastical architecture—one of Denton's particular interests—and during his long career he had been responsible for restoring several churches. In the event, the visit was not a moment too soon, since Ashbee died the following year.

Helen Roeder had a vivid memory of the day.

When I was running the Artists' Refugee Committee there was a man called Horst Nessler, a refugee, who married a girl who, I think, was Ashbee's grand-daughter, and I went down and told Denton this quite incidentally, whereupon Denton was like a pack of hounds and said we must go and see Mr Ashbee. You know what a collector of famous characters he was.

And so we went together to this beautiful Queen Anne house near Sevenoaks in Kent, but it was the sort of house that would by nature have had white panelling inside; however, when you went in—and I remember feeling quite stunned—the sitting-room was an absolute tornado of William Morris chintzes, William Morris curtains, William Morris paper and William Morris carpets, and they were all splendid, though in this quiet Queen Anne setting they nearly knocked one senseless!

Denton was in a state of ecstasy, and of course he got on terribly well with the old gentleman, and was terribly polite and attentive to him, calling him 'sir' and getting his stick for him, fetching his cup of tea, and so on, and before you could say 'knife', the old man was walking around the room with his hand on Denton's shoulder showing him things. Denton was very thrilled.[49]

The late Betty Swanwick remembered that Denton had once come into the work-room they shared at Goldsmiths' and had asked, 'Betty, how many famous people do you know?' She had been embarrassed by the gaucheness of the question, but appreciated that such things meant a great deal to her friend.[50] Now that he was in the process of finishing *Maiden Voyage* and also attempting to get his painting recognized, it occurred to Denton that maybe he should think of finding himself a patron, someone who could offer the odd word of encouragement and, if he was lucky, perhaps might even help promote his career. A figure from the world of literature or art would be the most suitable candidate.

He had been reading a book called *First Childhood*,[51] an autobiography covering the early life of Gerald Hugh Tyrwhitt-Wilson, the ninth Lord Berners. Berners, then fifty-eight, was an extraordinary figure, who, despite pursuing careers in art, literature, diplomacy and music, listed his recreations in *Who's Who* as 'none'. He was just the type of wealthy eccentric whom Denton thought might be worth cultivating. In *First Childhood* his eye had been caught by a fanciful monochrome photograph of the peer in his boyhood dressed as Robinson Crusoe, with a large macaw sitting on his shoulder. Denton decided to make an oil painting from it. He set about the task with the greatest of care. Not only was it necessary to exert some discretion in the choice of colour, but there was also the ever-present danger that the whole effect might appear grotesque and ridiculous, especially since the parrot was practically as big as the fur-clad child (see illustration).

'I've been copying out my book and painting a picture which I hope to sell to an interesting personage,' Denton wrote to Maurice Cranston in August;[52] and soon he had contacted Berners himself, asking if the peer would like to see the portrait before it was finished. Denton's pretext was that he wanted him to suggest any alterations that it might need. A meeting was arranged at the Randolph Hotel in Oxford some time in September. Unfortunately, things did not go as Denton had hoped. Although Berners came out with the favourable verdict that the picture was 'perfectly charming', he failed to take the bait, and a disappointed Denton was forced to return to Kent with nothing to show for his Oxford jaunt other than a few notes of improvements that had to be made to the picture and an inscribed copy of Berners' book *Far from the Madding War*. There had been no hint that he was interested in buying it. The only small crumb was that he had asked Denton to send him a photograph once it was finished.[53]

Denton had too much tenacity to be discouraged for long. Over the years he had invested a great deal of time and energy in his painting and he had no inclination whatever of dropping it in favour of writing. There was a boost to his morale in October, when one of his flower-pieces sold to a Geoffrey Howard for twelve guineas at the prestigious and enterprising Leicester Galleries in London. In the same month he tried his hand at a little teaching. Katharine Moore helped run the Oaks Youth Club in Sevenoaks and she asked him to take on a voluntary class for young boys and girls of fourteen upwards. Mrs Moore recalled that Denton wasn't terribly good at it, and the class petered out after quite a short time.[54] One can conjure up the image of him scanning the daubs of untalented teenagers with a growing sense of frustration, and wondering how he might possibly extricate himself from the situation.

Looking back over the months of 1941, Denton could justifiably have felt a certain sense of satisfaction. He had been able to sow the seeds of a working career. The Hop Garden provided a very pleasant environment and he was now well into the revisions of his book. On 27th November Gerald came down for the last time before being posted overseas, and on 3rd December there was a rare visit from his brother, Paul Welch. Denton and he discussed the possibility of buying The Hop Garden from Colin Lucas. After dinner that evening they went over to Crouch to have coffee with Frida Easdale. The two brothers were sitting back and relaxing to the sound of their hostess playing a Chopin Mazurka when suddenly the telephone rang. It was an emergency. The Hop Garden was on fire.

They rushed back in the car. Denton tried to reassure himself that the situation couldn't be that serious, since the house was built mainly of concrete. They returned to find firemen in control.

> As we turned into the drive I saw the long thick hose like a fat worm. I ran up the path to find the house alive with people. Squirt and hiss of water and flame in the kitchen, and trampling feet and pools of swimming water in the drawing-room. I ran to take the Nativity from the wall. It was hot! And I felt a sort of sweat on it. I ran with it into the garden, then I went back for the Etruscan head and great-great-grandfather's sword. This last was floating in its box on the black water which swilled over the floor. I held on to the arm of Amos the policeman as he helped me over the armchair and the rolled-up carpet. I could not bear to look at my things. Curls of burning paper had fallen from the ceiling and stuck to the covers and carpets.[55]

The portrait of Lord Berners was on an easel in the studio upstairs. Denton dashed in to fetch the panel, hardly able to open his eyes because of the smoke. It would be dreadful if several months of painstaking work had been wasted. The picture was due to be sent to the Leicester Galleries for their New Year's Exhibition in a few weeks time. He was relieved to find it basically undamaged, even though the paint had become sticky. Later that night, when the other people had gone away and left them in peace, the brothers prepared to camp down in the midst of the squalor and get what sleep they could. Denton suddenly had an awful thought. The family silver he had brought back from Shanghai was in the kitchen, the room where the fire had started.

> I ran down and searched under the wreck of the burnt trolley; the black wet mass was still hot. I raked over it with a stick. There was what remained of my mother's family's silver. Whole 'nests' of spoons and forks had melted together. What had not lost its shape was burnt black and terracotta red.
>
> This was the final thing. I had always longed for this silver, and nine years ago had actually got possession of it. Now it was burnt and melted and twisted. I gave out a cry to Paul and he said 'So awfully sorry, Punky.'[56]

The next day, having salvaged as much as he could from the chaotic site, Denton had to think of finding somewhere else to live.

Chapter Seven

Pond Farm and Pitt's Folly Cottage

With Christmas only three weeks away, it was hardly a propitious time for anyone, let alone a semi-invalid, to set about house-hunting. As a result of the war very little property was changing hands in the area, and Denton found it virtually impossible to rent an unfurnished cottage. He and Evie were in the hapless position of having to take anything on offer—and so, after May Walbrand-Evans had put them up for a week at the Brown Jug, they jumped at the opportunity to move into rooms at Pond Farm, a large house a couple of miles away and nearer the Medway.

Standing back from the road and surrounded chiefly by hopfields, Pond Farm belonged to Cecil Gardener. It was his wife Jane, however, who ruled the roost, and she allowed Denton to have a pair of upstairs rooms on either side of the front door. According to Helen Roeder, he was quite sure they were haunted. Evie occupied a smaller one along a corridor in the centre of the house. On 10th December all the remaining possessions from The Hop Garden were transported to this temporary home.

Jane Gardener and Denton were by no means strangers. They had gone on several excursions to country auctions together, and in conversation with the author Mrs Gardener admitted that the better part of her knowledge of china derived from what she had managed to pick up from the young man. Nevertheless, their temperaments were less than compatible. Whilst admiring his extraordinary expertise in being able to differentiate makes of porcelain merely by touch, on a more personal level she soon developed very definite reservations about her new tenant.

> I didn't really see very much of Denton whilst he was living with us, but I thought there was something rather secretive and sly about him. He was a very fastidious little man. Evie would pander to his whims, although I remember him very often shrieking at her. Denton didn't usually get up till 11 o'clock and then he would have his bath. If he found a hair in it there would be hysterics! A neighbour of ours, Colonel Petherick, once asked me, 'Well, is he a gentleman?', but despite all our problems with Denton, I liked him.[1]

Unfortunately, as Denton makes quite plain in the Journals, the feeling was not mutual (the strongest comments about his erstwhile landlady had to be excised from the published versions). It was simply a case of two strong and unbending personalities rubbing one another up the wrong way. Each took offence far too easily.

In spite of the underlying friction, the six months or so spent at Pond Farm was a productive period, with Denton being able to maintain a real momentum in his work. In February 1942, he completed the final draft of *Maiden Voyage*,[2] and within a few weeks there was a typescript ready that could be shown to one or two carefully selected friends. Francis Streeten had the honour of being the first to read the book. Sadly, his comments have not been preserved.

At some point whilst he was waiting for the manuscript to be typed, or maybe when somebody else was reading it through, Denton began working on an essay that proved to be not only his first published piece of prose, but also the single most significant component in the launching of his literary career. It was the humorous article that recorded the disconcerting visit to Sickert back in 1936. Originally given the title, 'A Glimpse of Richard Sickert',[3] Denton wrote the first version in a notebook that had already been used for a brief account of the meeting with Berners the previous year.

As far as his activity as a painter was concerned, although the portrait of the peer had failed to sell, the Leicester Galleries was still happy to show his work. One of Denton's still-lifes went into the spring exhibition, 'Imaginative Art Since the War', whilst another, 'A Gothick Flowerpiece', was finished in time for the 'Artists of Fame and Promise' series that opened in July.[4]

From this date until the time of his death six-and-a-half years later, the Leicester Galleries demonstrated a really wonderful faith in Denton's talent as an artist—and it was not a case of them exhibiting the works of a figure who had already made a name as a writer and had built up a literary following. At the time the Berners portrait was accepted Denton could have sported nothing in print save four poems in the obscure *Abinger Chronicle*.

The painter Carel Weight, who through Helen Roeder had kept in touch with Denton since their time together at Goldsmiths', recalled his friend's association with the adventurous gallery:

I used to see most of Denton's pictures at the Leicester Galleries, since I was showing very much in the rather remarkable 'Fame and Promise' series.[5] There was a man named Oliver Brown, a director of the gallery, who was one of the very few art dealers that all the painters adored. He was both amusing and very kind—his criticisms were very much liked by artists.

Denton began showing there. It seemed to be a sort of dream place for the up and coming. You'd send your pictures in and they'd be nicely hung; not against one by a contemporary artist, but next to a Monet or a Sickert or some other very splendid picture—and there were some very splendid pictures around at that time—and so it was everybody's delight to have something there.

I think that Brown must have seen that Denton was a very unusual character. One of the little jobs he handed out to young artists was to design the invitation cards for the next exhibition, such as the 'Fame and Promise' and on one or two occasions he asked Denton to do them—and they were delicious.

Denton had quite a little success with his pictures at the Leicester Galleries; they were quite unlike anything else being shown. He was certainly well-known as a character there, but he had no real reputation as an artist.[6]

However much Denton may have been gaining in confidence regarding his career, it was impossible to stave off the day when his antagonism to Jane Gardener would get the better of him. An absurd quarrel erupted between them after he was accused of taking good light-bulbs from her part of the house and replacing them with duds. Denton, with his distinct feelings of being persecuted, simply refused to be bullied into admitting he was in the wrong. It was not in his nature to lose face to someone he did not respect. Very shortly Cecil Gardener was given the duty of asking him to leave by the next rent day, the 10th June. As things turned out, Denton was gone from Pond Farm at the end of May.[7]

As one learns from an undated letter to Maurice Cranston, until the last moment Evie and he had no idea where they might go next. It even crossed Denton's mind to ask his elder brother Bill's mother-in-law if they could come and stay at her 'late Victorian mausoleum in South Kensington'. Happily, their worries did not last long—May again managed to turn up trumps; she found them somewhere to live, practically on her doorstep.

Her house, the Brown Jug, stood in the position of a lodge alongside a pair of large gate posts surmounted by concrete lions that proclaimed the drive leading to Pitt's Folly. Since 1939 the elaborately constructed Colt house had been inhabited by Mary Sloman, the estranged wife of a retired headmaster of Tonbridge School. The place had been built about thirteen years earlier for an interior decorator, Guy Osborn, but whilst extending their new home, the Slomans had swept away much of the original opulence of the rooms. Next to this wooden house, and joined to it by a covered way, was a slightly twee garage, over which there were living rooms for a chauffeur. This was to be Denton's new home. Regrettably, the author has been unable to locate a contemporary photograph of the building.

Despite the obvious drawback of its size, Denton knew that Pitt's Folly Cottage would suit him perfectly well for the time being. Furthermore, the first floor featured a modest gothic window at either end and this somehow lent the otherwise dull exterior a semblance of style. To a certain extent these windows succeeded in distracting the gaze of the aesthetically minded from the indignity of the garage doors.

Three years after he had moved in, Denton was commissioned by *Vogue* to paint a picture of the interior. The little gouache shows a cavernous chamber dominated by a gothic window, the two huge wooden angels flanking it on either side. To the left, crammed against a Regency chair, is the Dolmetsch harpsichord, with Denton's bed, festooned in bows, opposite it on the right.[8] This magazine illustration prompted one of his literary admirers to write telling him how captivated she had been by the 'perfect fairy house'![9]

Although Evie had her own room and there was a kitchen downstairs, it was in this single cramped room that Denton wrote and painted, worked and slept. If he wished to do any entertaining, there was just enough space to have one or two people in. It is not surprising that Hector Bolitho's reaction to Pitt's Folly Cottage after visiting Denton in June 1945 was that his living quarters reflected 'some of the claustrophobia of his life'[10] and that, coupled with the restrictions on movement dictated by his illness, the whole ambience lent itself to self-analysis.

But Denton was never one to stay inside all day long. If he chose to turn left out of the drive and follow the main road for a few hundred yards in the direction of Maidstone, he came to a pub, the Rose and Crown, and a lane branching off that wended its way towards the Oxon Hoath estate. With its spacious park, its Alphabetical Avenue and Cedar Walk, Oxon Hoath became his favourite retreat—a haunt for countless picnics.[11] When Denton felt in the mood he might sit down and do some writing there, or he could sketch the rushes on the banyard (a small lake) and look across it to the unusual mansion that had been altered in the mid-nineteenth century to imitate a continental villa (see illustration).

Oxon Hoath was the seat of Sir William Geary, an eccentric baronet who had formerly been Attorney General in Accra. He kept an African butler, was a keen huntsman and had quite an eye for the ladies—although sadly he had no heir. Much to Denton's approval, the old man had steadfastly avoided making any modernizations to the estate; it appeared to have been neglected for decades. In the midst of the war Oxon Hoath was Denton's timeless haven and sitting there in the long grass and cow parsley he could give free rein to his imagination.

It was soon after his life had taken this more secure and relaxed turn that on 10th July 1942, Denton began his Journal. When he came to make the last entry, on 31st August 1948, four months before his death, it had filled nineteen exercise books. The Journal was written with a definite eye on posterity and contains not only a sporadic record of daily activities, but also of how his career was progressing, of his aesthetic likes and dislikes, his emotional reactions to various incidents, his roamings about the countryside, the chance encounters with strangers, and, above all, an account of the unceasing struggle to live as normally as possible, whatever the circumstances.

Since Denton was primarily an autobiographical writer, to a certain degree the Journal also served to provide him with material that might be used at a later date. It took him some months before he was able to settle into it; a number of the earlier entries are reminiscences of incidents from his childhood and adolescence that bear no special relevance to the date on which they were written down. In the exercise books too one finds several poems interspersed between entries, but these were usually included purely for the sake of convenience when he had no other paper to hand.[12]

The reason Denton started writing his Journal on 10th July in particular was that to all intents and purposes the date marked the beginning of his literary career. The previous day he had received a letter from Cyril Connolly accepting 'Sickert at St Peter's' for *Horizon*. The periodical presented stories and articles by a galaxy of well-established and up-and-coming talents and was widely acknowledged as being one of the leading outlets for writers and artists of the Second World War years. Although 'Sickert at St Peter's' came out in the August number,[13] an edition which also featured a further instalment of Augustus John's autobiography and an article on the painter Matthew Smith by Richard Wyndham, Denton had to wait until the beginning of September before receiving any notable feedback about his piece.

In the meantime, *Maiden Voyage* was doing the rounds of various publishing houses, but without managing to take anyone's fancy. The manuscript had first been dispatched while Denton was at Pond Farm, and with that combination of impatience and excited apprehension familiar to every new author, he was 'almost in a state of collapse'[14] each time the postman came to the door. By the third week of August Jonathan Cape, the Bodley Head, the Fortune Press and Chapman & Hall had all been approached, but none of them wanted to take it.

Around this time, however, he succeeded in enlisting the support of the twenty-two-year-old novelist, poet and medical student Alex Comfort, the co-editor of *Poetry Folios*, whose own first book had been published when he was in his teens.[15] It seems likely that Denton had sent him some of his poems and in passing had mentioned *Maiden Voyage* and his lack of experience in approaching publishers. Whatever the precise sequence of events was, Comfort offered to read the novel. He was bowled over. He can be credited with being the first person to recognize Denton's flair as a writer. In an undated letter he gives his initial reactions to the book: even Denton, with his firm belief in himself, must have read its contents with a certain amount of incredulity.

. . . At first flush I think, quite honestly, that it is a work of something very like genius. But it is a visual genius rather than a literary one, perhaps. In spite of that, you have produced a book which is unlike anything I have read. It suggests Proust, but I like it better than Proust. You have analysed and revealed yourself so calmly and without any delight in victimizing yourself—yet everything you write is dead accurate in its effect. As a medico my chief interest is in the psychology of it, and its significance in this field compared with most autobiography is enormous. In addition to this fearless sort of self-analysis, you've a gift for small incident—the transvestism with the woman's clothes, the dead frog, to take two instances, which Proust had not, and which suggests Dickens.

That's all I can say. I admire the book enormously, from what I have read, and I'll send the whale of a letter with it. But be prepared to have all the psychologists about your ears if once it comes out. It's a happy hunting ground, and your case is just about 'textbook' in some respects.

Every good wish
in haste
Alex C.

P.S. You are my character Fyodor from *The Almond Tree* in every single respect. I too ran away from school[16]

With characteristic generosity, Comfort had written along similar lines to the seventy-six year-old Arthur Waugh (father of Alec and Evelyn), the chairman of Chapman & Hall, hoping to interest him in *Maiden Voyage*. He received a reply that was less than sympathetic to Denton's cause.

I have such a complete confidence and sympathy with your own work and your literary temperament, that it gives me actual distress when I find myself unable to agree with you in your enthusiasm for the work of your own friends. Of course, a certain gulf is inevitable. I stand in the relation of a grandfather to your generation, and it is not to be expected that we should see life or art in the same light.

But I must honestly confess that when you claim 'genius' for *Maiden Voyage*, and talk about Mr Welch out-Prousting Proust, I can only feel that we have got upon ground where we talk different languages. For three days I have concentrated on the MS, hoping that the light was about to break, which would reveal to me the subtlety of the author's interpretation. But the moment never came. The book seems to me superficial and disordered, and the character portrayed, so far as it emerges from the crowded environment of furniture, food and circumstance, strikes me as abnormally self-conscious and ineffectual. It is no good my spinning words about it all, for we are talking on different planes, and there is no arguing about tastes.

If you are right, I am wrong; and at any rate you have youth on your side. I shall be intensely interested to hear how the book strikes other readers. I only wish I could penetrate its purpose; for, as I have already said, I hate to be at odds with you in a matter of appreciation.[17]

Undeterred and quite confident in his opinion of *Maiden Voyage*, Alex Comfort suggested to Denton that next he should show the typescript to Herbert Read,[18] who was then a director of Routledge. Curiously enough, Denton had already written to the firm on 9th July proposing that they bring out a small book of his verse. When sending the novel he made the wise move of enclosing Comfort's wholeheartedly fervent letter.

Perhaps as a sop to distract him from his evident worries about *Maiden Voyage's* lack of progress, Comfort asked Denton to submit an article on 'Painting in 1942' for the journal, *New Road*, of which he was also an editor. It seems that it was intended to be a survey of the current scene in Great Britain. Denton worked at the essay for a few weeks—and with considerable difficulty ('I am far too hot-blooded to be a Nart Critic', he wrote to Maurice Cranston)[19], but although it was finished and mailed off, the piece never appeared in print and regrettably no copy of it has survived.

Evidently, Denton still had the ambition to search out some patron who might rally to his cause. The day before he agreed to write the article he had received a letter from the younger Sitwell brother, Sacheverell, thanking him for sending a photograph of the Berners portrait, which, as ever, remained unsold and generally unappreciated. The tone was courteous, but nothing more. Refusing to leave any avenue unexplored, within little more than a week Denton wrote to Edith Sitwell, enclosing a copy of her recently published collection of poems, *Street Songs*,[20] with the request that she should adorn it with her autograph. One wonders if he felt any pangs of guilt at making such a fawning approach: in the past he had referred to her as 'that old bag of bones'.[21]

In his Journals Denton describes the 16th September as having been 'the day of miracles'. Not only did the post bring two minor commissions and a request from W.J. Turner for him to correct the proof of a poem that had been accepted for *The Spectator*,[22] but there was also a 'plum, jewel, diadem knock-out' reply from Edith Sitwell. Writing to Helen Roeder five days later, he exuberantly quoted the most choice extracts:

'I cannot tell you how much my brother Obsert, with whom I am staying, and I, enjoyed your alarming experience with Mr Sickert. We laughed till we cried—though really in some ways it was no laughing matter. But one thing came out very clearly and that is, that you are a *born writer*!' She goes on—'Nothing could have been more admirable, for instance, than your description of the stringy man about to lose his hair.'

There are four lovely pages of it. She ends by saying this—'As I say, we were full of admiration for the *writing* of your adventure, and my brother Osbert was going to write to Mr Connolly to tell him how very greatly we admired it. . . '

Wasn't this the most wonderful present to receive straight out of the blue? I wonder if Osbert *did* write to Connolly. . . She asks me if I am writing anything else and I have mentioned the book, saying that I would send it to her if she wished me to. . . [23]

and in the Journal entry written on the 17th one senses that almost instantaneously he came to rely on Miss Sitwell as the fount of all the encouragement and advice that he needed to pursue his vocation as a writer:

It is very intoxicating when a great person takes up a thing exactly as you intended when you wrote it—shows you by their remarks that nothing has misfired. One quickly gets the megalomaniac's outlook—that all who pick holes are swine, and that in future you will only keep your pearls for the great because they have minds like your own and do not tediously misunderstand you. It is fatal I see. O I have fed on her letter all day. It is perhaps what I live for, this sort of appreciation. I can never hope again to get quite such a generous dose, sent straight from the blue sky.[24]

What Denton had not mentioned to Helen was that, taking the bull by the horns, he had asked Edith Sitwell if she would graciously consider accepting the dedication of *Maiden Voyage* (even though as yet the work had failed to find a publisher). She agreed.

Things began to develop very rapidly. By now Herbert Read had already written to Denton acknowledging receipt of the typescript.[25] He explained that he did not want to commit himself until the book was seen by his colleagues at Routledge. Later in the month Read sent another letter asking him to lunch at the Reform Club on 28th September. Denton replied at once and of course made a point of mentioning the good news about Miss Sitwell's acceptance of the dedication. Childlike in his enthusiasm, he wrote in the Journals

> May lunch on Monday be successful and delicious. May he like me, may I like him. May the book be published with success. May I be paid and famous. My book is almost lovely. I know it. But for the cloud which is me in it, as well as the loveliness which is me in it. Miss Sitwell has taken it for her present. I would write something fulsome and beautiful and florid at the beginning for her, but I may not dare.[26]

The day after the meeting had taken place Denton, bubbling over with even more good news, wrote to Helen Roeder telling her all about what had happened.

> Herbert Read's taken it! Not in writing yet, but he tells me I'm to take it as an accomplished fact. Apparently two directors don't see what he and another sees in it, so he will have to use a little gentle persuasion. They (the not so keen ones) seem quite willing, if I don't stand out for any extravagant terms! Needless to say that I stood out for no terms whatever!
>
> We had the most delightful talk and lunch at The Reform Club. My behind fitted into the niche made in the chair by Henry James after many, many years of taking his lunch in the same corner. Wasn't it nice to give me Henry James's seat on purpose?
>
> He, Read, is quiet, shy, seemingly a little cold, but perhaps not at all underneath. He told me fascinating anecdotes ranging from Queen Mary's gift of a common piece of modern Wedgwood to someone who had worked laboriously for *love* on a catalogue of her bibelots, to stories of how he used to make omelettes for Edith Sitwell.
>
> I told him K. Clark[27] had the other copy, and he said 'Well if you can get his patronage, it will perhaps be even more useful than Edith Sitwell's.' I am not certain whether he meant that K.C. would help me in a literary way as well. Poor K.C. if indigent authors are going to bombard him, as well as painters!
>
> He didn't discuss my book till after the coffee. Then he suddenly said, 'Let's talk about your book. Some people might think it precious. . .' then he gave a long pause. I couldn't bear it any longer, so I piped up desperately, 'But I am precious!' 'Exactly,' he flashed out with a smile. 'It's

your personality and that's that!' He went on, 'It struck me in a strange way as being very contemporary, or of your generation. I say strangely, because it is not full of ideology or any of the things that we are told youth today is interested in.'[28]

Read suggested that Denton should make his own decorations for the dust-jacket and title-page, and almost immediately he set to work on these with gusto. This was the first time he had undertaken any sort of illustration work and he looked on it as a welcome opportunity to add a further personal dimension to the book. When *Maiden Voyage* was published the following year, aside from the dust-jacket and title-page, the novel also contained decorated end-papers, a frontispiece, an ornamental dedicatory page to Miss Sitwell, a decorated border for her foreword and three highly elaborate full-page chapter numbers, all designed by Denton. For this time-consuming work he was paid £10, but only after he had asked Routledge for something extra in addition to the advance on royalties of £30.[29]

But before *Maiden Voyage* could go into production, there were some problems over libel that had to be confronted. Denton was told to arrange an interview with Oswald Hickson, a well-known lawyer who advised Routledge in such matters, and in a state of some unease he was soon using May's telephone to get through to the man's offices in Surrey Street, W.C.2. In the brief conversation that followed Hickson said it was chiefly references to Repton that he wished to discuss. The school was mentioned by name in the book, and this, he thought, gave rise to some difficulties.

It was the last thing Denton wanted to hear. His time at Repton had been miserable and he was incensed at the prospect of having to tone down the descriptions. What is more, he felt that he had already 'bowdlerized' *Maiden Voyage* quite enough. 'The English public schools deserve all the mud that is thrown at them,' he wrote to Helen Roeder, 'the only pity is that we still only dare to throw such very refined mud.'[30]

The actual meeting, it transpired, was a complete anti-climax, with him thinking that Hickson's objections, far from being sinister or depressing, were really rather funny.

> Oswald Hickson was superb! The complete example of straining after gnats and swallowing camels. I now realize exactly how the mind of the censor must work. No logic, no taking into account the spirit behind the written word; only a peculiar jumble of prejudices inherited from a non-conformist childhood.
>
> He only wants me to change nine things, eight of them ludicrous. The Alfred Douglas bit[31] must go, but I don't mind, as it was only 'dragged' in anyhow! The other objections are almost too absurd to write down. He tells me to cut out that the maid *smelt*, that there was a *suspicion of bad breath* about the art master, that one of the boys *wore a truss*, that Geoffrey said 'lucky bugger' (I have seen this in print three times at least—he didn't mention the good-bye kiss!). It appears that I must not call

someone an *unpleasant man* or say that another wore black pyjamas and had black hairs on his chest!

This last is the most grotesque objection of them all, I think. I was so dazed by the whole extraordinary episode (not one single thing had been mentioned that I thought *might* give grounds for complaint) that I rushed to Herbert Read at once after the interview, He was out, of course, so I shall have to write and tell him I think his libel lawyer *almost* mentally deficient.[32]

At the beginning of December, amidst various negotiations with Routledge over the illustrations for *Maiden Voyage* and the joy of receiving the odd letter of encouragement from Edith Sitwell, Denton heard that his father, Arthur Welch, had died at an internment camp in Shanghai the previous month. Apparently he had been smoking sixty cigarettes a day; the cause of death was cancer. One learns from the Journal entry of 7th December that Denton had looked on his father as little more than an affluent provider; there had been virtually no affection, at least not on his part. At once thoughts turned to the matter of his own security.

A statement of his income for the financial year 1942/43 shows that the annual allowance from Mr Welch had been £150. On top of this Denton received a further £125 from investments, the majority of which had been bought with the compensation money from the accident. Now he had to face the possibility that his income effectively would be halved; as yet there was no way of predicting how much he might expect to earn from writing.

Even though Denton's candour about his lack of emotional response to the news reveals a deep ingratitude towards the man who had attempted to look after his welfare, one can understand how the altered financial situation must have seemed a very real threat both to his lifestyle and his work. He had a firm determination that nothing should distract him from the enjoyment of his newly-found success.

By Christmas the first batch of proofs had arrived from Routledge, together with a note asking, 'Would you like to retain your own individual punctuation?'[33] On the last day of 1942 Denton took stock of all that had occurred since the disaster of the fire.

Now this year ends and I look back to the things that have happened to me. In painting not very much, but more than before—my Berners picture was illustrated in *Vogue*, and Jan Gordon mentioned another picture in *The Observer*.

But the chief thing is in writing.

My Sickert article was taken by *Horizon* and then I had the amazing letter from Edith Sitwell. I got in touch with Alex Comfort who cracked my book up. Then Herbert Read took it and now it will soon be out. W.J. Turner took a poem, and Middleton Murry two others. Henry Treece used one in *Kingdom Come* and others in *Decachord*, *Abinger Chronicle*.

Tambimuttu says he is going to use one in *Poetry [London]* too.

This may all be only a beginning, but it means something, and I must go on and on and on.[34]

Although he had to wait until the 21st April before being given a publication date for *Maiden Voyage*, Denton was so buoyed up with enthusiasm for what the new year might bring that his pen could hardly keep pace with all the schemes and ideas flooding into his mind. The contract he had signed with Routledge stipulated that they retained the option on a further two books, and so once the proof-reading of *Maiden Voyage* was behind him he started work on another autobiographical book.

'A Novel Fragment' can be viewed as an unsuccessful though by no means insignificant attempt to write a sequel to his first novel.[35] The story is centred on Denton's life at Goldsmiths' and his friendship with Gerald in particular. Quite apart from containing several descriptions that border on the libellous, at some stage, having written about 18,000 words, he came to realize that the projected book in no way succeeded in maintaining the intensity of *Maiden Voyage*. 'A Novel Fragment' was published later in *A Last Sheaf*, a posthumous anthology of Denton's prose and poetry.

At the beginning of March 1943, both Evie and he were laid up with a heavy bout of 'flu. Denton was afflicted with alarmingly high temperatures. Tenacious as ever, on the 5th he took up an exercise book and launched into yet another fairly substantial autobiographical essay, a work that was eventually published a decade after his death under the title *I Left My Grandfather's House*.[36] It is a loosely factual account of the walking trip he had made during the early summer of 1933, when he had just finished his first term at Goldsmiths'. Longing to shake off the residual feelings of squalor from his living in London, he had started out from Henfield and had then roamed westwards to Winchester, stopping at a succession of youth hostels for the night on the way. Apparently, Denton got as far as the edge of Dartmoor, but running out of money in Taunton, he had been forced to return unexpectedly to Waphams, much to the displeasure of Aunt Dolly. Disgruntled at his reception, he immediately set off again, this time with the intention of following the Pilgrims' Way, which runs from Winchester to Canterbury. The story, sprinkled with innocent escapades and containing an attractively poetic evocation of rural England in the inter-war years, breaks off at Cocking Churchyard, not far from Winchester, where he had stopped to paint a watercolour. The only clue one has as to how Denton might have finished *I Left My Grandfather's House* comes from some notes that were scribbled down on a scrap of paper.[37]

Work on the story must have been a painful reminder of the energy and vigour that were so much a part of his life in those days. Almost as soon as he had recovered from the 'flu, as if wishing to reassure himself that he was still not wholly spent, he made a tour of the countryside around Pitt's Folly that would have tired many a teenager. The route he took, cycling through Hadlow, Mereworth, West Malling, Borough Green, Ightham and Shipbourne, is certainly not less than twenty miles and on his return to the cottage Denton still had sufficient strength to write up a lengthy description of the afternoon in his Journal. The next day he started on the third and last exercise book containing *I Left My Grandfather's House*. In circumstances such as these one can perfectly understand how the majority of his friends and acquaintances were oblivious to the fact that he was seriously ill. There were things about him that simply did not add up.

To date Denton would have been quite justified in describing himself as a 'protégé' of Miss Edith Sitwell, but he could not have claimed that he knew her—they had never met. On 16th April, as he was drinking coffee with Maurice Cranston, Evie came into the room with a telegram that effectively put the icing on the cake.

> I took it expectantly, but telling myself it was sure to be nothing but disappointment. I read it not quite grasping, because of queer writing and bad spelling.
> 'Will you lunch here 12.45 Monday Stiwell [sic.] Sesame Club Grosvenor Street W1'
> In spite of 'Stiwell' I knew it was from Edith Sitwell, but because of my preconception that she would ask me to Osbert's Chelsea house I had the idea that I did not know where to send the answer.[38]

Determined that Miss Sitwell should receive his acceptance without any hitch, Denton sent a wire and then telephoned the Sesame Club.

> The woman at the other end would insist on calling me Madam, while I gave her my message. I wanted to be quite sure that Edith was staying there.
> 'Yes, madam,' the woman said.
> 'Don't call her,' I shrieked. 'I only want to leave her a message.'
> 'Is it Mr or Mrs Welch?' the woman asked right at the end, still definite in her own mind about my sex. I wanted to laugh.
> 'Mr,' I said, 'Mr Welch.'[39]

Although the morning of 19th April was rather wet, Denton decided to cycle the three miles to Tonbridge station.[40] The train was late and the journey itself turned out to be an inauspicious start to what he sincerely hoped would be one of the great days of his life. There were soldiers everywhere. It was impossible to find a seat. When the train did eventually reach Charing Cross—he had sat on someone's strong suitcase for much of the way—Denton decided he would walk the short distance to the Leicester Galleries to look at one of his pictures. In the event he did not go in; he was uncertain whether exhibitors were expected to pay the entrance fee or not. The next port of call was the cloakroom at the National Gallery, a convenient place where he could get spruced up, ready for lunch.

Inside the Sesame Club, Denton announced himself to the receptionist and then went to sit in a basket chair between 'two old ladies who appeared to be solitaries'.[41] His diagnosis had been wrong and almost immediately they entered into a lively conversation with him trapped in the middle. All the while Denton was keeping a firm eye on the foot of the stairs and the passage. It would be inexcusable if he missed Edith Sitwell!

> Then suddenly, when I turned once more to look over my shoulder, a tall figure, dressed all in black, was standing there, in the mouth of the passage-way. Black hat, black cloak and black dress to the ground. The draught from the door swept the folds of the cloak against her, and a powder-white hand held the hem at her throat. Two enormous rings glittered on her fingers. The lovely palest reservoir blue stones reached from the first to the second joints. They flashed, and flashed again. And from under the sweeping brim of the hat, which was a Spanish-trilby-witch's hat to me, two eyes were looking out, and a mouth and a nose were considering me. The mouth was not red, but flower-pink. The curve of the nose made me think of a sword, the nostrils of curling tendrils.
>
> I felt that all the features in the mother-of-pearl face were saying 'Is *this* the person we have asked to lunch? It would be foolish to make any mistake, so look a little aloof, a little severe, even surprised.'[42]

Summoning up all his courage, Denton went over and introduced himself. In a moment or two the austere-looking poetess and her irrepressibly alert companion were making for the bar, before going in to lunch. Once drinks had been ordered, Miss Sitwell, with true beneficence, produced a copy of her newly published *Poet's Notebook* from under the funereal cloak: the inscription inside the cover read, 'For Denton Welch from his friend Edith Sitwell'.

Conversation soon turned to *Maiden Voyage*, and with all the sincerity he could muster Denton thanked her for such generous patronage. He went on to explain that the book was delayed at the binders. He had heard it was 'oversubscribed before publication.' ' "It's due entirely to your Foreword," I pushed out of my mouth. More nervousness. Hot, red. "No it isn't. I think it's due to your article on Sickert." Here a laugh.'[43]

Miss Sitwell having asked the waitress to bring some beer to drink with their meal (not one of Denton's favourite beverages), they proceeded to the dining-room.

> Edith Sitwell took the seat in the corner and asked me to sit opposite. 'Will you sit there?' she said, 'then the window won't be too much for you.' The menu was brought.
>
> 'The tongue is very good today, Madam', the maid said.
>
> 'Shall we have tongue, or would you like soup first?' Edith Sitwell turned to the maid and added, 'What is *potage paysan*?'
>
> 'Sort of vegetable soup, Madam.' This was an older maid, quiet and resigned-looking. Edith Sitwell called her Mrs 'Something'. We both decided not to have the soup, but to begin with the tongue.

When it came it was soft and sweet-tasting, and there was Russian salad and some lettuce. Edith Sitwell had no lettuce. We both began to eat quite hungrily. Tall glasses of pale beer stood beside our plates.[44]

She questioned Denton about his family, but on hearing of his father's recent death the topic was soon abandoned. He would have treasured some extravagantly gothic description of the Sitwell family home, Renishaw, but none was forthcoming. After a pause they returned to the subject of *Maiden Voyage* —it was something that both could discuss with safety and enthusiasm.

'Now I think is the time for you to do something violent and vulgar,' she said.

The words struck a bell in me.

'That's what I'm longing to do,' I said.

'That bit in your book about the terrible Chinese hotel—quite remarkably terrifying.'

Silence for a moment.

'I will tell you what your danger is; it is your ingrowing toe-nail. Everything in, in, in.'

She bent her very dignified head and brought her two hands up to it in movements rhythmical, swirling, in-turning.

'It is perfect in that book, but you must not do it again.'[45]

Miss Sitwell implied that she considered the Sickert article to be the more effective piece of writing. Finding Denton's Achilles' heel with deadly accuracy, she reminded him of the one sentence in the story that she knew would be quite impossible to explain away. Having quoted Sickert's mischievous remark that 'ugly ones like us haven't got a chance when there's someone like Eden about', Denton, so offended at 'being lumped together with Sickert in ugliness' had written: 'I hurriedly tried to compensate myself for the humiliation by telling myself that, although it may not be saying very much, I was undoubtedly by far and away the best-looking person in the room, and this in spite of my long illness.'[46]

It is a measure of his hypersensitivity to criticism, particularly from those whom he admired, that he felt it necessary to include an explanation of this humorously arrogant remark in the essay 'A Lunch Appointment', which is an alternative account of the meeting with Miss Sitwell. 'Inexperience had made me yield easily to that temptation to be preposterous which comes to most writers at one time or another',[47] Denton writes—indeed, he had already squirmed a little when he read it in print in *Horizon*. The fact that Miss Sitwell had singled out the sentence made him feel doubly ashamed and he could not save himself from giving her a long and elaborate explanation as to why he had written it. In doing so he revealed rather more inner discomfort than was his intention. He stopped talking and looked at her. She was quite evidently amused. He did not mind. He could not have suffered the indignity of having bored her.

After lunch they talked about the literary world and then adjourned to the lounge for coffee. Denton had to dart back in to the dining-room to retrieve the inscribed book, which in a state of blissful agitation he had left at their table. At half-past two, suspecting he was very probably outstaying his welcome, he said to Miss Sitwell that he ought to think of making a move.

'No, no, you can't go' she protested, 'Osbert said "wait for me till a quarter past three. I'll try to come if I possibly can." I'm sure he'll come; he's the one who really introduced me to your essay. He came into my room, sat down on the bed, and rolled about with laughter. He says he'll dance the minute he sees you, as Sickert did at the tea party.'[48]

When Osbert Sitwell arrived a moment or two later, the conversation took a faster and more gossipy turn. Denton was told that he should try and write more things along the same lines as his *Horizon* article. He rejoined that he didn't really know any other famous people, to which Osbert replied, ' "Well, it must be arranged." '

Finally he took his leave of Miss Sitwell and shared a taxi with her brother, dropping the latter off at his home in Chelsea. Denton went on to Edith Road and had tea with the Dallas sisters before making the return journey to Kent.

Although he waited until the next day before writing an account of the trip in his Journal, back at Pitt's Folly that night, as if drawing inspiration from his contact with a famous poet, Denton did manage to scribble down a few words, to put a seal on the experience. 'The nightingale sings;' he wrote, 'it tears open its throat and sinks through all the night. The moon shines—all is cold after the heat. I live, am growing older, ever-dying now.'[49]

As soon as a few copies of *Maiden Voyage* were available from the printers, Routledge's managing director, T. Murray Ragg, sent one off to Denton. It arrived two days after he had seen Edith Sitwell. In an accompanying letter Ragg at last was able to give a publication date—7th May.

It has often been stated that *Maiden Voyage* was 'sold out before publication.' Although the first edition of the book did indeed go very quickly, a correspondence between Denton and his publisher demonstrates that this had not been the case.

April 21st 1943

Dear Mr Ragg,

I was very pleased to have received the book, and I like the cloth cover and the printed spine very much.

A friend of mine wrote to the Book Society ordering a copy of the book, when it should appear. They wrote back to say that they could not supply one as *Maiden Voyage* was already reprinting and no date had been given for the reprint. Thinking that there had been some mistake, I wrote to them myself telling them that the book was not even published yet. I received this answer, 'we would inform you that *Maiden Voyage* is out of print before publication as all copies have been subscribed.'

Am I to take it that this is true, or are they still making some muddle? They seem so uncertain of their facts in both letters that I was almost inclined to believe it.

Miss Sitwell invited me to lunch last Monday and kept asking me when the book would appear so I think I will send her the copy directly. Her brother, Osbert, who came in afterwards wanted to know all about it too.

Yours sincerely,
Denton Welch.[50]

On 27th April Denton was informed that the Book Society had made 'a stupid mistake'; he was reassured that Routledge's sales manager would get in touch with the organization and put matters right. In a further letter Ragg was able to write:

> . . . The mystery is now solved. Unfortunately, a book of the same title, *Maiden Voyage* was published in 1939—also a first book—and is now out of print and reprinting. . . I am afraid that it is too late to do anything about this now by way of changing your title, but since the other *Maiden Voyage* is out of print and apparently likely to be so for some time, I do not think it's existence is likely to cause us much trouble.[51]

By now Denton's other five presentation copies had arrived; he made a list of the people he wished to send them to. Margot, Countess of Oxford and Asquith, Lord Berners and E.M. Forster all received *Maiden Voyage*, and each wrote a letter. Whereas Forster, and to a lesser extent Berners, produced the level of adulation and encouragement he was hoping for, Lady Oxford, who earlier had admonished him for mentioning the 'glistening white W.C.' in 'Sickert at St Peter's',[52] only managed to squeeze out a meagre note that confirmed his suspicions of her as being pompous and not really worth bothering about. 'I thank you for your book,' she wrote, 'I am not a good person to give books to! I am too severe in my criticisms. Nevertheless, I would be very pleased to have such praise as Edith Sitwell has given you in her "Foreword". Yours sincerely, Margot Oxford.'[53]

Edward Sackville-West at the B.B.C. and Sir Kenneth Clark, then Director of the National Gallery (and a great friend of Helen Roeder), were sent the book too, and Denton also either lent or gave copies to a couple of friends living locally whose opinion he valued: he knew that anything the artist Tom Hennell said would be sensitive and wholly honest, Mildred Bosanquet the same. On 18th May, she wrote telling him that she had liked the China episodes much better than those about Repton. With considerable insight into the complexity of Denton's character, Mrs Bosanquet added, 'I wonder if you feel most people are bogus somehow?'

By the end of May several reviews had appeared in the press. Perhaps the most prized of all was James Agate's in *The Daily Express*. Others that published notices were *The Observer*, *The Evening Post*, *The Birmingham Post*, *The Listener* and *New Statesman*.[54] Soon Denton received an invitation to lunch from Edward Sackville-West and on 27th May Edith Sitwell sent a letter saying that she could not remember another first book that had been so well received.

Since it was chiefly in writing and receiving letters that Denton kept in touch with the outside world, the high point of his day was very often the delivery of the morning post. Apart from copies of reviews and the occasional fan letter forwarded from Routledge, he now heard from several friends and acquaintances with whom he had lost contact in recent years. There was, for instance, a letter from his old house-master, Harold John Snape, who had retired from Repton to run a pub in north Devon, and another from a Tony Muspratt Williams, someone he had known in Shanghai. Both had enjoyed *Maiden Voyage*. In the middle of June Denton wrote to the artist Basil Jonzen (another fellow-pupil at St Michael's) thanking him for sending a congratulatory telegram. He continued the letter with a discussion of his current plans:

I am writing another book. I have really begun three! I don't know which will be finished first. I have been painting very little because of all this mad activity. I am now wondering what I shall do in the future—whether I shall paint chiefly to please myself, or whether I shall try to keep both things going almost equally. What do you feel about this? When you write, does painting fly out of the window, or can you hang on to it?[55]

It cannot be said that Denton followed Edith Sitwell's advice that his next book should be 'something rather more violent and vulgar' than *Maiden Voyage*. Although the earliest work done on his second novel had apparently coincided with (or possibly been inspired by) the arrival of her invitation to lunch,[56] the first exercise book devoted to *In Youth is Pleasure* bears the date 'April 20th 1943', the day after he had been to meet her at the Sesame Club. The book yet again portrays an exceedingly introverted adolescent, although here 'Orvil'[57] (easily identifiable as Denton, despite being referred to in the third person), is a slightly younger boy than in *Maiden Voyage*. The setting of *In Youth is Pleasure* is a large well-established hotel, where the affluent 'Mr Pym' and his three sons have come to stay towards the end of the summer holidays. Writing in his Journal in 1948 Denton confirms that the hotel was Oatlands, which is near Weybridge in Surrey and remains open to this day. The rather ramshackle red-brick house is on the site of a royal palace; Elizabeth I and her court used it on several occasions as a retreat during hunting expeditions or when there was some epidemic raging in London.

But from the architectural point of view, the most remarkable feature at Oatlands was the famous grotto, which by the time Denton went there, in about 1930, had fallen into a sorry state of disrepair. Built in 1747 for the 9th Earl of Lincoln, it had been one of the most elaborate follies of the age. The interior, with its three chambers, had walls encrusted with giant clams and other shells; artificial stalactites hung from the ceiling. The Duchess of York, who lived at Oatlands in the nineteenth century, would play with her dogs and monkeys in the grotto, and her deceased pets were buried in a little cemetery nearby.[58]

Almost as soon as Orvil has arrived at the hotel he makes off to explore the grounds. The grotto and its terraced gardens draw him like a magnet, the broken-down bat-ridden folly appealing to the teenager's already developed preoccupation with all things Gothick. It is this morbid place that is always lurking in the background. The curious setting colours the reader's attitude to all human contacts that subsequently occur in the book.

The following day, free to spend his time doing whatever he likes, Orvil wanders down to the nearby river. The scene is idyllic. 'Trees hung right over the water, making a thick green shade. . . The sun filtered through in round spots that trembled like jellyfish.'[59] Orvil lies down in the grass.

> After some time he heard the sound of distant singing. Gradually it grew nearer and he recognized it as the sea-shanty 'Rio Grande.' He waited expectantly, ready to back through the hedge if he did not like the look of the singers.
>
> Suddenly a scarlet canoe appeared round the bend of the river. It was paddled by a young man, and two boys about Orvil's age. They wore khaki shorts, and their chests and arms were brown as burnt sugar. Orvil saw the Adam's-apples rippling up and down their throats as they sang lustily. They were grinning and laughing and swearing at each other under cover of the song. One of the boys splashed the man wickedly, and the man called him to order by beating him with his wet paddle.[60]

Orvil longs to be part of this healthy outdoor life, so he goes to buy himself a bathing-slip and hires his own canoe.

It turns out that the man and the boys are camping in a wooden hut by the river; he is a schoolmaster working with an East End mission that organizes holidays for deprived children. Their camaraderie is irresistible to the shy Orvil, who in voyeuristic fashion spies on them whilst they have a meal in the open air.

It is more than likely that Denton's inspiration for the episodes of the schoolmaster and the boys originated in what he knew about the activities of the Repton Boxing Club, a charitable organization that still exists in Bethnal Green. It was a well-known scheme by which East End boys would gain instruction in 'the noble art' from representatives of the public school. A number of them would actually go up to Derbyshire and visit Repton.

In Youth is Pleasure presents a succession of colourful incidents associated with Orvil's stay at the hotel, and the scene of the master living in the hut is developed throughout the book, with Orvil returning there on two further occasions and getting into conversation with the man, who is now alone and is awaiting the next contingent of youths. Orvil accepts him as his confidant and pours out all his worries and frustrations. He ends up by giving the school-master a deeply moving account of the last time he saw his mother, when he had been at prep school.

Orvil lay back on the ground after this outburst and put his arm across his eyes. He didn't want the man to see any part of his face. He hated the man because he had talked to him.

The man was silent. He was playing with a dead leaf, poking holes in it with a little twig. At last he said: 'But you can't stop still at your mother's death.'

'Nobody wants to stop still,' shouted Orvil, jumping to his feet. 'I'm not going to stop still, I'm going now. That's all made up, what I told you; and you thought it was real!' He tried to jeer at the man.

'Shut up. Don't be a fool; of course it's real,' said the man, catching hold of Orvil's arm and jerking him sharply down to the ground again. 'Talk about this sensibly,' he said.

Orvil subsided close to the man, without saying anything more. He was submissive now but silenced. He felt that he could never speak again.[61]

In describing the inner pain he suffered as a teenager, Denton was giving vent to feelings that he had recently expressed in a letter to Alex Comfort: 'Early adolescence was to me what I can only describe as a sordid and fearful time,' he wrote, 'I was frightened of everything and everything seemed sullied and slimed over with this fear. It is only just lately—I am now twenty-six—that I have come to realize what an unpleasant time it was.'[62] It is this fear, so closely associated with the desperate loneliness and insecurity resulting from his mother's death that is central to Orvil's outlook on life too. The pain communicated in *In Youth of Pleasure* is only alleviated by the retreat into a world of aesthetic symmetry and Gothic reverie.

In contrast to the theme of Orvil's love for the open-air life, and his quirkily unboyish scale of values (we read of him purchasing a painted scent-bottle in a junk shop), Denton also underlines the degree to which the main character is ill at ease staying in the hotel, where conventional social behaviour is the order of the day. 'Charles' (based on his elder brother Bill), is made out to be the oppressive villain of the piece, humiliating him at every given opportunity. Even though Orvil is able to form a close friendship with a young married woman, 'Aphra',[63] this too is spoiled when one night he goes again to the grotto and stumbles across the two of them making love: one is left with the impression that they have desecrated his territory.

In the novel the spirit of Denton's mother is never far away. It is as if she exists as the paragon against which all other young women are inevitably compared. She alone was unsullied by sexual contact. In Denton's descriptions of young women as a whole, one has the feeling that, unless he knew a girl personally and liked her, he visualized her as being either lifeless or a potential whore. This tendency to view people in terms of one stereotype or another was a severe barrier when it came to forming relationships. There can be little doubt that Denton suffered from the trait.

The title *In Youth is Pleasure* is the refrain of a song from a masque by the Elizabethan Robert Wever.[64] The lines are included in *The Oxford Book of English Verse*. Denton quoted the second stanza in the frontispiece of his book (see illustration). Commenting on his choice of title shortly before the book went into production (the original typescript also bore the subtitle, 'A Fragment of Life Story with Changed Names', but this was omitted), he wrote to Mr Ragg at Routledge, explaining he had 'meant it to be mildly ironical, as the hero seems to find his own youth rather difficult at times.'[65]

One suspects that there was more to it than that. The dedication 'To Rosalind Bassett'—significantly his mother's *maiden* name—is deeply touching. *In Youth is Pleasure* describes a period when Denton was growing in the consciousness of his own individuality, and he included the devotion to the memory of his mother's death as being a very important aspect of this.

Although one does sense that the hero of the novel has gained some experience of life during the course of the story, the author seems almost to be revelling in a state of emotional retardation. The reader may warm to Orvil's fervid awareness of beauty, but it appears that Denton, perhaps taking his cue from Herbert Read's observation that preciosity was an inescapable facet of his personality, has here exploited the trait to an almost perilous degree. In writing *In Youth is Pleasure*, Denton knew full well he was producing something consciously self-indulgent.

It is not generally appreciated that although he went to considerable lengths to present a descriptively consistent setting for each of his stories, Denton was not above taking some experience or detail from one context and placing it in another. For instance, the hotel's 'pretty "Elizabethan" plaster lodge' bearing the date '1846', described at the beginning of Chapter Two in the novel, belongs not to Oatlands, but to Oxon Hoath, and there is a further connection with the Kentish estate in that it, too, lies no great distance from a river, the Medway—a place where Denton would frequently go to watch boys fishing, swimming or canoeing. When he was living at Hadlow Road, he thought of taking over an empty scout hut near the river and using it as a temporary studio.

On 3rd July, in the midst of writing *In Youth is Pleasure*, Denton was down at the lock gates near East Peckham admiring two boys taking turns at diving.

> Ginger disappeared into the long grass by a mound, and I caught glimpses of clothes being pulled into the air, and the sudden dead whiteness of his shoulders.
>
> He rushed out of the grass, dead pearly white except for his freckled face, with little, lumpy, rather over-developed stomach and pectoral muscles. A rather broken up, not pretty, surface fussiness. Different from his friend's smooth lazy-looking body.
>
> Pulling his mouth back and showing his teeth in a wild, mad, excited gesture, he rushed at the water and dived, going so deep and straight down that his legs almost turned a somersault.
>
> 'He dives too deep,' I said to the friend.
>
> 'Yes,' he said indulgently. Then, when Ginger came up spitting and gurgling, 'Get up on the board and do your dive!'
>
> 'I can't,' Ginger said with assumed babyishness, quavering, making his limbs tremble.

'You're a bleeding liar,' the friend said.

'You got to come too,' Ginger insisted.

'I'll go off the lower one; I hit my head last time,' said the first boy.

Ginger got on the top board, about eight or ten feet up, and dived again very deeply. The other boy shouted, 'Coo, you've hit the bottom, look at the mud.'

Ginger swore and said he hadn't. The other boy dived off the lower board quickly to get the ordeal over. Then they both swam about, talking and spitting and dragging their hair back. Ginger's hair now looked metallically shiny and yet dead at the same time.

At last they both came out of the water and sat down on the grass beside me. The first boy lay flat on his back and half shut his eyes. He looked charmingly coarse and young-animalish now, with thick brown neck, smooth arms and hairs round each brown-red nipple. Ginger turned his extremely white and knobbly back to me and almost bent over his friend, talking to him about his work, and how he had been late because he had been staying at home, pressing his trousers for the dance that night.[66]

Pleasures such as these were nothing more than diversions. Twelve days later Denton had 'a poetry bout on' and despite being genuinely gratified by Elizabeth Bowen's good review of *Maiden Voyage* in *The Tatler*,[67] could not save himself from writing about a sense of utter dejection—perhaps the result of dredging up painful memories associated with his adolescence. It seemed as though nothing had changed. If he set all the adulation aside, he was still the same alienated boy that he had written about in *In Youth is Pleasure*.

> The little rabbits die
> between the cruel jaws—
> And so must I,
> Behind closed doors—
> No one to love me
> No one to see
> What troubled me my whole life through
> So mightily.[68]

Chapter Eight

Eric Oliver

Denton always had an incurable fascination for people whom he considered to be 'phonies'. He cultivated their friendship, and then when their backs were turned would ridicule them to others. Whether it was because they pretended to be poorer than they actually were, or that they adopted airs and graces that he thought incongruous with their rightful station in life, he would sniff them out and delight in the knowledge. There was the industrial psychologist who posed as a savant of the publishing world (and yet his book 'that would change the world' remained unwritten);[1] there was the middle-aged amateur artist who had insinuated himself into Augustus John's household and had then proceeded to divest the painter of scores of his drawings that he conveniently considered to be cast-offs.[2] But, most of all, there was Monté. It was in the second week of August 1943, that Monté appeared, as if from nowhere. He had spotted May Walbrand-Evans at a bus stop and recognized her from the early days of the war as the artist who had kindly invited him in for a cup of tea when he had discarded his bicycle in her garden. At this second meeting he was soon regaling her with stories of how he had been a fighter pilot in the Battle of Britain, had been awarded the D.F.C. and was now a warrant-officer. It was his idea that she should paint his portrait, resplendent with uniform and medals. May, who was much taken with Monté, asked him along for coffee on 19th August and commandeered Denton too, so that he could meet this 'ravishing young man'.

In the event, he did not find May's description at all apt:

> I was called Denton in the first few seconds and almost patted on the back. I looked at the ravishing young man. This was certainly not the right description. He was saturnine, black, harsh-featured with thick waving hair and rather small square white teeth. Thick black hairs covered his arms and sprouted at the base of his throat. He wore an Italian shirt of white towelling, with chord lacing at the neck. His trousers were dirty blue corduroy, patched on one knee. He was rather tall and rather heavy looking, somehow not quite thin enough at the waist. He spoke with extreme exuberance, directness and simplicity in a slightly cockney accent. It was impossible not to respond to his friendliness.[3]

Monté claimed to have been at Tonbridge School and, as he was telling Denton about Italy and 'honourable capitulation' (being careful to use an aspirant 'h' in honourable), another person joined the party. Elizabeth Plummer was now nineteen and a student at the Slade; she lived a few hundred yards down the road with her widowed mother. Monté glanced at the newcomer and at once turned to Denton, saying ' "I think Elizabeth's very shy of me, I wish she wouldn't be." '4 Then it was back to his stories of the war and various other escapades. Eventually, Monté said it was time he was off to Sevenoaks, and Denton, who was quite mesmerized by the chap, decided to take his bicycle and follow him some of the way until he reached a suitable spot where he could have a picnic and get on with some work.

As they were cycling along the road in the summer heat, Monté told Denton that he was descended from the Sieur de Montaigne (in reality he was John Henry Bones and had been born in the East End of London5). He also confided in 'Den' that he had fallen for Miss Plummer.

' "What a nice person Elizabeth is; has she got any money?" '

' "No," ' said Denton. (He later reported to friends that he had given all the right answers.)6 Just before the two men parted, Monté, who was amused by his 'highbrow' companion, came out with, ' "oh, you're not going to write, you devil" ' and then in a quite disconnected way told him that he had been at Christ's, Cambridge, which to Denton, who was not quite sure of his colleges, sounded suspiciously bogus.

Within a few days Monté and Elizabeth were engaged. For some inexplicable reason Mrs Plummer hurried along the union at a relentless pace, refusing to ask any of the pertinent questions about the young man and his circumstances. Much to Denton's horror, Monté took it for granted that he would be best man at the wedding. He told Denton rather unflatteringly that he reminded him of a pilot in the R.A.F., whom they had nicknamed 'Louise'. This Louise would wear satin pyjamas and was very fastidious about dirt.

' "He was very brave, you know, and very cruel," ' said Monté. ' "You're brave and cruel Denton, aren't you?" '7

Very soon cracks began to appear in Monté's stories, and yet the marriage was to take place within a week or two in a registry office by special licence. Monté, obviously desperate for money, tried to sell Denton a typewriter, and May felt she had to lock her doors, for fear of being burgled. On 3rd September things came to a head. As Denton and May were talking the matter over in her house, they saw a man walking up the drive towards Denton's cottage. It was a detective. He showed them photographs of Monté and asked them if they knew him. The inspector wanted to know what Monté had told them about himself. They both realized that he was in serious trouble.

The next morning Denton heard from May that there had been a dreadful scene at the Plummers' house the previous evening, with the police paying a visit shortly after Monté had shown Elizabeth the wedding-ring. Two plain clothes officers confronted him and read a warrant for his arrest. When the time came for him to be taken away, he became so violent that they had to call on three Newfoundland soldiers to restrain him.8

Following a trial, Monté was sentenced to three months hard labour for masquerading as a warrant-officer, a grave offence in time of war. He wrote to

Elizabeth from prison, asking for her forgiveness, and obviously hoping to take up with her again after his release, but not surprisingly she would have none of it. He then wrote another letter putting a curse on her![9]

The court case reached the headlines of the local newspapers and was also reported in *The News of the World*,[10] with both May's and Mrs Plummer's gullibility being laid bare before the public. Denton, much to his relief, was not called as a witness. He hated to think of Monté facing the degradation of being treated as a common criminal and was torn between being shocked by the enormity of the lies and a feeling of sympathy for such a likeable rogue. (Monté, a highly talented mechánic, spent much of the rest of his life along the same lines, and his illusions of grandeur frequently got the better of him. He was never able to apply himself to hard work and would spend most of his time pursuing women and dreaming of what might have been had his father not worked on a farm.)

Denton left a full account of the affair in his Journals and later worked it up into what is perhaps his most brilliant extended short story, 'Brave and Cruel'.[11] That he should have chosen Monté's off-the-cuff description is certainly revealing; it indicates a deep self-knowledge. Denton *was* brave in his determination to put his handicap behind him and lead as normal a life as possible, and he was cruel in that he never hesitated to note down other people's foibles and shortcomings of character (and turn these to good advantage in his writings).

A short time after the business with Monté had quietened down and his life had returned to some semblance of normality, Denton found himself in a position to write yet again about an unusual episode he had witnessed, only this time his victim, rather than being a working-class man, was a titled lady from one of the most exalted families in the land. On 2nd October, an invitation from the poetess Dorothy Wellesley, later Duchess of Wellington, arrived at Pitt's Folly Cottage, asking if he would care to' attend a Poetry Reading in Tunbridge Wells the next day.

Omitted from the purportedly complete edition of the Journals, published by Allison & Busby in 1984,[12] Denton's irresistibly amusing description of the outing opens with him boarding a bus for Tunbridge Wells. He arrives in the genteel town and soon spots Peggy Mundy-Castle alone in a tea-shop near The Pantiles. Clad in Donegal tweeds, grey pleated shirt and a thin khaki tie, Denton goes in to meet his friend and the two of them then set off for the hall where the event is to take place. After showing his invitation card to a perhaps slightly illiterate attendant (Lady Wellesley had scrawled some special instructions on the back), he chooses a seat fairly far up on the left, but then realizing that Peggy's is at the back, he gives it up and joins her.

At five o'clock Vi Sackville-West, looking long-nosed, 1924 bobbed-hair a little frizzy, cold, very English country dowdy not-quite-brown tweed skirt and not-quite-red jersey, with long rather delicate legs, got up to say that: Lady Wellesley had at first thought that she might not be able to appear, owing to the death in action of her nephew, the Duke of Wellington, but that she had decided after all that public duty should take precedence over private sorrow and so she had decided that she would appear.

This little speech delivered in a cold, rather Lady de Burghish deadness with that blank, completely unreceptive, eye. One rather felt against this stuffed Vi.

Then the reading began. Shane Leslie, bald in battle-dress, came onto the platform and began to read a piece of his 'Epic of Jutland' and then Rudyard Kipling's 'Mine Sweepers'. The stage was appalling. Two terrible Japanese screens and a lamp had been borrowed from a shop. The poets read off a box covered in red plush.

Shane Leslie told an anecdote in a boring way of how his uncle in India was one of the first to see Kipling's *Plain Tales of the Hills*. He sent them to the *Daily Telegraph*, who said that they were excellent, but not quite up to the standard of their paper. Everyone laughed.

After Shane Leslie there was a pause, because Louis MacNeice had not turned up. Ruth Pitter came on at last and declaimed with artificial gestures, but very sweetly, her 'Lament for the Handless'. One somehow took to her very much, whimsy gestures and all. Her curious black velvet cow-pat hat was somehow endearing too. After this one poem, which she recited by heart, sometimes using different words to the printed ones, she seemed to disappear for good. I was sorry.

Another poet, Peter Yates, had not turned up also, so someone read, I think, C. Day Lewis.

Then Clinton Baddeley, in a very heavy, rather thrilling voice, read a poem by Lady Wellesley. It rolled out well, professional, making the other speakers seem scratchy and messy. He looked rather nice too, brownish, nice strong neat grizzly hair, old-young, rather particularly male, especially when he said, 'the candle, manly and erect' (Lady Wellesley always seems to be speaking in these phallic symbols).

After this, Vita did something of her own and one began to like her more—to feel that there was something rather nice and sad and quite quiet and feeling beneath the stiff English horse shell.

In the interval I went to the man at the door and asked him to find Mrs— for me, for she was the woman who was going to introduce me to Lady Wellesley. Just as the man was going to find her, Lady Wellesley herself, with another mousier older woman came into the vestibule and dilly-dallied, as if they could not make up their minds whether to go outside or stay in.

The man, pressing my arm rather urgently, said, 'just a minute', and leant right across me towards them. He seemed very nervous and solicitous about something; I guessed that this woman must be Lady Wellesley, although I did not know for certain. She carried a studio stick with an agate top, was dressed in frumpish black, had one of those rather corpsy, dumpish figures, which seem to have too fat a back. Her face was blotchy, mottled under powder, and the hair was screwed up into a curious, rather 'helped', fair colour. Something tantrummy, druggy, and petulant hung about her. I hoped she was not Lady Wellesley.

I could not hear what the man was saying to her, but at last he left her and went to the stage door. Then he beckoned me.

Clinton Baddeley, who had been looking in my direction quite a lot in the interval, with a piercing, worried, interesting look, got up quickly from his seat and went through the stage door before me. I stood in a dark passage and waited. Mrs— bustled up to me and said, 'Oh, you're Mr Welch, aren't you? I'll go and fetch Lady Wellesley.'

When she left me I was alone for a moment with Clinton Baddeley in the passage. He came closer and there was a difficult silence in which we both, I think, wanted to say something, but didn't. The light caught his cheekbones. His face had good bone formation, and good smooth shiny brown skin. I saw that his suit was rough and hairy like mine.

Suddenly Shane Leslie appeared behind me and said, after staring at me, 'Now what are you? Have you come to help us out? I'm sure you're a poet—you look like one. Here we are, short of living poets. Can't you get up on the stage and do something for us?'

'Oh no,' I said nervously, 'I can't.'

'I'm sure you look like a poet; a lost poet,' said Shane Leslie, putting his hand on my arm. I wanted to say, 'Not so much of the lost', but of course did not.

Clinton Baddeley again seemed about to talk, when the door opened and Mrs— brought back the woman I had seen in the vestibule. There was very little expression as she held out her hand to me and said perfunctorily, 'How are you?' I got more and more the feeling that she too was a modern Lady de Burgh. The mottled face and the queer yellow hair added to the illusion. Mrs— was trying to make things smooth. Lady Wellesley said, 'I haven't yet had time to read your book. I must let you know what I think of it when I have.'

'Is it your first book?' said Mrs—, who I suppose must be the sort of quiet female toady companion. I liked her. I nodded my head. 'Very interesting', she added.

I said something about Edith Sitwell and immediately Lady Wellesley pricked up her ears and said, 'Oh—where is Edith now? At Renishaw with her brother, I suppose.' This led to a talk about the Poetry Readings in London. 'I read at the second', Lady Wellesley said truculently and sharply.

I longed to say, 'Yes, we all know that at the first you fell down drunk and then sat down when the Queen came in, so that you had to be taken back to your hotel, where you wept on the steps outside for a long time.' Osbert had told me all this as anonymous scandal, but I knew that it was Lady Wellesley.

The meeting was so sticky, stupid, meaning nothing. 'At any rate, we got you over here,' said Lady Wellesley. 'The audience is bad; there aren't nearly enough people.'

'Oh, I think the hall is nearly full,' I said placatingly.

Lady Wellesley turned to the other speakers and poets. 'If only all you others would go out in front and swell the audience, instead of hiding back here—', she said. No one answered. I said, 'I must be going back to my seat, I expect the interval is nearly up.' Mrs— murmured, 'Yes.' We all melted away. Lady Wellesley stumped off. I felt her feet were stumps for some reason. I went back to Peggy and we listened to Vita and then Lady Wellesley. She ended her poem on a shout. Shane Leslie stood on the platform with her for some reason, looking anxious. I began to think that she might be mildly tight, which would explain her curious, dead meeting with me.

'She's tight,' I said to Peggy. We giggled. It probably wasn't true.

Vita's recitation grew nicer and nicer. Towards the end people began to leave the hall in batches. Soon there were bald mangy patches in the audience. The utter incompetent dreariness of the whole thing was brought home to me and I felt that the poets should have felt ashamed to take part in such a squalid show.[13]

Much to Denton's satisfaction, interest in *Maiden Voyage* was undiminished and he had every reason to think of himself as a rising star in the literary firmament. The Readers Union was considering the possibility of bringing out its own edition of the novel, and on 22nd July, a month before the Monté affair, Denton recorded in his Journal that he had 'just heard Viola Garvin cracking my book up on the wireless—saying that Edith Sitwell had laid hands on my head like a priestess blessing a young neophyte or something'.[14] Not only was Routledge poised to reprint, but the firm was making some effort to find an American publisher as well. The initial feelers, however, were not promising; on 2nd November Ragg sent Denton a letter explaining that, owing to the war, only two per cent of new British titles were now being published in the United States, and so far his firm had approached Putnam, Knopf and Macmillan, but none wanted to take *Maiden Voyage*.

Although the role of the writer is, of necessity, a solitary one, Denton more than most had developed a particular way of life that left little room for serious relationships. Referring to an encounter with a 'superior-voiced soldier' the previous year, he had written

. . . I can never be true friends with anyone except distant women—far away. For I wish for communion with the inarticulate and can only fray and fritter with the quick. . . Yet I love myself and my own company so much that I would not even ask the soldier to come in for fear of his becoming a regular visitor. I even feel that people pollute my house who come into it.[15]

And it is true that the only persons that he now saw at all regularly were three middle-aged ladies: Evie, of course, May Walbrand-Evans and, to an increasing extent throughout 1943, Noël Adeney. Mrs Adeney's link with Denton—they first met whilst he was living at The Hop Garden—had been that she was the sister-in-law of his friend Ellen Easdale; in the 1930s she had built a holiday home close to the Easdales in Crouch, a small village neighbouring Platt. Noël Adeney wrote to Denton in September 1942, congratulating him on the Sickert article—and the friendship between them dated from then.[16] No doubt impressed by the rumours of his association with Edith Sitwell, one could describe it as being the attraction of a slightly lurid-minded and sometimes melodramatic older woman for a young, highly talented and, as she perceived him to be, vulnerable homosexual.

The incongruous pair did, however, share various interests. Mrs Adeney was a solidly accomplished artist, having studied at the Slade from 1910 to 1915, after which she had worked as a dress designer. Augustus John's celebrated portrait of the cellist Madame Suggia apparently shows the sitter wearing one of her creations. Noël Gilford, as she then was, had met Bernard Adeney, also an artist, in 1918 and following their marriage she took up painting again and exhibited as a member of the London Group.

From the earliest days Denton was very much in two minds whether or not he really liked 'Fringie', as he nicknamed her. Nevertheless, he could appreciate that she was well-read, that she had an impressive knowledge of porcelain and, what was perhaps more relevant, that unquestionably she could be of use to him. He liked to think he was in control of the relationship. The only price he had to pay was to take her into his confidence. As they came to know one another better, she would press him to reveal as much as possible about his homo-sexuality and, more especially, about his illness, neither of which Denton thought were any of her business. She was determined that he should regard her as his confidante, the one person who understood him. But whilst Denton almost taunted her to dig deeper into his personality, he would repulse her when she did so. She wanted to see him as being the apotheosis of the 'doomed artist'; he resolutely refused to co-operate.

When Noël Adeney was away in London (the family had a house in Hampstead) they would keep in touch by letter. By the autumn of 1943, she had become his most regular correspondent and it was in a postcard of 6th November that Denton told her he had just been introduced to 'a hearty landboy', a new friend of Francis Streeten's. The landboy's name was Eric Oliver. As things turned out, Eric was to become Denton's most devoted friend and companion—and the object of Mrs Adeney's most profound jealousy. In the Journal one reads a full description of how Eric and he had first met:

> . . . I was ill in bed with high temperature and terrible headache. Noël and May had been sitting in my room half killing me with their talk. Just as they had left and I was trying to simmer down, I heard voices below and then Francis talking to Evie. I had told her not to let anyone else upstairs, but as the minutes dragged on and I still heard the talking, I shouted out, 'Francis, I'm ill in bed. What is it?'

Evie answered, telling me that Francis had arrived with a friend and could they both come up for a minute. I consented and saw, walking into the room after fat Francis, someone in green battle-dress trousers, Wellingtons, and a jersey and white shirt, open, also white tops of pants showing above the trousers, large leather belt, face red-brown, with very good throat.

This person looked at me in the bed and Francis said babyishly, 'Oh, this is Eric, I've brought him to see you.'

I felt so ill that I couldn't entertain them properly. I tried to be very bright; but it was an awful strain. They had been drinking in a pub and had come on to me later. They were still mildly redolent of the pub and beer. They talked a little wildly.

When they left, Eric turned at the door and gave me a long sharp look. 'Why don't you get up and come and have a drink with us?' he had asked the moment before. Now he knew I was ill and he was sorry and he liked me.[17]

Although nearly fifty years had elapsed, Eric too retained a vivid memory of the day:

I had met Francis Streeten when I was working for the land army. I hadn't known him for long when, one rainy day—it was too wet to work—he came up to me and asked in his rather squeaky voice, 'Would you like to meet a friend of mine?'. I seem to remember we were working at East Farleigh and we got onto trains and buses and eventually came to Pitt's Folly near Tonbridge, where Denton lived. Francis really hadn't told me anything about Denton beforehand. And first of all Miss Sinclair opened the door and said that Denton couldn't see anybody, because he was upstairs and wasn't alright; and then he must have changed his mind, because he called us back and that was the first time I saw him.

I didn't think of him being ill. I just thought that I had never seen anybody like him before. I knew at once he was something out of the ordinary. Yes, I was interested in Denton right from the word go, although I don't think I was physically attracted towards him.[18]

Eric Oliver also could be described as being 'something out of the ordinary', but for entirely different reasons. The fifth of six children—there were three older brothers—he was the odd man out in the respectable middle-class family. Ill at ease with any kind of authority, Eric had hated school and Mr Oliver, who owned a small factory that manufactured jewellery-cases and died three weeks before his youngest son's twenty-first birthday, had been very concerned about his future. Of the different jobs Eric tried, only farming was at all congenial. A career in the Army lasted just eighteen months (Eric was in the Pay Corps), after which he was perhaps tactfully 'excused' on account of high blood pressure; his war work continued with the land army in Kent.

Eric's ambition always was to lead as uncomplicated a life as possible. He preferred to spend most of his time alone. The trouble was that in his twenties he frequently allowed himself to be led astray by older friends and, aside from trying to commit suicide by taking two hundred aspirin tablets, he had generally drunk a good deal more than was good for him.

On the face of it, one wonders how such a person, with whom Denton would appear to have had very little in common, could have come to be accepted as his closest friend and companion. The contrast in their looks, for instance, were extreme. Denton, though well-proportioned, was small in height, had tiny feet and walked with a slight limp. He had rather 'doggy' eye-teeth, restless, darting eyes, a high and aristocratic forehead with unusual tightly-curled dark auburn hair[19] and ears that turned down at the top. Despite this unflattering description, there was something complete about his appearance and people who knew him have said that in his own way he was good-looking.

Eric, on the other hand, had strong and handsome features. Not only could he boast 'a good neck', but his overall physique was muscular and well-developed. The face was dominated by a Roman nose that has been compared to the Duke of Wellington's. Even at twenty-nine, his age when they first met, Eric's light blue eyes were surrounded by lines. Denton noted that his looks could change more than any other person he had known. Totally lacking in vanity regarding his appearance and clothes, to the outsider Eric appeared to be a normal, healthy young man.

But apart from the very obvious physical attraction, Denton soon discovered that his new friend was highly sensitive, acutely observant of other people's personalities and, above all, intensely insecure. As such, Eric posed no threat to him. A wonderful gentleness and an inability to intrude upon another person's thoughts or way of life were qualities that Denton came to value highly as the friendship deepened.

Just a fortnight after the first unpromising meeting Eric, who was then living at lodgings in Maidstone, received a letter. 'I thought it was very young writing,' he remembered, 'and I wondered who it could be from. It was from Denton, asking me to have tea with him. I was surprised to get it and rather curious.'[20] He duly made the journey to Pitt's Folly Cottage the following Sunday and the two of them got on well, with Eric telling Denton quite a few stories about his background—some of them hair-raising.

There was also some sexual contact between them, though this aspect of the relationship quickly fizzled out and Eric Oliver later denied quite firmly that he and Denton were ever 'lovers', at least in the sense of being sexual partners. What is more, he hardly found the description flattering, especially since Denton had to use a plastic sheet in bed so as to cope with his incontinence. In short, it was Denton who was physically attracted to Eric, but not *vice versa*. Despite at first being upset by Eric's lack of response, Denton soon came to accept the reality of the situation and things were left at that.

Cynical by nature, Eric had often thought in retrospect that Denton very probably had another strong motive for befriending him. He believed Denton knew quite well that his health would deteriorate and that eventually he would need someone on hand to tend to his needs—someone rather more sympathetic than Evie Sinclair. Although there may well be an element of truth in this, as is perfectly clear from the numerous highly-charged emotional letters he wrote, Denton was in fact very deeply in love with Eric.[21]

All this attention had the effect of making Eric feel rather guilty—he worried that he was using Denton. He tried constantly to analyse his own motives, but to little avail; Eric could not admit to himself that he was sympathetic and caring and that Denton loved him almost entirely for his rare combination of delicate sensitivity and manly good looks.

The friendship progressed on a fairly even keel until Christmas of 1943 and as likely as not it was Denton's infatuation with his new friend that rendered Henry Treece's rejection of the story 'When I was Thirteen' fairly insignificant.

'When I was Thirteen',[22] certainly one of Denton's most consistently admired short stories, caused quite a controversy when it came out. Treece received the manuscript right at the end of November, but deemed it 'too amoral for publication' in the periodical *Kingdom Come*.[23] On the 17th, making use of one of the Christmas cards he had designed (with a cockerel crowing out 'Nowell, Nowell!' from the top of a brick wall and himself snuggled up cosily in a sleeping-bag underneath—see colour illustration), Denton wrote to the somewhat prudish poet that Cyril Connolly had taken the story for *Horizon*. 'I have just finished my new short book,' he informed Treece, then could not resist adding, 'I wonder if you'd think it very sexy.'[24]

The setting of 'When I was Thirteen' is a skiing holiday he had spent in Switzerland in the company of his elder brother. Denton had been thirteen in 1928, when he was still a pupil at St Michael's. Bill was up at Oxford. Denton tells how his brother (who is unnamed in the story) would go off for the day with his own friends, leaving him alone in the hotel to devote his time to reading and enjoying the various domestic comforts on offer.

It is in the hotel—he probably had the skiing resort of Wengen in mind—that Denton meets a fellow undergraduate of his brother's.

> He had broad shoulders, but was not tall. He had a look of strength and solidity which I admired and envied. He had rather a nice pug face with insignificant nose and broad cheeks. Sometimes, when he was animated, a tassel of fair, almost colourless hair would fall across his forehead, half covering one eye. He had a thick beautiful neck, rather meaty barbarian hands, and a skin as smooth and evenly coloured as pink fondant.[25]

In the story the young man is called 'Archer', the identical surname that is used for 'Jim' in 'The Fire in the Wood'—a name that for Denton symbolized strength and virility, as well as having the rustic association he found so appealing.

Archer and Denton get to know one another after striking up a faintly improbable conversation about literature: the young man is reading the auto-biography of the weirdly fey Queen Marie of Roumania, whereas Denton has precociously tackled Tolstoy's *Resurrection*. At something of a loose end, the undergraduate invites Denton to go on a skiing trip with him the next day.

They set off early and Archer shows a protective concern for his young companion. In the rest-house at the summit of their ascent he gives Denton strong coffee to revive him (which Denton hates), pieces from his own bar of chocolate and, whilst they are finishing off their packed lunch, as the author narrates, he 'then began to skin pigs of tangerine very skilfully and hand them to me on his outstretched palm, as one offers a lump of sugar to a horse.'[26]

Not particularly adept on his skis, Denton falls into a deep snowdrift as they are speeding down the slope. Archer picks him up and brushes the snow from his clothes. When they have returned to the town Denton goes back to his friend's quarters—a sort of annexe to the hotel—for a bath. That evening they have dinner together. Denton gets rather drunk and spends the night in Archer's rooms, since he is not in a fit state to look after himself.

On the doorstep of his hotel the following morning Denton meets up with his brother, who has been on a skiing trip. He is asked where he has been. It is Archer who offers an explanation. A few moments later Bill accompanies Denton to his room; he sees the bed has not been slept in. Still feeling a little sick from drinking too much the night before, the thirteen-year-old has put his face in cold water. To his utter amazement, his brother, with surprising violence, holds his head under and starts hitting his backside. Denton frees himself, but Bill, still violent, corners him, 'yelling in a hoarse, mad, religious voice, "Bastard, Devil, Harlot, Sod!" '[27]

The implication, of course, is that he thought Denton had acquiesced to a seduction, whereas in fact the whole business had been merely one of a young man treating a teenager as if he were his brother, or at worst his girl-friend. Although the hero-worship of Archer with its undertones of homosexuality is quite plainly the theme of the story (though not perhaps its message, which is more concerned with the unreasonable stigma attached to such a relationship), the descriptive content is kept wholly clean and innocent, since Denton portrays the undergraduate as being a friendly, affectionate, uncomplicated and rather charming companion.

The story's publication in April 1944 was yet another feather in Denton's cap, and yet nothing, not even the achievement of literary recognition, nor the exciting new experience of his friendship with Eric, could postpone an inevitable deterioration in his health. Dr Tuckett, who incidentally saw him quite rarely, now said that he should think in terms of seeing a specialist at half-yearly intervals. In recent months Denton had been forced to spend a day or two in bed nearly every fortnight and his high temperature attacks were becoming increasingly frequent. In an otherwise newsy letter to Noël Adeney of 7th December, he revealed that he was well aware things were changing for the worse. 'I hate falling to bits,' he wrote, 'it is so repulsive.' One suspects that the great disparity between Eric's robustness and his own increasing frailty served to heighten this feeling.

He hoped his new friend would provide a pleasant diversion at Christmas. Denton sent a letter inviting Eric over for lunch on Christmas Day if he thought he was going to be free. Evidently, there was no reply. When the day came and Evie had 'made a nice meal with make-believe turkey, soup and plum-pudding'[28] and there was no Eric, Denton started to get agitated. A telephone call hailed him to the main house, but it was only Rosemary Mundy-Castle, Peggy's daughter. Not wishing his Christmas to fall completely flat, Denton asked her over for coffee. When he got back inside the cottage he found Eric there waiting for him.

I took him upstairs and sat him down at the table. I told him how late it was, and that we had begun to eat. He bowed his head on his knee and groaned. It was quite real. He held on to one of my hands and didn't speak.

'I thought someone else was going to be here, and I couldn't face them, so I got up a little Dutch courage on the way.'

I smiled at him and said, 'A good lot, I should think. Now begin to eat; you're about two and a half hours late.'

'I'm not drunk,' he said in an affronted, bewildered voice.

Again his hair was sticking out in a bush and he wore an old thick jersey, and grey flannels tucked into Wellingtons. . . .

He hardly drank his soup, continually stopping to fix me with his eye and ask why my invitation was not more explicit. . . The whole letter was cold and unsatisfactory. He was angry about it. I wasn't a true friend. I was cold and ungenerous.

'Oh, Eric, you're like a child,' I said, worried and exasperated.

Again he looked deep, deep into me and seemed to be floating in a mist and a cloud; then he brought out in a voice which was a curious mixture of clearness and stutter, 'Denton, you're just talking for the sake of talking.'

I felt snubbed, for some reason. I poured out the Algerian wine, which Eric had opened badly. I poured out the dark wine and we drank it. It was like iron water.[29]

The atmosphere lightened when Rosemary Mundy-Castle appeared, 'a little Christmas merry from drinks'. She had never met Eric before and at once they got on well together. One senses Denton becoming slightly jealous. The three of them sat on the floor in front of the fire, and later on, after supper, they bicycled along to The Rose and Crown, the pub just a few hundred yards down the main road. When the time came for Rosemary to return to Cage Farm, she asked Eric if he would accompany her some of the way. Denton was annoyed and suspicious.

Eric did not return until after midnight—one suspects that he had spent most of the time in another pub. He was in a terrible state.

He began to pour out all that had happened and all his own troubles and shortcomings. He poured it all over me and I just sat back in the chair and listened and watched. Then suddenly I began to cry. Everything seemed so frightfully muddled and stupid and sad, and utterly hopeless.

Eric understood. We were terribly morbid and gloomy and felt that
we were both going to die.[30]

In all these early meetings and escapades with Eric, which are so graphically
recorded in the Journal, it is clear that Denton saw his friend as a poignant
figure; naive, otherwordly and lost. He took it upon himself to comfort him and
to make his life more interesting and purposeful. Each of them was obsessed
with death—it was something embedded in their psyches—and the obsession
itself became an unusual spiritual bond. In the moments when Denton faced the
ghastly limitations of his own life, he found that Eric was the ideal person to talk
to. His sympathy was instinctive. In some ways he had much lower expectations
of life himself, never thinking that he would live to be very old. Denton gives an
insight into their spiritual affinity in the description of a winter picnic they had
in a field during February 1944. Uncharacteristically, this time it was Denton
who was the worse for drink.

It seems unbearably sad now to think of that picnic, so unsuitable for
the time of year, so lost in the wood and in time and with only two tiny
points of humanity to remember it. It strikes at me and bites for some
reason whenever I think of it. . . .

There we sat and knelt, smoking our pipes. I knew I would remember
it afterwards and always. It was too sad to forget. And there was a lovely
quality too, because of the drink and the wood and our hunger for the nice
food.

Eric saw how sad I was and he kissed me and lay down on the ground
and shut his eyes. We both felt then, I think, how doomed we were, how
doomed everything was. We saw very clearly the plain tragedy of our lives
and of everybody's.[31]

There were perhaps also more specific reasons why Denton had been feeling
so low. At the beginning of January Henry Treece had responded to the pro-
vocative Christmas card by virtually accusing him of misusing his talents: he
considered that to produce a story dealing in a self-indulgent manner with
homosexuality was verging on the callous, given the then current circumstances
of the war. Treece thought that a conscientious writer should be concerning
himself with more serious matters. Never was Denton moved to defend himself
more strongly than in his reply of 4th January:

I think you imagine that I am out of the war and away from the
horrible crimes against humanity which you mention because I am a
conscientious objector, who, by some legal miracle, is allowed to live a life
of ease, completely unmolested.

I am reluctant to explain myself to anyone who has proved so
insolent and unstable; but, so that there shall be no more misunderstanding
on this point, I shall tell you that I have complete military exemption *only*

on account of my health, which was shattered in a very serious road accident when I was nineteen [sic]. My spine was fractured and there were many other injuries. I leave you to guess whether life has been made any easier, or not, as a result. . .

And on the 8th evidently in answer to a more conciliatory letter, Denton chose to give Treece a spirited defence of his artistic and moral credo. As such, it is virtually unique.

> I would be the first to admit a lack of robustness in the subject matter and the treatment of my stories; and in some moods I regret this lack very much. But I bitterly resent being attacked on this score; it seems so pointless and mean. I am what I am and there the matter must remain.
>
> It really has been horribly difficult, all through childhood and adolescence, resisting the pokes and prods of parents, guardians, brothers and even friends. And now that I am independent I absolutely refuse to cloak what transparency and honesty remain in me in conventional cloaks of heartiness, sophistication, irony and satire, which most people seem to find so useful.
>
> I am conscious of the embarrassing qualities of my stories (so easy to guise effectively), but it would be dishonest of me to write in a more adroit and worldly-wise way. Perhaps it is wrong-headed of me to write of what I do, as I do, at this particular moment in the world's history, but it is certainly not mere frivolity or exhibitionism that prompts me. If this were the case, then the embarrassments, difficulties and misunderstandings caused by *Maiden Voyage* alone, would have cured me long ago. I am quite prepared to make myself appear ridiculous if in the process I gain experience as a writer. This is the thing I want most.[32]

One realizes in reading this that Denton's quest for his *own* truth was the paramount priority in his work. Helen Roeder recalled him speaking on the subject:

> Once he said to me, 'If you think life is a work of art, you'd want it to be a good work of art, wouldn't you?' and that he'd want to tell the truth, the absolute truth. He did try to tell the truth about his motives and everybody else's, and I think you couldn't ascribe motives to Denton that he hadn't got. On the other hand, people didn't always understand his own code of morals, which were rather splendid in a way. He had great courage and passionate artistic integrity.[33]

Nowhere are these qualities more evident than in his final autobiographical novel, *A Voice Through a Cloud*,[34] which deals with the trauma of the accident. The fair copy of the manuscript has the date 'January 11th 1944' inside the cover of the first exercise book, thus indicating, significantly, that Denton started work on it only three days after writing the second letter to Treece. On 16th January he reported to Noël Adeney that he was finding the book 'agonizing to write'.

The unrelenting intensity of *A Voice Through a Cloud* is in quite a different category to anything he had previously attempted and one can appreciate how draining it must have been to have worked day after day on the episodes dealing with his harrowing experiences in hospital, the more so since he was aware of the recent decline in his health. Writing to Eric on 14th May Denton described the difficulties he still experienced in coming to terms with the lasting effects of his injuries:

> I have also had to tell you things about my accident which never cease to give me pain, humiliation, embarrassment. I can't tell anyone hardly about these things and I've tried to go on from day to day pretending to everyone that I'm really perfectly alright—it puts a pretty good strain on me and I sometimes feel fit to bust [or burst]. The fact that I used to be so hardy and free from all that sort of thing makes my present messed-up state very hard to bear with good grace; it's given my conceit and pride a smack which it won't ever forget. . .

Not everything, though was quite so gloomy at this time. On 29th December Denton had written to Herbert Read with the news that *In Youth is Pleasure* was just back from the typist and that Edward Sackville-West was reading it through for him. He also let slip the fact he had posted a carbon copy off to John Lane of The Bodley Head to enter the novel for a competition. In his reply Read advised him that it was possible this could cause a delay in Routledge's publication of the book, and so Denton hastily wrote to Lane saying it might have to be withdrawn. As soon as the original typescript was returned, Denton sent it to Herbert Read, mentioning that Sackville-West had liked *In Youth is Pleasure*, had read it 'at one stretch' . . . but had advised him 'not to publish such a book'.[35]

On 17th January Herbert Read himself gave Denton his first impressions of the novel. To a great extent he was in agreement with Sackville-West's cautionary verdict.

> I have read your new book with the greatest possible interest. There can be no question that it fully maintains the brilliant qualities which distinguished your first book and any reservations that we may have are not strictly speaking of a literary or critical kind, nor for my part are they in any sense ethical. I confess to a certain disappointment in that it is a continuation of the theme of your first book and does not yet show your ability to go beyond the autobiographical medium. But the real trouble —and here I agree with Sackville-West, is one which is personal to you and one which you must decide. The picture of the hero you present is one which most people will find perverse and even unpleasant, and however unjust this may be it will undoubtedly affect the attitude of the public to your future work. I would suggest, therefore, that you give this consideration very careful thought, and if you are still of a firm and settled opinion

that you would like to proceed with the publication of the book we on our part are perfectly willing to agree. It may be that in the interests of the sales of the book two or three phrases may need amendment or deletion; but this is a question which need not raise any real difficulties.

Please let me know what you think about these reactions of mine, which are fully shared by my colleagues here. Incidentally, I would say that your ability to write quite objectively is indicated by your portrait of the scoutmaster, which seems to me quite the most vivid and substantial piece of writing you have yet done.

Yours sincerely,
Herbert Read

Denton had no reservations whatever in wanting the publication of his book to go ahead.[36] Aside from being rather pressed for money (the Readers Union had recently offered what he considered to be a paltry advance of £20 for their edition of *Maiden Voyage*), he had no intention of letting all the hard work on the novel go to waste. What is more, Denton was uncertain how much longer he would be able to continue writing. He replied to Read's letter at once.

. . . I suppose no one likes being labelled (the labels never seem really to fit the particular case) and I agree with you in thinking that many people after reading this book would like to stick a label on me and then dismiss me as not to be taken seriously.

If publishing this book prejudiced people against reading any quite different books I may write in the future, I should be sorry; but I feel that on the whole I must probably take this risk.

What I wanted to show in this small book was the secret, lonely life of an adolescent boy, quite different to his life on the surface with other people. I suppose in writing of this hidden life I have stressed his quirks and oddities. Of course, he does not seem particularly bizarre or unpleasant to me, but I am quite willing to believe that he might appear so to other people.

If you feel that in spite of this, enough interest attaches to the book to make it worth publishing, *I should like you to do so.* I think that I must not concern myself too much with other people's reactions. If I consider the effect I am producing, I shall get completely bogged. It seems to me that I really ought not to mind too much.

Edward Sackville-West also regretted the fact that I seemed to break no new ground. This was one of his chief complaints. But I think the time is not quite ripe for that yet. I still seem to write naturally only in this vein. . .[37]

Amidst the continuing chaos of his relationship with Eric and his concerns with completing decorations for *In Youth is Pleasure*, a photo of Denton appeared in the March issue of *Vogue*, and in her 'Spotlight' column the authoress Lesley Blanch, then the magazine's literary editor, devoted a paragraph to sketching in her impressions of his lifestyle, based on a recent visit. 'He abhors ugliness,' she wrote, 'the sort of uglification of drab colours, badly arranged foods, the wrong texture, the conventional bourgeois interior, the cliché in decoration, or way of living. He himself lives in a little sham Gothic folly in Kent, surrounded by trees and all the beautiful booty of his much-travelled life.'[38]

It was Lesley Blanch who had been responsible for reproducing the Berners portrait in *Vogue* two years previously. It had shared a page with a drawing by Augustus John and photographs of Phyllis Calvert and a young Robert Morley. In the meantime Denton had come up with some delightful tiny pen-and-ink illustrations for Miss Blanch's article, 'In School, Out of School', published in the August 1943 number; but evidently the magazine found him a difficult personality to classify, for in this March issue the peculiarly languorous photograph of Denton—one of the series that Gerald had taken—was placed below a glamorous one of Greer Garson!

He is seen standing in front of the mantelpiece at Hadlow Road wearing a dark overcoat, with a lumpy hand-knitted jumper underneath, hiding his shirt. The nonchalant, hardly elegant pose, with its intriguing hint of cussed suspicion, was just too much for three of *Vogue's* readers who soon put pen to paper and sent him 'absurd fan letters'. The first correspondent, it seems, was a Rose-Marie Aubépin, the second an amateur artist called Guy Allan (he wrote in green ink from a studio in Chelsea), and there was another from someone intent on coming down and painting a portrait. 'I keep them all at bay,' Denton recorded in the Journal, 'being terrified of their disillusion if they should know me.'[39] Nonetheless, Mlle Aubépin, a Free French 'Volontaire', whose father was a naturalized Englishman, turned up at Pitt's Folly Cottage out of the blue (he found her rather easier-going than he had anticipated) and soon he was to establish a somewhat uneasy friendship with the highly eccentric Guy Allan.

Denton had not ventured up to London since October, but now on 3rd May he had an appointment to see the urologist Dr Yates-Bell in the consulting rooms at 86 Brook Street—the building where he had suffered the unpleasant contretemps with the psychiatrist several years before. Once the appointment was out of the way, Denton got into a taxi and went round to visit Guy Allan in Glebe Place. Eric was later given a full account of what happened:

. . . He came to the door and ushered me into a large, very high studio with huge skylights. Here were stacks of his and his boyfriend's pictures all round the room and the most arty and ugly hangings and furnishings, all rather dirty. After I'd admired everything I was taken into his cubby-hole under the stairs, where he slept. I confess I began to get rather uneasy. I talked very brightly about the photos on the wall. . . there was a signed one of Prince Yussupov, who killed Rasputin—he was all dressed-up in his great grandfather's clothes—fur hat, boots, dagger and embroidered coat. With all these photos was a picture of me he had done from the *Vogue* photo. Opposite the bed was a horrible sort of throne made of wood, ivory, leather and trimmed with lyre-birds' feathers; really hideous. Guy next took me and showed me the little room up a little flight of stairs with a window looking down into the studio. This is the one he has offered to me whenever I like to use it. So, Eric, come one night and Christen Guy's upper chamber bed. He'd probably be furious if I went chaperoned, but still I think I'd rather. Just before tea the front door-bell rang and a woman who used to be a model of Augustus John's came to fit Guy for a coat she is making for him. She stayed to tea, which we drank out of dark earthenware bowls. I ate a very large Jewish currant bun, but left the rounds of herring paste dressed with radish. There is no bath in the studio, only a shower, so you wouldn't be able to pee in the bath. After tea God was kind to me, for he sent two other visitors, both male. I was saved from being left alone with Guy. One of the males was an artist called, I think, Roger Decombes, who was Belgian; he looked rather like a tougher, swarthier, more negroid me. He wore a yellow pullover. He talked to the other visitor, while Guy and I sat on the bed and looked at snaps. . . Guy pressed me to stay to supper, but I said I had to get back. He asked me if I would like to come here next Wednesday. I'm afraid he may have fallen in love with me, though it sounds conceited to say it, but he seems so very protective and he has bought a Chinese earthenware teapot for me. He had it already wrapped up when I arrived. I think he has a very nice nature, but. . .[40]

Guy, Denton discovered, was also a Christian Scientist. Whilst living in Paris he had made a miraculous recovery from anthrax and had joined the church out of a sense of gratitude. Rather improbably, he was now in the Navy, though at fifty-five his war work consisted chiefly of going up and down the Thames towing mines, often in the company of A.P. Herbert. Denton and he were to remain in touch for several years and on three occasions or more Guy brought down his young artist friends to visit him in Kent. At one stage, fired with an enthusiasm for Covarrubias's book on Bali,[41] he even proposed that Denton might like to go and live with him on the island. In a letter to Noël Adeney of February 1945, Denton voiced some doubts as to whether *quite* such a radical change would be to his taste: 'I don't think I shall move to Bali just yet,' he wrote, 'just a little too much jungle and undergrowth.'[42]

Guy and Eric did not hit it off. 'I was a fly in the ointment,' Eric recalled. The older man could not understand why his new friend was attracted to someone who appeared to have virtually no interest in art or literature. However, it was not Guy who was guilty of playing with Denton's emotions during the spring of 1944. Noël Adeney, much to his alarm, was growing increasingly possessive, and one day, sitting on the banks of the Medway in the April sun, she assailed him with the extraordinary question, 'Does Eric know how much I love you?'[43] Inwardly he must have recoiled in horror. 'Her scenes shock me,' he told Eric in a letter of 18th May, '. . . I wish very much Noël wasn't fond of me. . . I have no love or affection for her.'

Denton, needless to say, was still besotted with Eric, but the relationship was very one-sided. Whilst having an appreciation of the difficulties Denton was suffering, Eric, lacking in self-confidence, could not really understand why he had been befriended in the first place, especially since he had made it plain to Denton that he was 'not his type'. The whole affair was preying on Denton's mind. 'When you long with all your heart for someone to love you,' he wrote in the Journal, 'a madness grows there that shakes all sense from the trees and the water and the earth. And nothing lives for you, except the long deep bitter want.'[44] Rather than being able to work uninterrupted on his new book, he was now wasting a great deal of energy in writing extremely long letters to his friend, either berating him for a lack of constancy, or indulging in protracted heart-searchings that he hoped would eventually help sort out their true feelings for one another. Eric, totally inexperienced in close relationships, read these letters with incomprehension and a certain amount of unease. Looking back, he admitted that his behaviour to Denton *had* been pretty appalling.

The exasperation at Eric's refusal to acknowledge he meant anything to him became so acute that towards the end of May Denton sent a letter saying they ought to call the whole relationship off; his frustration had finally boiled over.

> . . . If you set out with the express idea of being beastly, you could not have treated anyone more cruelly than you have treated me. You have hoodwinked and cheated me and then tried to explain all your past behaviour away by saying that you did it all because you were hypersensitive and did not want to hurt my feelings. This would be disgusting enough if it were true, but because it is not entirely true it becomes even more disgusting. I would warn you against ever being kind to anyone again in the same way, as they will not thank you for it. The whole stupid situation arises from ignorance and wishful thinking on my part, and a crooked insincerity and selfishness on yours.
>   . . . I have been utterly idiotic over the whole thing, in fact my foolishness has been quite indecent. Therefore I deserve to be bamboozled and made to look a fool. But to be told there has never been anything but cheating on your part, no real feeling at all, only fatuous pretence, is too much. It is enough to make me hate you for the rest of my life and it is obvious, of course, that I can never trust another word that comes from your mouth.[45]

As the month was drawing to a close Denton became desperate. 'My work has somehow died to nothing,' he recorded in the Journals, 'and I think of nothing but dying or killing myself. . . How nasty the talk of suicide, yet how inevitable it sometimes seems.'[46] In addition to the problems with Eric, one suspects that he was also depressed at Routledge's refusal to offer him any more than a £50 advance for *In Youth is Pleasure*. In the first place he had found it undignified to have to write to them on money matters, but to be offered no greater improvement in terms other than their agreement to pay £25 for the book's decorations must have shaken his self-confidence.[47] Given the success of *Maiden Voyage* and the fact that he had recently had stories either published in or accepted by *New Writing and Daylight*, *Horizon* and *English Story* (as well as a poem in *The Spectator* and a couple in *Life and Letters*),[48] Routledge's treatment seemed frankly rather mean.

Denton once again was suffering from that same suffocating mental agitation he had experienced during the obsession with Jack Easton. In the evenings the only way he could cope was to cycle around the country lanes in search of something to distract his thoughts from Eric. Evie was no help at all; her truisms were aggravatingly banal. May was quite oblivious to his homosexuality, and what is more, she did not have a particularly sympathetic temperament. On 28th May Denton realized that his only course of action was to go up to London and make an attempt at sorting things out.

Eric was staying at his mother's flat in Streatham for the Whitsun holiday. On the Sunday afternoon Denton and he went into St James's Park and, as we read in the Journals, they 'decided only to be friends and not to quarrel.'[49] But the weekend turned out to be a disaster. When evening came there was the inevitable draw of the pub and this time it was Denton who got drunk—eight gin and limes would surely be enough to make any healthy person's head spin. The next day things went from bad to worse and, unable to bear the atmosphere any longer, Denton stalked out and returned to Kent.

I packed my satchel. Eric said nothing. I asked him what bus to take. He said, 'I'll come to the station.' I said, 'What for?' as freezingly as possible.

Then I went and said goodbye to Mrs Oliver and flapped out of the house with Eric following me.

I walked fast and he kept up behind. Just as we reached the stop a 59 bus approached. Without looking at Eric I heard him say, 'This is the bus.'

I didn't turn, but marched on to the bus as if I had never known him in my life.

Suddenly as it was moving off I had the longing to see if he was looking after me. I dodged this way and that, and I thought I saw the grey Aertex of his shirt stretched across his broad back but the conductress stood four-square, worrying for my fare, obliterating. I went right up to the front of the bus upstairs, and then I began crying in total disregard of all the passengers. I had dark glasses on, but I suppose no one who looked could fail to see the tears trickling down. I really felt done for in some way.[50]

A few days later Denton sent off another long letter. This time the line was more conciliatory. He was convinced they were destined to be together and could not bear the thought of them drifting apart. Despite certain rather glaring distortions in self-perception, this time he managed to admit that some of the problems between them might just have been as much his own fault as Eric's.

Please let me say that I have *never* tried any psychological tricks on you. No-one could ever have been more open, transparent and generally simple with you than I have been. In fact, I think I've been much too simple. I have more or less given myself to you on a plate, a thing I've done to hardly anyone else in my life. If I have appeared to cross-examine you, it is only that I *love* to talk.

What is a human relationship if there is no communication—and you talk so well and simply, if only you can get it going. I love to know what you or anyone else is really thinking; sometimes even if it hurts, and I feel that it is such a terrible waste of time simply to sit about like farm labourers, just grunting and chewing our pipes. You agree with me really in this, although you are more inhibited. I have known that you are a slower, more silent person than I am and I often try *not* to be a gadfly, but at others I felt that you really needed to be bitten into life. It was impertinent, and you probably didn't like the process, but why the hell should you sleep all your life away? You won't get another.[51]

His possessiveness of Eric, and perhaps the wish to 'improve' his friend's personality lay at the heart of their difficulties. Denton told Noël Adeney of his absolute determination to make the relationship work, even if this meant going against his better judgement.

Gradually Eric became less suspicious. Although he had never thought of himself as the sort of person who could be close friends with an artist or writer, he liked the idiosyncratic lifestyle at Pitt's Folly Cottage and was flattered that someone so obviously his intellectual superior could have fallen for him.

From June 1944 the friendship between them became more stable, with Denton even acknowledging that it was having a constructive effect on his emotional development. No longer did he hanker after the romantic life of a recluse. 'I've tried to live up to now shut up in my own little private box,' he wrote, 'and it's burst upon me that this is the wickedest, stupidest thing that anybody could try and do.'[52]

With the relationship now running rather more smoothly, Denton could resume work on *A Voice Through a Cloud*—though not for long. The arrival of the initial batch of proofs for *In Youth is Pleasure* during the second week in August forced yet another interruption and they continued to flood in over the next six weeks. Agreeably, there was little that needed correcting. On re-reading the short novel, however, Denton came to realize that he no longer had much appetite for making further use of the 'over-sensitive child' theme and in subsequent works he largely abandoned using material from this period of his life. Eric looked at some pages of *In Youth is Pleasure* and said he thought the book 'readable, but unwholesome' (the latter being the same adjective he had applied to Guy Allan!) and after this unfavourable judgement Denton tended not to show him things he had written, nor did he ever discuss with Eric which of his pictures he especially liked.

Denton enjoyed enough days of tolerable health in the summer months to be able to return to his wanderings along the banks of the Medway and to eat several relaxed picnics in the park at Oxon Hoath. As he mentions in the journals, on Saturday, 24th June he even made a new friend.

. . . I went down to the river near East Peckham, and just as I had crossed the wooden bridge where a man was fishing and his woman was watching him, I stood irresolute, wondering which way to go and where to spread my coloured handkerchief for my picnic.

Suddenly there poked up from behind the hedge near the little curling tributary where the children bathe, a very blond head that flashed gold in the sun.

I had often seen people bathing there, but for some reason now something suggested that I should go and have my picnic near whoever was behind the hedge. I just had the feeling that it would be suitable and right.

When I turned the corner of the bush I expected to see a bathing party, but instead there was only one youth there lying on his stomach with no clothes on at all, reading the *Reader's Digest.*

He jerked his head up and we confronted each other and smiled spontaneously, if rather nervously. With no more ado I plumped down on the ground quite near him and began to unpack my picnic, asking him how warm the water was.[53]

The golden-haired youth's name was John James Bloom and he was spending the weekend with his grandmother, Rose Bloom, who fittingly grew flowers and fruit in her garden and sold them locally. He was employed in a music publisher's shop in London and, as Denton discovered, had also been a patient of Jack Easton. John, who was by no means an intellectual, accepted Denton's invitation to go back to Pitt's Folly Cottage for tea.

Whilst Denton was making the most of these chance encounters and continuing to bask in his success, the inhabitants of the surrounding district were more concerned with the bombs and shrapnel falling from the sky. The Germans had just unleashed the V1 rockets and were inflicting considerable damage on the area. Because of the danger from the 'doodlebugs', the Adeneys for the time being had abandoned Middle Orchard, their holiday home in Crouch, and on 8th July, without any warning, Eric appeared at Pitt's Cottage saying that his hostel at Appledore had been hit and was quite ruined. He asked if Denton could put him up for a while. As it turned out, Eric stayed for the rest of Denton's life.

On 13th September Denton wrote in the Journal that he and Eric had been living together since July. He had found it 'the strangest thing in my life to share almost my whole existence like this'. What he omits to record is that in the meantime there had been a potentially disastrous upset between them. It occurred when they were taking care of Middle Orchard for the Adeneys. The couple returned for a night and, before going out to dinner with friends, Bernard Adeney unwisely invited Eric for a drink at The Chequers, Crouch's tiny pub. Noël came along a little later to join them, leaving Denton at Middle Orchard. In *No Coward Soul*, a book that charts her up-and-down friendship with Denton (and her antipathy towards Eric, who, for reasons of libel, is transformed into the oaf-like 'Gina'), Noël Adeney writes about the pub incident in minute detail, relishing the display of a less attractive side of Eric's nature:

At the door I met Austin [Bernard] who was leaving too soon. Why was he escaping, I wondered, but I went in and sat down with my half-pint at the dark iron-bound mahogany table, feeling puzzled, when Gina [Eric] suddenly began to speak in a curious whining voice, curling her thin lips, 'I'm going, Merton [Denton] *makes me sick*,' leaving no doubt of her meaning or intention. These foreboding words used in relation to Merton's poor injured body seemed utterly shocking and cruel and my thoughts swung in loathing from the brutal tone of the banal remarks to pity of the distress which occasioned them; they were suspended between and I could not find words, while Gina rambled on about her sexual inclinations, explaining and boasting. . . I thought of Merton's sensitive nature, and in a flat measured voice I made trite remarks about considering more, not leaving at once, and we shambled out of the pub, shamefaced and estranged.[54]

Later that evening, when they were alone together, Eric, who had been behaving rather oddly, made a full confession of what he had said. Denton was distraught. In a letter to Noël Adeney he repeated their conversation word for word. '"Shut up! I've heard that all before," ' he had shouted, ' "What are you doing here if that's your state of mind?" '[55] Eric replied that he knew what he'd said had been 'treacherous' and he lamely made a promise to be more loyal in the future. Denton tried to throw him out of the room. He was still capable of becoming violent when really angry.

The atmosphere eased considerably during the days that followed, though the incident continued to prey on his mind. On 11th August, having virtually accused her of being responsible for planting the 'treacherous' thoughts, Denton wrote to Noël Adeney saying that at last he thought he was beginning to come to grips with the complexities of Eric's personality. He described his friend as being 'so unnecessarily puzzled and distrustful' of his motives. He continued:

Because of his knockabout aimless life, he has so much quite useless cynicism and disbelief that he cannot enjoy the most straightforward things. In a bad mood nearly everything that is said to him is looked on as a sugared bait and a threat to his liberty! I don't want only my own way with him. I don't want to swallow him alive. What I do want is to look after him and to make his life as pleasant as possible. This may be considered domination of the worst kind, but I can't help that. In his own way he is in an even more peculiar state of health than I am and he will just go and get drunk in a ditch, if no-one pulls him out. He says that I am selfish and am pleasing no-one but myself with my mission work, and I suppose he is right.

Denton added that '. . . I answer perfectly to the quiet, submerged, almost lost side of his nature.' A poem written that same month gives a vivid idea of the relationship between them at this stage.

Understanding and Fighting

My friend and I
Are close and blind and warm,
—Sometimes.
And then we find
All happiness in being still
And knowing the dark earth.

But other times
Our hearts are far apart.
No darkness sings,
No stars keep guard;
Only the cruel words are said
And ancient wounds remembered.[56]

Chapter Nine

An Inevitable Decline

Eric Oliver is certain that Denton sensed he had only a limited amount of time left; it was therefore imperative that he should grasp every opportunity to carry on with *A Voice Through a Cloud*. Maurice Cranston remembered him describing the project with characteristic modesty as 'something I shall do very badly if I don't do rather well.'[1] But unfortunately, during the second half of 1944 his ambitions were frequently thwarted. Eric's presence in the cramped upper room at Pitt's Folly tended to upset the train of thought, especially since he also had the habit of staying in bed late into the morning.[2] Denton was used to working alone. Whereas painting was quite possible in company, writing was not. Only towards the end of the year did the situation sort itself out, with Eric gradually developing a greater feeling for the rhythm of his life, and he, in turn, completely accepting Eric's companionship.

The absence of any entry in the Journals between 11th July and 13th September is evidence of the degree to which Denton's routine was interrupted that summer. Apart from the unpleasant consequences of Eric's outburst in the pub, a further distraction occurred during the first two weeks of August when Guy Allan and his young German refugee friend, Vernon Fox, came down to camp in May's garden (a 'thistle-patch', as Denton described it to Noël). Quite understandably it was Denton that the two artists wished to see, and so they were entertained with picnics and trips down to the river. Otherwise, it was a frustrating time of waiting. Routledge had told Denton that *In Youth is Pleasure* would most probably be published in the early autumn, but it became delayed and he did not receive proofs for the dust-jacket until November.

With the summer over—he always preferred the winter months for working—Denton was able to go back to his novel. Late in September Noël devised the idea of painting a portrait of Eric, thus getting him out of the house in the mornings,[3] and by 18th October Denton had reached the part of the narrative where he is put in a wheelchair in the common-room of the hospital in Queen's Square—approximately a third of the way through the book.

Alongside the writing he also possessed sufficient drive to undertake a few commissions in his role as artist. Just before the business with Monté had broken the previous year, he had received four photographs of a pug called Alex, with the request that he should paint a picture of the animal in an imaginary setting. The commission came from the dog's owner, a Mrs Julian Goodman. 'I think storm clouds would be a *perfect* background,' she had written, approving of a suggestion Denton had made, 'his eyes are dark with blue irises. . . he has a beautiful snore.'[4]

It was not until October of that year, by which time he had completed the picture, that Denton discovered Julian Goodman to be the daughter of the much-fêted Bloomsbury hostess, Lady Ottoline Morrell, and not the 'rich Jewish financial gentleman'[5] he had initially suspected. Still in the family's possession, the painting depicts Alex standing with his feet in a pool; there are some mauve irises growing on the bank. Whether Denton had misunderstood the reference to 'irises' in the letter, or whether they were included as a conceit, is unclear. He described the pet's expression as being 'broken-hearted'. Quite satisfied with the finished work, he had made one of his rare trips up to London and had delivered the picture to Mrs Goodman in person at her home in Gower Street. She was enthralled (see illustration).

On the strength of his success, Mrs Goodman now wanted Denton to paint *her* portrait, again based on photographs. 'She is supposed to be seen by moonlight,' he wrote, 'and there are bits of bramble and barley and ivy about, also a little bat in the sky!'[6] One has the suspicion that the picture was too exaggeratedly fantastic for comfort. When it was taken up to London for Mrs Goodman's inspection at the end of October Denton was told that he had got the colour of the eyes wrong; they should have been grey-blue, rather than brown.[7] He took it home.

In November the painting of Alex was reproduced in the 'Spotlight' page of *Vogue*, and there was also mention of another novel in the pipeline from 'the versatile author of *Maiden Voyage*.'[8] A couple of months previously Denton had met with the magazine's art editor, John Parsons, and had been asked to contribute a feature-length article for them, which he could illustrate as well.[9] The association with Vogue lasted for some time and consisted chiefly of Denton providing small illustrations, mostly in pen and ink, for a monthly cookery column written by Doris Lytton Toye. The first of these drawings appeared in the July 1945 issue and the last in August 1947.[10] In many respects they were little more than glorified doodles and Denton would usually work at them in bed—and on any scrap of paper that was to hand. Their individuality and childlike charm nevertheless reflect his idea that the skilful presentation of food constituted an art form in itself.

Around the time he was writing the article for *Vogue*, Denton received letters from two new correspondents who showed a specific interest in his work as an artist. The first concerned an oil with the intriguing title, 'A Gothick Flowerpiece'. For two years it had remained in stock at the Leicester Galleries without attracting a buyer. At last Denton heard that it had sold, and on 10th October he received an appreciative letter from the purchaser, Dr Bennie Press. Replying the following day he revealed the process he had used in painting the still life, with its predominantly crimson-brick-red colours.

It first began as a very direct painting done straight from a bunch of autumn flowers and leaves. Then gradually I evolved the rather ghostly background and the fragment of building and the figure of a nun. The texture of the painting too was built up slowly, first by ordinary painting with a brush (hog and sable), then by scraping with a little metal tool that I have, and by the use of a wood-carver's knife (also sand-paper, I think!)

So you can see it has grown into what it is by rather a slow process. Evolution, not planning! that is how I like to paint pictures, and how I think they really should grow. The drawback is, of course, that it is a gradual building up, and one can never tell what the final result will be. . .[11]

Monica Booth, who had been a fellow-student at Goldsmiths', recalls how one day she went into a grocer's with Denton. There was a marble pillar in the shop and, much to her surprise, she saw him lick it quickly when no one was looking. His feeling for texture was always acute. As with the delight in handling beautiful porcelain, he wanted to make the best possible use of the surface of a painting, so as to create an individual effect and add to the 'dimension' of the work. The device of partially scraping away one layer of paint to reveal another (or to obtain a rubbed and abraded surface) was especially effective in the depiction of masonry or coarse-grained wood, or when used with stronger, brighter colours, to give a translucent quality to flowers or domestic ornaments.

Between the two letters, though, one reads an entry in the Journals describing a technique that is radically different: it is something much more delicate and unusual. As ever, Denton's preoccupation with texture is to the fore:

I am painting a new picture, which I have done first of all in pencil outline, carefully, then with turpentine to darken and strengthen the line. Now I put on, rub on, colour very gingerly, very little. The board is whitened and rubbed down, so that the mahogany shows a little in places. Now I think that in some ways I have found the technique for my painting, direct, simple, permanent and utterly unlike what is usually understood as oil painting.[12]

It seems, however, that Denton very soon decided not to restrict himself to this technique. When answering a fan letter from Aircraftman J.E. Parker just ten days or so later he makes no direct mention of it. His reply to Parker reveals that two years after completing the 'Gothick Flowerpiece' he was still perfectly happy to use the identical formula of a still-life dramatized and expanded in context by the inclusion of a figure, an animal, a shell or some other artefact. One could say with justification that it was the only style he adhered to for any length of time.

I've just finished a small still-life, which I rather like, of an urn holding some barley, poppy-pods and ivy; some mushrooms are on the table and a shell, and in the background is a sort of mer-cat, which I have invented, and a tall rock with a bell on it. . .

Living as I do in a tiny place, I've taken to doing small pictures and I enjoy it, as I sometimes aim at a jewel-like quality. Most of my pictures are in oil or a sort of mixture of water, paint and chalk, which I varnish. But I am always drawing and scratching and scraping with a variety of tools that I have, so that they hardly ever have the ordinary surface of an oil painting or watercolour.[13]

As the winter months took their hold, so Denton became increasingly miserable. The final week of November was spent in bed and on one occasion his temperature rose to 103°. He made a quick recovery—then, throwing caution to the winds, overdid things. Whilst trying to cycle over to Trottiscliffe with Eric, probably with the intention of visiting Mrs Carpmael, he became so ill that they had to terminate the journey at Middle Orchard. The Adeneys were away. Unable to summon up enough strength even to ride back down the hill to Pitt's Folly, Denton was forced to stay in bed there for several days, leaving Eric to tend to such things as cooking and keeping him warm with fires. He was in and out of bed right up until Christmas.

On New Year's Eve they heard that Sir William Geary, the owner of Oxon Hoath, had died at the age of eighty-five. It was inevitable that changes would now be made on the estate; Denton wished to cling to his memories of Oxon Hoath as a magical place where time seemed to stand still—he had always felt secure and untouched by the grimness of everyday life when in the lazy expanse of the park. Eric had been walking there a couple of days before and, as Denton recorded in the Journal, his friend too was struck by the lovely otherworldly atmosphere:

Eric said in the moonlight it was wonderful the other night—with a horse moving soundlessly over the grass and the lake reflected. In the Cedar Avenue he smelt a strange smell, and looked up at the gate pillars and thought of Sir William all his life walking between them from a little child to old age.

All still in the moonlight, spun into a glass picture.[14]

The one high point in what Denton described to Helen Roeder as being 'the most frightful winter of solid invalidism'[15] was the publication on 23rd February 1945 of *In Youth is Pleasure*. His presentation copies had arrived during the second week of the month and Denton had been mildly irritated to notice that the title-page still bore the date of the old year—it seems nobody at Routledge had spotted the error—otherwise he was perfectly happy with the overall quality of the production. Mr Ragg had obviously done his best.

But now *In Youth is Pleasure* was out Denton expressed a degree of paranoia about how Bill might react to it: his elder brother could scarcely fail to recognize himself as the boorish and uncaring 'Charles', whom he had portrayed as attempting to humiliate and patronize 'Orvil' at every given opportunity. It was bad enough that the hero had come across Charles with his hand down the dress of a married woman, but potentially much more embarrassing was the impression the book gave that Denton harboured a fear almost amounting to hatred of his brother.[16]

Denton was also a little fearful of how the book would be received more generally. Given the cautious words of Edward Sackville-West and Herbert Read, he must have wondered whether the critics could possibly respond to his new novel as warmly as they had to *Maiden Voyage*. He need not have worried. Although there was a bad review from Kate O'Brien in *The Spectator*, the critic of *The Observer* hailed *In Youth is Pleasure* as 'a brilliant and dreadful little book'[17] and there were also favourable mentions in the *New Statesman* and *Horizon*. Edith Sitwell remarked on the same level of vitality that had so much attracted her to *Maiden Voyage*, and this time, making up for previous silences, Lord Berners wrote Denton a letter telling him that the book 'had caused a sensation in this house'.[18]

There were fan letters too. Denton valued these almost as much as he did praise from friends. On 3rd March he started corresponding with a tall, middle-aged lady from Colchester, Peggy Kirkaldy, who wrote to him of her 'sharp joy' at reading the new novel. In his reply Denton mentioned the doubts he had about how the book would be received; he told her he had been 'preparing for quite a lot of rudeness'. The letter continues:

> When one is writing one is so cut off from the rest of the world that one hardly realizes that other eyes will soon be reading what one has so roughly put down on paper.
>
> I must admit that when a book first comes out I hate the thought of others reading it. I suppose this feeling may wear off in time, but I always have it now, so you can guess how nice it is to feel that someone else enjoys and approves.[19]

As with Noël Adeney, Mrs Kirkaldy had a penchant for cultivating budding literary figures, yet a natural sense of propriety guaranteed that she never made any demands on him. Although she did come down to Kent on three occasions, theirs was essentially a pen friendship—but with a difference. She virtually bombarded Denton with books, antique spoons and suchlike, many of which were for him to keep, others to he returned. Delighted at the attention, he accepted her extraordinary generosity with little protest, and one might add that her interest was an important element in easing the frustration and boredom of his last years, when it was often impossible to muster sufficient energy for work.

One topic Denton could not resist telling her about was the remarkable dolls' house that he first began to repair in 1941, when he was living at The Hop Garden. Since the move to Pitt's Folly the bulky thing had been stored away in May's garden-studio. Now that the evenings were getting longer (one suspects Denton had not yet developed much strength to get back to walking or cycling), he resumed work on the house and found it to be an ideal means of relaxation after the concentrated mental effort of writing.

The four-and-a-half foot long structure really belonged to Mildred Bosanquet and one winter's day when Denton had been to visit her in Seal she had taken him down into the cellar and shone a torch onto the then very dilapidated toy. It had belonged to her mother's family. The cellar was soon to be converted into an air-raid shelter for the village and had to be cleared. Denton offered to look after it; he had plenty of room. After about a fortnight's wait the dolls' house was delivered to The Hop Garden. Denton gave Peggy Kirkaldy an enthusiastic description of its condition and of the many improvements he was in the process of making:

. . . the sad thing about this mid-eighteenth century house which I am repairing is that it only has about two pieces of old furniture left—a little Pembroke table with tapering legs, and a chest of drawers. The generations of children have smashed all the rest.

Until it came to me it had been in the same family—the Littledales—somewhere up in Yorkshire ever since it was made. Indeed, it is supposed to have been made by the estate carpenter; but this of course can't be verified. It is on a stand with two drawers, painted with a charming Chinesey fret pattern. There is one old brass handle, the other I've replaced.

The dolls' house itself has four rooms—dining, drawing, bed & kitchen—each with a differently designed mantel with the most delicate mouldings. The bedroom has two perfect little cupboards on each side of the fireplace, and the doors are mahogany in white surrounds, an arrangement I always love. The landing upstairs has an arch in blue with white keystone and moulding—another charming touch. The stair-rail is almost entirely gone, but I am nearly certain that it was a Chinese Chippendale fret (like the pattern on the stand drawers) and I'm slowly but surely designing and remaking it.

I'm most proud of having reconstructed the balustrade, which originally ran along the cornice of the house, joining the pediment. Quite by chance, a friend saw two terrible Arabian brackets with turned balustrading on them. I went to look at them, and the height and shape was exactly right, so we bought them at once and tore them to pieces, and now the balustrade looks marvellous on the skyline! I've also made two missing chimneys.

Inside the rooms are all wainscoted halfway up. The most awful job has been stripping layer upon layer of paint off. Some parts were completely clogged with it.

I feel, at the moment, that work will never stop on it, but I suppose one day I shall finish. It really is worth preserving, although, when it was first given to me it seemed almost a ruin. The structure was alright, but all the refinements had been lost or overlaid.[20]

'The problem is,' he had written in his previous letter to Mrs Kirkaldy, 'where in this wedding-cake of a room can the dolls' house be put when it is mended!'[21] After nine months at Pitt's Folly with Eric, it gradually dawned on Denton that the three of them really had to think of moving to a larger home. Aside from the fact that they were living in very close proximity to one another, he had some suspicion that the landlady, Mrs Sloman (who after all was only a few yards away in the main house), wished to interfere.[22] On one or two occasions she had made the mistake of trying to get Eric and Evie to do small jobs for her, and Denton, highly attuned to details of punctilio when it suited him, took offence.

Having asked all sorts of people if they knew of somewhere possible, he set his sights firmly on the Adeneys' home, Middle Orchard. Eric and he stayed there again for ten days in May and, possessed with a kind of spring fever, he was soon writing to Peggy Kirkaldy about all the improvements he would make to the interior, given the chance. The welcome change of surroundings only served to emphasize just how constricted he felt at Pitt's Folly, with Eric, Evie and 'the ladies' (Mrs Sloman and her friend Brenda Cobb) living almost on top of him.

While they were at Middle Orchard Denton performed an act of kindness that demonstrates an unexpectedly sympathetic and engaging side to his personality. Writing in his Journal he describes how one day he had been out on his bicycle and had come across a woman trudging forlornly along Seven Mile Lane, the road that leads straight through the considerable expanse of the Mereworth Woods. Hauling a heavy suitcase, she was travelling around from place to place in search of her husband, who was supposed to be in an army camp somewhere in the area. By now desperately tired, the woman told Denton that she had no place to go for the night. He volunteered that if she had failed to find a bed by the evening, she could come over to Middle Orchard and they would put her up. He gave her the exact address. She memorized it.

Later, after we had finished supper and Eric had gone to bed, I suddenly heard a movement, and there she was looking up at the back door, peering, frowning.

'Come in,' I said boisterously. And she plunked on to a hard chair in the sittingroom, not the arm one I had tried to steer her towards. She sat there breathing hard, talking in a whisper of exhaustion.

'It's not right,' she kept saying.

I quickly made some tea and gave her that with cake, while I heated up the remains of the macaroni cheese. I expected her to be quite uninterested in food, but she wasn't when I mentioned it; she seemed touched, made vital for the first time. But when she came to eat it, she was moderate, not greedy.

She said, 'God's good, he sent you to me!' but there was no real conviction. Life was on a level of amazing flatness. . .

Long after she had gone to bed, Eric and I talked in his room. At midnight I left, but I was feeling very restive and I lay in a half-awake state for a long time.

All at once I heard a movement on the landing, and I felt ridiculously scared, imagining that the woman had come up to steal my money. I lay there hating everything, not awake enough to be sensible. . .

Of course the poor woman had only gone to the W.C., as I was to discover in the morning, for she was too considerate to pull the plug.[23]

The entry for 17th June is entirely taken up with a minutely detailed two-thousand word report of Hector Bolitho's visit the previous day. The New Zealand-born author was hurriedly invited to lunch after he had written to Denton proposing to come down and see him in Kent. The interview would be used as the basis for an article in the American magazine *Town and Country*.

On receiving the letter, Denton had asked Noël Adeney what she knew of Bolitho. Her neighbour, Joanna Potter, had a *Who's Who* to hand, and so Noël was able to fill in something of the man's career. Denton was quite familiar with the name, of course, ('so harsh, Byzantine', he wrote), but he was not sure how it should be pronounced, nor whether he might be confusing him with Philip Guedalla. Mrs Potter's *Who's Who* yielded the solid information that Henry Hector Bolitho was born in Auckland in 1898 and had been publishing books since 1920—mostly with an historical bias, but certainly not in any sort of competition with Guedalla's weighty tomes on Palmerston and Gladstone.

Denton went to great lengths to make the lunch as entertaining as possible. Miss Sinclair did what she could to brighten up the usual basically vegetarian fare, leaving him free to fuss around upstairs making the marble-topped chess table as pretty as he could in preparation for the meal. He laid out lace mats that had belonged to his mother, a large salt-cellar and a Gothic toast rack; in the middle he placed a white and gold sugar basin containing a selection of garden and wild flowers. Bolitho was bound to be impressed. Eric had instructions to absent himself for the duration of the meal.

'Hector Bolitho came yesterday, rather early for lunch, while Evie and I were still getting things ready,' Denton wrote in his Journal.[24] Having paid the taxi, the visitor was ushered up the steep dark staircase to meet his host—at the top a little rosewood *chiffonier* graced the entrance to the main room. Denton turned on the light and 'saw a small tubby man with large heavy rimmed glasses and a rather square "German" head with bushy white hair'.[25] In spite of this somewhat unappealing first impression, he found Bolitho to be a 'very easy' if voluble guest and soon he was making himself comfortable on the bed, with the author sitting back and proceeding to tell him a great deal about his *own* life.

The New Zealander's account of the lunch is one of the most atmospheric descriptions that we have of Denton in his home environment:

I settled into a chair, and while Welch went into the kitchen for ice I looked about me in the crowded room. There was an unfinished portrait on an easel[26] and brushes in a straight line on a table; a pile of books neatly stacked beside the bed, and a small inlaid dining table, all so close together that I could imagine Welch painting, reading, writing, playing the spinet, and eating within the space of a few square yards. Although he could walk in the garden and work at one of his tasks for a little time each day, he spent most of his time in bed and in the room with too many objects. One absorbed some of the claustrophobia of his life, and the self-analysis such a pattern encourages.

But there was absolute tidiness. I realized later when I watched him cutting a cake with the timid precision of a surgeon that the talent for tidiness in his words and his painting, the delicate music of the spinet, the birdlike caution of his movements, the gentle kindness in his manners were all one talent. Each word, each movement, each pencil line, each striking of a match, each time he filled my glass with golden cider, all grew out of his inability to be clumsy or vulgar, in mind or movement.

His eager spurts of curiosity over the world and the people beyond the angels and the gothic window saved his introspection from becoming too selfish. I found that he was interviewing me, and being an eager talker and not a willing listener, I was easily trapped. I had to remind myself of the purpose of my visit.[27]

Denton's observations were similarly personal. In the Journal entry he notes down not only the drift of their conversation, but also his visitor's table manners and appetite. Having started off with some asparagus and melted butter, they 'went on to a dish of new peas, hard boiled egg, split lengthways, sardines, new potatoes with mint and butter, salad hearts and sweet dressing.' He continues that Bolitho 'was quite greedy and couldn't resist things that were pressed on him, saying that things tasted far better in the country.'[28]

Starved of news, Denton wanted to hear as much as possible of the London scene, of other writers and so on. After this the conversation turned to *In Youth is Pleasure*, which, he learnt had broken down Bolitho's defences to such a degree that following a quarrel with the man whose house he had been staying in the previous day, he had retired to his room sobbing! Not knowing whether Bolitho was being 'genuine' or whether it was 'all a fancy thing' to titillate him, Denton couldn't muster up anything more than the comment, 'how awful that my book should do that.'

There were more stories of the famous. At around three o'clock—Bolitho's taxi was late—Denton suggested they should go for a walk in nearby Pittswood. Eric was at the cottage on their return. During a moment when Denton was out of the room Bolitho said to him, ' "How nice it is to meet someone who is unspoilt by his success." ' The comment is recorded in the Journal, and the entry concludes:

When the car came at last, we took him out to it, and he pressed both our hands with a meaning look. Something most understanding—put on, of course, but likeable, for in spite of all the little insincerities, that even a great person can't entirely weed out, he seemed to wish one well, 'to want to live and let live,' as Eric put it.

Eric said the moment he was gone, 'Well that went off like a house on fire. What do you think he'll write? Something pretty good.'

And we talked about it all, and I suddenly felt quite exhausted.

The war in Europe had ended on 7th May. Denton describes a rather irritating Victory Day spent first of all working at the dolls' house in May's garden (he had decided that the momentous nature of the day merited a break from work), and then entertaining Noël and May to a hurriedly arranged supper, which Miss Sinclair, ever-resourceful, had been persuaded to stretch at short notice. As the evening wore on Denton became more and more tired; the situation was not made any easier by the blatant animosity between the two middle-aged lady artists. 'May as usual had been rude to Noël,' he writes, 'Saying "Perfect!" in a sneering voice, because Noël was making up her face to cover up her boredom with the King's speech.'[29] Denton had been twenty-four at the outset of the war—now he was thirty. During the night he experienced great difficulties sleeping; he was aware of the 'awful thoughts and anxieties in the air—the breaking of something—the splitting apart of an atmosphere that had surrounded us for six years.'[30]

Eric and he were yet again given the opportunity of spending some days alone together at Middle Orchard. It was the week of the post-war General Election. On 5th July, before going to Crouch, they called in at the local polling station in Hadlow School and, as he writes in a letter to Noël Adeney, 'of course did everything wrong and began to chat in those secret horse boxes, so that a man rushed round and said, "You can do what you like at home, but you mustn't do it here!" '[30] After a delay of three weeks, during which the servicemen's votes had to be gathered, the results were announced and Denton, by now back at Pitt's Folly, learnt that the Socialists, the party he had supported, had won by a landslide.

Still concerned with the idea of moving house, Denton was finding his now ever-increasing lack of mobility hard to bear, and shortly after Peggy Kirkaldy had driven over to visit him for the first time, he wrote to her with the news that Eric and he were eagerly awaiting the arrival of their own driving licences. Denton had bought May's Austin Cabriolet. On 3rd August the two friends took the vehicle out and went up to Gover Hill on the edge of the Oxon Hoath park, where they had a typical picnic of tomatoes (which Eric had grown), cheese, hard boiled eggs, Darvita, chocolate and plums. It was an idyllic summer's evening that reminded Denton of the pre-war years; the sun, he wrote was like 'a crimson hot plate sinking down into the dusty, mousy clouds.'[32]

And so now they had the car the search for a new home became quite a pleasurable pastime. Middle Orchard was definitely out the running for the moment. When they were staying there back in May, Eric had written to Noël Adeney asking if she might be prepared to part with it for £2,500, but, as is made plain in her novel *No Coward Soul*, she had had no intention of letting the house go for that sum. Though Denton decided he really had to leave Pitt's Folly Cottage in the near future, there was no real rush; he felt perfectly at liberty to indulge his imagination.

. . . my fancy roves from medieval to gothic revival; but I think my heart is really fixed on something classic, in spite of flirting with other ideas.

As a schoolboy I used to think that the most delightful thing would be to live in the corner of a ruin—either a Greek temple or a Norman castle! One would have just one or two habitable snug rooms and look out onto the grand ruins. I suppose most children have this sort of romanticism in them. I still have it at moments, though I am horribly matter-of-fact at others. Then I think that only quietness, cleanness and warmth are of any importance.

This other mood, I suppose, is brought on by the great difficulty of finding anything even bearable in the present-day world. What would really suit us would be a little eighteenth-century cottage, lodge, or villa, but that, of course, is like asking for the moon.[33]

The closest he came to settling into 'the corner of a ruin' was a hopelessly impractical plan to take over Old Soar, a tiny medieval manor near the village of Plaxtol—only a mile or so from Gover Hill. Joined to an eighteenth-century brick farmhouse, until twenty years previously the stone-built ruin had been used as a store. The farmer allowed Denton to look over it. Soon he was writing to The Society for the Protection of Ancient Buildings with the proposal that they should buy Old Soar and restore it. 'I've said I'll put up as much of the money as I can manage, if I'm allowed to live in the place!' he told Peggy Kirkaldy, adding, 'these things are managed sometimes, but I daresay nothing will come of this attempt.'[34] Nothing did. The following month Denton wrote at length describing an empty old house they had found near Pembury; here it was a seventeenth-century staircase 'with amazingly thick carved posts and ample bulging balustrade'[35] that sent him into a state of rapture.

Progress on *A Voice Through a Cloud* was painfully slow. In answer to a request from Routledge for information of any future literary plans, he had told them about the novel, but gave no inkling as to when it might be finished. He referred to it quite misleadingly as 'a book which is drawn from my experiences as an art student'.[36] Although two-thirds of the way through *A Voice Through a Cloud* by the autumn of 1945, Denton was writing to his fellow-author Stephen Bagnall that once the fair copy had been completed there would still be a 'third revising and general refurbishing'[37] to do. No mention is made of the difficulty he was having in deciding where to end the narrative; such was the seriousness of the quandary that it lay unresolved at the time of his death over three years later.[38]

One does not want to give the impression that more generally Denton had particular trouble in putting pen to paper. Aside from the fifty-four entries in his Journal for 1945 (the longest of which extends to nearly two thousand words), there also exists a notebook with seventy-eight poems written during the year. Every week there were letters too. Even when Eric was in London for a few days seeing his mother Denton would keep him up to date with any news, and Eric, in turn would send almost daily messages back. Taking a break from his work one Monday in late October Denton wrote to his friend in the evening telling him about the sort of things he would normally have recorded in his Journal.

Dear Dump,

I've just come in from a long day out in the car, first picnicking where we did with Peggy in front of Peckham Old Church. Then walking into the grounds of Mereworth Castle, where they pumped out the sewage. Further down the road I found a little ruined cottage or summer-house, octagonal, with a very pretty doorway. On the door soldiers had painted in bright red [a] skull and cross-bones and 'Danger High Explosives', and other ruder things too, but it was all deserted now and the roof would soon fall in. As usual, I imagined it all repaired and me living in it with a fire in the grate and some nice food on the table. It would be a fine little retreat, as it's in the middle of some magnificent old beeches and chestnuts.

At this particular moment I began to rumble inside, so I retreated into the bushes to do my duty, as the matron used to say. . . Judge of my foolish feeling when I looked up in the middle of the process and saw a lance-corporal only a few yards away picking chestnuts. I quickly dragged myself together and I'm glad to say he was too engrossed in his foraging to notice me. I went up to him and asked him if I was trespassing, thinking it best to take the bull by the horns. He said, 'Naw, you're nawt trespassing.' I can't write it, but he came from the North and seemed to think it was quite alright for me to wander anywhere I liked in the castle grounds. He said that further down was a prisoner-of-war camp and that there were only a few servants in the castle.

I would have liked to have gone right then, but I felt too tired, so after going a little further I turned back. When I looked over my shoulder I saw three Germans behind me in a line. I got the absurd notion they were following me to knock me on the head in the woods and take my clothes and money to escape with. The feeling was so strong that I got very hot and bothered and walked much too fast and began to feel very peculiar. I was looking everywhere for the lance-corporal, but he completely disappeared and when I looked round again the Germans in their grey peaked caps had also disappeared mysteriously. I imagined them lurking behind the huge gnarled trunks. It was rather a moment, and I wished you were there as moral support.

Denton tells how he continued on to the small town of West Malling, and then returned home via a lane that passes through the hamlet of Swanton, which had a large pool that he liked.[39]

I don't know why I went that rather unusual way; perhaps it was suggested to me by something in the air, for just before I got to Harmston's oasthouse,[40] I saw something black dangling out of one of the windows. Almost at once I knew there'd been a fire and the next moment I saw the place had been completely gutted. Two small boys were in the garden and I went up to them and asked them all about it. They said that it happened last night when Harmston was out. He banked up the fire too high, as he always does—he burnt the mantelpiece at Middle Orchard—and then went to Trot's. Absolutely every thing is gone—all his clothes, furniture, papers. Only the walls are standing; no floors, roof or window-frames. The bath and the water pipes are dangling in mid-air. He spent last night with Peggy at Cage Farm.[41]

Harmston appears in *No Coward Soul* as the shadowy, occult-loving 'Professor Stoneley Raymond'. He visits 'Merton' while he is staying at 'Deer's Farm' (Middle Orchard) and, playing the part of the experienced businessman, tells him he has been handling his publishers all wrong and that he shouldn't have given up the American rights on his 'long poem' (i.e. *Maiden Voyage*). In point of fact, Denton had repeated the gist of this conversation to Noël Adeney when he wrote to her in May and, taking on board the full import of Harmston's remarks, he had gone ahead and contacted the literary agents Pearn, Pollinger and Higham, who had been recommended to him by Edith Sitwell. He said he should like to take their advice before making any further agreements with Routledge. In the second letter to the firm he asked if they might be willing to approach editors of magazines on his behalf, or whether they saw their job as being restricted to placing whatever pieces he happened to send them. Would they, for instance, be prepared to deal with commissions for illustrative work? In closing this letter of 30th June Denton made a reference to *A Voice Through a Cloud*, saying over-optimistically that the novel 'may be ready in another five or six months. . . perhaps even sooner.'[42]

Denton had recourse to using an agent not because he wished particularly to obtain more commissions, but more so that he could divest himself of unnecessary distractions. Nonetheless, financial considerations were beginning to cause him real worry. It was bad enough that the second printing of the American edition of *Maiden Voyage* had been a fiasco—sales were exceptionally poor[43]—but what really disheartened him was the definite news that he would not inherit any money from his father's estate; at least, not in the foreseeable future. Bill, recently discharged from the R.A.F., came down and told him that Ada, their stepmother, had been left everything and was intending to run Wattie & Co. herself. Now that Denton's dreams of financial security were shattered, the pressure was on him to earn some hard cash. But what would happen if he became too ill to work?

On 20th November he noted down how all the commissions were piling up: he was struggling with a story for the American magazine *Harper's Bazaar*, something similar for *Kingdom Come*,[44] also one of his monthly drawings for the cookery column in *Vogue* (each of which paid six guineas), he had the book to complete, not to mention paintings for the Leicester Galleries and two for The Arts Council. 'How much of this will get done soon?' he asked ruefully, 'I am a snail worker turning out about four paragraphs a day and messing with my pictures until they are an obsession.' We learn from the next entry of the Journals that within the week he was laid up in bed with 'flu.

Denton was in every sense a perfectionist. He simply could not toss off any work that was destined either for publication or for exhibition. Even though the commissions were now accumulating in rather an alarming fashion, this did not prevent him from developing a new style of drawing that was the most intricate and time-consuming he had yet attempted. 'The Woodman's Cottage' and 'The Bust and the Toadstools', the small pictures sent in for the Leicester Galleries' New Year Exhibition,[45] are much more reminiscent of engravings than of pen and ink drawings, and the care with which each is finished should be seen in conjunction with the infinite pains he was taking over *A Voice Through a Cloud*.

As in so much of his writing, Denton takes a relatively mundane subject and adorns it with several idiosyncratically evolved distractions in order to create an ambiguous and symbol-laden composite. For instance, the inclusion of the phallic shapes of various fungi in the foreground of both of these pictures lends the already established morbid mood a subtly sexual content. Whilst this may not have been intentional, the impression is nonetheless powerfully projected. 'The Bust and the Toadstools', contrived as being more fanciful than 'The Woodman's Cottage', features a rather sinister skulking figure in the foreground with one of his hands buried deeply in a trouser pocket. Soon after purchasing the picture at the Leicester Galleries, Charles Neil, an early practitioner of the Alexander Technique, wrote to Denton saying, 'My wife is most suspicious of what the young man behind the tree is doing!'[46] and though highly decorative, there is certainly a happy air of scarcely repressed sexuality about it (see illustration).

The inclusion of mushrooms and toadstools in three pictures done at this time did not spring wholly from Denton's imagination. Early in October Mrs Kirkaldy had sent him John Ramsbottom's little book on fungi,[47] and soon Eric was scouring the fields for various edible varieties, leaving Denton to admire the illustrations and familiarize himself with the artistic possibilities of each. Several times he went out into the woods to sketch fungi and these drawings were incorporated into the above-mentioned pictures.

'The Woodman's Cottage' (there is no connection with Tom the Woodman), shows a tiny house flanked by a pair of leafless winter trees. A large barrel for catching rainwater is seen by one of the walls and the toadstools in the foreground only add to the feeling of dampness. The atmosphere of 'The Woodman's Cottage' is redolent of the special smell that one associates with trampling dead leaves and twigs underfoot (see illustration).

Local lore has it that the highwayman Jack Diamond once lived in this cottage, and it is interesting that Denton did not opt for something more sensational when deciding on a title for the picture. In fact he knew the Williams family who lived there; Mrs Williams used to keep the key for Harmston's oast-house which was just down the road at Swanton. Also very close to Oxon Hoath and approximately equidistant between Pitt's Folly and Middle Orchard, was The Coffin House, a curious habitable folly that is said to have been built by one of the owners of the estate to remind the family who lived at neighbouring Hamptons of their mortality. Denton's evocatively Gothic picture of The Coffin House, evidently influenced by Samuel Palmer's etching 'The Bellman' (1879), has two rabbits in the foreground, one of which is blind and is patting a mushroom with its left paw. Just above the animal one can spot the west lodge of Oxon Hoath. The pen and ink drawing is generally very accurate, especially in the architectural details of the cottage itself. As with the other two pictures, 'The Coffin House' is coloured with a light wash (see illustration).

During the late autumn Denton's prospects of getting his hands on Middle Orchard underwent a dramatic improvement. It happened that the Adeneys were trying to find another London home around this time and though they nearly settled on a property in Hampstead, the project came to nothing. In a moment of inspiration it crossed Denton's mind they might be interested in 34 Croom's Hill, the house where he had lodged with Miss Sinclair during his years at Goldsmiths'. It still belonged to her brother, Braxton, and the main part was empty. Initially, though, the Adeneys said they were not keen on moving south of the river, but by the end of November Denton, who had always loved the place, succeeded in convincing them that it was just what they were looking for. It had such an interesting combination of architectural styles; there was a lovely view across the park; the road was absolutely quiet, and so on. He manipulated the situation with consummate skill. A few days later Peggy Kirkaldy received a letter bubbling over with excitement:

> Now I must tell you my plum. . . I think it is now almost certain that we shall move to Middle Orchard in a month or two! The Adeneys fell for the Greenwich house I told you about and they're almost fixed up with the L.C.C., who had requisitioned it, to stay on in a part as their tenants. The rest they will live in. They want to keep the studio at Middle Orchard for themselves. It will be quite cut off from our bit, and I think it will be bearable; although it would have been nice to have had the complete place. We shall have all the rest of the house, and the garden and orchard.[48]

In spite of a last minute hitch over the transaction, a week before Christmas the Adeneys went up to sign the papers for Croom's Hill and on 19th December, his mind fully at rest, Denton made a trip into Tonbridge with Eric to do some shopping and also to search around for things they might need for their new home. As usual they were drawn to the old roller-skating rink, a glorified flea market, where in the past he had discovered many bargains. This day it was a striking Victorian red horsehair couch that caught his attention. At once Denton knew it had to be his, 'its ugly, Gothic, sharp parrot smartness simply calling out to be used, sat upon and loved'[49]—never mind the woodworm. Five pounds was the price and, enchanted, he gladly gave up the money without attempting to haggle.

Back at Pitt's Folly Cottage he started to clean the cushions with Eric's nailbrush; the couch itself was to be delivered to May's the following day. Denton cannot have realized how much all this activity had tired him. Later in the evening, as Eric and he were sitting upstairs waiting for Miss Sinclair to come and read to them, he felt something alter slightly in his left eye. Eric had a look and said it was nothing; Denton was just being 'a little neurotic'. The reading went ahead. What happened next is described in the Journals:

. . . I jumped up, not being able to stay still any longer, and went into the bathroom.

I saw there that my lid had dropped down and that the pupil underneath was huge, velvet black, almost swamping the tiny coloured rim. The other pupil was normally small. The whole effect of my face was wickedly languorous and lopsidedly un-me. I went back to the others to tell them and to show them, but they still pooh-poohed comfortably.

And so I settled down to a night of deep pain in the heart of my head like a tight little walnut. I took a Veganin tablet, and after that I seemed to be still in pain but too lethargic to be as restless as I wanted to be. My eye was weeping all on its own, apart from me, the water coursing down my cheek, and my heart was frightened. I felt abandoned. The watering of my eye seemed as gruesome as the dripping walls of a lavatory in an Industrial Revolution slum.[50]

In the morning there was no improvement so Eric was sent to telephone Denton's new doctor, Walter Ramsden. He was out. Eric then tried Jack Easton who had returned to Tonbridge earlier in the year following his discharge from the Army and had written to Denton asking if he wanted to be his patient again (rather confused at the suggestion, Denton decided to stick with Ramsden whom he liked). Anyhow, on this occasion Easton was free and answering the summons he came over almost immediately. It was the first time they had seen one another in years.

He came up the stairs without Evie saying anything to me, and I was not perfectly certain that I had not deluded myself until he opened the door and stood there. He was more or less the person that I had first seen ten years ago in the garden of the nursing home at Broadstairs; there was less hair on the top of his head. He was tireder, and I thought of all the disgustingness that he had had to deal with in Egyptian hospitals for the last four or five years.

The meeting would have been much more graceful if Jack had not suddenly said in a too social a voice 'How are you!' What was I to do? Respond in the same tone, or at once plunge into my anxieties over the eye? I compromised and said with rather a giggle, 'I'm quite all right if it weren't for this peculiar eye surprise.' There was a tremor of dislocation and surface silliness, then I told him what had happened and waited.[51]

The problem seems to have been a temporary paralysis of the third nerve. Dr Easton's prognosis was that it should right itself in anything between a few weeks and a couple of months. In retrospect he thought it was quite possibly a slight stroke. To begin with Denton may have revelled in the macabre sight of himself in the mirror with a black patch over the bad eye, but he knew quite well that the illness was symptomatic of a general weakening in his condition. Hopefully, things would be back to normal in the New Year; it was vital he should be well enough to cope with the move to Middle Orchard.

The recovery, happily, was rapid and by 14th January 1946, he was full of naughty gossip about a misfortune that had befallen Mrs Walbrand-Evans. A letter to Peggy Kirkaldy written ten days previously betrays the extent to which he was out of sympathy with his old friend. 'May,' he wrote, 'seems to get more unmixable from day to day. I think she should stop living in her over-stocked junk shop of a house with the mice gnawing at the floorboards and the fringes of the carpet.'[52] Now, to his considerable amusement, it seemed that divine retribution had been wreaked on her acquisitiveness: her house, the Brown Jug, was subjected to a most eccentric burglary.

> I feel she ought to be very pleased she slept right through it. Someone got into her drawing-room through the window in the early hours and took two Chelsea figures, a china box with raised flowers on it, a gun-metal watch, opera glasses, a little silver and glass bonbon box and her chocolate ration. He washed himself, polished his shoes, rested on her couch and spread marmalade all over the kitchen table![53]

The early New Year found Denton busily adding finishing touches to a number of poems earmarked for the editors of various magazines and periodicals. His first approach to Routledge, in July 1942, had been with the suggestion that they should bring out an illustrated volume of his verse, but resurrecting the idea in January 1944 he wrote self-deprecatingly, 'I have a lot of poems here, but many of them may be muck.'[54] Over the intervening years the quantity had grown by several hundred, and yet Denton's reservations about their worth were as strong as ever. In the first week of February 1946 he wrote to Mrs Kirkaldy that

> as soon as things come to this stage one begins to lose confidence in any poem one has ever written, and the more beautifully one copies them out, the more nervous one becomes about their content! One can only go on telling oneself that it is squeamish not to let others see what one has tried to say.[55]

There can be little question that his poems *are* very uneven. It appears that in several instances when Denton wrote down lines of verse he was not doing much more than exercising an ability to express his own imaginative thoughts.[56] It confirmed for him that he was indeed a literary animal. However difficult work on his book may have been on any particular day, it was relatively easy to spend twenty minutes or so drafting the odd poem. If some of them could be worked up into a publishable form, so much the better—there was nothing to be lost in cultivating the practice.

Confident in the knowledge that there was a readership who appreciated his work, Denton felt that as long as he was true to his personality he could afford to express himself with greater freedom than before. 'I must never be afraid of my foolishness,' he had written in the Journals, 'only of pretension.'[57] The two

40. Male nude, drawn by Denton in the life class at Goldsmiths', c.1934.

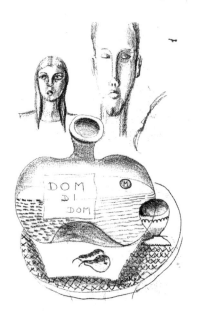

41. Page from a sketch-book that Denton used in hospital, 1935, whilst recovering from the accident.

42. Pen and ink portrait of Francis Streeten, c.1937 (cat. no. 105).

43. Oil painting of male nudes drying after swimming in the River Medway, 1936 (cat. no. 9).

44. Still-life, c.1936 (cat. no. 22).

45. A fantastic beach scene, c.1939, showing the influence of Edward Bawden (cat. no. 110).

46. 'Faces at the Stage Door', 1939 (cat. no. 104).

47. Lord Berners as a child, dressed as Robinson Crusoe, 1940 (cat. no. 48).

48. 'Alex', a pug, 1943 (cat. no. 57).

49. 'Harvesters', 1941 (cat. no. 47).

50 'Nina' (cat. no. 67), a painting influenced by Belgian artist, Reimond Kimpe.

51. The horse and the tower, a pen and ink drawing used in *Poetry London*, 1943.

52. 'The Milky Way', a pen and ink drawing used in *Vogue*, 1947.

53. A cow in the park at Oxon Hoath, Kent, a pen and ink drawing,
c.1943.

54. Tom the Woodman, detail from a pen and ink drawing from life, 1940
(cat. no. 117).

To **Rosalind Baſſett**

Methought I walked
still to and fro,
And from her company
I could not go—
But when I waked it was
not so:
In youth is pleasure,
In youth is pleasure.

LUSTY
IUVENTUS
by
ROBERT
OLIVER

55. The dedicatory frontispiece from *In Youth is Pleasure*, 1944.

56. A Christmas card, from a pen and ink drawing by Denton Welch.

57. Ornamented title-page for a projected anthology of his poetry.

58. Flowers and a Demon, an oil painting, c.1943 (cat. no. 63).

59. 'A Beauty Waiting in the Fields', a watercolour, begun earlier, but completed 1947 (cat. no. 94).

60. 'The Woodman's Cottage', Peckham Hurst, a watercolour, c.1946
(cat. no. 122).

61. 'The Coffin House', Oxon Hoath, a watercolour, 1946 (cat. no. 123).

novels and most of the short stories already published had dealt with his childhood and adolescence; quite possibly it occurred to him that the vagaries of character revealed in *A Voice Through a Cloud* might appear less excusable now he was portraying himself as an adult. Whereas the hero-worship of 'Archer' in 'When I was Thirteen' had been a common, if unmentionable, phenomenon, what would people think of his obsession with 'Dr Farley'?

Denton was well aware, however, that he had to avoid falling into the trap of writing about things that were beyond his own experience. On one or two occasions, admittedly, he did take a woman as the central character in a story, but this was done either to explore the feminine aspect of his own personality or, as in the case of 'The Fire in the 'Wood', to write about a relationship that would have been unacceptable if presented as a homosexual love story. Mildred Bosanquet's criticism of Denton's work was that it contained 'nothing of the universal', yet she had failed to grasp the point that his strength lay in convincing the reader that the hero, however peculiar and irritating he might be, was attempting to come to terms with an alien world that seemed to have been thrown together at random. Going very much against the grain, Denton tried to explain something of the scope of his writing to Stephen Bagnall, who had recently sent him the manuscript of his own first book:

> The fear of being petty, laboured and too particular makes us often cast our thoughts in the safer, grander and more generalized forms, but the more I write, the more I'm convinced that one can't be too individual, idiosyncratic even. You will see from this that I am prejudiced against broad statements that embrace all the world in a novel. The things that happen to one character are symbolic of much greater world happenings, and one can leave it at that, I feel.[58]

During the first week in March Denton was told by the Adeneys that he would definitely be able to rent Middle Orchard from the end of the month. Temporarily, he took on a new lease of life. In the weeks preceding the move not only did he go up to London for a meeting with Pearn, Pollinger and Higham (his first visit to the capital in eighteen months), but also, less than a week later, he drove over to Greenwich with Noël and Eric. Denton wished to convey to her something of his special enthusiasm for Croom's Hill and furthermore to point out a number of his favourite haunts in the area. The time at Goldsmiths' had been one of the happiest periods of his life and it was a strangely nostalgic experience for him to return to the house, knowing that in future it would be lived in by the Adeneys. Back at Pitt's Folly Denton wrote up an account of the day in the Journal and recalled his impressions on seeing the place for the first time in 1933:

> It had been all fresh and newly painted when at eighteen I had come upon it in my agitated, inexperienced and determined search for a room of my own. Eve [sic] had opened the door to me and been as moony and as

unattached as she still is. Strange to think that from that day to this she has been somewhere about the place. First I lived in her house; now she lives in mine. And she is as inhuman as ever.[59]

Miss Sinclair's present situation was giving cause for anxiety, the problem being that she did not fancy the idea of going to live at Middle Orchard. Noël was bound to be down very often to visit, and by and large Evie did not get on with her. Moreover, now Eric was an established member of the household, her own role had been relegated purely to that of servant; in short, Evie no longer felt indispensable. Eric believed that at the back of her mind, incredible though it may seem, her ambition had always been to marry his friend. 'She has now become so extraordinarily difficult, so glowering, and with such a sense of grievance,' Denton wrote to Peggy Kirkaldy, 'that neither Eric nor I can reason with her.'[60] The only solution, he thought, was that she should make a complete and possibly permanent break from them.

He persuaded her to answer a notice advertising the post of housekeeper to two sisters living in Cornwall. Fortunately they did not require anyone for a month, so she was able to lend a hand with the move. Eric spent much of the time at Middle Orchard supervising the cleaning and redecorating of the house. Two days before the great event got under way Denton, who had developed a high temperature, rested from all the frenetic activity and cast his mind back over his life at Pitt's Folly, the place which more than any other he associated with the launch of his literary career. The Sickert article and *Maiden Voyage* were both published whilst he had been living here, then another book, short stories too, 'and I was waiting all the time for something else to happen to me';[61] then, almost by accident, Francis Streeten had brought along Eric and he had nearly turned them away because he was ill in bed.

What would have happened if I hadn't suddenly changed my mind? Another door was opened on to a landscape that I thought would always be quite foreign to me. All those crags and pools and frowning storm-clouds; a degree of sharing quite outrageous if it had been prophesied to me; unhappiness and feeling of waste that I thought I had done with for ever; cosy snugness of friendship that I only remember very early with my brother.[62]

At 10.40p.m. on Monday, 25th March, totally uninterested in the then current drama of the Nuremburg trials, Denton opened one of his exercise books and wrote with a sense of triumph and relief:

It's happened, we are here. I'm in the quiet room all to myself and Eric is in his, sleeping already. The stiff new red, grey and fawn striped curtains are round me and I smell paint from downstairs. I ache all round the middle of me in a broad belt. There was an owl just now calling and calling.[63]

Chapter Ten

Middle Orchard

Middle Orchard is a little characterless. Its walls, both internal and external, as well as the floors, are made of cedar—the wood was quite light in Denton's day—and to some extent it was not really designed to withstand extreme weather. At either end of the long low house there is a veranda and Denton could get onto the roof of the one beside his bedroom through a french window. From this room there are views of open fields and, to the west, a small wooded valley; the atmosphere is restful and open.

It seems likely that Denton was attracted to the place because, as a quite modern holiday home, it did not have an especially strong 'lived-in' feeling. The Hop Garden had been the same. At last there would be enough room for all the furniture, and one of the first things Eric and he did was to put up the ten-foot-square French cartoon that had been kept in storage since his move to Pitt's Folly. The picture was so colossal that it became necessary to fold in two feet at the base and fix one end of it round a corner.

In the living-room downstairs Denton hung the green velvet curtains he had bought for the flat in Hadlow Road; a small Regency side-table fitted neatly between the windows. The handsome secretaire, which contained all his manuscripts (as well as money and various other documents), went up to his bedroom, the dolls' house too. Everything was positioned with fastidious care and very quickly the plain house with its light rooms was transformed into a veritable repository of antiques and works of art.

On 7th May Miss Sinclair finally left to take up her position as housekeeper to the sisters in Cornwall. Denton was extremely sceptical that the arrangement could work. 'Little do they know,' he wrote to Peggy Kirkaldy, 'that their "lady-help" will probably only stay a month!'[1] In the Journals he describes how Evie had come into his bedroom to say goodbye: she made 'two little running darts' in his direction, but could not summon up sufficient courage for a kiss. Just as Eric and she were leaving for the station he ran down in his cassock and waved her farewell. Despite all their rows, Denton knew he would miss her. 'She has a streak of madness, of course,' he wrote, concluding the day's entry, 'and that often makes her touching, infuriating and tragic.'[2]

Denton had always valued Evie's culinary skills very highly. Her potatoes roasted in nut oil were a perennial favourite. From now on he would have to subsist on the more basic food provided by Eric. 'Denton was, always very appreciative of what I produced,' his friend recalled, but I knew quite well that I was no cook.'[3] Matters were not helped by the continuance of rationing, which meant that it took considerable imagination to vary one's daily diet. Denton himself seldom spent much time in the kitchen, although occasionally he would turn his hand to cleaning the stove and Eric said that he treated the chore as if he were accomplishing a work of art.

Although he never really kept to any definite timetable at Middle Orchard—so much depended on how he was feeling—Denton usually rose fairly early in the morning and would then spend a long time in the bathroom, leaving Eric to make his bed and turn the mattress. Sometimes Eric came in and sat on the lavatory when he was in the bath and then, as a joke, would proceed to make the most excruciating noises. Denton then got back into bed and had his breakfast, which his friend remembered throughout the year consisted of porridge. Writing was next on the agenda, and on a good day this continued uninterrupted until it was time for lunch.

His medical condition proved to be as unpredictable as ever. Just a fortnight after the move he was suffering from internal bleeding, and yet within a couple of days he went out in the Austin exploring the network of lanes up on the North Downs. Even through the worst bouts of illness Denton managed to continue supplying a monthly drawing for the cookery column in *Vogue*. With regard to his writing, however, he decided to resist pressure from Pearn, Pollinger and Higham to channel his energies into producing short stories. Recently he had been working on a new one (this was 'The Fire in the Wood'), but after spending a miserable Easter of being so unwell that he could scarcely eat, Denton wrote to his agents saying he did not want to do any more and that now he intended to devote his time entirely to finishing *A Voice Through a Cloud*.

Yet whatever his ambitions may have been, Denton was virtually incapable of protecting himself from interruption, and soon a whole horde of people descended on Middle Orchard. On one occasion it was five relations; another time a man from The Medici Society who thought it might be nice to make a pamphlet about him and his pictures. Guy Allan and Derrick Sayer came down with a camera and took a number of photographs of Denton and Eric in their new home. The Adeneys, who retained the studio in the house, put in an appearance too. They perhaps were the least welcome of all 'Noël will come and sit on the bed and try to talk disquietingly, but then she remembers that she ought to go, and goes,' he wrote. 'Perhaps the secret of successful social intercourse is to mask your feelings very little, no more than makes for ordinary politeness.'[4]

It was only during the second week in May, shortly after Evie's departure, that Denton was entirely alone, Eric having gone up to London to see his mother. On the 14th he wrote in the Journal:

> The day is messy. I have done some writing, but things are sloppy. I am a melting jelly. It seems that my happiness only comes from being a monk; and when I am not a monk, therefore I cannot be happy. When I am dammed up and I will not force and break the dam, will not bore

through it and will not make the waters flow in however rough a channel, I am not happy. Idleness cannot be a happiness for me. It is too heavy a burden. But perhaps half-hearted work is a greater pain. It is like struggling in giants' entrails. To be trapped in the web of unformed work!

With the monk in his dedicated life he may waste some of his time, but he is not distracted, so that even his idleness is dedicated. But when one gives oneself in several directions one is naturally torn to pieces.[5]

Unfortunately, this is exactly what Denton allowed to happen: in the fortnight that followed he entertained the Dallas sisters to lunch one day, the author Stephen Bagnall another, he saw an old friend whom he had known in Shanghai and was gaily inviting Peggy Kirkaldy to drive over from Colchester. On the evening of 5th June Denton lay in bed revising the episode in *A Voice Through a Cloud* that describes how he had roamed about the streets of Broadstairs in the rain, blindly reaching out for something or someone to alleviate the pain of his loneliness. He was by himself in the house; Eric had gone to a pub. Deeply involved in the emotions he was trying to recapture, he suddenly ran from his bedroom, got out his bicycle, and rode off along a path into the nearby Shipbourne Forest. It was an extraordinarily ill-judged thing to have done. His idea was to make for a cottage in the woods 'where a dark-eyebrowed youth used to live,' a person he knew when he was at The Hop Garden. He only had a very rough notion of the direction. The track he was following led right into the blackness of the vast wood.

Denton soon appreciated the folly of his action. Desperate thoughts began to crowd in upon his mind. Reading the account of the nightmarish experience in the Journals, one senses the quest came to assume a peculiar significance. Denton felt that finally he was lost—and that he half brought it on himself:

'What if you should wander for hours,' I thought, 'what if you should be in here all night! You would very probably die. Already you are very strained and knocked about. You who lie in bed for days, will probably not be able to get home now, even if you do find the way, which seems unlikely. And when strangers find you, they'll not know what to do, and you'll have to ask, if you're still capable, to be taken home.' . . .

Because of the night I could not stop for a moment, I had always to be forcing forward. Strange that when one is afraid and lost one cannot stop to contemplate for a moment.

The tractor trail that I had begun to follow took one up and down hillocks, over bristling scrub that made me convinced that I was more lost than ever, through deep slush puddles. I fell down once. My face was streaming. I felt, 'That you should do this, play this idiocy for a whim! This is how people end themselves all in a moment—a wild impulse that dishes them.'

If I had been a strong person the largeness of the wood netted with false trails would have been intimidating; but for me it was appalling. And that it was in the heart of the tame countryside—people and houses and cars all about me—that was horrible.[6]

As fortune would have it he eventually came out of the wood right into the garden of the cottage. He saw a light in the window. Someone was moving about. Denton did not stop. From here he could get onto a track to Seven Mile Lane, a straight road from which it was easy to branch off and return to Crouch. On reaching Middle Orchard he discovered that Eric was not yet back. In a moment, though, he spotted the lights of their car advancing along the drive.

> I flew into the hall, pulled off coat and gloves, climbed the stairs, kicked away the muddy shoes, then got under the eiderdown of the bed and pulled my notebooks and pen up from where I had left them.
> He found me writing, just as I had been when he left.
> I had the wish to tell no one of my fright and my journey into the black wood.
> And though we drank tea and stayed talking for a long time, I said nothing at all about it.[7]

Very probably one of the reasons why Denton resorted to working on the book in the evenings was that in recent days he had been busy with another project—and it carried the fixed deadline of 1st August. The poet José Garcia Villa had written from America asking him to contribute something for a special number of the journal *Harvard Wake* dedicated to Edith Sitwell. This was a commission he simply could not refuse.

Given a completely free hand as to length and content, at once it became obvious that he had to put together an essay about his meeting with her at The Sesame Club, back in April 1943. He had written an exuberantly comprehensive account of it in the Journals; this could form the basis. At first glance the work seemed to be quite easy, but Denton rapidly became aware of certain pitfalls that had to be avoided. The last thing he wanted was to give his patroness any cause for embarrassment. 'I am anxious not because I have any unfavourable things to say,' he wrote to Peggy Kirkaldy, 'but because it is so easy to offend unintentionally, either by mentioning small, unimportant details or by repeating careless snippets of conversation that are never meant to be repeated.'[8] One might remark that he had seldom demonstrated any such qualms before.

Denton wrote to Miss Sitwell requesting her permission. Immediately she set his mind at rest, saying in her letter that the idea gave her 'a mixture of really *extreme* delight and some trepidation'—the latter when she considered his wicked account of the tea with Sickert. 'But at least,' she wrote, 'I did not, as far as I can remember, dance or sing.'[9] In the course of this friendly letter she twice mentions that she would appreciate seeing the essay before he sent it off, a request with which Denton in due course complied.

In the event, all the work was wasted. 'A Lunch Appointment' was not used; there was no issue of *Harvard Wake* for 1947. On the last day of July Denton was writing again to Mrs Kirkaldy, saying he had just heard *Maiden Voyage* was about to be translated into German, 'which reminds me,' he added, 'that I must get back to my third book, which is taking so long. I shall have to closet myself with it and think of nothing else.'

In the meantime; as he had predicted, Miss Sinclair was sacked by the sisters in Cornwall. Apparently she refused to eat her meals *en famille* and there had been a scene. Now she was in the employ of a lady doctor in Truro. In August the woman went on holiday and Evie invited Denton and Eric to come down and stay with her in the bungalow. Much to his regret, Denton had to decline and so on the 8th Eric set out by himself, taking the recently finished picture 'A Cat Waiting for its Master' to the Leicester Galleries on the way.

What should have been an ideal fortnight for him to catch up on revisions to *A Voice Through a Cloud* did not materialize as such. The following day he was writing in the Journal that Noël was still there, 'although I've made it quite plain that I'd rather be alone,' and having mentioned receiving a letter from Commander Hugh Corbett, R.N., who had bought a flowerpiece from a recent Artists International exhibition, Denton went on to list requests for work that had come in from the *New York Post* and *The New Yorker*, aside from which *New Writing* and a little magazine for adolescents, *Junior*, wanted him to contribute illustrations for single numbers. 'I would like, whenever I am asked for something, to be able to do it,' he wrote, 'but I cannot, and so I feel confused by requests and wish to be left alone to finish my book.'[10] A poem dating from the same month expresses the extent to which the accumulation of things was contributing to his worries:

> One day all the rages of my fever brain
> Shall die down to pleasant life again;
> And I shall be a clear white stone,
> An ivory, a polished bone,
> A smooth egg lying on the shore,
> Breathing out love for evermore.[11]

To cap it all, on the 13th he received a letter from the artist Michael Ayrton saying he was putting on an exhibition at Heal's featuring about sixteen young painters. Would he like to participate? The pictures were to sell for under £40. Denton was nonplussed. He had heard Ayrton speak on the B.B.C.'s 'Brains Trust' programme and formed an instant dislike to him. 'He seems to be insisting rather school-girlishly on his charm,' he wrote, 'when all the time I feel quite unwilling to give him any credit for any charm at all.'[12] Nevertheless, flattered at being asked to exhibit, he was soon adding the finishing touches to two pictures: one, a small oil of a hand and flowers by a seashore, and the other 'The Coffin House',[13] which is regarded as one of the most striking works he ever produced. Ayrton wanted all the pictures to arrive by 15th September, since the exhibition would open early the next month. Unfortunately, he had not done his homework: it transpired that six of the selected artists were forbidden by their dealers to take part and the whole scheme was scrapped.

Other than his friends from Goldsmiths', Denton had very little contact with fellow artists and he never met Michael Ayrton. By coincidence, however, on 26th August the painter Keith Vaughan telephoned to ask if he might drop in at Middle Orchard that afternoon, as he was going to be in Sevenoaks, only a few miles away. It seems that in referring to him as 'a Keith Vaughan' Denton was not familiar with his work (which is concerned almost exclusively with a timeless and symbolic depiction of the male nude), although he certainly knew the name and had every reason to be well-disposed towards him. In May 1944 he had received a letter from Vaughan praising *Maiden Voyage* in terms nearly as extravagant as those used by Alex Comfort. It was a letter Denton had kept. There was one sentence in particular that could well have stuck in his memory:

> Apart from Kafka, you are the only writer I know who has that unique power of saying something quite simple and making it mean a great deal more—an absolute preciseness of image, and the power of concentrating into an exact statement of fact a world of significant feeling.[14]

Described in the Journals as 'fairly small and slight, very smiling, hair a little thinning, dressed in corduroys,'[15] Keith Vaughan arrived at four o'clock. Immediately, the conversation flowed easily and Denton even went downstairs to get the tea himself. As the evening wore on he listened to a fair amount of talk about the artist's mother, though the most welcome piece of news was that John Lehmann had bought 'The Woodman's Cottage' picture at the Leicester Galleries.

After spending week after week confined to his room, Denton grew a little stronger. Making use of the car on various days in September, Eric and he took a picnic to Mount Ephraim in Tunbridge Wells, attended the sale of Victor Cazalet's possessions at Fairlawne (he bought a pair of small eighteenth-century Chinese mirror paintings for twenty-four guineas) and also made a trip to Rochester. Early in October they went to Rye, the nearest point on the South Coast, where, with a mixture of disapproval and delight, he was able to observe the antics of 'an absurd clergyman' who was seen standing in front of the church 'showing off to some workmen on a scaffold and any other parishioners who would stop to listen.'[16] Later on in the month, amidst a veritable bombardment of letters written in coloured inks from a highly eccentric naval chaplain, Richard Blake Brown,[17] Denton made what was to be his last long journey: the two friends drove up to Greenwich to have lunch with Noël Adeney.

He had wanted to see all he could of the outside world before winter set in. Denton was never able to do so much again. The state of invalidism, described in the Journals as 'a sort of wicked acceleration of one's life', now became to all intents and purposes permanent and there was only the occasional day's remission when he could venture out in the car. Worst of all, his work too was severely affected:

> The feeling has come over me that I must let everything melt away, that I am no longer in command at all. And in my idleness all I can think of are rich strange dishes wonderfully cooked, amazing little houses in fine gardens, rare and lovely objects for these tiny palaces, and then wills and bequests both fantastic and more down to earth.[18]

They persuaded Miss Sinclair to come back in mid-November and she tended to their needs over Christmas. The idea was to give Eric a break, but to begin with all their former housekeeper wished to do was to sit around and regale them with stories of her doctor-employer in Cornwall and the enormities of the woman's children, whom it was her duty to look after. Happily, the spell away had done Evie good and there were no more domestic upsets for the time being. On Christmas Day Denton and Eric invited a twenty-one-year-old German prisoner-of-war, Harry Diedz, over for lunch. Conversation in broken English was perhaps a little trying, but Eric in particular was so impressed by what he heard of Germany that for several days afterwards he talked of little else.

During the first three weeks of 1947 Denton lay closeted upstairs, unable to collect his thoughts, let alone work. The objects in the bedroom began to worry him; they seemed to assume a threatening life of their own. He found it impossible to eat normally and had to be prescribed a type of protein food, tasting like 'artificial manure'. Every four hours Eric injected his thigh with penicillin to curb the inflammation in the kidneys, but it did not help.

Life at Middle Orchard was becoming terribly difficult. Denton could barely walk at the beginning of February. To make matters worse, the latter half of the winter proved to be one of the harshest on record. Although his electric fire was kept on all night, the taps froze and then within a few days there were power cuts. Denton's hands were so cold that he was unable to write. On the 24th, taking up his orange fountain pen, he discovered the ink had solidified. Once it thawed he turned to the Journal and yet again recorded details of the work that had yet to be started. *Junior* had taken his story 'The Packing Case House and the Thief' and now suggested he might provide illustrations to go with it;[19] *Vogue* this time required two drawings for the cookery column. The commissions were not in themselves taxing, but close intricate work was a strain on his eyes and frequently brought on a blinding headache. In the entry Denton mentions too that there was a 'long-short story'—almost certainly 'Brave and Cruel'—waiting to be revised.

Later on the same day he wrote a poem, 'The Secret Pug', which also bears the alternative title, 'The Fear and the Monkey':

> And we shall lick each others' sores.

> I
> I had a secret in my jacket
> It wasn't a bird or a toad or a rabbit;
> It wasn't a tortoise or a feeble newt.
> It was my secret dark as soot.

> Nobody knew that under my vest
> It laid its head on my bare chest
> The breath from its tiny monkey nose
> Made dew drops on my woollen clothes.

Its perfect little monkey face
Would look up with a soft grimace
Whenever I pulled off my shirt;
And its fairy voice was pert.

It had transparent paper ears,
Eyes like blue needles weeping tears,
A ruff and hood of Persian fur;—
It was a peerless comforter.

As every day I walked through the grass,
Watching the puff-ball cloudlets pass,
I would sing loud, it is my Joy,
My living doll, my breathing toy.

From the river bridge I dived to swim
He clutching me, I soothing him;
Then we lay dreaming in the sun,
Until each lovely day was done.

II
But later came another time,
I restless with my pug would climb
To where great beech trees lined the hill;
There in the leaves I sat quite still

The trunks were scarred with lovers' names,
The squirrels' tails stood up like flames,
But I was heavy in the leaves
As one who for his treasure grieves.

The monkey knew it, he could tell
That my spirit was not well;
The tiny teeth began to gnaw,
And he would tap me with his paw.

I felt him there beneath my shirt,
Sometimes his sober love-bites hurt.
But I wanted him there close to my skin;
He was my doll, my manikin.

He was my plaything and my pet,
My perfume and my fountain jet,
My silver popinjay of stars,
Sweeter than rose leaves in closed jars.

He was my happiness and life
My diamond-hilted stabbing knife
He was my emperor and pope,
My desperate song and brittle hope.

III
Now in the cloister I knelt down,
Under the ruined wall's grey frown.
The dandelions flecked the breeze,
Wasting their faces on my knees.

I had been told that dead monks lay
Under the broken flags and clay;
I tried to know them through the stones
To touch their ancient skulls and bones;

For the pug was working in me now,
Burning and churning like a plough
A silver-bladed plough to bite
Through diligently day and night.

I thought of each monk in his shaped stone box,
I told the time on the flower clocks,
I tried to make a singing sound. . .
And then I fell down on the ground.

The monkey's head was in my flesh
Tearing the muscles' bleeding mesh.
This moment he had waited for;
He had his body through the door.

My misery had let him in,
It was my weakness and my sin.
When I was happy all day long,
He was my joy and I was strong.

But now he scrambled to my heart
And tore the crimson wide apart.
He lapped at blood with lustful joy
As if such drink should never cloy.

And when the screaming heart was raped,
Then to my gut he wildly scraped,
With teeth and claws of acid fire
He worked the wreckage of desire.

He had the bowels, the gall, the spleen,
He licked till the stomach walls were clean;
Then he leapt out of the bloody cave
And I saw him racing like a wave.

Over the flags of the cloister garth,
Leaving a dripping crimson path.
The rose foam glistened on the weeds
And held feathery flying seeds.

He never paused, he never turned,
Cold, cold now where his claws had burned,
I lay there hollow as a tree,
And the chill wind blew through me.[20]

It is in reading extracts from the Journals of around this time that one comes to appreciate the symbolic power of the pug-monkey. As Denton's physical state deteriorated, so the sense of a division within himself became increasingly alarming. On the one hand there was his body, which he refers to as being 'like a dead asleep thing hanging on me, bearing me down,'[21] on the other, the same old life-force inside, exemplified by an irresistible eagerness to be up and about and to continue exploiting his talent to the full. So long as the two aspects of him were working in tandem, then everything was alright, but in this poem Denton is depicting how, when death comes into sight, the life-force, still strong and vigorous, claws wildly to preserve its own existence—it feeds on the body and, once sated, flees.

The dreams of 'wills and bequests both fantastic and more down to earth' before long were brought to an abrupt end. With no immediate prospect of inheriting anything from his father's estate, Denton had recently turned his attention to Cissie Carpmael, whom he looked upon as an unnecessarily wealthy surrogate aunt. At the beginning of December he had speculated that her fortune might stand at 'anything between £50,000 to £80,000',[22] and in his mind's eye he had selected two Georgian teapots and some Persian rugs as being the most desirable items amongst her possessions.

On 3rd March, as if in answer to a prayer, he received a letter from Irene Dallas telling him that Mrs Carpmael, her closest friend, had 'passed on' two days earlier. Apparently, she had fallen on the floor of her studio at the oast-house in Trottiscliffe and broken her thigh. Since the household consisted entirely of Christian Scientists, Miss Brown, the mad sister Connie's companion-housekeeper, had not called a doctor until it became clear that she was critically ill. He could do nothing. She died on the Saturday evening. The Dallas sisters came straight away from London to take things in hand.

It seems that Denton *was* genuinely upset. Cissie had been the person who first introduced him to painting. She had taken him seriously. She had done her best to make him feel welcome in the school holidays. What lent the news a particular poignancy was that it reached him on the anniversary of his mother's death twenty years earlier. However, once the shock had worn off—and it did very rapidly—Denton's mind turned to the contents of the will, and with the snow blowing around Middle Orchard in a blizzard, he lay wrapped up in bed growing more and more obsessed with the matter.

The following days were not easy. Denton worried that he might be expected to deal with Mrs Carpmael's huge canvases and Eric, seconded to help with moving things from the oast-house, had a violent quarrel with Evie. It was not until twenty days after the funeral that Denton felt able to take up his pen and write about the outcome of the will in his Journal. The document, which had been drawn up years before, had proved to be a severe disappointment. There was no codicil in his favour. He was left nothing. He asked Miss Dallas if it might be possible to have one of the teapots—there was a matching cream jug, and both were embossed with fruit, flowers and scrolls—but even this turned out to be difficult.

> Somehow this wrangling about a teapot depressed me even more than the news that Cecil [Mrs Carpmael] had not bothered to remember me at all. I was dirtied by it, turned into a vulture on such a tiny scale. I had thought so often of Cecil's Will when she was alive, hoped so much that she would leave me a cosy fortune. That had been quite simple and natural and friendly. Now there was a sort of pointless resentment that fixed itself round the teapot, but really spread out far and wide.[23]

As late as 12th June Denton was still venting his anger in an excessively virulent diatribe against the formidable Miss Dallas, who he considered had arranged her deceased friend's affairs in an unnecessarily ham-fisted and insensitive manner. Enfeebled by illness, the whole experience had bruised his self-confidence to a barely comprehensible degree.

With the appalling winter now over, Denton began to revive a little, and shortly after celebrating his thirty-second birthday on 29th March he was well enough to resume work on one of his pictures which he had come across stored away in a cupboard. The watercolour, 'A Beauty Waiting in the Fields', is a thing of pure fantasy (see illustration). He records in the Journal that he started to make 'all sorts of little changes and additions' to it[24] and very soon his pen was running riot in filling the paper with an extravagant range of decorative effects.

In the background there is a moonstruck cow peering over its shoulder at the subject of the picture, a sedate, outrageously overdressed lady, who one presumes is out for a stroll in the country. She has eyes reminiscent of those dreamlike sirens in the paintings of Paul Delvaux. The frieze-like ornamentation on top of the hat brings together such incongruous companions as a bird and two fishes, a rose and ears of corn, and her sexuality is given a curiously indeterminate aspect by the plain cross hanging around her neck below the mustard-yellow scarf with its fabulous bow. The cross seems to signify the attitude, 'in spite of all this nonsense, I am chaste'—a gesture perhaps saying something of the conflict within Denton's own personality between his Christian Science upbringing and the self-indulgent fantasy of his adult mind. As with so many of his portraits, the 'Beauty' is more akin to an icon than a living, breathing person.

More than ever Denton could not count on being well enough to earn any regular income. Although some money was coming in from foreign editions and reprints of his two books, he realized that unless either *A Voice Through a Cloud* or a volume of short stories was published fairly soon, he might be forced to cut back on his expenses. This was the last thing he wanted to do now his health had become so precarious. There were still his shares in Canadian Pacific and Imperial Tobacco, but if these went he would be without any guaranteed income whatever.[25] Bill had sent £100 for his last birthday, but this year there was only the assurance he would step in if things became too desperate. Needless to say, Denton had no intention of being dependent on the charity of his elder brother.

Apart from the disappointment of Mrs Carpmael's will and his anxiety over a massive electricity bill, he found Noël's indecision about what she wanted to do with Middle Orchard increasingly unsettling. The present arrangement was that he rented the house at £96 a year. Early in July, however, Frida Easdale told Eric over a drink in the local pub that Noël knew she could be getting far more for the property. Eric, true to form, immediately repeated the conversation to Denton, who, having recently received a cheque for £100 from Routledge, was by now considerably more confident of his financial state, and subsequently he wrote to Noël saying he realized he *should* be paying more. His calculation was that if he did so, she would be much less likely to want him to quit. In the letter he suggested that in assessing a fair rent she should treat him as she would any ordinary tenant, in fact as she would 'a stranger'.

It was an unfortunate term to have used. Noël fancied herself in the role of Denton's benefactor—perhaps of more real use to him than Edith Sitwell had been—and now in her eyes he was attempting to distance himself in a manner that seemed cold and even rather disingenuous. On 5th July Noël posted Denton a letter that was intended to put him in his place:

> . . .You suggest that I write about Middle Orchard as I would to a stranger, but I think that would not be easy, would it? And before we freely discuss the rent, and so on, there is something that seems to me to be more important, and that is whether the sharing is proving a good arrangement, as it seems to be straining on friendliness. I think a good example, perhaps a glaring one, of what I mean happened on our last visit.
>
> Evie's rudeness, Eric's misreporting—I do not know if this was consciously mischievous—would be impotent with us without the lively hostile action of yourself.
>
> I do not think it's possible to be at Middle Orchard each ignoring the other, though there could be some pretence. I should like to know what you feel could better the arrangement, apart from the unfairness to us if we never visited.

Much as Denton denied that such a 'lively hostility' existed, this was in reality a very accurate description of his attitude towards her. She had made herself indispensable to him and he bitterly resented it. If one is to believe Noël's version of events as told in *No Coward Soul*, there was still a very definite rapport between them, particularly when they were alone, but over and above this Denton felt no compunction whatever in exploiting the friendship to the bounds allowed by decency; if things did become very strained, he knew that he could always fall back on his considerable resources of charm to paper over the cracks.

He managed to get out into the fields for a few afternoons in the third week of June and by the beginning of August had completed a new short story, 'The Trout Stream', which was mailed off to Rosamund Lehmann in her capacity as an editor of *Orion*.[26] On the 6th, however, Denton was suffering such agonizing pain that Eric had to summon Dr Easton to give him morphia and atropine. He writes in the Journals that the effect of the drugs was surprisingly pleasant:

> When he had gone away I floated off, not to sleep but into a pleasant stupor where I heard the infants squacking [sic] and screaming outside the cottage at the end of the orchard, heard the birds and the aeroplanes, but didn't care anything about them. The killing pain lost its grip, became playful even, nagging a little, jabbing, dancing, settling down at last to a comfortable thrumming.
>
> Later when he[27] came in to me, I opened my eyes and smiled. Something made me pick up a bit of mirror and hold it above my head.
>
> My lips were thick and warm and red, my lids thick and creamy. Underneath, my eyes looked happy and deliciously sleepy. My whole face seemed transformed by my drowse.[28]

It is difficult to determine exactly when Denton reached the decision that his next book should be a collection of short stories. We do know, however, that in May 1947 he sent nine of them to Routledge, hoping the firm might be persuaded to make them into an anthology. The idea was rejected, which left him free to approach another publishing house with the project. At the end of September he got in touch with Hamish Hamilton.

Back in April 1944 Hamilton had attempted to explore the possibility of his firm bringing out just such a collection, but Denton had quashed the proposal by informing him that, apart from being contracted to Routledge, he had only a meagre four short stories to his name. But now the situation was quite different. In his letter of 25th September Denton was able to tell Hamilton that the four had grown in number to nine and that he was in the process of completing another one roughly eleven thousand words long, as well as 'a slighter thing'.[29] He was very keen that Hamish Hamilton should publish them. Fortunately, the Scotsman had lost none of his admiration for Denton's work. 'It was good of you to remember the interest I expressed in "When I was Thirteen"', he wrote, 'and I shall be delighted to consider your collection of short stories. Most publishers when impressed by the quality of stories enquire whether the author intends to write a novel next, so I hope you won't mind my asking you the question now, in view of the fact that I am certain to enjoy the stories, judging from what I have already read.'[30] Denton replied telling him of the 'long thing' he had been working on for the past three years (i.e. *A Voice Through a Cloud*) and he said he thought the novel could be finished by adding something in the region of ten or twenty thousand words to the eighty thousand odd he had already written. 'I have not touched it for months,' he continued, because of short stories and pictures I have been doing; but I shall go back to it now with fresh eyes, I hope. I have been wondering a little about its fitness for publication, since it is turning out to be so very autobiographical. Does this put you off?'[31]

Unaware of the gravity of his illness, Hamilton's response was to try and coax Denton into producing the novel first and, if this proved to be impossible, at least letting him have it soon after the short stories. Either way, he was delighted at the idea of numbering Denton Welch amongst his authors. On 4th November Denton wrote back saying that he would much rather tackle the novel after the stories, 'since they at least are finished; and it is just possible that I may be hung up in the last chapters of my book.'

In the event, the process of assembling the collection proved to be far more worrisome than he could have anticipated. Six of the stories had already been published and therefore presented no difficulties—these were: 'The Coffin on the Hill', 'The Barn', 'Narcissus Bay', 'At Sea', 'When I was Thirteen' and 'The Judas Tree'[32]—but he had yet to complete 'The Fire in the Wood' (the eleven-thousand-word story referred to in the initial letter) and he was also in a bit of a dither whether to include 'Leaves from a Young Person's Notebook', since under its former title, 'The Sound of the Sea', it had already been rejected by both Reginald Moore and John Lehmann back in the autumn of 1944.[33]

What came as a profound blow, however, was that Hamish Hamilton, himself a qualified barrister, on learning that the longest one, 'Brave and Cruel' very possibly contained certain indiscretions and needed to be shown to a lawyer, wrote saying that if the story really was based on fact and involved people living in the area, it could be 'very dangerous indeed'.[34] He considered it would be unwise to start setting the book until the question of libel was cleared up. Denton intended 'Brave and Cruel' to be used as the title of the collection as a whole and at once recognized that if his account of the curious scandal surrounding Monté had to be excised, the viability of the entire book might be put in jeopardy.

The hitch could not have come at a worse time. Denton was very poorly throughout the first fortnight of November and on three occasions Eric had to correspond with Hamilton on his behalf. Slightly improved by the 14th, he conceded to the publisher that 'Brave and Cruel' was quite possibly not a suitable thing to bring out, though he doubted very much whether Monté himself would object to the story's content. Moreover, he argued, nothing he had written was untrue. In a subsequent letter a by now deeply depressed Denton said that he could not change the story without virtually rewriting it. 'I shall remember in future,' he added despondently, 'never to choose a theme so close to me in time and place again.'[35]

The whole dilemma turned out to be no more than a storm in a teacup. By 18th November Hamilton's partner had read 'Brave and Cruel' and did not consider that it warranted such caution. The publisher wrote to Denton telling him that while the portrayal of Monté was probably acceptable, maybe that of 'Mrs Bellingly' needed some modification, though he added, 'if she is a close friend of yours, she is unlikely to make trouble.'[36] Heartened by the change of tone, Denton at once began to make various alterations—'Den' became 'Dave'; 'La Fontaine' was transformed into 'Beaumont'—and in an altogether easier frame of mind he informed Hamilton that he didn't expect 'Mrs Bellingly' (May Walbrand-Evans) to raise any significant objections (even though she had been made out to be a gullible fool). 'She will probably feel that I have caricatured her, but she would never think of bringing an action. Of that I feel sure. . .'[37] In writing an accompanying note to the corrected manuscript, Denton reveals himself to have been gloriously naive, or perhaps insensitive, to the feelings of those who counted themselves as his friends:

My idea had been to let people discover the book for themselves, then to explain, if necessary, that no offence was meant, that the characters in the story were not intended to be portraits of living people, although the story was based on a real happening.[38]

Hamilton was satisfied. By the beginning of December the bulk of the book had gone to the printers. 'The Fire in the Wood' was posted off at the last minute, with a letter from Denton instructing that it should be forwarded to his agents if the publishers did not wish to include it in the volume.[39] All that remained was to design a jacket for the book, but Denton decided he wanted to leave this until after Christmas. Immediately the stories were out of the way he went back to *A Voice Through a Cloud*, which had been put aside for over a year. Another pressing concern was to finish a couple of pictures in time for the New Year Exhibition at the Leicester Galleries.

One would like to know what stage the novel had reached, but unfortunately it is impossible to determine this with any degree of accuracy, as Denton's own estimates of the length vary a great deal. One cannot be sure whether the wordage he refers to is corrected, worked-up text, or merely an overall amount, some of which had yet to be revised. It should be remembered, however, that back in September 1945, he told Stephen Bagnall over two-thirds of the book was already completed, though this draft had still to undergo a third revision. Writing to Hamish Hamilton on 9th December 1947, Denton mentions fifty-six to sixty thousand words, and although this differs from the eighty thousand of his earlier letter, the author is inclined to believe that this does indeed refer to fully revised text. *A Voice Through a Cloud*, as published, extends to something in the region of ninety-five to one hundred thousand words.

His health began to worsen still further. The spasms of pain were so frequent that Dr Easton found it necessary to show Eric how to administer morphine.[40] In spite of this, Denton never lost interest in what was going on about him. On 19th December Eric went along to a sale of Mrs Carpmael's possessions in Trottiscliffe with instructions to bid for one or two pieces, and although the affair turned out to be a disappointment (he returned with a pair of highly elaborate ormolu sconces that didn't look quite right at Middle Orchard), one good thing, at least, did emerge from the expedition: Eric ran into Graham Sutherland, a neighbour of Cissie Carpmael's, and the artist, always friendly, told him he had heard someone mention Denton's name to Somerset Maugham, who had replied that he considered him to be 'a very good author indeed'. Denton was a bit suspicious of the reported conversation. 'I wonder what really was said,' he mused in the Journal, 'how many qualifying clauses were added?'[41]

His Christmas present from Eric was much more attractive than the sconces with their pouting cupids: it was a late eighteenth-century glass mustard-pot in the shape of an urn. Denton kept imagining what it had been like when new. 'I think of it standing on the white damask,' he wrote, 'coming down through all the hundred and fifty years safely to me.'[42] Otherwise, Christmas Day itself ended up by being a very quiet affair. There was no Evie to see to the cooking; she had disappeared in October and now they didn't even have her address. Eric managed to rustle up a lunch of turkey (from a tin), chestnut stuffing (with sage and onion mixed in for good measure), potatoes and Brussels sprouts, which he had grown in the garden, and afterwards they tucked into a Christmas pudding given to them by his aunt. Denton made 'a hard sauce with butter and sugar and almond essence' to go with it. 'As we were having lunch,' he wrote 'great gusts of rain spattered the windows; the glass grew steamy, because of the warmth inside.'[43] That afternoon, ignoring the bad weather, they went for a drive in the car and it was the first time he had been out of the house since October.

Denton felt somewhat better for several days. On 6th January he wrote a poem in his notebook, the first for over two months, and two days later a thank-you letter to Peggy Kirkaldy, which is in a fast, well-controlled hand that bears no trace of the mental confusion he had suffered in November. One is amused here to note him making what was most probably a subconscious association between the Adeneys and the American novelist Edith Wharton:

Dear Peggy,

What delightful little books! I shall enjoy them; and what charming Victorian notepaper! I really have three separate things to thank you for.

I am so sorry that you are not feeling well. I hope it clears up as quickly as possible.

Eric and I go to the dentist today. As a compensation, we hope to find something interesting in the Sevenoaks antique shops.

Those were amusing extracts from the Stanley letters. I have ordered Percy Lubbock's book on Edith Wharton. She sounds horribly self-centred and dominating. I enjoy reading about impossible people, although I can't bear them in the flesh. I wonder why this is. We haven't seen the Adeneys for a long time, but they keep saying that they are coming down for a few days.

My new sister-in-law in Hong Kong is most attentive;[44] she keeps on sending us lovely food parcels of butter and tuna fish and delicious strawberry jam. It takes a complete stranger to do this sort of thing, I suppose? If she keeps it up we shall feel very well fed.

Eve Sinclair wrote a long letter from Cambridge, where she spent her Christmas holidays, but still not a word about her new job or address.

The agreement for my short stories is signed, but the agents say I mustn't expect the book until the autumn at the earliest.

Headaches are frightful; they stop one doing anything. I do hope yours disappears soon. Thank you once more for my little books.

Love Denton.

The Adeneys did indeed put in an appearance before long. They were staying in the studio at Middle Orchard the first weekend in February and on the Friday Eric drove Noël and Denton over to Brenchley, a small village just the other side of Paddock Wood about ten miles away. The plan was to attend the preview of a sale at the 'Ponds', a house Denton describes as being 'a sort of twentieth-century flattened-out Tudor'[45] in style. He sat in the back of the car, cosily wrapped in a big fur-lined army coat wearing Donegal tweeds, a polo neck sweater and yellow scarf; it was the thickest clothing he had.

The rain was beating down when they arrived. The first thing they did was to have a picnic. 'Huddled together under the dripping roof we drank scotch broth from the thermos and ate the sandwiches filled with a sort of foie-gras from Australia—very good. I delighted in the barley at the bottom of my bowl, each grain a tiny palish peach with the crack down the centre.'[46] Written the following day at the unusually early time of 7.30a.m., the Journal entry continues with Denton recounting how, leaning on a stick, he had managed to struggle up the drive to the 'flat, bleak, pointless little house.' He tells of the china they found inside, the cabinets, 'stuffed with Kang-shai blue and white or famille verte.'

Noël too describes the same outing, though with rather a different end in mind. She mentions that the three of them were due to meet up with May Walbrand-Evans, and in *No Coward Soul* the incident is used to draw attention to a less than appealing side of Denton's character. In writing as she does, one comes to realize that when Noël was feeling out of sympathy with Denton, her assessment of the true nature of their relationship—and at this stage one hesitates to employ the word 'friendship'—could be remarkably clear-sighted. Referring to May, she continues:

She was ill, lonely and unhappy since she had turned her house, unsatisfactorily, into two. She had asked Merton [Denton] to drive her home to tea, obviously needing his few minutes' friendliness there to warm and create it into a home. He said he had no petrol. She was walking wearily down the drive, after the sale view, when we overtook her. Merton was purposely neglecting to drive her the quarter mile to her bus. . . I do not know what I said, but he stopped and she came into the car, which had belonged to her, and Merton dropped her too soon. The last I ever saw of Amy [May] was her flagging, dispirited figure, painfully attempting to run or trot to catch the bus; her thick legs enclosed in doll-like warm stockings with socks over them. And we drove on, miles and miles around, had tea in a café and arrived home after dark. I must have exuded disapproval all the time. . .

When next I saw Merton alone I said, 'You're a little queen and need your subjects; you like to keep elderly people on a string. Amy and doubtless I are your convenient Aunt Sallies; we bear the full brunt of your brick-bats now that Ivor [Evie] is away.'

'. . .*One always bites the hand that feeds one.*'

'O yes, indeed, in adolescence, I know all too well. Some people grow up and you should.'[47]

'In *The Times* I read that Amy had died. I was shocked and telephoned Deer Farm. Gina answered and said at once, "She's left Merton the chandelier." '[48] These two sentences open the next chapter of Noël Adeney's book and they follow on directly from the above extract. Presumably the aim was to add substance to her portrayal of 'Merton' as a person who had lapsed into a state of indifference to other people, something that had been fostered through his association with the good-for-nothing Gina, but the way in which she presents the situation gives a grossly misleading impression of Denton and Eric's reaction on hearing of their sixty-eight-year-old friend's unexpected death; indeed, it is a venomous misrepresentation.

May had been admitted to the Tonbridge Cottage Hospital suffering from a prolapse. This involved a minor operation and she was expected to recover in a matter of two or three weeks. Denton and Eric went in to town to visit and, attempting to cheer her up, brought along some books, dates and barley sugar. 'She seemed rather miserable still, lying quite flat, looking as if she had been through an ordeal; but she often assumed a suffering expression when she wanted to fix one's attention on her, so I thought little of it.'[49] They had meant to go and see her the next Sunday too, but, as Denton continues in his Journal, 'the snow was so thick we could not move from here.' Up to the very last moment Denton had been justified in considering *himself* the iller of the two and the news of her passing came as a complete shock. 'May had so much bounce that it is terribly hard to think of her as dead,' he wrote to Peggy Kirkaldy, 'I felt she would live for years and years.'[50] One finds an engagingly vivid portrait of her in the Journal:

I think of May in great cartwheel hats with scarves, in crooks' slouch caps jammed over her eyes, in surprising widow's bonnets with streamers. I see her tiger-skin bootees, her mustard-yellow satchel, the coral and olive green of her one-time best afternoon dress. I see her heavy maquillage masking every inch of her real complexion, the vaseline on her eyelids, the mascara on her lashes.

I remember what a cook she was. The first time I ever had lunch with her there was hot-pot with tiny sausages and mushrooms in it.[51]

May *had* kept Denton in mind when she made her will; she left him a wonderful Queen Anne mirror in a broad walnut frame (Noël's chandelier was an invention). It was a piece he had always admired. Nor had she forgotten Eric; he was allowed to choose twelve books. Offering an interpretation of the significance of May's gift, Noël, in a superb piece of sub-Jungian mumbo-jumbo, ventured: 'I wondered if Amy was the witch cult-victim, and the chandelier the miracle-working relic.'[52] Her hypothesis was surely very wide of the mark. Denton's affection for May had been sincere. Noël realized this and was deeply resentful.

Just before he heard of May's death, Denton had begun a short story about his first encounter with the hapless Francis Streeten. It is called 'A Picture in the Snow'.[53] The narrative opens in the present, with the author and his companion 'G' (this is Eric Oliver, whose middle name was George) going to their 'nearest town' (i.e. Tonbridge) to do some shopping. Having failed to lay their hands on a spare part for the car, they decide to take a drive and see what they can of the dazzlingly picturesque winter landscape. Their route takes them up Tonbridge High Street. Past the public school they turn left into the London Road, and some distance along Denton recognizes the Streetens' former home, 'High Hilden', which stands back from the road on raised ground. They follow the drive up to the house and investigate. This is the cue for Denton to start telling how, nine years earlier, when walking in the town, he had been assailed by Francis ('Danny Whittome' in the story) with the wonderful opening gambit, '"Oh—you look interesting; do tell me about yourself."'[54]

One visualizes that in writing 'A Picture in the Snow' Denton was taking a break from the exacting work of completing *A Voice Through a Cloud*. An entry in the Journals for 16th March indicates that he had become thoroughly frustrated with the process of bringing the manuscript up to scratch:

> How I am aware of the thinness, the affectation and strain of what I write! Revising, correcting, is hateful, fishy, shaming. I would knock the posturing out of words, bash them into shape, iron out their obstinate awkwardness. Wishing violence means impotence.[55]

But rather than going back to concentrating exclusively on his novel, very soon he launched into 'The Hateful Word', another story inspired by something he had come across while out in the car. On this occasion, however, he had been to West Malling, very probably collecting medicine from the chemist. In the street his attention had been drawn to a rather vain German prisoner-of-war. Denton's description of the man appears first in the Journals and is a continuation of the 16th March entry:

> On Saturday, I remember the German in Malling, standing on the pavement in his too-romantic, rust-brown cloak ending in graceful points. With a furtive movement he glanced at himself in a shop-window, then drew out a black comb and sleeked back the close-fitting skull-cap of his

fair hair. It was thick, horribly smoothed and trained, catching the light and glinting. It seemed a pathetic little triumph and glory—his golden hair cherished in captivity.

'The Hateful Word', on the other hand, has a 'Flora Pinkston' noticing the man as she is coming out of the ironmonger's.

He stood near the bus stop, wearing a too-romantic rust-brown cloak which fell to his knees in graceful points. His long hair fitted his head so sleekly that it looked like a thick gold skull-cap. Its regularity repelled her a little; she wished the wind would ruffle it. She was not surprised when she saw him glance furtively in a shop window, then draw out a little blue comb and run through the shining strands.[56]

Flora offers him a lift in her car. They talk in rather broken English. It dawns on her that quite possibly he had not been meaning to go anywhere in particular, that he was just ambling around to fill in the time, and so she asks him back to her home for a drink. Flora's attitude is perhaps breezily patronizing, but here Denton is attempting to portray a female who displays none of the vulnerability of 'Mary' from 'The Fire in the Wood'—at least not until the very end of the story.

The young prisoner-of-war is called 'Harry Diedz'; it was the name of the German Denton and Eric had invited over for their Christmas lunch in 1946, and much of the conversation here is taken from this source. After she has plied him with various stock questions about his family, his work, whether or not he likes boxing, and so on, Flora is relieved to hear her husband returning home from work. Her hope is that he will engage the young German in everyday manly conversation. But Pinkston is tired and his only wish is to relax.

Flora shows Harry around the garden before he leaves and it crosses her mind that he might like to come over some evenings and help with the 'less interesting jobs' outside. He jumps at the opportunity. And so the story proceeds with Flora maintaining her shallow, self-consciously middle-class outlook and Harry's attitude towards his exploitative benefactors being one of almost grovelling appreciation.

One rainy afternoon he appears unexpectedly early at the house, his usual landwork having been abandoned for the day. By this stage Harry has proved his efficiency and needs little supervision. He offers to clean the greenhouse. Flora invites him for tea and asks afterwards if he will go upstairs with her to help move some furniture in her bedroom. Bending down to pick up a drawer, the German is transfixed by 'a small collection of old fans, scent-bottles, beadwork purses and early Victorian nosegay holders.' Flora wants to know if he likes coming to the house, and here it is that Denton slips in the twist to the story:

He looked up at her with his most brilliant smile. A raindrop still glistened in the little cup at the base of his throat. The unmistakable soldier smell rose from his warm damp battledress.

'I like here like my home. Before I was very sad—nowhere to go; now I think every day, tonight I go to Mr Pinkston.'

'You like my husband?' Flora asked, barely conscious of her wish for him to say something appreciative of herself.

'Mr Pinkston *very* good man, very clever, very strong. . .' Harry left his sentence in the air, finding it impossible to put his admiration into English words. He blushed a little and looked down again at the drawer to hide his awkwardness.[57]

Impulsively, overcome by 'an irresistible urge to treat him as a small boy', Flora leans forward to put her arms around him. She starts crying. Not surprisingly, Harry is soon on his feet and making a hasty excuse to escape from the embarrassing scene. He thanks her for having befriended him. ' "You are like mother to me," ' he gets out in a rush of words, ' "—my English mother." ' The story ends with a sentence that is most probably an unintentional rhyming couplet: 'He was out of the room and down the stairs, leaving the hateful word tingling in her ears.'[58]

Eric Oliver recalled that in writing 'The Hateful Word' with its almost wholly fictional plot, his friend had tried to produce something that might appeal to a magazine readership; only now was Denton perhaps willing to compromise his standards in the interest of financial security. He followed it with 'The Diamond Badge',[59] also intended for a similar market. The latter story is more convincing, for in depicting 'Andrew Clifton', a physically deformed writer, and his friend 'Tom Parkinson' as the main characters, Denton is quite obviously thinking of himself and Eric. The story is told from the point of view of a fan, 'Susan Innes',[60] who pays them a visit in their country retreat.

In mid-April Evie Sinclair came back to Middle Orchard and stayed for two nights. Recently she had been employed by a Scotswoman of eighty who lived in Clacton-on-Sea, but the lady had sold her house and so Evie decided to take a few days off before starting another job. Passing on this and other bits of news to Peggy Kirkaldy in a letter of the 25th, Denton continued:

Noël Adeney half plays with the idea of selling this [house] for £4,500. A horrible price, but I suppose someone will be willing to pay it, if I don't. We have seen a tiny house near Tunbridge Wells advertised at £3,900. It sounds very good for us: 2 bedrooms, large living room, kitchen with refrigerator, and walled garden—that is all, but it may not be nearly so good when one goes to see it.

I've just had a visit from the prosperous farmer of the village. I've been trying to get him to pay for a new fence between us and the squalid cottage at the end of the orchard. It's his cottage and fence; but we were so genteel that money wasn't even mentioned. He went away calmly giving me permission to have a new fence erected, I suppose at my own expense. . .

I've found a pretty little late 18th century table on Tuesday, very delicate pedestal and tripod feet—so delicate that it had been badly broken. It was £4 15s 0d, quite enough; but the mahogany is interesting, very dark and smoky with lighter almost faded patches. I had to strip off thick strawberry jam varnish. It now has a lovely waxed surface. . . Perhaps it is a bad policy to buy broken things, but I always fall for those spindly, fragile pieces, and they've nearly always been maltreated. . .

There is not a hope of course, but if you do see a tiny house in the country round you, do let me know. I have this for one more year, that is all.

Unfortunately, the muddle and indecision over Middle Orchard never did reach a satisfactory conclusion. The studio made an ideal bolthole for the Adeneys and the last thing they wanted to do was to sell their home to Denton and then, after his death, find themselves having to rent the room from Eric. Another suggestion of Denton's was that he might build a small place in the orchard. Not surprisingly, this too met with a similarly negative response.

And so the process of house-hunting had to begin all over again, though now in rather a half-hearted way. Denton was really beyond being able to cope with the thought of any radical change. Even though recently he had started work on two pictures—one of a woman in a huge hat holding a little dog, the other a flowerpiece—his mood was one of ever-deepening hopelessness, as is reflected in this touchingly poignant poem:

> How sadness comes to sit
> A little more each year
> In the corner of the room.
> Her back is turned,
> She bows down;
> Each year her dress is fuller,
> Filmier, more elaborate.
> She will sit there,
> Growing like a grey signet.
>
> If she is not there
> Silliness is there instead,
> Rattling her head,
> All full of peas.
>
> Why must I choose
> Sad face or silly face?
> Can't I have (a) smooth face
> My own face, my true face?[61]

There was no picnicking or going out into the fields this summer; apart from an excursion to the village of Wateringbury in April, most of the trips in the car were now concentrated on finding a possible new home. It seems that Evie was no longer thought of as being a member of the household, even though Denton longed for her return so that she might do some cleaning and relieve poor Eric, who usually went away for a holiday in the summer. The down-trodden Evie agreed to come on 9th July and once back she told Denton that Middle Orchard was really rather more congenial than Clacton. But their house-hunting itself proved to be depressingly unproductive. Denton could not afford to spend more than £3,000 and nearly all the places in this price-range turned out to be either aesthetically unattractive or inconvenient from a practical point-of-view. Noël did nothing to alleviate his worries. Writing in his Journal on 18th August, Denton describes her as behaving in a 'rather jerky and witch-like'[62] manner and though in subsequent days he yet again proposed that one way of solving the problem would be if she increased his rent and treated him as an ordinary tenant, his efforts to gain her co-operation were in vain.

The previous week a young undergraduate called David Carritt had paid a brief visit to Middle Orchard.[63] He came fresh from seeing Vita Sackville-West and Harold Nicolson at Sissinghurst and brought the news that the couple would very much like to meet Denton when he felt better. One assumes Denton must have contacted them without delay, for soon a firm invitation arrived and it was arranged that Eric and he should go over to the castle for tea on Friday, 27th August.

Although at first Denton doubted if he would ever actually get there, on the 27th itself his health was tolerably stable. Nevertheless, it still required a supreme effort to appear normal; the last thing he wanted was to be pitied by the Nicolsons. Eric, who was going to do the driving, would be there in the supportive role of his 'secretary', a title he could now lay claim to with some justification, since recently proofs for *Brave and Cruel* had arrived, and he was helping by reading them out aloud.

They took the day at as relaxed a pace as possible. Denton felt a real sense of occasion and, as one reads in the Journals, decided to seize the opportunity and dress up in his smartest country clothes: 'I put on my Pekin grass-cloth shirt, my Donegal tweed suit and old "patinated" shoes with lolling tongues. The back of the car was filled with two velvet cushions, gold and terracotta, and the green-and-black Nairn tartan rug Paul brought back from fighting in Italy. I lay there with my feet up, preserving myself fanatically.'[64]

Keyed up with enthusiasm, he digested everything of interest *en route*, though since they were a little late in starting, the drive turned out to be rather more fraught than was originally intended. Near Goudhurst they stopped to ask an elderly road-sweeper the way, Vita Sackville-West having sent a map only for the final stage of the journey. Denton had never visited Sissinghurst before. His initial impression of the castle was one of disappointment: 'it was so almost ugly, so featureless and unruinous,' he wrote, 'It had the quality of a granary, a barracks, or an enormous stable.'[65]

We drove into a little gravelled square where another car was just about to depart. A tall woman, whom I took at once to be Vita, was bending down, saying good-bye to the man through the car window. She wore cord riding-breeches which disappeared into tall laced canvas leather boots which were very slim. Above the knees she gradually bulged until she [?] came to some blowsy reddish, jersey thing, I think belted at the waist. This part of her body seemed soft and full. On her head she wore a large straw hat, floppy and flimsy, woven in pink-red checks, the sort of large nondescript hat that might be kept for years to wear in the garden and on the beach.[66]

After she had reassured herself that the two young men in the Austin were indeed the expected guests, Vita Sackville-West came over and greeted them. Denton had not seen her since the ignominious Poetry Reading five years previously.

> Her manner was a little withheld, a little torpid. It was not quite social or bright enough to make a first meeting really easy; but, on the other hand, it would be wrong to call it boorish or neglectful. Can I describe it as sluggishly dignified? Her voice was slow and rather sleepy too—almost drawling. She said that it was good of us to come so far, and that I must be certain not to walk too much.[67]

They were led to a shady spot in the garden, beneath a semi-circular wall covered with unripe fruit. They sat down and Vita produced cigarettes 'from a leather case, like a man's note wallet.' Denton wanted to hear all about the history of Sissinghurst, about the old house that had been demolished in the mid-eighteenth century, but his hostess proved to be somewhat reluctant to impart information. Eventually they were joined by Harold Nicolson, who, according to Denton, 'seemed in rather a hurry, as if we were keeping tea waiting by lolling on the seat under the nectarines.'

In a moment or two the party was walking across the lawn to the Priest's House, where they were going to have the meal. Denton describes this as 'the stickiest part' of the visit, the trouble being that the Nicolsons made scarcely any attempt to keep the talk flowing. 'I felt a little resentful,' he wrote, 'as if I were being forced to try to make up for their deficiency and when my efforts failed, they were holding me responsible.'[68] Quite possibly it also crossed his mind that he had not succeeded in inspiring them to rise to a more interesting level of conversation.

There was another guest for tea, a rather unprepossessing old lady who at first he suspected might be an aunt 'or perhaps some old nurse of Vita's.' When introduced however Denton was delighted to find himself shaking hands with Lady Colefax; she had been a society hostess of the pre-war years and he knew her name well. Having described in detail the intriguing combination of jewels strategically placed to liven up her appearance, Denton, determined to omit nothing he had found interesting, then went on to write about the interior of the Priest's House:

> . . . I saw a long Spanish table with pointless spikes and curves of wrought iron running along its stretcher close to the floor. The table was only laid with a large farmhouse cake and cucumber sandwiches, but there was an

air of richness and profusion. Perhaps this was caused by glasses as well as cups being at each place. There was also a large old silver shell, rather beautiful, holding about half a pound of butter patted and spanked nicely with ridged wooden boards. At our approach a manservant retreated behind a curtain. The room had a mullioned window, an arched brick fireplace, brick floor, high beamed ceiling, Oriental rugs, fragment of tapestry behind a little medieval wood carving of a saint. Our chairs were William and Mary with high caned backs. I tried, unthinkingly, to rest my arm along the back of mine.

Harold Nicolson said, 'There's cider, tea or water—who wants which?'

Eric and Vita chose cider: The rest of us had tea, Lady Colefax and I in thick, large Italian peasant cups, Harold in some smaller straight-sided, less clumsy thing. Tiny flies had got into the keg of cider, and Vita fetched an old silver wine funnel through which to strain it. I was glad that I had chosen tea.[69]

Although Denton does mention various things that were said, he gives the impression of having been happy just to sit back and let the others do most of the talking. His account of the trip to Sissinghurst concludes:

In writing down our conversation, flatly, quickly and rather clumsily, I am very conscious of its inanity and purposelessness; and yet in reality it had another character. Lady Colefax made it bright, quick-moving; Harold and Vita were beginning to feel at home again in their own house; Eric was enjoying his cider, and I felt warmed and protected by the richness of the room. Almost everything stopped short at the seventeenth century. For once it was refreshing to see nothing from one's own favourite eighteenth and nineteenth. Taste which is not one's own is a sort of holiday. One criticizes but enjoys. I wished I could be left alone to look about me. Even now, as I write. . .[70]

This is the point at which Denton's Journal comes to an end; the entry tails off in mid-sentence.

During the four remaining months of his life Denton was hardly able to do any work. The only writing accomplished was a handful of poems, possibly the rounding-off of 'The Diamond Badge' and, of course, further revisions to *A Voice Through a Cloud* (though still no conclusion). The final batch of proofs for *Brave and Cruel* was posted to Hamish Hamilton at the beginning of September.

The four poems written between 23rd October and 14th November are piercingly sad reflections of Denton's state of mind as he approached death. It was not a time of peace. He felt a sense of utter waste and misery.

> Jerk out your lip,
> Spit, blaspheme,
> Thicken the atmosphere
> Of your black dream.
> Swings round your head
> In wild uproar;
> They whisper about you
> Near the door.
> You are the filth
> In the royal gutter,
> The ornamental pat
> Of rancid butter.[71]

Dr Bates noticed that the task of nursing him was taking its toll on Eric—Denton could not bear the thought of having to end his days in hospital. Evie was persuaded to return and help with the running of the house. As ever quite out of touch with reality, she told Denton that if only he got out of bed and dressed, things would be perfectly alright.

He rallied a little at the end of November and managed to write some letters. At the beginning of December the six presentation copies of *Brave and Cruel* arrived, and writing to Hamish Hamilton on the 4th in a very neat hand, Denton thanked his publisher for sending them.

> I think the book is *very* nicely produced. . . . I was very pleased with the jacket. I shall send a copy to Edith Sitwell for Christmas, and she might like to tell other people in America about it. I have been terribly held up over my new book; every effort to get back to it has been frustrated. But perhaps l really am a little better now; tho' I still have to have morphia every night, and this keeps me in rather a cloudy state for all the next day. I hope the evidences of this are not too apparent.

The remission did not last long. Aside from being afflicted with a severe asthmatic condition, dropsy set in and Denton's legs expanded to an enormous size. Eric came and slept on a mattress in his room; only now did he realize his friend was dying.

On Christmas Day Evie cooked a duck. Denton was just able to force down a few mouthfuls. Eric, who had won £100 at the races, gave him a lovely early nineteenth-century vinaigrette decorated with flowers; from Peggy Kirkaldy he received Truman Capote's *Other Voices Other Rooms*.[72] Writing to Hector Bolitho on the 28th, Eric tried to keep up appearances by telling the author something of the progress of *A Voice Through a Cloud*. 'Denton is on the last two or three chapters of his long book,' he wrote, 'and says it should be finished at least in the next few months.'[73]

The morning of Thursday, 30th December was one that Eric would never forget. Much of the time Denton was distraught, crying out in fury and frustration that he was not ready to die. A letter had come from Paul, but when Eric showed it to him, he just waved his hand aside, too weak to take an interest in it.

Finally, Denton achieved some calm. He told Eric that in his mind's eye he could see children climbing over a gate. It was the last thing he said. Eric was sitting beside the bed when at two o'clock in the afternoon Denton died.

On the mornings that followed, Eric, unable to face the reality of the situation, found himself running upstairs to Denton's room to show him what had arrived in the post.

Appendix One:

The Packing-case House and the Thief

When I was ten years old, my mother had a little house made for me out of a large packing-case. The packing-case had held an old lacquer chest for fifty years and was very well made and strong, and the carpenter who converted it was clever. He cut a small door and window, then thatched the roof with straw. Inside he made a miniature dresser, corner cupboard and window seat. That was all he did. The painting and decoration were left to me, as I had asked for them to be.

I made the door red, and the window-frame and inside paintwork white, but when I came to the walls I hesitated, because they had been papered. The sides of the packing-case were too rough and furry for paint.

I was afraid that I should never be able to do the cutting and pasting neatly, and the job was put off day after day. The house stood in a far corner of the garden on the edge of a clump of evergreen bushes, rather like a miniature dark wood. When I came in from it in the evening, I would say to my mother, 'I haven't dared to begin papering yet.'

At last she said, 'We'll do it together.'

Even then I had misgivings. I was still afraid that we should spoil the sprigged paper she had chosen so carefully, but she seemed quite confident, so one autumn afternoon we began in earnest. We made a huge basin of paste on the kitchen stove, then carried it, with the rolls of paper, two pairs of scissors, and two large brushes, across the sun-spotted, leaf-strewn lawn.

Being the smallest, I stood inside the house, while my mother, half in, half out of the door, cut the paper carefully, and passed it to me, telling me to use as little paste as possible.

The rulers, the measurements, the endless patience. But how rewarding to see at the end of the day, just before the light faded, smooth fresh walls where there had been only splintery wood; to touch it with your fingers and to see how perfectly it fitted, with only the slightest smear of paste round the shelves and the window-frame!

I was so delighted with our work that in the night, after my father had read to me and I had eaten my milk and bread and butter supper, I ran out into the garden, instead of going upstairs to bed, as I should have done. The dewy grass made my felt bedroom slippers feel as if they were made of soaking moss. The bottoms of my pyjama trousers were wet through.

I undid the little padlock on the door and peered in. For a moment I was spellbound, because the moon had suddenly come out, and *real* moonlight was falling through the real, opening window on to the real dresser. The thought that this little house was mine gave me the purest pleasure that I had known.

I ran my fingers from sprig to sprig, enjoying the satin feeling of the paper. I planned in my mind the little fence I would make round the house, the brick paths, and the flowers I would plant. At last I made myself leave it, and climbed back to the veranda, where I slept winter and summer.

In the morning I was up long before breakfast to collect my valuables together; my mother's old toy tea-set, which she said I could use in my house; some leather books, some beautiful fossils and shells, and some coins. Then I went round the house looking for a very small rug. Outside a bedroom door I found a grey one that pleased me. I rolled it up and went out to the house. There was the final clearing up to be done after the papering. I hummed to myself, swept, dusted, rubbed, polished, unrolled the carpet on the floor and admired it from every angle, then went outside and looked first through the shut window, then through the open one. The effect with the wall-paper was indeed lovely, and all that was needed now were curtains for the window.

At breakfast, over scrambled eggs, I implored my mother to make curtains for me as soon as possible. Would she begin as soon as she had finished her coffee?

My mother laughed and said that she must see to her own house first, so after long ordering of meals, making of laundry lists, instructions for turning out rooms, I dragged her to the chest where the scraps of material were kept, and asked her which I could have.

I chose in the end some yellow striped cotton, very pretty to my eyes. We went to the house with the work-box and my mother began to sew it, while I arranged my things on the dresser.

My mother sat at the door of the house, in the still warm sunshine. She was not an experienced needle-woman, and she did things like making knots and licking the cotton. As my mother worked she smiled. I sat at her feet and began to try to stitch the rings on while she was doing the bottom hem. There was pulling and laughing and grumbling. We were very happy together.

When the curtains were nearly finished, I got up secretly, and took the doll's tea-set to the kitchen. I made the tea, filled the milk jug and sugar basin, cut sponge cake into miniature fingers, and chocolate biscuits into dice. I tried, too, to make toy sandwiches, but these were less successful.

With the tea things on a tray, I walked back to the house, where I found my mother just hanging up the curtains. The yellow stripes, the pink and green sprigs on the walls, the cream paint, the grey rug, the books and my collections of objects—could anything be more satisfying? We gazed at the delightful thing we had completed. Then I insisted on shutting the door and having tea inside the tiny house.

After the house was finished, I spent nearly all my spare time in or near it. I would have slept in it, of course, if there had been room, but only my dog could lie down; I had to sit or stand.

My dog seemed to be very fond of the house too. He would be curled up on the grey rug, keeping an eye on me through the open door as I tended the small garden I was making.

One evening, perhaps a month after the finishing touches had been put to the house, I left it, as usual, when called in to have my bath. I snapped the little padlock together, then flattened my face against the window, as I nearly always did, to have another look at the inside. Someone had just given me a small spirit kettle and oil lamp, and these were the things I looked at most of all.

I was not to know anything was going to happen to the house, but I always left it and went indoors reluctantly, as though there was some chance of my never seeing it again.

When supper was over and I was in bed on the veranda, I flashed my torch through the iron railings to where my house stood. The beam was not very strong and I only caught a dull gleam on the window, and then the shaggy fringe of the thatched roof. The house was in utter stillness, which gave me the feeling that it was waiting for somebody. Because it was night and I was alone, I imagined ghosts; ghost animals as well as humans, going into my house, sitting on the window seats, drinking out of the cups, pretending to read my books, cackling and muttering in their own particular ghost way. I was half frightened, half excited, by these imaginings.

Then I must have fallen asleep, for I then knew no more until it was daylight. My mother was calling me, telling me to come in and have my fruit while she drank her early morning tea. Before I ran in to kiss her good morning, I only had time to give my house a hurried glance. It looked as it should have done from the distance of the veranda. I noticed nothing.

I had just settled myself on my mother's bed and was cutting an orange in half, when my father came in rather slowly and said in his bored voice, the one he put on when he didn't want anyone to know what he was thinking:

'My dear, there have been burglars. They've left their filthy bootmarks and burnt matches all over the dining-room and drawing-room. Slip on a dressing-gown and come down; it's quite a sight.'

'But, Arthur!' my mother said, 'what have they taken? Have you looked? Is the silver still in the sideboard?'

'The cupboard doors seemed to be open, darling,' my father said, even more drawlingly, 'but you'd better come down and look for yourself.'

I jumped out of the bed and ran downstairs at once. My mother quickly followed. We stood by the glass folding doors leading from the hall to the drawing-room, and gazed for a moment at the trail of matches and garden mud all over the polished floor. It was as if some giant snail had been crawling here and there about the room, visiting every piece of furniture. All the drawers of the cabinets and chests were open, and some of the things that had been in them were on the floor, as if the thief, enraged to find them only porcelain or bronze, not precious metal, had abandoned them.

My mother said nothing. She covered her sadness and her anger by going quickly to work. She had soon made a list of all the missing objects in the drawing-room. I helped her a little, but I was too excited to be methodical. I kept running in to other rooms to discover what had happened there. I found the forks and spoons that my mother was so fond of, because they had belonged to her family for a long time. By some marvellous chance they had been taken into the pantry the night before. They were saved, because the thief had not gone in there, but the old boat-shaped salt-cellars, the tall pepper-pot and mustard-pot were gone from the sideboard cupboard, also the Sheffield candle-sticks from the mantelpiece.

The thief had got in the house by chipping the putty away round a pane of glass in one of the French windows. He had then lifted out the pane, slipped in his hand and unfastened the latch in the usual burglar's way. While I was gazing at the empty frame, admiring this cleverness, my father strolled into the room and said:

'Of course that dog of yours never raised a squeak. He only barks at me and at our best friends. Oughtn't you to find out if he's still alive and snoring?'

My father always taunted me in this way, pointing out how useless, greedy, and badly trained my dog was. I know that my father quite liked him, but he never showed it, so I had always to be protecting my dog's character from him.

'If you didn't make him sleep in the downstairs cloak-room, he would have heard everything,' I said. 'He would have bitten the thief and woken us all up with his barking. How can he hear through two thick doors?'

I threw this last sentence at my father as I ran to let my dog out. I had forgotten all about him in the excitement, and now I had the fear that the thief might have drugged him or even killed him.

I was relieved when I opened the cloakroom door and saw him still curled up in his basket on the coloured tiles. He came towards me crabwise, with his tail tucked under, and his ears flat to his head. He was shy and sleepy and wanting to please me and be loved.

'Did you hear nothing, Taff?' I asked rather sadly, feeling that my father would never forget this lapse.

Taff only wagged his lowered tail, did a little curving dance, and finally woke up and ran into the front rooms.

Of course the smell of the burglar was fascinating to him; he sniffed, greedily following the trails from room to room. I watched him for a moment, wondering what to do next. Then it rushed on me that as I had forgotten Taff, so had I forgotten my little house.

Calling Taff to follow me, I ran across the lawn in my dressing-gown. Not until I was quite near could I see that anything had happened. The first thing I noticed was the gaping padlock, then I saw that part of the fence had been trampled down. I hardly dared to look inside, and waited for a moment with my hand on the door.

Before I pulled it open, I had hardened myself a little, and I don't think my face showed anything when I saw most of the toy tea-set smashed on the floor, the beautiful shells and fossils swept roughly together, my books gaping and splashed with the tea left in the pot. The wall-paper was splashed too, and the thief had smeared it with his black hands. He had even torn down one of the curtains. At first I thought this the most stupid, wanton act of all, but I was soon to discover his reason.

While Taff ran about rooting and sniffing, I stood in my little house, gazing at the wreckage, hating the man with all my might. I felt that I would never have the heart to work at it again. No one would ever give me new cups and saucers. The books were dirtied. The wall-paper, which had been so difficult to cut and fit and paste, was spoilt for ever.

Without picking anything up, I sat down on the window seat and waited. I don't know what I was waiting for; I suppose it was for someone to tell me what to do. My own mind had gone dead.

Taff found me there and jumped up, putting his paws on my knees and trembling. He seemed to want me to go out to play with him. Mechanically I got up and followed. He ran into the dark bushes behind the house and began to make loud growling snorting noises. I took very little notice, because I was trying to imagine the scene of last night, when the thief broke in. Another boy had once told me that thieves sometimes stripped naked, then covered their skin with black oil to make themselves almost invisible in the night, and to make it very difficult for anyone to hold them if they were caught.

Because of this story, I imagined my thief creeping up to the house, all naked and black, smashing the padlock—here my imaginings were broken into by Taff's return. He was *determined* that I should go into the bushes with him.

He had been digging in the ground, pretending, I suppose, that he was unearthing a rabbit or a buried bone; but when I bent down I saw that he had half-buried under his pile of earth two round pads of old green baize. I picked one up, but could not think what it was, until it flashed on me that it was the covering for the base of one of the old Sheffield plate candlesticks. I had often turned them up and seen the stained green cloth.

I knelt down at once and started to feel under the pile of earth, but there were no candlesticks there. It was clear that the thief had just pulled off the baize to discover if the candlesticks were of solid metal.

I was thrilled by the find and kept saying to Taff, 'Good dog, good dog, go on, seek him out.'

By 'him' I meant any other things that may have been dropped in the garden. I was about to give up hope and to feel that the two round pads, like pen-wipers, were all that we should find, when Taff began sniffing along the back of the house, where there was a crack, between the ground and the bricks on which the house stood.

I was the first to see a gleam of yellow, and I darted forward just as his nose reached it and he began to pull at the corner of the cloth with his teeth. It was the missing curtain, done up into a Dick Whittington bundle.

I shall always remember sitting on the ground there under the dark bushes, with Taff dancing about, scratching me when he put his paws on my thin pyjamas, and my hands shaking and being clumsy as I tried to undo the knot.

The first thing I saw was the mustard spoon, long and curving like a whip. Under it were three salt spoons and, greatest find of all, one of the four boat-shaped salt-cellars.

As I held it in my hand, gloating on its smooth gleam, longing to spring it on my mother, then watch her face, yet saving up the moment as something precious, not to be thrown away in a hurry, I felt happy for the first time that morning. It seemed wonderful to me that even these few things had been saved. Why had the burglar tucked them into the crack under my house? I could only guess that he had had too much to carry, and that he meant to return for the bundle later.

I thought again of how my house had been spoilt for no reason, and although I still had great bitterness, I felt, too, a strange new satisfaction. I was pleased that my house had not escaped, was almost proud that it had been damaged. It made it even more real to me, deeper and more interesting.

As I ran back to the big house to show my mother what had been found, new thoughts were bubbling up in me.

'I can do it all over again,' I told myself, 'if I take time. I know how to do the papering now, and someone will give me some china.'

Then the delightful thought came to me that I would be able to tell my father that Taff had found the missing things.

Before I end my story I shall just say that nothing else was ever recovered. The police came, took some fingerprints and scratched about in the garden, but that was all they did. The rest of the table silver, the cigarette boxes and other little objects in the drawing-room were gone for ever. This made my mother treasure the one remaining salt-cellar very much indeed.

Just in case the thief should return, I waited one night in my house for what seemed a long time. I was a little fearful, but I had Taff with me and a good sailor's whistle. But nothing happened. The clouds hurried across the night sky. There was a bird calling sometimes from the bushes. I sat in the doorway with my arm round Taff, thinking of all that my house had seen.

This short story was written in the latter part of 1946 for the periodical Junior *(see Bibliography, no.39); this is the first time that it has been reprinted.*

Appendix Two

The Big Field

The two young boys walked round the Big Field arm in arm. This was not according to school habit, but the slightly older one with 'dirty' coloured fair hair had been so carried away with his own story, that he'd seized the other's arm on an impulse and had not let it go again. Spitting very slightly in his excitement, he was saying, 'And then they carried her up to the top of the tower and put her under the sky, and the vultures and all the other birds came and pecked out her eyes and her tongue and all the other parts of her. They built nests with her red hair and then nothing was left but the white skeleton, just like chalk, from the rain and wind. If you go up there now you can still see her skeleton. I know, because I've been.'

The other boy said nothing for a moment—he seemed uneasy and restive—then broke out with, 'But Thompson, how could your grandmother have been left buried on top of a tower instead of being buried properly? They'd never allow it in this country.'

'A special licence was got,' the older one said grandly. 'If you don't believe me, I'll take you to the tower at the bottom of her garden, if you're ever near Wokingham!'

They walked on in silence. Thompson had not quite convinced his companion, but he knew that he had caught his interest and had intrigued him a little. He left his grandmother on top of the tower and returned to the subject of their dead mothers, the one thing that had bound the two rather dissimilar boys together.

'Of course, when my mother died, I thought that I couldn't go on,' he said importantly, 'Life seemed to mean nothing. There was only the horror of school looming in front of me. It wasn't good enough. I suppose you felt that too. . . But somehow one manages to get through the day and they say that time is the greatest healer of all.'

The grown-up use of 'one' and the cliché 'time the healer' were to be expected from Thompson. He was nearly always searching for effect, trying out new words and mannerisms. Marshall, the younger boy, felt a little uncomfortable, but said nothing. 'Of course, that's why I failed my Common Entrance. I was all to pieces, and nobody realized it, until I told. . .

Possibly written c.1941, this fragment relates to the time when Denton Welch was a pupil at St Michael's, Uckfield and had recently received news of his mother's death in Shanghai.

Appendix Three:

Reading My First Review—In Spring

I remember so well the first review I ever saw of my first book, *Maiden Voyage*. I had been picnicking alone on the banks of the river near Tonbridge; and afterwards, as I lay in the long grass and let my thoughts wander, I remembered that I had shopping to do in the town—toothpaste to buy at the chemist's; ink and exercise-books at the stationer's—so I got on my bicycle again and pedalled back along the narrow towpath.

It was a lovely afternoon, early in May, with the sun hot on my back. I will not deny that my thoughts all the time were churning round my book, which had just come out. 'When I get to the public library,' I told myself, 'I can go in and look at the magazines; not that there will be a review yet; it is *much* too early.'

Propping my bike against the worn brick wall and taking the pump with me, so that it should not be 'lifted' while I was quietly reading inside, I entered the, to me, rather sinister building. Sinister, because of the forlorn-seeming people who bend over illustrated encyclopaedias, or murmur and whisper to one another as they crackle the newspapers on the tall stands—and sinister too, because at that time, 1943, the front door was draped in several heavy black-out curtains, the colour of a broken-down priest's cassock—not black, not green, not 'rusty'—an indescribable colour.

In this labyrinth of curtains school children used to hide; and all around you in the hot, sticky darkness boys and girls were giggling, teasing, mocking. Sometimes, as you hurried through, feeling rather desperate, you were even lightly slapped, tickled, or thumped on the back.

Well, after this ordeal I found myself in the quietness of the magazine room. I was sweating slightly from the almost summer heat, the awfulness of the children, and perhaps from my own excitement. I *knew* there would be no reviews, and yet I was excited. My eyes darted from table to table, and seeing only unillustrated periodicals, I remembered hearing the librarian once say 'We have to hide all the shiny ones. If we didn't there wouldn't be one left. People who want to look at them must come and ask.'

I decided at once not to ask for anything, but to content myself with the *New Statesmans*, the *Time and Tides*, the *Spectators*, and the curious technical magazines that were there.

The latest *Spectator* was nearest to me, so I took it up at once, and after the first fluttering of pages to get to the reviews, I found myself suddenly face to face with my own name in print and the name of my book, under the heading 'Growing Up.'

It was a real, though smooth and silky, shock. The sort of shock that makes you convinced that your face, your being is changed, that the people round about *must* notice.

But after the first completely self-coloured moment, I realized that the people at the tables were *not* aware that a writer had seen the first review of his first book. They were quite calm—just as the people on top of the bus are always calm, though the young person in love, sitting in their midst, is always afraid that the outrageous indecent state is obvious to all.

I sat down at the yellow oak table and started to read in earnest. I was so delighted to have any review that I don't think I feared its being a bad one. I would have taken that as part of my fate.

But it was not a bad one. It struck me as both sensible and appreciative. I felt that the woman who had written it was right about me, in her own way; and when she said '. . .he lives for us in these pages with an almost embarrassing vividness,' I was strangely pleased, not made uncomfortable.

I read it all over again and gazed at it for a little time with my eyes focused far beyond it, then I turned to the other magazines; but nothing else had come out yet, and for this I was almost grateful. It allowed me to concentrate entirely on the first encouraging notice.

Before I left, I again remembered the librarian's words, and they put the idea into my head that I too might take the people's property to myself. But I didn't. I imagined too clearly the furtive crackling of the *Spectator* stuffed down my shirt-front.

* * *

After that there were many reviews. They came trickling in steadily. I would sit up every morning and read them in bed, before I had breakfast. I found myself paying far more attention to adverse criticism than to praise— extravagant or moderate. Perhaps this is usual. It was as if disapprobation always bore the mark of truth on it—although I might still consider it wrong-headed— whereas praise presented itself to me as pudding, as stuffing, as insincerity put out to trick me into some ridiculous position. I understood now why, in old novels and letters, flattery is almost invariably considered insulting or cruel.

I wonder if I was influenced by reading all those reviews? They certainly made me more self-conscious about my work, more aware of its possible effect on other people; for before I was published, I steadfastly refused to think of the impression my words might leave behind. I knew that it would muddle me to consider any one but myself. What pleased, what amused, what touched, what horrified me must be put down as well as I knew how; but everything else must be swept away. There must be no titbits for special types, no appealing to a public I knew nothing of.

But now I *had* to consider other people's impressions. When the reviewer of the *Listener* finished his mingled praise and blame with the extraordinary statement that all women were to me 'just shapeless, repulsive, silly bags,' I was bound to be affected by the words. I was bound to rake over my book in my mind, in an effort to find anything that could have led him to such a preposterous opinion.

And when James Agate said: 'If he is not extremely careful he will grow up into another Proust,' I had to stop and decide whether this meant anything at all—or was it just to be taken as gay newspaper extravagance?

Was I also not to take too seriously Miss Elizabeth Bowen's references to the 'faultless form' of my book and to the 'errant genius' of the sixteen-year-old 'I' in it? Was the *Liverpool Post's* 'a painful picture of adolescence at its most gawkish period' more worthy of my attention?

I revolved all these questions in my mind, with many more as well; and in the end I think I came to the conclusion that the generosity, the encouragement, the sneering, and the patronage were all rather unreal, and that although I could never again be unaware of them as I was at first, still I must *never* let them prevent me from going my own sweet way.

Reprinted here for the first time, this article was written for Readers News *(an organ of the Readers Union book club) in 1944/5 and appeared in the latter year with the same painting of the interior of Pitt's Folly Cottage that was used in* Vogue, *June 1945.*

Notes

sources abbreviated:

ALS	—	*A Last Sheaf*, John Lehmann, 1951
AVTAC	—	*A Voice Through a Cloud*, John Lehmann, 1950; Penguin reprint, 1983
FLS	—	*Fragments of a Life Story; the Collected Short Writings of Denton Welch*, Penguin, 1987
ILMGH	—	*I Left my Grandfather's House*, Allison & Busby, 1984
IYIP	—	*In Youth is Pleasure*, Routledge, 1945; Oxford Paperback, 1982
Journals	—	*The Journals of Denton Welch* (ed. Michael De-la-Noy), Allison & Busby, 1984; Penguin, 1987
Maiden Voyage	—	*Maiden Voyage*, Routledge, 1943; Penguin reprint, 1986

other abbreviations:

coll.	—	collection
DW	—	Denton Welch
HRC	—	Harry Ransom Humanities Research Center, the University of Texas at Austin
NYPL	—	New York Public Library

The Bibliography, Catalogue of Pictures and List of Poetry referred to in these notes apply to the tables to be found before the index in this volume.

Chapter One
1. Details of the accident are to be found in Chapter Four.
2. The work has been published with the title 'I Can Remember'; see Bibliography, no.3.
3. The late Maurice Cranston expressed this opinion in his article on DW in *The Nineteenth Century and After*, CXLVIII, 884 (Oct. 1950), pp.237-45: 'His mother—it seemed to me from what he told me—must have been disappointed in him, and far from loving him to excess as the youngest of her three sons, was vaguely put out by his being such a pretty child and yet a boy. I suspect he had been something of a doll to her—to be dressed in pretty clothes and handed round the drawing-room; something quite different from the other boys' (p.243). He was christened Maurice Denton Welch.

M. De-la-Noy in *Denton Welch: the Making of a Writer*, p.23, mentions another child, Tommy, who died in childhood. DW makes no reference to him in his writings.

Regarding the origins of his family, in answering a request for biographical material from the American publisher Fischer, DW's publisher, Routledge, supplied a blurb containing the following information: 'Denton Welch. . . was born in China of English and American parents. Mother's people were early English and Dutch settlers, who made their homes at Boston and surrounding countryside. New Bedford was named in honour of one of her ancestors whose surname was Russell. Father's people were originally Scotch and claimed John Knox as an ancestor.'

DW's first cousin, Thomas Kane, kindly supplied information to the author that their Welch grandfather, Joseph, originally came from Standish in Lancashire, and in 1866 had gone to Shanghai as an apprentice in the tea trade. The name Denton derived from the surname of DW's maternal grandmother, Katherine Denton, a New Englander.

4. Sir Elly Kadoorie (1867-1944) was an industrialist, businessman and philanthropist, born in Baghdad, who founded companies bearing his name in Shanghai and Hong Kong. He had a London home at 6 Princes Gate in Kensington to which DW as a young boy and his mother were invited for lunch, c.1925. DW later wrote a short story around the event, calling it 'At Sir Moorcalm Lalli's'; see Bibliography, no.44.

5. In his Journals (p.152) DW refers to his mother having been at a convent in Florence; the dates of her visits come from an autograph book that she kept during the years preceding her marriage. The book also shows that she had met Arthur Welch several years before they were married.

6. This extract in conversation with the author. Enid Saunders Candlin in *The Breach in the Wall* (Cassell, 1974, p.74) recalls: 'Then there was *Dear Brutus*, which attained the level of a really great performance with Rosalind Welch as Margaret. When the artist realises that she is nothing but a midsummer night's dream, the actor's anguish was so moving that I doubt anyone who saw the play has ever forgotten it.'

Marjorie Penton (née Parsons) remembered Mrs Welch as being 'petite', with curly golden hair, whereas Arthur Welch was 'large and a bit matter-of-fact.'

7. 'I Can Remember', *FLS*, p.15.

8. Extract from letter of 12th January 1946 (private coll.); these reminiscences also feature in 'I Can Remember', *FLS*, pp.15-16.

9. Founded by James Alexander Wattie, the firm functioned as a general trading company, especially in rubber. Wattie himself retired to the Guildford area and features as 'Mr Mellon' in the short story 'The Trout Stream'; see Bibliography, no.40. Bill and Paul Welch at various times worked for the firm in Shanghai. Following the Second World War, Arthur Welch having died in 1942, DW's elder brother Bill returned to Shanghai to reopen the company, soon transferring it to Hong Kong. Bill Welch ran Wattie & Co. until his death in 1965, the firm then passing to his brother-in-law, K.H.A. Gordon, who subsequently sold it to the Kadoorie brothers.

10. *Maiden Voyage*, p.81.

11. In conversation with the author.

12. Arthur Welch's return to Shanghai around December 1919 features in the diary of the writer Stella Benson (Dept. of MSS, Cambridge University Library). In *Stella Benson, a biography* (Macmillan, 1987, pp.144-5) Joy Grant describes how Welch had been more than attentive to Stella Benson, even giving her 'a gold lacquer cigarette case to remember him by.'

13. 'I Can Remember', *FLS*, p.19.

14. ibid., p.22.

15. Hutchinson, 1942, p. 79.

16. 'Narcissus Bay', *FLS*, p.74.

17. Mrs Blanche Bois was the sister-in-law of DW's paternal grandmother. It was in 1922 also that Stella Benson met the Welches in Sussex: 'Denton, the youngest of their three sons, she recalled, "was always my friend." He was seven now. "A flea would despise the

amount of lemonade I've got, Mother", he quaintly remarked, in a slow, earnest, thought-ful voice... which is most charming.'" (Joy Grant, op. cit., p.193).

Later in life DW took a phrase from Benson's last book, *Mundos, an Unfinished Novel* (Macmillan, 1935) as the first line for a poem, entitled 'Heart's Will'. The line runs 'Yes, muscles sweat their pride and strength away,' (HRC coll.).

18. 'I Can Remember', *FLS*, pp.27-8.

19. ibid., p.28. 'Wooly' (the author has been unable to discover her real name) also features as the subject of a short story, 'Velvet' (see Bibliography, no.34), which describes a visit she paid to DW in January-February 1940.

20. 'I Can Remember', *FLS*, p.35.

21. ibid., p.37.

22. ibid., p.38.

23. ibid., p.49.

24. ibid., pp.49-51.

25. ibid., p.51.

26. ibid., p.51.

27. ibid., p. 51; for 'The Coffin on the Hill' see Bibliography, no.32. The picture, a water-colour, featured as no.15 in the catalogue of the posthumous exhibition of DW's work at the Leicester Galleries, 1954, and possibly corresponds with a painting of a corpse and funeral in the HRC coll. (no.66.72.25), although the author considers the latter not to be of sufficient quality to have been exhibited.

28. ibid., p.52.

29. ibid., p.53.

30. ibid., pp.58-9

31. See Bibliography, no.22. DW refers to the setting as Brook House, whereas the correct name was Brookside.

32. 'The Barn', *FLS*, p.117.

33. Originally DW had written ' "Now go back, you silly little bugger" ', a phrase that John Lehmann, editor of *New Writing and Daylight* (in which the story first appeared), insisted should be toned down for publication.

34. 'I Can Remember', *FLS*, p.64.

35. This is taken from an unpublished fragment, the MS in HRC coll.

36. 'I Can Remember', *FLS*, p.66.

37. DW describes two such trips at this time: one to see J.A. Wattie (ibid., pp.67-8) and another to a Mrs Aldridge (Journals, pp.53-7).

38. Journals, p.37.

39. ibid., p.38.

40. It was about this period that Stella Benson again met DW and considered him 'the nicest little boy I have ever met... he always wants to understand everything to the last degree. "How did they know, Stella, at the beginning, that a terrier's tail would look nice cut short? Did one have its tail cut off by mistake? Or did they take two dogs and cut off the tail of one and put them side by side?" All very determined and emphatic.' (Joy Grant, op. cit., p.193).

41. In conversation with the author.

42. Michael Astor, *Tribal Feeling*, John Murray, London, 1963, p.88. St Michael's still exists as a school, but is now at Tawstock Court, Barnstable, Devon; the buildings in Uckfield are at present a school run by a religious order.

43. Jocelyn Brooke, *The Military Orchid*, Penguin ed., 1981, p.46.

44. The MS of this last fragment, which is published here for the first time (see Appendix Two), is in the Berg Collection, NYPL.

45. 'Mrs Hockey', *FLS*, p.155-6; see Bibliography, no.12.

46. Letter dated Monday, October [1926]; private coll.

47. For publication and details see Bibliography, no.28.

48. 'At Sea', *FLS*, pp.91-2.

49. ibid., p.94.

50. Extracts from letters of 19th and 25th November, and 17th December 1926; private coll.

51. The cause of death was Bright's disease.

52. 'C' refers to 'Cissie' (Cecilia) Carpmael. Irene (1883-1971) and Hilda Dallas (1878-1958) were friends of DW's mother and had known her since she was young. The sisters were brought up in China, their father, they claimed, having been tutor to one of the Emperors. Hilda was the prettier and more feminine of the two, and was also an accomplished artist.

53. Journals, pp.324-5. C.K. Adamson, a fellow-pupil at St Michael's recalls that he offered to share his school 'garden' with DW, thinking that it might help to take his mind off his mother's death. Mr Adamson remembers DW as having been 'somewhat delicate.' Another pupil, David Atkins, who later followed DW to Repton, recalled that the news had come through on a Saturday. All the boys had been to the tuck-shop to buy sweets. DW was called out by Mrs Hockey and told of his mother's death. The rest of the school was informed that evening and Mr Atkins remembers that nearly all the boys offered DW their sweets. DW was crying gently, but managed to smile to them.

Chapter Two

1. David Atkins, 'Writers Remembered: Roald Dahl', *The Author*, CIII, No.1, Spring 1992, p.24.

2. Roald Dahl, *Boy*, Penguin, 1986, p.150.

3. Roald Dahl, op. cit., p.145.

4. In correspondence with the author, 2nd May 1990. DW was at Repton for only seven terms. The printed academic results of each term demonstrate that during the course of his stay, although he started well in English and French, DW's position soon slipped, with him routinely placed at the bottom end of the class in Maths and Science. His exam results tended to be marginally better. Only in Drawing was he either always first or second.

5. Letter from Kenneth Blackburn to the late Richard Newton; date unavailable. Blackburn appears as 'Bradbourne' in *Maiden Voyage*.

6. In conversation with the author. The Rev. John Lisney appears as 'Whitney' in *Maiden Voyage*.

7. *Maiden Voyage*, p.42.

8. ibid., p.48.

9. Letter of 25th October 1945.

10. MS in Berg Coll., NYPL.

11. *Maiden Voyage*, p.10.

12. MSS in HRC coll.

13. *Maiden Voyage*, p.12.

14. In a letter to the author of 14th April 1991, George Ziffo, who was in the same house as DW at Repton, recalls: 'Both Denton and Paul were considered as "girl substitutes" by some boys and this was not considered strange.'

15. *Maiden Voyage*, p.13.

16. Commonly known as the Poultry Cross.

17. *Maiden Voyage*, p.23.

18. ibid., p.26.

19. ibid., p.27.

20. ibid., p.30. There was indeed a boy named Iliffe with DW in Brook House, but rather than having 'left at the beginning of last term', the real Iliffe was two years younger than DW and first arrived at Repton during DW's final term.

21. ibid., p.39.

22. ibid., p.41.

23. See *FLS*, pp.185-92.

24. DW calls the Captain 'Newman', whereas J.H. Human, who had indeed been Captain of games, had left Repton the previous term.

25. *Maiden Voyage*, p.54.

26. ibid., p.66.

27. ibid., p.69.

28. ibid., p.71.

29. ibid., p.77.

30. ibid., p.86.

31. ibid., p.109. It is worth noting that during the early months of 1932 Shanghai was undergoing a period of extreme instability. On 2nd January the Japanese had proclaimed the Manchukuo Republic in Manchuria and on the 28th their forces occupied Shanghai, the Chinese forces being driven out on 3rd March.

32. It should be mentioned that DW's choice of names for the only sympathetic main female characters in his novels (i.e. 'Vesta' in *Maiden Voyage* and 'Aphra' in *IYIP*) carry definite mythic associations, Vesta being goddess of the hearth. The resonance of these associations is discussed in Robert S. Phillips, *Denton Welch,* Twayne Publishers Inc., 1974.

33. *Maiden Voyage*, pp.117-8.

34. The journey is described in *Maiden Voyage*, pp.122-63.

35. ibid., p.122.

36. ibid., p.140.

37. The author has been unable to trace the location of this town. However, it should be noted that Yiching is a type of pottery with which DW would have been familiar.

38. *Maiden Voyage*, p.158.

39. ibid.

40. *All About Shanghai: a Standard Guidebook*, University Press, Shanghai, 1934-5 ed., p.186. Of the Chinese porcelain DW acquired during this period, he kept a blue and white bowl for grinding medicines ('Kang-he 17th Cent. bought in Shanghai $1'), a big blue and white jar with symbols of the Seasons ('Ming $16'), a small purple cup with a raised pattern of storks and lotuses ('$5—slightly broken. Kang-he or perhaps Ming'), a rouge pot with a brocaded motif all over in gold, pink, red and green with blue, with a pomegranate and two flowers on a twig, the inside tortoiseshell ('Chien-lung late 18th century, $1 Shanghai'), as well as a blanc-de-chine lion ('$10 at Ki-feng foo. May 1932') and a blue and white artist's brush pot in the shape of a drum, with ducks and lotus ('$20 at Ki-fengfoo'). The descriptions in brackets are taken from a MS notebook in the Berg Coll., NYPL.

41. *Maiden Voyage*, p.169.

42. ibid., p.171.

43. ibid., p.174. DW's friend Gerald Mackenzie remembered being told about the incident with the soldier and was quite sure it was true.

44. ibid., p.178.

45. Letter to the author, 2nd November 1987.

46. *Maiden Voyage*, p.183.

47. ibid., p.194.

48. *All About Shanghai* lists a St Anna Ballroom in Love Lane, which offered dancing

nightly between 8pm and 2am (pp.72, 77); it seems likely this was the establishment DW had in mind.

49. *Maiden Voyage*, pp.207-8.

50. Sir Harry Fox's first wife, Josephine (née Bassett, d.1900), was the sister of DW's mother. 'Aunt Dos' (Dorothy) was Sir Harry's second wife.

51. *Maiden Voyage*, p. 239.

52. ibid., p.242.

53. These are preserved in the HRC coll. There are ten watercolours, four of which are of fruit (accession nos 66.72.3.1-10).

54. ibid., p.246.

55. ibid., p.255.

56. Letter of 17th February 1944. Pocetta's sister, Enid Saunders Candlin, who also knew DW well and appears as 'Elaine' in *Maiden Voyage* was much less sympathetic to the book. In a letter to the author of 19th July 1990 she writes: 'He had a great sense of visual beauty and was very materialistic, very sensuous; also, when it came to writing, ruthless and cruel. Many of his old friends, and his mother's, felt this keenly when they read what he did to them in his books—they asked him to stop, but he wouldn't. For instance—a mutual friend was on the ship which took him from China; she had been through a dreadful time (her husband was found to have 'borrowed' from his friends when he could never pay it back), and she and her daughter were going back to the U.K. at the expense of the Council—Denton described her in a malicious, vicious way. Naturally we all knew who it was, and her children suffered keenly to see her so handled. He did the same with us, while assuring us that we meant more to him than he could possibly express. Indeed, he had treated our home as his. . .'

Chapter Three

1. Stanley Anderson (1884-1966), elected R.A. in 1941, was a well-known and highly accomplished artist of the day. At Goldsmiths' he taught etching, drypoint and wood-engraving, though there is no evidence that DW received instruction from him. Anderson was a close friend of James Bateman (see below), the two men having a particular interest in depicting the rural life.

2. Journals, p.79.

3. 'The Earth's Crust', *FLS*, p.207.

4. Extract from letter of 4th November 1947; in catalogue for exhibition of Clive Gardiner's work at the South London Art Gallery, Camberwell, 1967. Clive Gardiner (1891-1960) continued as Headmaster and then Principal of Goldsmiths' College until 1957.

5. DW studied with all three of these teachers, especially Bateman and Mansbridge. James Bateman (1893-1959) was a painter and wood-engraver, who specialized in landscapes and cattle. As with Gardiner, he had trained at the Slade. He was elected R.A. in 1942. Ernest Michael Dinkel (1894-1983) was a landscape artist too, but also a designer, as well as a glass-engraver. Multifaceted, he exhibited as a sculptor and also worked in watercolour. Aside from teaching at Goldsmiths' on Mondays, Dinkel was also on the staff of the Royal College of Art. John Mansbridge (1901-81) joined the teaching staff at Goldsmiths' in 1929 and concentrated on portraiture. His work is in the National Portrait Gallery and Imperial War Museum. He taught at Goldsmiths' until 1966, after which he published a *Graphic History of Architecture*. At the time of his death he was working on a mammoth book, *Ways of Seeing: the Recreation of Man*, described in his *Times* obituary as 'an illustrated philosophical view of man's progress through the creative and scientific world from the beginning of recorded history to the present time.'

6. 'The Youth Rang the Bell', *FLS*, pp.215-6. Evelyn Dorcas Sinclair was born in 1894 and

died at a nursing-home near Margate in 1976.

7. *AVTAC*, p.73.

8. An account of the walking tour is given in the posthumously published book *I Left my Grandfather's House*; see Bibliography, no.19.

9. Helen Roeder in conversation with the author recalled: 'Denton liked having dumpy little girls about. He was very charming if you were a companion. He was like having another jolly sister. He was so sympathetic to women, in a way, and he was very easy to get on with. All women liked him, I think, partly because he was so frivolous. And very sympathetic. If you were at all unhappy or down on your luck he would be awfully sweet. He could tune into anybody—that was the novelist in him. You can see it in his books—how he was passionately interested in everything. I think if one had overloaded him with worries he would have got irritable, but who doesn't?'

10. Letter to the author, 20th July 1987.

11. Letter of 6th September 1945.

12. Catalogue of Pictures, no.110 (see illustration).

13. University of London, Goldsmiths' College, School of Art, Prospectus, 1933-4, p.3. Courses that DW appears not to have attended were those in architecture, etching and wood-engraving, stage setting and scene painting, commercial art and fashion-plate drawing.

14. 'A Novel Fragment', *FLS*, p.218. The name 'Mme David' is an invention (she was, in fact, Mme Paul), nor were pulleys used. Cedric Rogers, a fellow-student, suggests that the association between the name 'David' and the pulleys may derive from DW learning that the French artist Jacques-Louis David (1748-1825) sometimes used the device when setting up poses.

15. ibid., p.221.

16. Frederick Halnon was in charge of this class.

17. 'A Novel Fragment', *FLS*, p.246. 'Madge and Jane' were the Lean sisters, Peggy and Joan; the wrestler's name was Rothwell—he came from the North of England. Another of DW's nicknames, according to Betty Swanwick, was 'Bubbles', because of his similarity to the child in the famous Pears Soap advertisement.

18. Letter to the author, 18th December 1988. In a letter of 8th December 1987 Rogers writes of DW: 'Without the benefit of hindsight it is easy to forget that before the accident he seemed the least likely student to make a mark in the world—a character from light comedy, not high drama.'

19. 'A Novel Fragment', *FLS*, p.229.

20. Gerald Mackenzie coll.

21. Journals, pp.181-2.

22. 'Strange Discoveries', *FLS*, p.317; see Bibliography, no.33.

23. Gerald Mackenzie coll.

24. Gerald Mackenzie remembered that the shop was near the bottom of Croom's Hill and that he had been the one who originally saw it. DW lists the painting in his 'Catalogue of Pictures' (Berg Coll., NYPL), giving the date of its purchase.

25. Although in 'Strange Discoveries' (*FLS*, p.319) DW states he paid 8/- for the work, in his 'Catalogue' he gives this price, and also, again, the date of purchase.

26. 'A Novel Fragment', *FLS*, p.265.

27. ibid., p.270-1.

28. The version printed here is pencil-written, whereas the great majority of DW's mature writings were penned in ink.

29. DW was, in fact, twenty. The description of 'Ian's' bathing-dress bears an uncannily close resemblance to that of 'Rupert Sandstone' in Francis Streeten's novel *Frolic Welcome* (p.168): 'He was representing Adam. The foundation of his costume was a bathing slip,

and to it he had attached a number of leaves, which, with praiseworthy historical veri-similitude, were mostly fig ones.' The extract relates to a fête held at 'Castle Careless' (inspired by the Streetens' former home, High Hilden, in Tonbridge). DW and Streeten became friends around 1937. A reference to *Frolic Welcome* is made in the short story, 'A Picture in the Snow' (*FLS*, p.334).
30. In reality Betty Swanwick.
31. The sculptor Ivor Roberts-Jones.
32. Monica Booth, who later married Roberts-Jones.
33. Betty Swanwick's sister, Aileen.
34. MS in private coll.; the author has been unable to identify the nun.
35. Cedric Rogers's two cats.
36. Ian Smith (or 'Little Smith', as he was known, to distinguish him from another stud-ent of the same name), was a dwarf. DW makes no reference to him in his writings, although the two stayed in contact for some time after the accident.
37. The painter Leonard Appelbee.
38. Cedric Rogers MS copy enclosed in a letter to the author, 8th December 1987.

Chapter Four
1. Other students who went on the holiday included John Lewis, Jack Miller, Corinne Snow (and her sister Betty, who was not an art student) and Joan Waymark. They stayed at a guesthouse called 'Ingleneuk'.
2. For the Wednesday, 7th June 1944 entry in his Journals (p.151) DW writes: 'What a day of aching and giving up! The day nine years ago on which I was run over and my health ruined for ever. . .' It has been assumed from this that the accident occurred on Friday, 7th June 1935. However, the date appears to be incorrect. Mrs Phyllis Timber-lake, DW's first cousin, whose parents' house at Leigh he was trying to reach, was almost sure that it was a Sunday, which is confirmed by Gerald Mackenzie's diary note written contemporaneously—'Denton run over on Whitsunday.' Furthermore, the two news-paper reports quoted below specify 'Sunday afternoon.'
3. This is the last town mentioned in his account of the journey given in *AVTAC* (p.10).
4. *AVTAC*, p.31. The road on which the accident happened is the A23.
5. ibid., pp.10-11.
6. The accident was also reported in the *Croydon Advertiser*, which confirms the location of the accident. M. De-la-Noy, op. cit. incorrectly states that DW was taken to Lewisham Hospital (p.98).
7. Bernard Kane drove up from Leigh with his mother. Writing to his sister, the late Beatrice Kane, in January 1975, he recalled: 'I can remember the policeman coming to the door and asking for Mum, and the general kerfuffle before we got started, as no-one knew exactly where the place was. It was fairly late when we got to the hospital, but they let us in and the ward was more-or-less in gloomy darkness. Mum stayed for a fair time, but I broke for the fresh air, as the "hospital" smell was too much for me.'
8. *AVTAC*, p.17.
9. One can identify 'Clare' as being Hilda Dallas from an early draft of *AVTAC* (HRC coll.), in which DW writes the name 'Hilda' instead of 'Clare'.
10. ibid., p.21.
11. In conversation with the author. Corinne Snow and Joan Waymark appear as 'Cora' and 'Betsy' in *AVTAC*. It has previously been wrongly assumed that 'Betsy' was Betty Swanwick, who did certainly visit DW in hospital, but not on this occasion, and not with Corinne Snow. In a MS draft of *AVTAC* DW actually writes 'suddenly I saw Joan and Corinne, two girls from the Art School, coming towards me. . .' (HRC coll.).
12. ibid., p.42.

13. This small sketch-book containing pencil and ink drawings is in the HRC coll. (accession no.66.72.4). It bears the inscription, 'Done in my first days in the hospital, June 1935.' The doodles include abstract composition designs, various heads, vessels and plants.

14. *AVTAC*, p.48.

15. This daydream (see *AVTAC*, pp.55-7) can be compared with a previously unpublished extract from a journal kept early in 1936: 'Then gradually I returned through the dripping park under the trees laden with rain across the soaking grass. Until I came to the fosse that divided the park from the garden. Wearily I clambered down and up the other side, when I saw it twinkling through the beeches, the lights of the house.

'How welcome it all was. The great porticos seemed to draw me on and when I lay before the fire in the deep warmth of the panelled room I longed only for my tea, which came on a silver tray steaming and comforting, and with it hot little scones and cherry jam. [There follows a description of dinner.] Then slowly I rose and made my way up the great staircase lighted by the six candles on the Georgian chandelier I carried. My room was dark, with rain beating against the panes, but I drew the curtains and lit the silver sconces that illumined the soft colours of the tapestry. I lit the fire in the grate and fell asleep.' (MS in Gerald Mackenzie coll.).

Similar dream-like episodes occur in the Journals (e.g. pp.25-6, 83).

16. *AVTAC*, p.64. Although this passage is surely an example of 'poetic licence', it is probably an accurate reflection of DW's state of mind when contemplating death.

17. Gerald Mackenzie, in conversation with the author. A slip of paper inserted into his diary of the time records: 'Denton run over on Whitsunday. St Alphege's Hospital—on danger list for four days, then after three or four weeks moved to National Hospital for Nervous Diseases, Queen's Square. Broken ankle; at first no feeling in buttocks or left leg and unable to stand. After treatment (Sept. 1st) able to walk to the bathroom in the hospital and regained feeling in leg, etc. The nerves controlling the bladder are not yet in order.'

18. *AVTAC*, p.94.

19. ibid., p.99.

20. Mrs Betty Walters (Corinne Snow's sister) in a letter to the author of 12th August 1989 writes: '. . . Later Denton became mobile and was able to walk in the hospital grounds. Eventually he walked round the corner to a pub and began talking to some medical students, who inadvertently told him what was the matter with him and that he would not recover.' The story is confirmed by John Lewis, another fellow-student from Goldsmiths'; see also J. Lewis, *Such Things Happen*, Unicorn Press, Stowmarket, 1994, with refs to DW.

21. *AVTAC*, p.105. The exterior of the front of the building remains entirely unchanged.

22. MS in HRC coll.

23. *AVTAC*, p.115.

24. ibid., p.116.

25. On 18th November 1935 Gerald Mackenzie wrote in his diary: 'Dr Easton, late of King's College Hospital, tells me that Denton will never get any better. Nothing seems to be able to help him.'

26. *AVTAC*, p.117.

27. ibid., p.124.

28. ibid., p.131.

29. ibid., p.136.

30. M. De-la-Noy, op. cit. suggests in a footnote (p.111) that 'Denton took the name "Farley" from the village of East Farley [sic] in Kent. . .', but since the correct spelling of the village is East Farleigh, the author considers this unlikely. In an early draft of *AVTAC* DW used the name 'Dr Ashley' for Easton, Ashley being the first name of Dr Herman,

senior partner in Easton's Tonbridge practice.

31. *AVTAC*, p.143.
32. MS in HRC coll.
33. *AVTAC*, p.161.
34. ibid., p.163.
35. ibid., p.164.
36. ibid., p.171
37. The date is determined from Gerald Mackenzie's diary.
38. 'Sickert at St Peter's', *FLS*, p.323.
39. ibid., p.324.
40. ibid., pp.324-5.
41. ibid., p.326.
42. ibid., p.328.
43. *AVTAC*, p.188.
44. ibid., p.189.
45. Regrettably the author has been unable to identify the newspaper from which this cutting was taken. Another such cutting in Gerald Mackenzie's coll. informs us additionally that '. . . Mrs Annie Hutley, of Woodyate-road, Lee, S.E. was driving the car, which was owned by Mr William George Falconer, transport contractor, of Silwood-street, London, and both were made defendants.' The £4,000 damages was awarded with costs.

Chapter Five

1. In a letter to the author, 9th May 1987. In a further letter of 12th June 1991 Dr Easton gave another account, which differs slightly in detail: '. . . By this time [1936] I had realized my mistake in settling in Broadstairs and had found an ideal practice in Tonbridge, where I could probably get on the staff of the Tunbridge Wells Hospital as a consulting physician. It could have been only a few days after arriving there that Denton suddenly appeared crying and collapsed in my garden. I drove him to the Nursing Home and contacted Hugh Raven. My wife thinks he stayed three or four days in the Home before I put him back on the Broadstairs train, with a sigh of relief. He got off the train at Ashford and returned to Tonbridge, landing again in my garden, this time spotted by a policeman.'

Dr Easton had no recollection of Miss Sinclair having been in Tonbridge during these visits, and it is possible DW has compressed events.

The Berg Coll. (NYPL) has one of DW's notebooks in which he made the briefest jottings of how he might conclude *A Voice Through a Cloud*: '1/Martin. Christmas. 2/Hilda—against. 3/Gerald, Aunt Dos. 4/Lawyers. 5/Jack going. 6/One other night. 7/House hunting. 8/Terrible tel. talk. 9/Paddock Wood. End.' It is possible, however, that these jottings are simply for a chapter, but the author considers the word 'End' to imply something more definite and final.

2. From extracts of DW's journal kept in February 1936; Gerald Mackenzie coll. A further extract about Dr Easton: 'The love you bestowed on your little dog made me bite my lips. Your smile: I think of it all day long. When I think of you I realize how little I love other people. How little value I set on their friendship. I don't want it. I don't want them or anything: only you.' This journal, from which Mackenzie copied out these passages, was almost certainly destroyed when DW attempted suicide in 1938/39.

3. Journals, p.137.
4. Elizabeth Guyatt, in conversation with the author.
5. The club expanded considerably over the years and it was still operating in the 1970s, its name having been altered a number of times.
6. Accession no.70.3.2.

7. Mrs Mundy-Castle was published by Arrowsmith, Chapman & Hall and John Murray.

8. Noel Cousins, in conversation with the author. Amongst DW's nicknames for her were Myrtle and The Harlot. In the Journals she is usually referred to as 'Eve' (not 'Evie', as printed). Eric Oliver recalled that DW had a surprisingly strong voice in his shouting matches with her! According to Elizabeth Hasell-Walker he also possessed an attractive baritone voice, taking a solo in 'The Holly and the Ivy' at West Peckham Church during a Christmas service.

9. *AVTAC*, p.159.

10. The exhibition was shared with works by John Craxton, and ran during May and June 1954.

11. Cat. no.1141.

12. See Catalogue of Paintings, nos 6,7,8. There exist also six portraits of DW by other artists, including Gerald Mackenzie, May Walbrand-Evans and Noël Adeney. A 'self-portrait' reproduced on the cover of the Penguin ed. of the Journals is certainly not by DW; the author has been unable to identify the artist. Nor does it appear to be a portrait of DW.

13. In a letter to Peggy Kirkaldy of 20th March 1945 DW writes: '. . . Collecting is a vice, I think too, if it gets too all-absorbing. It can drain one of nearly all original impulse; for nothing can be more delightful than just hunting, furbishing, mending and preserving the charming things of other centuries. But severely kept in its place it makes the perfect relaxation.'

14. His bride's name was Ada Henderson (like DW's mother an American), who had been a confidential secretary in the firm of the millionaire, C.V. Starr.

15. The correspondence, which is in private hands, consists of forty-two letters.

16. The mansion part of the house was demolished in 1951. See Joan Thirsk, *Hadlow Castle: a Short History*, Hadlow Historical Society, 1985.

17. Amongst other artists who designed Shell posters for 1937 were: McKnight Kauffer, Tom Gentleman, Rowland Suddaby, Paul Nash and Graham Sutherland. DW's original painting of Hadlow Castle is part of the Shell Art Coll., housed at the National Motor Museum, Beaulieu, Hants.

18. Mrs Rosamund Owen recalls being taken by her father to watch Streeten speaking on a soap-box near Tonbridge Station, and him being pelted with tomatoes!

19. Francis Streeten appears in the book as 'Wilfred Manton'. See also Chapter Three, note 29.

20. 'A Picture in the Snow', *FLS*, p. 330.

21. M. Cranston, op. cit., p.242.

22. In a letter to the author, 30th January 1989.

23. M. Cranston, 'Denton Welch, sketch of an oddity', *Readers News*, November 1951, Vol.14, No.5, p.4; Cranston also wrote about DW in *The Spectator*, 1st June 1951, p.724.

24. This was 'Parliament Square' (see List of Poetry at end of volume). The others were: 'O moon, so sonnet-tawdry' (*Dumb Instrument*, p.13), 'For a dead Conscript' (*ALS*, p.218), 'Babylon' (*ALS*, p.219), 'Window Display' (*ALS*, p.232), 'Friday Night' (*ALS*, p.224), 'Two Cats' (*ALS*, p.232) and 'Before Bed' (*ALS*, p.224).

25. Letter of 19th December 1938; HRC coll.

26. 'A Fragment of a Life Story', *FLS*, pp.340-52 (see Bibliography, no.17). Here the following incident is set in a 'late January afternoon at the beginning of the war.' However, the period December 1938 to January 1939 is almost certainly correct.

27. Dr Easton and his wife recalled DW had indeed entered their house surreptitiously on more than one occasion.

It seems probable the 'parish hall' referred to in the Journal account was St Saviour's, now the Red Cross Centre, Tonbridge. See also 'I First Began to Write'; Bibliography, no.6. Gerald Mackenzie remembered that quite soon after DW moved into the Hadlow Road flat he had made an attempt to gas himself.

28. See *FLS*, pp.373-82; Bibliography, no.30.

29. Letter of 18th February 1939; copy in private coll.

30. Jocelyn Brooke, 'The Dual Role: a Study of Denton Welch as Painter and Writer', *Texas Quarterly*, VI, 3 (Autumn 1964), pp.120-7, 123.

31. See Catalogue of Pictures, no.104.

32. 'Faces at the Stage Door', *FLS*, p.383.

33. *FLS*, p.388.

34. M. Cranston, *The Nineteenth Century and After* (op. cit.), p.240. In 'Touchett's Party' Cranston appears as 'Markham', Edward as 'Wilmot' and Streeten (in this extract 'Oswell') as 'Touchett'. The late Maurice Cranston was unable to remember the identity of 'Edward' (the name used in his article on DW), someone who he suspected anyhow may have been a composite character in DW's short story.

35. The Journals, p.144 gives the number as 26 Brook Street, but this is an incorrect transcription from the MS.

36. Gerald Mackenzie, in conversation with the author.

37. 'The War Breaks Out', *FLS*, pp.398-9. The piece is published incomplete in the latter ed.; the remaining 200 or so words are to be found in MS at the Berg Coll., NYPL.

38. One learns from the Journals (p.256) that DW left the Tonbridge flat in January 1940 and moved into his new home later the same month.

Chapter Six

1. For a floor plan and information about the construction of the house, see F.R.S. Yorke, *The Modern House*, The Architectural Press, 3rd ed. 1937, p.166.

2. From an early draft of the story 'The Fire in the Wood'; HRC coll.

3. In conversation with the author.

4. Letter of *c.* February 1940.

5. Her stay is related in the unfinished story 'Velvet', *FLS*, pp.400-4.

6. Extracts from diary entries for 27th and 31st March 1940. 'J.M.' refers to the publisher John Murray and 'F.F.' possibly Faber & Faber.

7. In conversation with the author.

8. Journals, pp.193-4.

9. See *FLS*, pp.407-42 and Bibliography, no.36. In an early draft of the story (HRC coll.) DW calls the man's mother first 'Mrs Johnson' (crossed out), then 'Fletcher' (crossed out), and finally settles on 'Archer'. In making enquiries as to the identity of Tom the Woodman, the author spoke to a Mr T. Bailey of Sherborne, Dorset, formerly the foreman of a timber business in Kent, and himself a Yorkshireman, who, without prompting, came up with the surname Fletcher. He mentioned a friend of his in Yorkshire who had known this Tom Fletcher (a woodman from Yorkshire who certainly had worked in Kent), but was unable to contact the friend, since he had either died or changed his address.

10. In a discarded early version of 'The Fire in the Wood' DW writes: 'Mary as unobtrusively as possible settled herself against a bush and started to draw the two men kneeling. She started on the haunches and the tucked-up legs, but when she got to the shoulder and the swinging arms, she could only attempt the merest indication. . .'

11. This drawing too has survived and is in a private coll. in Holland.

12. From an early draft of 'The Fire in the Wood', entitled 'Pine Wood'; HRC coll.

13. ibid., *FLS*, p. 424.

14. ibid., p.428.

15. From an early draft; HRC coll.

16. The whereabouts of the picture is unknown.

17. From an early draft; HRC coll.

18. Journals, p.97. In the index of this edition another reference is given (p.49), but this results from a misreading of the MS. The reference is to 'Trot's cottage' (not 'Tom's cottage', as printed), Trot Mann being the sister of Phyllis Ford, a friend of DW's, who lived in rooms at Peggy Mundy-Castle's house. The White Cottage, the home of Trot Mann and her friend Prue Selfe, is referred to elsewhere in the Journals.

19. Gladys Ellen Killin (pseudonym of G.E. Easdale), *Middle Age 1885-1932, an Autobiography*, Constable, 1935. She counted Leonard and Virginia Woolf amongst her friends.

20. In conversation with the author. See Katharine Moore, *A Family Life 1939-45*, Allison & Busby, 1989 (with refs to DW on pp.71, 73, 87-8, 93, 97, 100-1, 103, 108, 133).

21. In conversation with the author.

22. The precise date and circumstances of their first meeting are unknown; the date is inferred from a reference in the Journals (p.354) to Mrs Walbrand-Evans, 'whom I have known so well, seen so much of, for the last ten years.'

23. In the Journals (p.355) DW writes: 'I think of her now as she must have been forty years ago, when Lavery painted her all in black as an Edwardian beauty. She had pink roses in her hands and was leaning on a grand piano. Then there is his other portrait of her in a pink balldress with pearls in her hair.' The two portraits of Mary Delmar-Morgan (Mrs Walbrand-Evans) mentioned here are in the National Gallery of Modern Art, Rome (the first, with the title 'Polyhymnia') and the International Gallery of Modern Art, Venice ('A Lady in Pink'). Apparently, there is also a third, described as 'a small oval'. The author is grateful to Kenneth McConkey, Professor of Art History at the University of Northumbria at Newcastle, for supplying this information on the location of the pictures.

24. Accession no.66.72.34.

25. 'A Mews Flat in the Country', *FLS*, pp.451-3. Blair Hughes-Stanton (1902-81) was known especially for his book illustrations; see Penelope Hughes-Stanton, *The Wood-Engravings of Blair Hughes-Stanton*, Private Libraries Association, Pinner, 1991 (especially illustrations pp.174-6).

26. *Dumb Instrument*, p.14.

27. M. Cranston, *The Nineteenth Century and After* (op. cit.), p.240.

28. Journals, p.194.

29. See Bibliography, no.3.

30. Aside from the account that follows, in the Journals (p.232) DW describes witnessing at close hand the crash of a German plane. The incident is written up in greater detail in 'Fear', *FLS*, pp.443-5.

31. Journals, p.20.

32. ibid., p.194.

33. Chatto & Windus were the original publishers.

34. Journals, p.194.

35. Indeed, his friend Gerald Mackenzie stated quite definitely that DW did have a quantity of notebooks in the years before he embarked upon his career as a writer. One might conclude that he destroyed the diaries or notebooks relating to *Maiden Voyage* once he had written the book and had no further use for them.

36. In a letter to Helen Roeder, c.1942, by which time the painting had been taken to Green & Stone's in London to be framed. Mrs Molly Townsend (née Ure) recalls seeing the 'Harvester' on DW's easel at the Hop Garden. She comments in a letter to the author, 5th July 1989: 'I much disliked the picture and wrote a poem about it, which had as its refrain, "O horrible headless woman with hideous breasts" and Denton said I wasn't the

only person who'd been moved to write about it. I felt bad about writing it, but the picture was just too strong to ignore.' Mrs Townsend remembers DW at this time as 'a beautiful young man, who was courteous, clever, and who had all the appearance of a heavenly choir-boy. He gave no indication whatsoever of being in pain. It was only after reading his books that I realized he was a brave man, as well as being a charming host.'

37. In the short story 'The Party' DW refers to Derain as being his 'new discovery' (*FLS*, p.295). The 'Harvester' bears some similarity, for instance, to Derain's *L'Age d'or* of c.1939 (in the Musée d'Art Moderne, Paris), though it is unlikely DW would have seen a reproduction of this picture in particular.

38. Peter Bishop appears as the bridegroom in 'Memories of a Vanished Period' (*FLS*, pp.529-40); see Bibliography, no.45. DW gives a very unflattering description of Bishop in his Journals (pp.274-5).

39. Better-known as the sculptress Karin Jonzen, whose husband Basil had been at St Michael's with DW. Basil Jonzen wrote an article 'A Visit to Mr Sickert at Broadstairs' (*Horizon*, VIII, 45 (September 1943), pp.194-203.

40. Neither of these pictures has been traced. DW made two other drawings of centaurs.

41. See Michael MacLeod, *Thomas Hennell: Countryman, Artist, Writer*, Cambridge University Press, 1988.

42. In a letter to the author and critic Frank Swinnerton (1884-1982), 16th July 1943, written following the publication of *Maiden Voyage*, DW recalled his state of mind whilst working on the novel: 'I am only just beginning to realize how personal, not to say ego-centric, that book is. All the time I was writing it, I hardly thought of its effect on other people. I had never published anything before and didn't know if anyone would take what I had done, when it was finished.' (HRC coll.)

Freddie Beale was a friend of Peggy Mundy-Castle; he was in the R.A.F. and was killed in action in 1942. He is mentioned a number of times in the Journals.

43. See List of Poetry. 'Jane Allen' was one of five poems by DW that the composer Howard Ferguson used for his song cycle *Discovery*, published in 1952.

Amongst other contributors to *The Abinger Chronicle* were the composer Ralph Vaughan-Williams, Max Beerbohm, E.M. Forster (who lived at Abinger Common), Desmond MacCarthy, William Rothenstein and G. Rostrevor-Hamilton, who later bought one of DW's pictures. In September 1941 DW had some correspondence with Forster concerning 'the Latham case'. The baronet and M.P. Major Sir Paul Latham was court-martialled and forced to resign his seat over 'disgraceful conduct while on active service', and attempted suicide. The result of the court-martial of 4th and 5th September was a sentence of two years imprisonment, without hard labour. The charges related to 'improper conduct with three gunners attached to Searchlights and with a fourth man who was a civilian' (*The Times*, 5th September 1941). DW was outraged at the harsh treatment meeted out to Latham.

44. The poem was first published in *Penguin New Writing*, 1950, (p.61), and subsequently in *ALS* (p.216). 'The animal-doctor should put you to sleep', which is the final line of the poem, was chosen by Eric Oliver as the title for DW's last completed watercolour (see Catalogue of Pictures, no.92).

45. See List of Poetry.

46. In conversation with the author.

47. Wednesday fell on 6th January in 1943, which is the presumed date of this piece. Printed in 'Thirteen Texts by Denton Welch', ed. Jean-Louis Chevalier, *Texas Quarterly*, Autumn 1972, pp.39-40.

48. *Journals*, p.194.

49. In conversation with the author.

50. In conversation with the author. At the same meeting Miss Swanwick revealed she

had thought DW had 'an eerie and sinister side to him', and that he reminded her of a satyr. 'He was narcissistic and only really liked himself.' Compare this description with that of Noël Adeney when she is writing about 'Merton' (DW) in *No Coward Soul* (The Hogarth Press, 1956, p.5): 'His curling burnished hair growing up from his face gave an even greater vitality to it, and emphasized two fulnesses at the top of his forehead, where incipient horns might have been.'

51. Lord Berners, *First Childhood*, Constable, 1934. The photograph described faces p.114 and bears the caption 'Myself aged eight.'

52. Letter of 13th August 1941.

53. DW's visit to the Randolph Hotel is written up in 'A Morning with the Versatile Peer, Lord Berners, in the Ancient Seat of Learning'; see Bibliography, no.9.

54. In conversation with the author.

55. Journals, pp.21-2.

56. ibid., p.22. 'Punky' was the Welches' pet-name for DW. Writing to her son on 3rd December 1926 Rosalind Welch started her letter 'My Darling Denton (known as Punky)'. It is curious that Miss Sinclair, who was very fond of cats (which he was not), used to call him 'Pusky'. Possibly she had misheard his brother Paul speaking to him.

Chapter Seven

1. In conversation with the author.

2. The date is ascertained from the MS in the British Museum (Additional MSS, 49, 062), which is in nine exercise books. Inside the cover of the first book is written 'Begun Sept.? 1940; Finished Feb.1942'. The eighth and ninth notebooks have his Pond Farm address inside, probably for the benefit of his typist.

3. The timing of DW's work on the piece is significant, since Sickert had died on 22nd January at Bathampton.

4. See Catalogue of Pictures, no.50.

5. Occasionally nicknamed rather unflatteringly 'Artists of Shame and Compromise', the series was held during July and August, some years extending through to September.

6. In conversation with the author. See Oliver Brown, *Exhibition*, Evelyn, Adams & Mackay, London, 1968.

7. In April DW had written to the sculptor and artist Henry Moore asking to buy one of his drawings. He was sent five small ones from which to choose. DW selected one of three seated figures, priced at £5. Moore's letter of 29th May, acknowledging receipt of the remaining four, had to be forwarded from Pond Farm to c/o Mrs Walbrand-Evans, the Brown Jug.

8. The picture appeared in *Vogue*, Victory Number, June 1945 with the caption: 'Denton Welch has given us a rendering of a room in his cottage in Kent, where colour plays an important part. He says "Do not think that brilliant colour is difficult to live with. It is always stimulating and refreshing; and change to a neutral-toned, colourless room would be extremely lowering and depressing" '.

9. Journals, p.197. The fan was Peggy Kirkaldy. The main house, originally called Pittswater, was written up in *Country Life*, LXXII, 2nd July 1932, pp.10-11.

10. H. Bolitho, 'My Friendship with Denton Welch', *Texas Quarterly*, X, 4 (Winter 1967), p.236. The article is a new and expanded version of 'In Welch is Youth', *Town and Country*, C, 4284 (May 1946), p.150.

11. In a letter to Barbara Cooper, secretary to John Lehmann, of 29th October 1943 DW gave his hobbies as 'old glass, china, furniture, little pictures and picnicking alone.' The Alphabetical Avenue no longer exists and, sadly, the Cedar Walk was devastated in the storm of October 1987.

12. Eleven of these poems were printed in the text of *The Denton Welch Journals*, ed.

Jocelyn Brooke, Hamish Hamilton, 1952, but all are omitted from the Penguin ed. of the Journals.

13. See Bibliography, no.11.

14. Letter to Maurice Cranston, written when DW was still at Pond Farm, c.May 1942.

15. This was *The Silver River*, 1938. Comfort's third book, *The Almond Tree* (also Chapman & Hall) was published in 1943, after which he became a Routledge author. A pacifist, he had a noted career as a physician, gerontologist and writer on medical matters.

16. Routledge Archive, University of Reading Library.

17. Letter of 14th July 1942 (MS Coll., University College, London); in a further letter from Waugh to Comfort, the former refers to DW as being Comfort's 'Golden Swan'.

18. Herbert Read (1893-1968) edited *The Burlington Magazine*, 1933-39 and was knighted in 1953. Aside from being a poet, critic, publisher and editor, he was one of the most influential and enlightened writers on the arts that Britain has produced.

19. Letter of September 1942; HRC coll. *New Road* was co-edited by Comfort and John Bayliss. The 1943 number acknowledges DW's assistance, but in it was published an article by E.H. Ramsden: 'A Critical Survey of the Work of the Younger Exhibitors'.

20. *Street Songs*, Macmillan & Co., London, 1942.

21. Recalled by Noel Cousins, in conversation with the author.

22. 'My House'; see List of Poetry.

23. Letter of 21st September 1942. Edith Sitwell's letter to DW was written from Renishaw Hall on the 14th. In it she suggests that he should write 'a reminiscence' of a meeting with the artist Percy Wyndham Lewis (along the same lines as 'Sickert at St Peter's'), even though DW had had no contact with him!

24. Journals, p.10.

25. Letter of 7th September 1942.

26. Journals, p.10.

27. Sir Kenneth Clark was a friend of Helen Roeder, who helped in the rehanging of pictures at the National Gallery, of which he was then Director.

28. Letter to Helen Roeder, 29th September 1942.

29. At their meeting in London Herbert Read had offered DW an advance of £50. However, on reading through his contract, which arrived by post at the end of October, DW found the sum had been reduced to £30.

30. Letter of 9th October 1942.

31. DW later used the excised description of travelling in the same Pullman car as Lord Alfred Douglas for an episode in his second novel, *In Youth is Pleasure* (pp.105-6), but Routledge still insisted that Lord Alfred's name should be omitted.

32. Letter to Helen Roeder, 16th October 1942. Oswald Hickson had died by the time DW submitted his second novel to Routledge. The eminent libel lawyer Peter Carter-Ruck recalls DW having come to the office to see Hickson.

33. In his article on DW for *The Nineteenth Century and After* (op. cit.) Maurice Cranston writes: 'He used to confess. . . that he did not know how to punctuate a sentence; he was awed by a profession of letters, about which he knew nothing.' (p.241).

34. Journals, p.44. The Berners picture appeared in *Vogue*, January 1942, p.42; Jan Gordon mentioned 'A Gothick Flowerpiece' in *The Observer*, 9th August 1942, p.2; the poem W.J. Turner took for *The Spectator* was 'My House'; the ones Middleton Murry took for *The Adelphi* were 'Jane Allen' and 'The Hungry Hour'; the one in *Kingdom Come* was entitled 'Poem'; the one for *Decachord* 'Parliament Square', for *The Abinger Chronicle* 'Can We No More' and 'The Anatomists'. For details of publication of these, see List of Poetry.

35. Since 'A Novel Fragment' begins with DW's early days at Goldsmiths', it virtually continues on from where *Maiden Voyage* left off, with a break only of about three or four

months.

36. See Bibliography, no.19.

37. The notes are: 'Winchester 2 o'clock in the morning (*ILMGH,* pp.146-7)—Follow Pilgrims' Way across ploughed fields (p.148)—Four Marks nasty people (pp.148-9)—walking with Welsh girls—paddling in stream—sleeping in crowded hostel with man and black beard—walking with tramp, stories of the kind vicar and the priest who blest the tent with incense—Godstone—Kemsing—Stansted, down the Vigo to Trosley [Trottiscliffe]—Boxley with the foreign students—sleeping in the stable—on to Charing—milk from the palace—and midnight bike-ride—be good—picked up by the Midland pair—are you a P.S.B.? [i.e. a public school boy]—all good humour—aeroplane ride, offering it to me—tea—can you afford it?—the Dutch boys—their rowdyism—the hostel—singing in the Court [?]—the Cathedral.'

38. Journals, p.66.

39. ibid., p.67.

40. DW no longer had his Baby Austin; he had had to give it up because of petrol rationing.

41. 'A Lunch Appointment' (see Bibliography, no.37); p.14 of MS in HRC coll.

42. ibid., pp.16-19.

43. Journals, p.69.

44. 'A Lunch Appointment', pp.28-30.

45. Journals, p.70.

46. 'Sickert at St Peter's', *FLS,* pp.326-7.

47. 'A Lunch Appointment', p.37.

48. Journals, p.73.

49. ibid., p.67. The words 'tears open its throat and sinks' are omitted from the published text.

50. Routledge Archive, University of Reading Library.

51. Letter to DW, 30th April 1943. Writing on 26th July Ragg informed him that copies of *Maiden Voyage* were still available from booksellers. A second edition was available on 22nd September, but the novel was out of print again by 2nd November.

52. Letter from Lady Oxford to DW, 20th August 1942; HRC coll.

53. Extract from letter of 10th May 1943, quoted in M. De-la-Noy, op. cit. (pp.165-6). A roughed-out list of other people DW intended to give copies of *Maiden Voyage* to includes Cyril Connolly, Graham Sutherland, W.J. Turner, Alex Comfort, Tambimuttu, Oliver Brown, Edith Sitwell, James Agate, Lord Howard de Walden, May Walbrand-Evans, 'Daisy' [probably Daisy Kane], Noël Adeney and Frida Easdale.

54. See Appendix 3. For a survey of the critical reception of DW's work, see the series of five articles by R. Whittington-Egan in numbers of *Contemporary Review,* June 1985—September 1986.

55. Letter of 16th June 1943. The three books referred to are *I Left My Grandfather's House, In Youth is Pleasure* and 'A Novel Fragment' (or possibly *A Voice Through a Cloud,* since one of the MS notebooks containing this novel is designated as a 'Fair copy', begun 11th January 1944).

56. See 17th April entry in the Journals (pp.65-6) for fragmentary draft of a beginning for *In Youth is Pleasure.*

57. The choice of the name Orvil, with its American connotations, is curious. However, one might bear in mind that the book is dedicated to DW's mother, who was American, and with whom he identified, whereas his two elder brothers, who appear as 'Charles' and 'Ben', were closer in spirit to Arthur Welch, who was English.

58. For descriptions of the grotto at Oatlands, see Barbara Jones, *Follies and Grottoes,* Architectural Press, 1953, pp.44-7, Marcus Whiffen, 'Vandalism Triumphant', *The*

Architectural Review, CIII (March-June 1948), pp.216-18, Lavender Westwood, 'The Grotto at Oatlands Park, Weybridge', *Country Life*, CIII (sic., 7th May 1948), pp.924-5.

The pets' cemetery was removed and re-established closer to the hotel; nothing remains of the terraced gardens or the grotto, which was demolished in 1948, although one or two shells taken from it have been used to build a small raised flower-bed in the hotel car park.

59. *IYIP*, p.30.
60. ibid.
61. ibid., p.139.
62. Letter of 5th January 1943; HRC coll.
63. Robert Phillips in *Denton Welch*, Twayne Publishers Inc., 1974 (p.81) comments that this is 'a name which suggests Aphrodite and the lure of heterosexual love.'
64. From R. Wever, *Lusty Juventus. An Enterlude called Lusty Juventus, lyuely describing the frailtie of youth: of natur, prone to vyce: by grace and good counsayll traynable to vertue*, Wyllyam Copeland, London, c.1565.
65. Letter of 18th February 1944.
66. Journals, pp.89-90. The Penguin ed. states that the entry was written at 3.25pm. 8.25pm is correct according to the MS.
67. *The Tatler*, 7th July 1943, pp.22, 24.
68. This poem follows the 15th July entry in the MS of the Journals. A similar short verse precedes the 3rd July entry quoted; it is printed in *The Denton Welch Journals*, ed. J. Brooke, pp.78-9.

> No one shall know
> If I don't tell
> The secret life
> Where all goes well.
>
> No one shall know
> If I don't tell
> The life that's lived
> In my private hell.

Chapter Eight

1. This was Alfred Harmston Seymour. The only work of his listed in the British Library catalogue is a pamphlet on projected improvements to school buildings, published by the National Union of Teachers.
2. The artist was Guy Allan. Augustus John mentions his escapades in 'Fragment of an Autobiography—XIII', *Horizon*, XI, 64 (April 1945), pp.260-1, though he misspells the name 'Allen'.
3. Journals, p.100.
4. ibid., p.101.
5. In the Journals (p.107) DW states his 'real name was Bone.' Bones is correct. Throughout the MS of the Journals DW is careful to write Monté, whereas in the Penguin ed. the name is printed as Monte. In fact, Monté or Monty was a name that Bones used for many years, and his nephew told the author he had always known him as Uncle Monty.
6. The conversation was relayed verbatim to Mildred Bosanquet, who reported it in a letter of 23rd September 1943 to Gerald Mackenzie.
7. Journals, p.104.
8. There were Canadian soldiers manning anti-aircraft guns very near to Pitt's Folly Cottage. In Mrs Bosanquet's letter to Mackenzie there is a description of DW's reaction

to the detective calling at May's house very different from the one in the Journals: 'Denton was standing in May's garden and they were discussing the whole thing. A man walked in at the gate, a portfolio in his hands, with folded arms—he stood and looked steadily at them before speaking. Denton turned white and then red. Afterwards he is furious at this. He said to me, "Wouldn't you change colour if somebody suddenly came in and gazed at you?" But the thing that panicked him was the man's comment to May: "I think your little friend must be either very nervous or have a guilty conscience." '

9. Elizabeth Hasell-Walker (née Plummer), in conversation with the author.

10. In 19th September 1943 ed. The article in the *News of the World* reveals that Monté had once jumped bail and had stowed away on the *S.S. Kurdistan* to Canada, from where he had been forced to work his passage home. '. . . de Montaigne told stories of how he had shot down a German plane,' the report of the case continues, 'sank a submarine' and 'showed them photographs of a destroyer he said he had attacked.'

11. See Bibliography, no.38.

12. Aside from leaving out the Poetry Reading episode, the Allison & Busby/Penguin ed. of the Journals omits a further 600 words, excluding poetry.

13. This constitutes the Sunday, 3rd October 1943 entry in the Journals. It has been published in 'Thirteen Texts of Denton Welch', *Texas Quarterly*, (Autumn 1972) pp.45-9.

14. DW originally had hoped that Frank Swinnerton would broadcast on the book. In the event Viola Garvin mentioned it in 'What I am Reading Now.'

15. Journals, p.11.

16. M. De-la-Noy, op. cit., p.152.

17. Journals, p.125.

18. In conversation with the author.

19. In the poem 'Will it Twine at Last' (*ALS*, p.238) DW writes of 'my gingerbread hair' and in an early draft of the story 'The Fire in the Wood' he describes it as being 'fox-coloured'.

20. In conversation with the author.

21. All surviving letters from DW to Eric Oliver are in the HRC coll.; there are fifty-two in all.

22. See Bibliography, no.24.

23. In a letter to Noël Adeney of 7th December 1943 DW states that Treece had rejected the story for *Life and Letters*. On the subject of eroticism, in a letter to Treece of 9th June 1943 DW had written, 'I find myself continually annoyed and upset when I think of the huge tract of human experience which has to be left untouched,' and in a further letter of 1st December 1943 he wrote, 'You are the only person so far who has stressed the amoral, erotic, call it what you will, side of my writing.'

24. Quoted in M. De-la-Noy, op. cit., p.185.

25. 'When I was Thirteen', *FLS*, p.169.

26. ibid., p.175.

27. ibid., p.184.

28. Journals, p.127.

29. ibid., pp.127-8.

30. ibid., p.129.

31. ibid., p.133.

32. The letters are in the HRC coll.

33. In conversation with the author.

34. On 3rd September 1949, some nine months after DW's death, Eric Oliver wrote to John Lehmann thanking him for coming up with the title of the novel; Lehmann published *AVTAC* the following year.

35. Letter from DW to Herbert Read, 4th January 1944.

36. In a letter of 20th January 1944 to Peter Gamble, an employee of the Readers Union, concerning *IYIP*, DW wrote: 'I am so tired of all this insistence on ordinariness; dullness; so-called normality. . . that I wrote at once to say that I didn't mind being plastered with mud if they [Routledge] didn't mind publishing. . . All this makes the book sound terribly scatological and "naughty" and of course it's nothing of the sort. It's really rather prim, I think; but I suppose I have stressed the hidden fantasy life of the "hero". It seems as mild as milk to me, when I think of what goes thro' my head every moment of the day!' (HRC coll.)

37. Letter of 18th January 1944.

38. *Vogue*, March 1944, p.78.

39. Journals, p.140. From this date onwards DW frequently answered fan letters with an invitation to come down and see him, and from his Journals and correspondence one knows of over fifteen individuals who made visits to Pitt's Folly, or subsequently, to Middle Orchard. DW came to value these visits very highly.

40. Letter to Eric Oliver, 3rd May 1944. Roger Decombes (sic) exhibited at the Redfern Gallery and did a number of rather whimsical fashion drawings for *Vogue*.

41. Miguel Covarrubias, *The Island of Bali*, Cassell & Co., London, 1937.

42. Letter to Noël Adeney, 6th February 1945.

43. Letter to Eric Oliver, 11th April 1944.

44. Journals, p.145.

45. Letter of 22nd May 1944.

46. Journals, p.148.

47. In a letter of 14th May 1944 to Ragg, DW asked to be paid £25 for the decorations, rather than the £10 Routledge had offered, also for 12% royalties, rising to 15% after 2,000 copies sold; Routledge's reasoning for refusing to improve the terms of the contract was that *IYIP* was a smaller book than *Maiden Voyage*.

48. 'The Barn' appeared in *New Writing and Daylight*, 'When I was Thirteen' in *Horizon* and 'At Sea' in *English Story*. The poems were 'A Mistake' in *The Spectator* and 'A Rhyme' and 'Ashford Train' in *Life and Letters* (see Bibliographies for details of publication).

49. Journals, p.149.

50. ibid., p.150.

51. Letter to Eric Oliver, 2nd June 1944.

52. Letter to Eric Oliver, 27th June 1944. In a further letter of 4th July DW wrote: 'I have so often turned away from them [i.e. personal relationships] thinking that it was a grand thing to live in isolation; always criticizing, despising, seeing thro' people, thinking nobody good enough for me. But I know now suddenly what all that egoism leads to. It leads to death, negation, nothing. It is as if one were still alive and yet had committed suicide. If one does no good, gives no happiness, goes out to no one, what is the point of living at all?'

53. Journals, p.158. The second, third and fourth sentences of this extract have been omitted from the printed text.

54. *No Coward Soul* (Hogarth Press, 1956), pp.76-7. Eric had originally appeared as 'Fred' in Mrs Adeney's MS, Miss Sinclair as 'Letty'. The real 'Gina' was an Alsatian bitch that belonged to Mary Sloman, DW's landlady at Pitt's Folly. Eric Oliver was fond of the dog, though DW seems to have been afraid of it. In a letter of c.21st July 1945 to Peggy Kirkaldy he writes of the real Gina: 'She is not supposed to bite, but she manages to pull buttons off people's clothes and I for one feel that she should be put under restraint.'

55. Letter of 22nd July 1944.

56. *Dumb Instrument*, p.27.

Chapter Nine
1. M. Cranston, *The Nineteenth Century and After* (op. cit.), p.244. In a letter to Eric Oliver of 22nd June 1945 DW writes: 'I wrote rather well this morning and didn't feel agitated, but I'm afraid the book may sound awfully peculiar and I expect nobody will like it. I must finish it tho', as I myself like it best of all.'
2. Eric Oliver slept on a mattress on the floor, under the Gothic window.
3. The present whereabouts of the portrait is unknown (if it was not destroyed). It is reproduced in M. De-la-Noy, op. cit., illustr. 15. In December 1945 Mrs Adeney was working on a portrait of DW, which he described to a friend as 'rather unfortunate'.
4. Letter from Julian Goodman to DW, 3rd August 1943.
5. Journals, p.91.
6. Letter to Peggy Kirkaldy, 12th June 1945.
7. In a letter to the author of 28th January 1989 the late Mrs Vinogradoff (Julian Goodman) told what she remembered of the portrait: '. . . I was turning my head sideways. The colour was yellow and green, and I found it unattractive.' She gave it to a policeman during the years when she still lived in Gower Street.
8. *Vogue*, November 1944, p.48.
9. The article was to be on ghosts and dreams. It was not published by *Vogue*. Either DW failed to complete it in time, or the magazine rejected the MS. The short story 'Ghosts' (*FLS*, pp.193-6, Bibliography, no.29) is probably the piece in question. There also exist three fragments that appear to be related to the project; these can be found in *FLS*, pp.197-201. The only article by DW published in *Vogue* was 'Strange Discoveries'; see Bibliography, no.33
10. During the latter part of this period John Minton contributed some of the drawings and subsequently took over the column when DW became too ill to continue. There is no evidence that the two ever met or had any contact with one another.
11. Noel Cousins, who frequently went out painting with DW in the Hadlow Road years, remembers that DW did not have a very clear idea of what the finished picture would be like—he tended to fill the page/panel as he went along.
12. Journals, p.171.
13. Letter of 5th November 1944.
14. Journals, p.176.
15. Letter of 13th February 1945.
16. In a letter of 2nd March 1945 to Herbert Read, referring to the blurb on the dust-jacket of *IYIP*, DW wrote: '. . . it is inclined to give people the impression that this new book is as frankly autobiographical as the other [i.e. *Maiden Voyage*] and I should like this book, since it is written in the third person, to be regarded as a fiction; chiefly because of my family. It would never do for my eldest brother to identify himself completely with the brother in the book. I have told him that it would be absurd to do so, except in the less important details, and it would be best if other people as well did not look on the book as cold fact.'
17. Alan Pryce-Jones in *The Observer*, 25th February 1945, p.3.
18. Letter of 26th February 1945.
19. The eighty-three letters from DW to Peggy Kirkaldy are housed in the Berg Coll., NYPL.
20. Letter of 4th April 1945. The Dolls' House is now in the Museum of Childhood, Bethnal Green. It is illustrated in Constance Eileen King, *The Collector's History of Dolls' Houses*, Robert Hale, London, 1983—see pp.570-3. Coincidentally, of the books that DW took out from the Library at Repton, one was Ibsen's play *A Doll's House*.
21. Letter of 20th March 1945.
22. It appears that DW's paranoia was getting the better of him; Peter Sloman, her son,

assured the author that his mother regarded DW as a model tenant.

23. Journals, pp.195-6.

24. ibid., p.199.

25. ibid.

26. This was the portrait of Julian Goodman, to which he was adding finishing touches. In a letter of 23rd June to Mrs Kirkaldy he wrote that Eric had finally delivered it to Mrs Goodman. 'I've got to hate it,' he wrote, 'and I feel she must hate it too.'

27. Hector Bolitho, 'My Friendship with Denton Welch', *Texas Quarterly*, X, 4 (Winter 1967), pp.235-40; this extract p.236.

28. The visit is described in the 17th June 1945 entry of the Journals (pp.199-203).

29. ibid., p.190.

30. ibid., p.191.

31. Letter of 7th July 1945.

32. Journals, p.212.

33. Undated letter to Peggy Kirkaldy, c.20th May 1945.

34. Letter of 9th August 1945. Old Soar actually belonged to the Oxon Hoath estate; in 1950 it was bequeathed to the National Trust.

35. Journals, p.221.

36. Letter to T.M. Ragg, 24th May 1945. Though one might conclude that this description better accords with 'A Novel Fragment', DW's reference to having worked on the book 'for the last year and five months' would seem to establish it as *A Voice Through a Cloud*, since Notebook One of the 'Fair Copy' of the latter bears the date 'January 11th 1944', whereas Notebook One of 'A Novel Fragment' has 'Begun Monday. January 19th 1943'. See Bibliography, no.18.

37. Letter to Stephen Bagnall, 22nd September 1945.

38. The only evidence to have emerged as to how DW might have concluded the novel is found on the notebook sheet described in note 1 of Chapter Five. The MS notes also contain the sentences 'I concentrated on the rhythm of my breathing. I felt glad that I should always have this with me till I died.' It is possible this may have been intended as the conclusion of the novel.

39. This is described in the fragment 'The Secret Life', *FLS*, p. 201.

40. Alfred Harmston Seymour. The actor John Mills lived at the oast for a time.

41. Letter of 22nd October 1945. 'Dump' was short for 'Dumpling', one of DW's several nicknames for Eric Oliver.

42. The original correspondence between DW and his agents apparently no longer survives, though typed copies of a number of DW's replies exist (private coll.).

43. Despite advance sales of nearly 5,000 copies and an exceptionally favourable review from W.H. Auden in the *New York Times Book Review* (18th March 1945), on 28th September Ragg wrote to DW that the American publisher Fischer had 'got stuck' with a great number of reprints of *Maiden Voyage* and that Routledge were taking 2,000 to sell in the U.K.

44. 'The Coffin on the Hill' was rejected by *Harper's Bazaar*; subsequently it was published in *Life and Letters* (see Bibliography, no.32). However, it seems that DW had intended to write a different story for the American magazine, but was unable to complete it; nor did a new story appear in *Kingdom Come*. 'At Sea', which had first appeared in *English Story*, 1944, was reprinted in *Harper's Bazaar* in June 1949 (pp.73, 126-8, 130, 132).

45. 'The Woodman's Cottage' was reproduced in *Penguin New Writing*, No.3, 1947 (between pp.128-9) and *A Last Sheaf*; see Catalogue of Pictures, nos 122,87.

46. Letter of 13th March 1946.

47. John Ramsbottom, *Edible Fungi*, King Penguin, London, 1943.

48. Letter of 9th December 1945.
49. Journals, p.240.
50. ibid., pp.241-2.
51. ibid., p.242.
52. Letter of 4th January 1946.
53. Letter to Peggy Kirkaldy, 22nd January 1946.
54. Letter to Herbert Read, 16th January 1944.
55. Letter of 3rd (?) February 1946.
56. On 9th June 1943 DW had written to the poet Henry Treece: 'I still find it almost impossible to formulate to myself what I am trying to do when I write a poem. I just want to do it; and consequently what comes out of me will probably be rather shapeless, rather sexy and probably rather trite.'
57. Journals, p.197.
58. Letter of 30th December 1945. Bagnall's book was *The Crater's Edge*, Hamish Hamilton, London, 1945.
59. Journals, p.257.
60. Letter of 19th March 1946.
61. Journals, p.259.
62. ibid.
63. ibid., p.261.

Chapter Ten
1. Letter of 10th April 1946.
2. Journals, p.270.
3. In conversation with the author.
4. Journals, p.271.
5. ibid., pp. 271-2.
6. ibid., p.278.
7. ibid., p.279. The entry was written at 11pm that evening. Although DW writes that he 'said nothing at all about it', Eric Oliver had the habit of reading entries in the Journal at the end of the day, when his friend was in the bathroom.
8. Letter of 10th July 1946.
9. Letter of 15th July 1946.
10. Journals, p.293. It appears that DW had to turn down the requests from America, whereas he did provide six pen and ink drawings for *Penguin New Writing* and two pencil and two pen and ink drawings for Katherine Mansfield's short story 'The Voyage' for *Junior*; see List of Illustrations.
11. *ALS*, p.224.
12. Journals, p.296.
13. The description of the first picture is similar to 'By the Sea', but the author considers it must have been a separate work, which is untraced. 'The Coffin House' later went to the Leicester Galleries, where it was purchased by the writer Rose Macaulay; see Catalogue of Pictures, no.123.
14. Letter of 14th May 1944.
15. Journals, p.299.
16. ibid., p.304.
17. Blake Brown was the author of fourteen published books, including *Bicycle Belle: the Journal of a Jolly Journey*, Fortune Press, 1937. His brother, Lincoln, was married to the sister of Francis Streeten.
18. Journals, p.312.
19. See Appendix for text of the story, also Bibliography, no.39.

20. *Dumb Instrument*, pp.35-7.

21. Journals, p.321.

22. ibid., p.313.

23. ibid., p.327.

24. ibid., p.329; the title of the picture was DW's.

25. M. Cranston in 'Denton Welch; Sketch of an Oddity' (*Readers News*, 14, no.5, November 1951) commented: '. . . I doubt if he was ever tempted to touch his capital. He had Victorian principles of thrift; and so to spend his capital would have been to acknowledge that he was soon to die—one truth he could not bear to face.'

26. See Bibliography, no.40. In 1946 DW had had a poem, 'Skeleton Child', published in *Orion III* (see List of Poetry).

27. 'He' is correct; the Penguin ed. substitutes 'Eric'.

28. Journals, p.335.

29. The 'slighter thing' was 'Evergreen Seaton-Leverett', which Woodrow Wyatt was to reject for *English Story* in July 1948 (not 1947, as in M. De-la-Noy, op. cit., p.279); see Bibliography, no.25.)

30. Letter from Hamish Hamilton, 29th September 1947; one wonders if Hamilton's appreciation of 'When I Was Thirteen' was coloured by his fondness for skiing.

31. Letter of 30th September 1947.

32. 'The Trout Stream' too was finished, but as yet had not been published.

33. As 'Leaves from a Young Person's Notebook' the story was also rejected by Woodrow Wyatt in July 1948, though subsequently it was published in *Brave and Cruel*. The title 'Leaves from a Young Person's Notebook' had originally been used for 'A Fragment of a Life Story', the essay about DW's suicide attempt; see Bibliography, no 17.

34. Letter of 10th November 1947.

35. Letter to Hamish Hamilton, 18th November 1947.

36. Letter of 28th November 1947.

37. Letter of 30th November 1947.

38. Undated letter of c.5th December 1947.

39. The contents of *Brave and Cruel* when published were: 'The Coffin on the Hill', 'The Barn', 'Narcissus Bay', 'At Sea', 'When I was Thirteen', 'The Judas Tree', 'The Trout Stream', 'Leaves from a Young Person's Notebook', 'Brave and Cruel' and 'The Fire in the Wood'.

40. Easton continued as DW's physician until August 1948, when Dr Bates from the practice in West Malling took over. Easton considered that Crouch was too far from Tonbridge for convenience.

41. Journals, p.344.

42. ibid., p.343.

43. ibid.; entry of 26th December. This sentence is omitted from the Penguin ed.

44. This was Bill Welch's second wife, Judy.

45. Journals, p.351.

46. ibid.

47. N. Adeney, *No Coward Soul*, pp.182-3.

48. ibid., p.184.

49. Journals, p.354.

50. Letter of 3rd March 1948.

51. Journals, p.355.

52. N. Adeney, op. cit., p. 184.

53. See Bibliography, no.41.

54. 'A Picture in the Snow', *FLS.*, p. 330.

55. Journals, p. 356.

56. 'The Hateful Word', *FLS*, p. 572.

57. ibid., p.582.

58. ibid., p.583.

59. See Bibliography, no.43.

60. 'Susan Innes' is a composite character, with aspects of Peggy Kirkaldy, Rose-Marie Aubépin and Count Gian-Carlo Rusconi, a young Italian nobleman who first contacted DW in April 1948 and subsequently came to stay at Middle Orchard. As Eric Oliver recalled, it was he who cried out in the night. A portrait entitled 'Susan Innes' was exhibited at the Leicester Galleries in July 1949 (in the 'Artists of Fame and Promise' series—see Catalogue of Pictures, no.96), though not in the same gallery's 1954 commemorative exhibition (thus suggesting that it was sold at the former event). It remains untraced.

61. *Dumb Instrument*, p.40.

62. Journals, p.366; the entry is in fact a continuation of the previous one, which is incorrectly dated 10th August in the Penguin ed.

63. In a letter to Peggy Kirkaldy of 8th October 1945 DW described Carritt, a friend of Guy Allan, as 'rather excitable and exhausting—like a firework'. Carritt later became a well-known art expert and dealer, working at Christie's and later establishing his own firm. Apparently, the references to him in the Journals (especially p.223) caused him considerable embarrassment.

64. Journals, p.366.

65. ibid., p.367.

66. ibid.

67. ibid., pp.367-8.

68. ibid., p.369.

69. Journals, pp.369-70.

70. ibid., p.371.

71. *Dumb Instrument,* p.43.

72. *Other Voices Other Rooms*, Heinemann, 1948.

73. This extract is misquoted in M. De-la-Noy, op. cit. (p.290) as 'Denton is on the last two or three chapters of his long book, so if his health improved the book should be finished in the next few months.'

Bibliography

1. The Published Writings—a selection of the most significant English and American editions

Maiden Voyage, Routledge, 1943; Fischer, New York, 1945; Penguin 1954 (with reprints).

In Youth is Pleasure, Routledge, 1945; Fischer, New York, 1946; Vision Press, 1950, Oxford University Press paperback, 1982.

Brave and Cruel and Other Stories, Hamish Hamilton, 1949.

A Voice Through a Cloud, John Lehmann, 1950; Penguin, 1983.

A Last Sheaf (an anthology of stories and poems, with reproductions of nine paintings), John Lehmann, 1951.

The Denton Welch Journals (ed. Jocelyn Brooke), Hamish Hamilton, 1952.

I Left My Grandfather's House (with an introduction by Helen Roeder and illustrations by Leslie Jones), Lion and Unicorn Press, 1958.

Denton Welch: Extracts from his Published Works (ed. Jocelyn Brooke), Chapman & Hall, 1963.

Dumb Instrument (an anthology of poetry, ed. Jean-Louis Chevalier), Enitharmon Press, 1976.

I Left My Grandfather's House (with an introduction by Michael De-la-Noy), Allison & Busby, 1984.

The Journals of Denton Welch (ed. Michael De-la-Noy), Allison & Busby, 1984; Penguin 1987.

In Youth is Pleasure (with a foreword by William Burroughs), Dutton, New York, 1985.

The Stories of Denton Welch (ed. Robert Phillips), Dutton, New York, 1986.

Fragments of a Life Story: the Collected Short Writings of Denton Welch (ed. and with an introduction by Michael De-la-Noy), Penguin, 1987.

2. Books About Denton Welch

Noël Adeney, *No Coward Soul*, Hogarth Press, 1956

Robert S. Phillips, *Denton Welch*, Twayne, New York, 1974

Michael De-la-Noy, *Denton Welch: the Making of a Writer*, Viking, 1984

3. The Works of Denton Welch—Prose Writings

This section of the Bibliography catalogues all Denton Welch's prose writings, excepting letters, that extend to more than 1,000 words, as well as a few shorter works that the author feels have a particular reference to the text of this book. The entries specify in which publication the relevant story first appeared. The author has aimed to give the context of each piece, including, where known, an identification of the real people behind the characters used. The works are listed in the order in which they were written.

Abbreviations:

ALS   *A Last Sheaf*, a collection of Denton Welch's prose writings and poetry, with illustrations of some of his paintings, John Lehmann, 1951.

FLS   *Fragments of a Life Story: the Collected Short Writings of Denton Welch*, Penguin, 1987.

1. *John Trevor*, a short story. 7pp.; written c.1939/40; first published *FLS* (incomplete, since 2pp. of the MS are lost)
Inspired by a school outing that DW undertook while at Repton, the house being Chatsworth (see *Maiden Voyage*, pp.49-51). 'John Trevor' is a young artist employed by 'the duke'. Some schoolboys come to the house and are shown round by the librarian, who is in charge of Trevor. In the evening Trevor goes to the nearby village with a young gardener and gets drunk.

2. *A Party*, a short story. 13pp.; written initially c.1939; rewritten 1948; first published *ALS*.
A fancy-dress party at the home of Betty Swanwick ('Bertha Swan'), set during the time when DW was a student at Goldsmiths'. The date of the party was May 1935.

3. *I Can Remember*, unfinished autobiography. 53pp.; written 1940; first published incomplete in *Texas Quarterly*, Autumn 1972, with missing parts in same publication, Winter 1975 (pp.97-115)
The work covers DW's childhood from his birth to the age of about eleven. It is possible that it was begun as a result of his reminiscing with his old governess, Wooly, who had visited him at The Hop Garden in January or February 1940.

4. *Maiden Voyage*, novel. 240pp.; with dust-jacket, endpapers, etc. drawn by the author; begun September 1940; first draft completed between 24th May-18th June 1941; final text completed February 1942; first published by Routledge, 1943.
For the nine notebooks of the rough draft the novel bears the title 'Youth's Journey'. The book starts with DW running away from public school (i.e. Repton) and subsequently going to China for about nine months to live with his father.

5. *Weekend*, short story fragment. c.1,700 words; written c.1940/41; first published *Words Broadsheet* 13, 1975 and subsequently *FLS*.
Seemingly the setting and content are fictional: a woman in her mid-thirties stays in the country for a weekend and has a brief 'fling' with a farm-hand.

6. *I First Began to Write*, prose fragment. c.580 words; written c.1940/41; first published *FLS*.
A description of DW's earliest attempts at writing, ranging from a Gothic poem at nine to the time of his attempted suicide aged twenty-three, when he burnt his old notebooks.

7. *In the Vast House*, short story fragment. c.1,800 words; written c.1940/41; first published *Texas Quarterly*, Autumn 1972, pp.51-55.
The author depicts himself as an orphan living with his (maternal) grandmother. He describes his admiration for her footman, 'Will'.

8. *Alex Fairburn*, a short story. 8½pp.; written c.1940/41; first published *Texas Quarterly*, Autumn 1972, pp.55-62.
Written whilst DW was working on *Maiden Voyage*: fragments of 'Alex Fairburn' interrupt the early draft of the first chapters of the novel. The setting has some similarities with The Hop Garden, where the author was living from January 1940 to December 1941. Alex Fairburn is a twenty-three-year-old woman who is recovering from the breakdown of her marriage to 'Jack' (evidently DW had Dr J. Easton in mind). A young man comes to her cottage in the evening and asks to spend the night in her barn. They end up sleeping together in front of the fire, she having fed him. 'The Cardboard Box' from

Memoirs of Sherlock Holmes has a character named 'Alec Fairburn'.

9. *A Morning with the Versatile Peer, Lord Berners, in the 'Ancient Seat of Learning'*, essay. c.820 words; written probably September-October 1941; first published *Time and Tide*, 5th July 1952.

The account tells of DW's brief meeting with the composer and artist Lord Berners at the Randolph Hotel in Oxford. The purpose of the visit was to interest the peer in a portrait DW had painted.

10. *In Brixham Harbour*, prose fragment. c.600 words; written some time between October 1941 and January 1942; first published *FLS*.

The setting is Brixham in Devon, where DW and a number of other Goldsmiths' students spent a holiday during the summer of 1934, staying at a guesthouse, 'Ingleneuk'.

11. *Sickert at St Peter's*, essay. 6pp.; written probably January/February 1942; first published *Horizon*, August 1942, pp.91-97.

DW's first published prose. The essay describes a visit DW had paid to the artist Walter Richard Sickert at his house, Hauteville, near Broadstairs. Sickert died 22nd January 1942, and it seems very probable the piece was written shortly after this. The rough draft of the essay bore the title 'A Glimpse of Richard Sickert'.

12. *Mrs Hockey*, prose fragment. c.1,000 words; written early 1942; first published *FLS*.

Mrs Hockey was the wife of the headmaster of DW's prep school, St Michael's, Uckfield. DW's mother comes to take him out.

13. *A Child Meets Church and State and Poetry in Strange Places: Lady Astor*, essay fragment. c.1,000 words; written the first half of 1942; first published *Texas Quarterly*, Autumn 1972, pp.40-42.

Describing an occasion at St Michael's when the politician Lady Astor, whose sons were pupils at the school, helped in preparations for a production of *The Mikado*.

14. *Full Circle*, short story. 6½pp.; written the first half of 1942; first published *World Review*, June 1949, pp.55-57.

In a letter to Maurice Cranston from Pond Farm (where he lived from January to June 1942), DW wrote that he had sent a 'horror story' to the magazine *Lilliput*. This almost certainly corresponds to 'Full Circle', a typescript of which bears the address 'Pond Farm'. Though published incomplete in *FLS*, the final page of the typescript was at HRC in 1975, but appears subsequently to have been lost. The *World Review* version is similarly incomplete. It is possible that a typescript 'Return Journey', which was sold at Sotheby's in July 1968, corresponds with the story. 'Full Circle' tells of the author bedding down for the night in a shed whilst he is on a walking tour (possibly that recounted in *I Left My Grandfather's House*). A young man comes in and sleeps in the hay near him. In the morning a much older man is lying beside him in the hay; he is dead.

15. *Journals*. 353pp.; first entry: Friday, 10th July 1942; final entry: Tuesday, 31st August 1948; first published in an abridged edition Hamish Hamilton (ed. Jocelyn Brooke), 1952; unabridged edition Allison & Busby (ed. Michael De-la-Noy), 1984.

Though numerous sentences and phrases are omitted from the unabridged edition, the only substantial entry excluded is that of Sunday, 3rd October 1943, the 'Poetry Reading in Tunbridge Wells', published in *Texas Quarterly*, Autumn 1972, pp.45-49. Unfortunately, the abridged edition also contains innumerable inaccuracies in transcription from the original MS.

16. *The Earth's Crust*, short story. 7pp.; written probably the latter half of 1942; first published *Contact*, September-October 1950, pp.29-30, 59-60.

This describes the author's earliest days as an art student at Goldsmiths'. Taking the content into consideration, it would seem likely that it was written before 'A Novel Fragment', which was begun in January 1943. The MS has DW's Pitt's Folly Cottage address, to which he moved in Summer 1942.

17. *A Fragment of a Life Story*, short story. 11½pp.; probably begun December 1942; first published *Horizon*, September 1949, pp.160-171 (as 'A Fragment of Life Story').
The story, which describes the author's attempted suicide whilst he was living at 54a Hadlow Road, expands on the Journal entry of 2nd December 1942. 'A Fragment of a Life Story' originally bore the title 'Leaves from a Young Person's Notebook', which at a later date was used for a different story (see no.30). On 1st January 1943 Cyril Connolly wrote to DW rejecting a MS that he said should not be published by itself, as it was obviously a section from a book; this could possibly correspond with 'A Fragment of a Life Story'. Possibly Connolly kept a copy of the MS and made use of it at the later date.
18. *A Novel Fragment*. 65 pp.; first notebook of the MS headed 'Begun Monday, Jan. 19th 1943'; first published *Life and Letters*, June 1950.
The work describes DW's life as an art student at Goldsmiths' College. Amongst the identifiable characters are his teacher James Bateman ('Mr Bridgeman'), his then landlady Evelyn Sinclair ('Miss Middlesborough') and various fellow-students, including Cedric Rogers ('Billings'), Gerald Mackenzie ('Gerard Hope'), Joan and Peggy Lean ('Jane' and 'Madge'), Ivor Roberts-Jones (the 'squat little Welshman') and Edward Bouverie-Hoyton (a student in a mauve satin shirt and velvet breeches). Frederick Halnon was the sculpture master and Rothwell the 'all-in wrestler' model in the sculpture class. Dorothy Welch is 'Robert's aunt'.
In a letter to Basil Jonzen of 16th June 1943, DW states., 'I am writing another book; I have really begun three! I don't know which will be finished first.' Doubtless 'A Novel Fragment' was one of these, the other two almost certainly being *In Youth is Pleasure* and *I Left my Grandfather's House*. On 8th November 1944 Routledge wrote to DW including a copy of the blurb to be sent to DW's American publisher, Fischer; this refers to 'an autobiographical book which he is working on at present—this deals with the period when he was an art student', which seemingly should be 'A Novel Fragment', though it could refer to *A Voice Through a Cloud*. Again, on 24th May 1945, contributing more career information for the American edition of *In Youth is Pleasure*, DW stated: 'All I can say about my immediate plans is that I am writing and have been for the last year and five months, a book which is drawn from my experiences as an art student'. Although this latter date would certainly more probably seem to refer to his starting *A Voice Through a Cloud* (see below), the description of the content better accords with 'A Novel Fragment'. The author has been unable to reach any definite conclusion one way or the other.
19. *I Left My Grandfather's House*, unfinished travel story. 135pp.; begun 5th March 1943; first published by James Campbell, 1958, also the same year by The Lion and Unicorn Press (with illustrations by Leslie Jones).
An account of an extended walking tour, mainly in the West Country, that DW undertook during the early summer of 1933. There is evidence that the account is not wholly factual. DW's ideas for concluding the story exist only in the form of a rough jotting (see note 37, Chap. 7).
20. *Touchett's Party*, short story. 10½pp.; written before April 1943, but possibly much earlier; first published *Chance*, April-June 1953, pp.47-55, with the title 'A Short Story'.
DW describes a dinner at the Leicester Arms, Penshurst, in the company of Francis Streeten ('Touchett'), Maurice Cranston ('Markham') and a Blackshirt (given the name 'Wilmot'). The latter is more likely to have been an anarchist, given Streeten's political sympathies; the late Maurice Cranston could not recall the man's identity, but considered it possible that he was a composite character. The party retires to DW's flat in the Hadlow Road, Tonbridge.
21. *In Youth is Pleasure*, a novel. 154pp.; with dust-jacket, endpapers, etc. drawn by the author; begun April 1943 and completed December; first published by Routledge, 1945.
The novel is set at Oatlands Park Hotel, near Weybridge in Surrey. DW ('Orvil') is

fifteen. Other identifiable characters include his brother Bill ('Charles') and Paul ('Ben'), as well as his father, 'Mr Pym'. Charles Terrot, a friend from DW's prep school days at St Michael's, appears as 'Guy Winkle'.

22. *The Barn*, a short story. 7½pp.; written Spring 1943; first published *New Writing and Daylight*, Winter 1943/44, pp.98-104.

The story is based on a holiday that DW spent with his parents and brother Paul, in the village of Benson, Oxfordshire in 1924. The house they took was properly called Brookside and the owner was Capt. Richard John Carey Oakes. The latter's wife was Mrs Elfrida St Lo Oakes. The barn itself still exists, but has recently been converted into a house.

23. Anna Dillon, a short story. 9pp.; possibly begun July 1943; first published in *The Stories of Denton Welch* (ed. Robert Phillips), Dutton, NY, 1986.

The inspiration for this story, in which DW adopts a female role, seems to derive from an encounter with a Norwegian soldier in the village of Shipbourne, near Tonbridge, Kent, as is described in the 21st July 1943 entry in the Journals (pp.92-4).

24. *When I was Thirteen*, short story. 16pp.; completed by the end of November 1943; first published *Horizon*, April 1944, pp.250-65.

The setting is a skiing holiday in Switzerland, where the author had gone with his elder brother (evidently Bill Welch, but unnamed in the story). The other main character, 'Archer', remains unidentifiable, although there had been an older boy with this surname in DW's house at Repton. DW also uses 'Archer' as the surname for 'Jim' (Tom the Woodman) in 'The Fire in the Wood'.

25. *Evergreen Seaton-Leverett*, short story. 10pp.; begun possibly 1943; reworked and completed September 1947 to March 1948; first published *Orpheus II*, 1949.

The character of the title is based on an eccentric lady, Mrs Hayes-Jackson, who lived in Molyneux Park Road, Tunbridge Wells. DW went to visit her along with his prep school friend John Hesketh ('Alec Gale'). The story was rejected by Woodrow Wyatt for *English Story* in July 1948.

26. *A Voice Through a Cloud*, unfinished autobiographical novel. 224pp.; the first notebook of the 'fair copy' of the MS has the date 'January 11th 1944', which might lead one to assume the rough draft was begun the previous year—by October 1944 DW was working on an episode which features in pp.89-92 of the book and by Autumn 1945 he had completed two-thirds of the novel (the fair copy); in September 1947 he wrote to Hamish Hamilton he had filled eleven exercise books (i.e. to Chapter 22), but had yet to complete it—he was to write a further six chapters and was working to finish the novel at the time of his death in December 1948; first published by John Lehmann, 1950.

The novel describes DW's road accident of 1935 and his subsequent struggle to recover his health. Whilst convalescing in Broadstairs, Kent, he falls in love with Dr Jack Easton ('Dr Farley'), whom he eventually follows to Tonbridge. The identifiable characters in the book include Edith Kane ('Aunt Edith'), Hilda Dallas ('Clare'), Corinne Snow ('Cora'), Joan Waymark ('Betsy'), Gerald Mackenzie ('Mark Lynch'), Miss Widdop ('Matron' in Broadstairs), Hugh Raven (senior partner of 'Dr Farley'), Mrs Noote ('my aunt's mother'), Martin Miles ('David') and Evelyn Sinclair ('Miss Hellier').

27. *Narcissus Bay*, short story. 6pp.; written March/April 1944; first published *The Cornhill*, July 1945, pp.394-8.

The setting is the island of Wei-hai Wei off the Shantung Peninsular in China. DW is a child of about seven and is staying there on holiday with his mother.

28. *At Sea*, a short story. 15pp.; completed by 15th April 1944; first published *English Story*, 1944, pp.54-68.

The setting is an ocean liner on which the author, as a child of about ten, is accompanied by his mother.

29. *Ghosts*, essay. 4pp.; started October 1944; first published *ALS*, pp.91-5.

This is almost certainly the article on 'Ghosts and Dreams', originally written as a feature for *Vogue*, which is referred to in the Journal entry of 8th October 1944. It was not published in the magazine.

30. *Leaves from a Young Person's Notebook*, short story. 10pp.; written during the latter half of 1944; first published *Brave and Cruel*, 1949, pp.119-130.

This story, rejected by both Reginald Moore (for *Modern Reading*) and John Lehmann (for *Penguin New Writing*) in October and November 1944, originally bore the title 'The Sound of the Sea'. The setting is a convalescent home in Broadstairs, where DW had gone to recuperate early in 1939.

31. *The Judas Tree*, short story. 9pp.; completed April 1945; first published *Penguin New Writing*, 1945, pp.71-81.

The story tells of the author's meeting with an eccentric schoolmaster. DW was then an art student. The man wishes him to paint a picture of a Judas Tree.

32. *The Coffin on the Hill*, short story. 11pp.; started possibly c.October 1944; completed June 1945; first published *Life and Letters*, June 1946, pp.210-20.

Almost certainly this is the story on China that DW wrote initially for a new magazine, *Eurasia*, which never took off. It was later submitted to his agents at the end of October 1945. The story expands on an incident written about in 'I Can Remember' (*FLS*, p.51); the author and his parents go up the Yangtze River on a houseboat at Eastertime, and the young DW comes across an old Chinese graveyard.

33. *Strange Discoveries* (or *Discoveries*), essay. c.1,800 words; written Summer/Autumn 1945; first published *Vogue*, December 1945, pp.68, 90.

A description of various pictures, pieces of furniture, etc. that DW found and purchased when he was an art student.

34. *Velvet*, short story fragment. c.1,600 words; written possibly the latter half of 1945; first published *Texas Quarterly*, Winter 1975, pp.116-9 (as 'An Unfinished Story').

This tells of a weekend visit from the author's former governess, Wooly (here called 'Velvet'). The actual visit took place in January or February 1940, when DW had recently moved to The Hop Garden, Platt.

35. *The Youth Rang the Bell*, short story. 4pp.; probably written November/December1945; first published *FLS*.

The setting is the Blackheath-Greenwich area of South London; the youth is DW. He was then an art student, and the story tells of him looking for lodgings. He finds a place with 'Miss Green' (in reality Evelyn Sinclair).

36. *The Fire in the Wood*, extended short story. 38pp.; early draft begun 9th February 1946 (as 'Pine Wood'); worked up and revised August to December 1947; first published *Brave and Cruel*, 1949.

This tells of the romance between 'Mary' and 'Jim' (Tom the Woodman).

37. *A Lunch Appointment*, essay. c.5,000 words; begun May/June 1946; completed 17th July; first published in limited ed. of 150 copies by Elysium Press, 1994 (with foreword by Edmund White).

This is an account of DW's meeting with Edith Sitwell at the Sesame Club in April 1943, expanded from the entry written in his Journal (pp.67-76). The essay was commissioned by the poet José Garcia Villa for the American Journal *Harvard Wake*, but never appeared in the publication.

38. *Brave and Cruel*, extended short story. 62pp.; begun possibly late Summer/Autumn 1946; revised February/March 1947; completed by 17th April; first published *Brave and Cruel*, 1949.

The story concerns DW's meeting with John Henry Bones ('Monté') and the scandal surrounding the latter's masquerading as an officer in the R.A.F. The affair, which happened during August and early September 1943, is written up in the Journal, pp.99-108. Identifiable characters in 'Brave and Cruel' include Monté ('Micki Beaumont'), May Walbrand-Evans ('Julia Bellingly'), Elizabeth Plummer ('Katherine Warde'), a Mrs Bernard ('Mrs Charles'), a Mrs Presland ('Mrs Minton') and Eric Oliver ('Ted').

39. *The Packing-Case House and the Thief*, short story. c.3,000 words; begun c.October/November 1946; accepted February 1947; first published *Junior*, September 1947, pp.2-11.

The setting is the garden of the Welch's house in Shanghai. DW has a playhouse, which is robbed during the night; the thief is surprised by his pet dog.

40. *The Trout Stream*, short story. 27pp.; written probably May/June 1947; first published in *The Cornhill*, Spring 1948, pp.131-54.

The story concerns two visits made by DW in his youth to the homes of James Alexander Wattie ('Mr Mellon'), the retired senior partner of Wattie & Co. The setting of the first section is a house called Pareora (now demolished), which was on the Epsom Road out of Guildford; the remainder of the story is set at Wattie's elaborate bungalow, 'Wo Yuen', Enton Green, near Milford, Surrey. Descriptions of both locations are accurate, and the death of 'Mrs Slade', the housekeeper, is factual; she did indeed drown in the trout stream at the foot of the garden. Wattie's adopted daughter, Molly Perry, appears as 'Phyllis'. After the tragedy the family emigrated to British Columbia, Canada. The story was first intended for *Orion*, but was returned by Rosamond Lehmann after she had ceased being associated with the publication. The gardens of Wo Yuen were illustrated in *Country Life*, 4th January 1941, pp.10-13.

41. *A Picture in the Snow*, short story. 10½pp.; written February-March 1948, first published *ALS*.

DW tells of his first meeting with Francis Streeten ('Danny Whittome') and of their visit to High Hilden, the Streetens' former home, off the London Road, Tonbridge. The house is now a nursing-home and is also the setting for part of Streeten's own novel, *Frolic Welcome* (Fortune Press, 1933), where it is referred to as 'Castle Careless'.

42. *The Hateful Word*, short story. 11pp.; probably begun shortly after 16th March 1948; first published *ALS*.

A virtually fictional story in which a German prisoner-of-war comes to garden for a middle-class married couple. 'Harry Diedz', the name the young German is given, had in fact been a prisoner-of-war whom DW invited from a nearby camp to share the Christmas lunch with him and Eric Oliver in 1946.

43. *The Diamond Badge*, short story. 21pp., begun around mid-July 1948; first section (*FLS*, pp.551-66) published as 'The Visit' *Penguin New Writing*, 1949, pp.12-29; full story first published *ALS*.

'Andrew Clifton', a cripple, and 'Tom Parkinson' act as hosts to a female fan, who has come to visit the former at his home in the country. The characters are loosely based on DW and Eric Oliver, the girl being a composite character made up from Rose-Marie Aubépin, Peggy Kirkaldy and Count Gian-Carlo Rusconi. This story and 'The Hateful Word' were recalled by Oliver as having been written rather quickly and with a popular publication, such as a magazine, in mind.

44. *At Sir Moorcalm Lalli's*, short story. 5½ pp.; thought to be one of the last stories DW wrote before his death in December 1948, first published *Contemporary Review*, March 1974, pp.134-40.

As a boy DW is taken by his mother to lunch with 'Sir Moorcalm Lalli' (in reality the well-known philanthropist and businessman Sir Elly Kadoorie, 1867-1944) at his home in Kensington. The two unnamed sons who appear for the meal were Lawrence (later Lord Kadoorie) and his brother Horace. In a letter to the author of 10th January 1991, the late Lord Kadoorie, commenting on the story, wrote: 'It is good to see ourselves as others saw us—even allowing for a substantial dose of poetic licence! Let us hope that old age, like old wine, has improved us over the years. . . My recollections of Prince's Gate are somewhat different from those of the author [i.e. DW]. I can remember French furniture and a collection of Persian carpets, many of which were transferred to Shanghai and later lost to the Occupational Forces during the Second World War. It may be of interest to you to know that the marble busts of my father and mother (no lace!). . . also 'went' with the rest of the contents of our house in Shanghai. However, some thirty years later we were informed that they had been put up for sale in a Communist curio shop in that city. This prompted us to take the necessary steps to retrieve them and to place them in our office, where they can be seen to this day. On a more serious note, and to put the record straight, my mother, who was admired and loved by all who knew her, lost her life in the fire which took place in our home by re-entering the building to rescue a governess in our employ; a tragedy which affected the course of our lives.' DW had written that the lady had been burned to death retrieving a pet parrot.

Writings of which the Dates of Compostion are Unknown

45. *Memories of a Vanished Period*, short story. 11pp.; first published *ALS*.
The MS is inscribed 'London, May 10th 1941', which is the date when the events took place. The wedding reception referred to followed the marriage of Peter Bishop, formerly a neighbour of DW's in Platt, and Odette Lees. Other identifiable characters who appear are Marcus Oliver ('Angus'), Helen Roeder ('Grace'), Carel Weight ('Randal') and Peter Culley ('Michael'), who was, like DW, an Old Reptonian.

46. *An Afternoon with Jeanne*, short story fragments. 6½pp.; two pp. of the MS missing; first published *FLS*.
Another vignette from DW's childhood. He is twelve and plays with a young girl, Jeanne.

47. *Constance, Lady Willet*, short story. 7½pp.; first published *The Stories of Denton Welch* (ed. Robert Phillips), Dutton, NY, 1986.
The character is based on the mother of Francis Streeten. She was an alcoholic, and the story, in which Streeten appears as 'Mark', tells of her making a trip to Tunbridge Wells, where she falls down drunk and is questioned by a policeman.

4.Poetry

This listing includes all poems by Denton Welch published during his lifetime (so far as the author has been able to trace). These are arranged in chronological order of publication. The first collection of Denton Welch's poetry appeared posthumously in *A Last Sheaf* (John Lehmann, 1951), which contains sixty-seven poems, including many of those listed below. Thirteen poems which are interspersed between entries in his Journal appear in *The Denton Welch Journals*, ed. Jocelyn Brooke (Hamish Hamilton, 1952). The first anthology entirely devoted to Denton Welch's verse is *Dumb Instrument*, ed. Jean-Louis Chevalier (Enitharmon Press, London, 1976), which contains fifty-eight poems, none of which had appeared in print before.

1. 'Where I Wander', *Abinger Chronicle*, vol.2, no.4 (June 1941), p.42
2. 'Our Maid Jane Allen', *Abinger Chronicle*, vol. 2, no.5 (July 1941), p.48
3. 'Can We No More', 'The Anatomists', *Abinger Chronicle*, vol.3, no.4, (September-October 1942), pp.45-6
4. 'Parliament Square', *Decachord*, vol. XIX, no.95 (September-October 1942), p.80
5. 'Jane Allen', *Poetry Quarterly*, vol. IV, no.4 (Winter 1942), p.147
6. 'Poem', *Kingdom Come*, vol.3, no.11 (Winter 1942), p.26. See no.14 below
7. 'My House', *The Spectator*, 27th November 1942, p.501
8. 'Philanthropist', *Opus*, no.14 (Spring 1943), p.29

9. 'Panacea', *Modern Reading*, no.8 (1943), p.60

10. 'Jane Allen', in *Wartime Harvest*, 1943 (anthology of prose and verse from *Kingdom Come*), p.78; the poem, however, appears not to have been printed in *Kingdom Come*.

11. 'Jane Allen', 'The Hungry Hour', *The Adelphi*, vol.19, no.4 (July-September 1943), p.101

12. 'A Girl's Poem', *Life and Letters Today*, vol.39, no.75 (November1943), p.120

13. 'A Mistake', *The Spectator*, 28th January 1944, p.79

14. 'A Rhyme', *Life and Letters Today*, vol.40, no.79 (March 1944), p.161. This is the same poem as no.6, above

15. 'Ashford Train', *Life and Letters Today*, vol.41, no.82 (June 1944), p.156

16. 'For a Drowned Friend', 'At Midnight in the Fields', *Dint*, no.1. (n.d.; probably Summer 1944), p.8

17. 'Night in Wartime', *Dint*, no.2 (Autumn 1944), p.8

18. 'Barricades', *Phoenix Quarterly*, vol.1, no.1 (Autumn 1946), p.55

19. 'The Skeleton Child', *Orion III*, (Autumn 1946), p.119

20. 'The Driving Power', *Modern Reading*, no.15 (1947), p.123

A Catalogue of Pictures

This is the first catalogue of Denton Welch's artistic work, and it aims to list all the pictures of note, as well as some others that have a special relevance to his writings. Inevitably, a degree of selectivity has been exercised in deciding which items to include, though the author has been careful not to leave out anything of interest on the grounds of his personal taste.

The dating of much of Denton Welch's work presents problems, for he seldom makes reference to specific pictures in his letters or Journals. It should be pointed out, however, that since he died at thirty-three, his entire output can safely be attributed to a span of fifteen years or so, i.e. 1933-48. Another factor that makes accurate dating difficult is that many of his pictures were started during one period, were put to rest for a few years, and were then worked on again and completed.

In light of the briefness of his career, one might expect the pictures not to vary very much in terms of style; anyone who has seen more than a few of them, however, will know that this is not the case. Within the fifteen years we find the artist trying his hand at Surrealist-inspired drawings, figure-paintings owing an allegiance to André Derain, very numerous still-lifes that demonstrate a knowledge of Mark Gertler's work (although the later ones, especially the flowerpieces, emerge as highly individual) and lastly, very detailed pen and ink-drawn watercolours that, whilst being loosely influenced by Samuel Palmer, whom Denton admired, are also strongly reminiscent of the closely-worked fantasy-illustrations that one finds in modern children's books. This latter style was one that predominated at the end of Denton's life.

It can be presumed that the Shell poster of Hadlow Castle (1937) represents Denton Welch's first commercial success—and very possibly it was also the first work he ever sold. The next year, 1938, finds him exhibiting a flowerpiece (priced at ten guineas) at the Redfern Gallery, and a similar oil the next year in the same salon. Two flowerpieces, at £8 each, featured at the New English Art Club exhibition of October-November 1939 and a further flowerpiece was at the Leger Gallery in the summer of 1942. However, from October 1941 onwards Denton Welch's work was shown at The Leicester Galleries, near Leicester Square in London. From the latter date until his death 1948 the gallery handled just over twenty of his pictures, and continued to exhibit one or two in the years that followed. The Leicester Galleries' association with Denton's work culminated in the posthumous exhibition of May-June 1954, which included thirty-nine works, twenty-five of which are included in this catalogue.

The other main exhibition of Denton Welch's work was held by Abbott and Holder at their former premises in Castelnau, London SW13 in November 1984, timed to coincide with the publication of Michael De-la-Noy's *Denton Welch: the Making of a Writer*. The exhibition showed around a dozen works already in private ownership, and a substantial quantity of watercolours and drawings, deriving chiefly from the artist's sketchbooks, which had come from an auction at Sotheby's on 23rd May 1984, and which Abbott and Holder were offering for sale.

Reproductions of nine of Denton Welch's paintings can be found in *A Last Sheaf* (nos 49, 53, 67, 92, 94, 95, 122, 123, 124 of the catalogue that follows). Several more of his works are illustrated in Sotheby's Modern British and Irish Paintings, etc. catalogues of the 1980s and 90s. The catalogue below does not lay claim to giving exhaustive information on the exhibition of the works listed.

Abbreviations:

A&H   exhibited at Abbott and Holder, picture dealers, London (followed by the month and year in question)

HRC   Harry Ransom Humanities Research Center, Art Collection, the University of Texas at Austin

LG   exhibited at the Leicester Galleries, London

n.a.   not available

priv. coll. private collection

S   (given after the measurement) signed by the artist

*   unseen by the author either in life or reproduction

Measurements are given height before width, and in cms.
Several of Denton Welch's oils painted on panel have another picture on the verso.

OILS

possibly pre-1936

1.	Still-life of three shells with figures inside	canvas	50x54.5	HRC
2..	Fantastic painting with a cat	canvas	40x44.5	priv. coll. (A&H 11/84; Barbican 5-7/87)
3.	A Farm	board	51x63.5	HRC
4.	Village scene—probably near the South Downs, Sussex Miss Evelyn Sinclair	board	51x76	priv. coll.
5.		canvas	35.5x30	priv. coll. (A&H 11/84; the author considers this painting very possibly to be by May Walbrand-Evans—if correct it would then date c.1942

1936-39 period

6.	Self-portrait in brown jacket and blue tie	board	57.5x52.5	HRC
7.	Self-portrait with layers of different coloured clothing	board	47.5x40.5	National Portrait Gallery, London (LG 5-6/54)
8.	Self-portrait with toggle around neck and suspicious eyes	board	c.52x38	priv. coll. (A&H 11/84)
9.	Three male nudes drying after bathing (1936)	board	76.5x91.5	priv. coll.
10.	Two girls in yellow straw hats	board	61x51	priv. coll.
11.	Naive painting of men bathing near trees	cardboard	40x58 S	HRC
12.	Young man with laurel wreath on head	pressboard	47x38	HRC
13.	Three stylized blond-haired figures at table with a dog underneath	pressboard	72.5x75	HRC
14.	Oriental woman holding a blond baby/verso: 'By the Lake'	pressboard	92.5x61	HRC
15.	Still-life with knives, vegetables and a jug of flowers	pressboard	55.5x61	HRC

16.	Still-life with a bottle, toothbrush, shell and basket	canvas	35x30	HRC
17.	Still-life with recurring Greek key pattern, egg with swastikas and a ewer of flowers	canvas	45.5x30	HRC
18.	Still-life with a brush and mug of spring flowers on a table	fibreboard	76x61	HRC
19.	Still-life with tape-measure and a brush	masonite	70x58.5	HRC
20.	Flowers in a Worcester teapot	board	70x48 S	HRC
21.	*'The Devil Jug'—still-life with bottle, shell and toadstool on an ornate table	?board	70x50	priv.coll. (LG 5-6/54)
22.	'The Loving Cup'—still-life with bottles, a china lion, a crassula, etc.	pressboard	51.5x6 S on verso	HRC
23.	Hadlow Castle—painting for the Shell poster (1937)	board	52x95 S	Shell Coll., National Motor Museum, Beaulieu, Hants (Barbican 5-7/87)
24.	Farmhouse at Yalding, Kent	fibreboard	76x61	HRC
25.	A church and cemetery	pressboard	55.5x80	HRC
26.	A road with various rustic buildings	board	55x80	HRC
27.	'Capel Church' (in fact Tudeley Church, near Tonbridge)	board	71x47	HRC
28.	A clothes line	pressboard	59.5x50.5 S	HRC
29.	Probably the back yard of 54 Hadlow Road, Tonbridge	board	65x51 S on verso	priv.coll. (?LG 5-6/54)
30.	Garden with a white chair	canvas	56x46 S	priv. coll.
31.	Portrait of Prince Serge Belosselsky	board	58x40	HRC
32.	Portrait of Miss Evelyn Sinclair	board	76x51	HRC
33.	Portrait possibly of the artist's brother Bill	board	61x44	HRC

latter part of the same period, or slightly later

34.	Young woman in yellow jumper	board	66x44	priv. coll. (A&H 11/84)
35.	Portrait of a handsome, unidentified lady in a dark blue cardigan, with crossed	board	70x51	HRC

36.	Dinner Serenade—with a figure playing a rebec and another blessing a table	pressboard	62x74	HRC
37.	A china dog and large blue and white vase on a brightly-coloured quilt	hardboard	48x56	priv. coll. (A&H 11/84)
38.	A King Charles spaniel near a red brick cubicle	board	72.5x61	priv. coll.
39.	A centaur drawing a bow, a miniature female nude on his back	pressboard	76x55	HRC (?LG 5-6/54)

1940-41 period

40.	*Tom the Woodman seated, with an axe on his knees	board	n.a.	lost
41.	A jug transformed into a human face, with fowers for the hair	board	51.5x32	priv. coll.
42.	'The Gilded Serpent'—a sea-serpent in the foreground, a face behind	tempera, house-paint, etc. on shingle	21x27.5	HRC (LG 5-6/54)
43.	Abstract collage—influenced by Blair Hughes-Stanton	masonite	28x49.5 S	HRC
44.	Flowerpiece—flowers in a large ewer	board	26x49	priv. coll. (LG 10/41)
45.	An elaborate flowerpiece with figures and a landscape in the background	panel	82x76 S	HRC
46.	*Two centaurs	?	n.a. (small)	lost
47.	'Harvesters'—a horse on the left, a barefoot woman dancing, another on a column, a bearded man	board	91x122	The Tate Gallery, London (LG 5-6/54)
48.	Conversation Piece—Lord Berners as a child, dressed as Robinson Crusoe	board	84x61 S	priv. coll. (LG 1/42, 5-6/54; A&H 11/84)

latter part of the same period, or slightly later

49.	'A Cat Patting Bluebells'—a hand-vase with a tulip and spring flowers (the cat added at a later date)	board	35.5x27 S	priv. coll. (Leger Gallery 7-8/42; LG 1/48, 5-6/54)
50.	'A Gothick Flowerpiece' —flowers in a jug with a Gothic window and building on the left	board	43x33.5 S	priv. coll. (LG 7-8/42)

51.	*'The Coffin House'—a coffin-shaped house surrounded by trees (see also no.123)	plywood	c.91x106	lost
52.	*Forest landscape—a cherub and a vase of flowers (possibly 'The Cherub Wood')	?	28x37	priv. coll. (?LG 5-6/54)

1942-46 period

53.	'By the Sea'—a female head with a horn and flowers in her hair, a hand-vase with flowers, the sea in the background	board	33x43 S	priv. coll. (LG 1/43, 8-9/51, 5-6/54; Barbican 5-7/87)
54.	Flowers in a jug, with mottled texture to the paint	board	49.5x29.5 S	priv. coll. (Barbican 5-7/87)
55.	*'Stillness in the Afternoon' —a still-life in the foreground, in the background sea	?	n.a. S	priv. coll. (LG 1/45)
56.	*Flowers in a vase resting on a book, with the artist's name on its spine	board	42.5x32 S	priv. coll. (Artists International Spring/46)
57.	'Alex'—a pug standing with its front paws in a stream (1943)	board	33x42	priv. coll.
58.	A cat sitting on its haunches	gouache, oil and pen on board	16.5x23	priv. coll.
59	Pond Farm, Peckham Bush, Kent	pressboard	55.5x80	HRC
60.	*'The Tower and the World Outside'	?possibly not an oil	n.a.	priv. coll. (LG 1/45)
61.	*Portrait of Mrs Julian Goodman	board	n.a. (small)	lost

latter part of the same period, or slightly earlier

62.	A Madonna-like female with flowers in her hair and horns, a baby mermaid reaching to her breast	board	40.5x22, the top rounded	priv. coll.
63.	'Flowers and a Demon'—a demon hovering above a jug with summer flowers	board	61x51 S	priv. coll. (LG 1/48; Barbican 5-7/87)
64.	Summer flowers and wheat in a hand-vase	board	61x45.5	Yale University Coll. (LG 5-6/54)

65.	*'Spirits above a Flower'	?board	n.a.	priv. coll. (LG 7-8/46)
66.	A white horse in front of a tree, beside it a statue, a hot-air balloon in the sky	board	18x23 S	priv. coll.

oils the date of which is uncertain

67.	'Nina'—a three-quarter-length woman in a hat, near her cat, with buildings in the background	?possibly mixed-medium or water-colour	n.a.	priv. coll. (LG 5-6/54)
68.	*'Lords and Ladies'	?board	n.a.	priv. coll. (LG 5-6/54)
69.	'Girl with a Choker'—another in the background, also a triumphal arch	board	41x33.5	priv. coll. (A&H 11/84)
70.	Flowerpiece—the vase edged with a Greek key pattern	oil & collage on board	30.5x25.5	priv. coll.
71.	Still-life with broken tile	board	n.a.	priv. coll.
72.	*A Cottage among Trees	board	63.5x75.5	priv. coll.
73.	*Caterpillars	?	n.a.	priv. coll. (LG 5-6/54)

WATERCOLOURS, GOUACHES AND MIXED MEDIUMS
1936-39 period

74.	Self-portrait with spiv-like hair and crude features	gouache on paper	34.5x27	priv.coll.
75.	Three rustic seats under trees (1936)	paper	25.5x36 S	priv. coll.
76.	The Postern, Tonbridge—a row of houses	paper	23x28 S	priv. coll.
77.	A lane with farm buildings and a chimney	paper	24.5x35.5 S	HRC

1940-41 period, or possibly later

78.	Still-life with a bowl of fruit and a large prawn	gouache on paper	23x29	priv. coll.
79.	*Design for an anti-war poster	gouache on paper	31x37	priv. coll.

1942-46 period

80.	'A Lion and a Pilgrim'—possibly inspired by Androcles and the Lion (1944)	pencil, crayon & gouache on board	15.5x28 S	priv. coll. (Barbican 5-7/87)

81.	'A Cat Waiting for its Master'—a cat with a bell around its neck on an ornately-coloured tiled floor (begun Feb. 1946	coloured pencils, water-colour, pen & ink on paper	34.5x22.5 S	HRC (LG 7-8/46)
82.	'A Horse by a Tower'	paper	6.5x10 S	Redfern Gallery (LG 7-8/43)
83.	Portrait, possibly of Mrs Brenda Cobb	paper	38x25.5	priv. coll.
84.	The Interior of Pitt's Folly Cottage (1944)—an illustration for *Vogue* (in June 1945 number)	gouache on paper	n.a.	unknown
85.	A house near Mereworth—a graveyard in the foreground	gouache on paper	38x28	priv. coll.
86.	*'Landscape in a Dream'	paper	n.a.	priv. coll. (LG 7-8/43)
87.	'The Bust and the Toad-stools'—a path leading to cottage in the background	paper	20x26 S	priv. coll. (LG 2/46)
88.	'Dream of a Poet, a Cupid and a Cow in the Park' (1944)	paper	17.5x24.5 S	priv. coll.

1946-48 period

89.	*'An Enchantress'	?a water-colour	n.a.	priv. coll. (LG 1/47)
90.	'Flowers by the Window, Middle Orchard, Crouch, Kent' (1948)	paper	18.5x24.5 S	priv. coll. (LG 7/48)
91.	A glass vase with pansies and small roses on a window-sill, a boy looking through from behind	paper	36x25 S	priv. coll.
92.	'The Animal Doctor Should Put you to Sleep'—a fat rabbit beside a cracked tea-pot with flowers in it (1948)	paper	30.5x28 S	priv. coll. (A&H 11/84)
93.	A garden with a path leading to a cottage, on the left under a tree, a young man, on the right in the foreground a dome-shaped object with a cupid (1948)	paper	37x52.5 S	priv. coll.

completed during the same period, but started earlier

94.	'A Beauty Waiting in the Fields'—a young woman with a large, fantastic hat (1947)	paper	36x26 S	priv. coll. (LG 5-6/54)
95.	'Now I have only my Dog' (or possibly 'Love me, Love my Dog')—a bonneted lady carrying a tiny animal	paper	35.5x20 S	priv. coll. (LG 1/47, 5-6/54; A&H 11/84)

watercolours, etc., the date of which is uncertain

96.	*'Susan Innes' (probably 1947/48)	?paper	n.a.	priv. coll. (LG 7/49)
97.	*A Harlequin	?paper	n.a.	priv. coll. (LG 5-6/54)
98.	*'The Coffin on the Hill'	?paper	n.a.	priv. coll. (LG 5-6/54)
99.	*'The Mausoleum in the Meadow'	?paper	n.a.	priv. coll. (LG 5-6/54)
100.	*'Little Bobby Davis'	?paper	n.a.	priv. coll. (LG 8-9/50; 5-6/54)

PEN AND INK DRAWINGS—WITH OR WITHOUT COLOUR WASH

Pre-1936

101.	Paul Welch reclining full-length on a sofa	with colour wash, on paper	25.5x37 S	priv. coll.

1936-39 period

102.	Bizarre scene with mythological figures in the foreground, a man walking up steps to a pavilion in the background	with colour wash, on paper	22x35 S	priv. coll.
103.	A Surrealist scene with three comically altered figures, a cat, a flying-machine, etc.	possibly with wash, on paper	?38x26.5	priv. coll.
104.	'Faces at the Stage Door'— four heads with curious, symbolic distortions (1939)	paper	28x35.5 S	HRC (LG 5-6/54)
105.	Portrait of Francis Streeten	paper	37.5x27 S	priv. coll.
106.	Portrait of a young man—possibly the artist's brother Paul	paper	35.5x25.5	priv. coll.

latter part of the same period, or later

107.	Self-portrait—without glasses, wearing a tie and jacket	with coloured chalk, on paper	30.5x24	priv. coll.
108.	Portrait of Miss Evelyn Sinclair	paper	35.5x25.5	priv. coll.
109.	Still-life with two head, fruit and cheese on two plates, flowers in a tankard	with colour wash, on paper	37x26	priv. coll.
110.	A Bawden-like fantasy picture—a man and woman in bathing costumes, another man in the recess of a door, a stone bell-tower	[?]	26x37.5 S	Redfern Gallery
111.	Fantasy picture—three infants in a boat, a male and female figure; in the background a classical	with colour wash, on paper	26x36 S	priv. coll.

1940-41 period

112.	Mrs Mildred Bosanquet lying under a bush	paper	25.5x35.5 S	Redfern Gallery
113.	*A cat licking its behind	paper	n.a.	lost
114.	A figure based on Evelyn Sinclair, reading	paper	37x27	priv. coll.
115.	John St Nicholas in a deck-chair, reading	paper	37x27 S	priv. coll.
116.	Tom the Woodman resting on the ground, beside him a shovel (1940)	paper	26x36	priv. coll.
117.	Tom the Woodman and his father sawing down a tree (two rough sketches, 1940)	paper	26x36	priv. coll.

1942-46 period

118.	A cow in the park at Oxon Hoath, the house in the background	coloured paper	c.30x23 S	priv. coll. (LG Summer/45; A&H 11/84)
119.	'A Sheep in the Sunset'	paper	16x20.5 S	(LG Summer/45)
120.	A horse under a tree, with two birds and a necklace on a branch	with colour wash, on paper	19x14.5	priv. coll.

121.	'The Moon was a Great Egg Born in Blood when I Trampled my Baby's Face in the Mud'—a Surrealist composition with three distorted figures, a dog and a bird, the rounded borderpartly with serrated patterns (1943)	with colour wash, on paper	25.5x35.5 S	HRC (LG 7/50, 5-6/54)
122.	'The Woodman's Cottage, Peckham Hurst'	with colour wash, on paper	18x25 S	priv. coll. (LG 2/46, 5-6/54; A&H 11/84)
123.	'The Coffin House' (latter half of 1946)	with colour wash, on paper	c.22x30 S	priv. coll. (LG 10/46, 5-6/54)

1946-48 period

124.	'A Cat Brooding'	with colour wash, on paper	26.5x36 S	priv. coll. (LG 1/47)

pen and ink pictures, etc., the date of which is uncertain

125.	*'Musician in a Landscape'	with colour wash, on paper	17x25.5	priv. coll.
126.	A Scarecrow	with colour wash, on paper	25.5x31.5	priv. coll. (LG 5-6/54)

PENCIL OR CHARCOAL DRAWINGS

127.	A sketchbook used by the artist in hospital (1935)	some pen and ink sketches	18x24	HRC
128.	Self-portrait	charcoal and pen and ink	38x26.5	priv. coll.

MISCELLANEOUS

129.	A bone cariving of a primitive head (finished 1943)		12.5 height S	priv. coll.

Illustrations

1. Books illustrated by Denton Welch

Maiden Voyage, Routledge, 1943: dust-jacket, end-papers, frontispiece, title-page, dedicatory page design ('For Miss Edith Sitwell'), surround for foreword, section divisions (decorated Roman numerals). All are pen and ink designs, save for the dust-jacket which is coloured in dark red and green, on yellow paper.

In Youth is Pleasure, Routledge, 1945: dust-jacket, end-papers, frontispiece, title-page, chapter numbers. All are pen and ink designs, save for the dust-jacket, which is a pencil design, coloured in yellow, grey and pink.

Brave and Cruel and other stories, Hamish Hamilton, 1949: dust-jacket only (an intricately-worked pen and ink design with the lettering coloured in purple and orange).

2. Posthumously published editions with illustrations by Denton Welch

A Voice Through a Cloud, John Lehmann, 1950: dust-jacket (most probably not from original artwork by DW), end-papers (using a design that had already appeared in the Christmas Number of *Vogue*, 1945), design on title-page, chapter heading motif. Save for the dust-jacket, all are in pen and ink.

A Last Sheaf, John Lehmann, 1951: dust-jacket (seemingly made up from an original drawing, with lettering copying DW's style), end-papers (not by DW), title-page part surround, a chapter heading design duplicated twelve times; before 'A Novel Fragment' a cracked bell with a ribbon bow; an elaborately worked frontispiece for the section of poetry; before the reproductions of DW's paintings an armless mermaid pierced by an arrow.

2. Magazines and Periodical Illustrations by Denton Welch

Poetry London, vol.2, no.9, 1943: five tailpieces, all pen and ink, comprising (a) an ornamental pen and ink shell with a sprig of foliage, (b) a fish skeleton, (c) a limbless mermaid/sea-snake, (d) a horse and a tower (see Catalogue of pictures, no.82), (e) a picture of a figure with corn in her hair and a cat, a building and the sun setting.

Vogue:
1. Illustrations for 'In School Out of School', an article by Lesley Blanch, comprising a decorated title and two small pen and ink drawings of a cat playing a harpsichord and a young demon near an urn, playing a viol. August 1943 ed.
2. A painting, reproduced in colour, of the interior of Pitt's Folly Cottage (the original probably a gouache). June 1945 ed.

The following fifteen items, except where specified otherwise, were commissions to provide title illustrations for Doris Lytton Toye's regular cookery column in *Vogue*. The recipes, along with the accompanying drawings (and those by John Minton, who took over from DW), were collected and published as *Vogue's Contemporary Cookery*, Condé Nast, 1947:

3. 'Serve Cold'; pen and ink, July 1945
4. 'The Sweets of Summer'; pen and ink, August 1945
5. 'Autumn Fare'; pen and ink, September 1945
6. 'Puddings and Pies'; pen and ink, October 1945
7. 'Savouries to Savour'; pen and ink, November 1945
8. 'On the Feast of Stephen'; two pen and ink designs reproduced as negative images; separately, a pen and ink design to accompany DW's article 'Strange Discoveries', December 1945
9. 'Children's Party'; pen and ink, January 1946
10. 'Fork Supper'; pen and ink, February 1946
11. 'A Chaplet of Herbs'; pen and ink, March 1946
12. 'Coffee and Cake'; pen and ink, April 1946
13. 'Fishmonger's Haul'; pencil, May 1946
14. 'Vegetable Variants'; pen and ink, June 1946
15. 'Salad Days'; pen and ink, July 1946
16. 'Cuisine Bourgeoise'; pencil, September 1946
17. 'The Milky Way'; pen and ink, August 1947

Junior 3, Winter 1946: title surround for 'How to Make your Own Sweets', by Monica Marsden, and accompanying the article a pen and ink drawing of a bag with fruit on it.

Junior 4, March 1947: four illustrations for 'The Voyage', a short story by Katherine Mansfield, comprising (a) a title surround in pen and ink, (b) 'Fenella, her father and Grandma', pencil, (c) 'Grandpa, Fenella and the Old Woman (her Grandma)', pencil, (d) the swan-neck of an umbrella, pen and ink.

Junior 5, September 1947; illustrations for 'The Packing-case House and the Thief', a short story by Denton Welch, comprising (a) a title surround in pen and ink, (b) the packing-case house, with a figure in the background, pencil, (c) 'Taff', a dog, pen and ink.

Penguin New Writing 30, 1947; seven tailpieces in pen and ink, comprising (a) an armless mermaid pierced by an arrow, (b) a broken bag with coins in it, (c) a shell with a face peeping out, (d) oak leaves, an oak-apple with an eye and a beak, (e) a small branch with three eggs at its base, (f) a branch with a chain, (g) leaves, twigs, etc.

In 1947 Denton Welch also produced two pen and ink drawings (similar to those for *Vogue*), which were intended for *Home and Garden*. The author has been unable to trace whether these were ever published.

INDEX

The names in inverted commas identify people appearing as characters in Denton Welch's prose writings, as well as one or two in *No Coward Soul* by Noël Adeney.